THE ULTIMATE PRACTICAL BUSINESS MANUAL

EVERYTHING YOU NEED TO KNOW ABOUT BUSINESS

(FROM LAUNCHING A COMPANY TO TAKING IT PUBLIC)

---

by Chris Haroun

The Ultimate Practical Business Manual

Copyright © 2016 by Chris Haroun

(Published by www.BusinessCareerCoaching.com)

All rights reserved. No part of this book may be reproduced or transmitted in any form or by any means without written permission from the author.

DEDICATION

To my incredible students at San Francisco State University!

I also want to thank the best professor I have ever had – Matthew Rhodes-Kropf who taught me the practical and entertaining way to learn business concepts at Columbia University. Matt now teaches at Harvard Business School.

Thanks Matt! :)

PLEASE READ THIS FIRST: PURPOSE OF THIS BOOK

Many business concepts are simply common sense. This book will focus on business concepts that you need to know that might not be common sense! This book will teach you everything you need to know about business....from starting a company to taking it public. Most business books are significantly outdated. This book leverages many incredible online resources and makes the whole business, accounting and finance process very easy! There are many incredibly engaging and entertaining video links in the book to YouTube and other sources; edutainment rocks! **I tried to visualize the content of this book as much as possible as this is a more impactful and enjoyable way to learn (think Pinterest versus the tiny words in the Economist)!**

The contents of this book are all based on my work experience at several firms, including Goldman Sachs, the consulting industry at Accenture, a few companies I have started, the hedge fund industry where I worked at Citadel and most recently based on my experience at a prominent San Francisco based venture capital firm. I also included helpful practical business concepts I learned while I did an MBA at Columbia University and a Bachelor of Commerce degree at McGill University. Think of this book as a "greatest hits" business summary from my MBA, undergraduate business degree, work experience in consulting, equities, hedge funds, venture capital and starting my own companies.

As the title of this book suggests, this is a practical manual to help you accomplish your business career goals. I have minimized "boring theoretical concepts" in this book in order to keep it as close to reality as possible. I hope you enjoy it! In addition to teaching at 4 universities in the Bay Area, you can find other courses that I teach online at :

www.tiny.cc/chris1

I hope you enjoy this book! I am a firm believer that 'edutainment' works best!

Thanks a lot,

Chris Haroun :)

WE WILL COVER THE ENTIRE LIFECYCLE OF A COMPANY!

We will start here in Chapter 1....

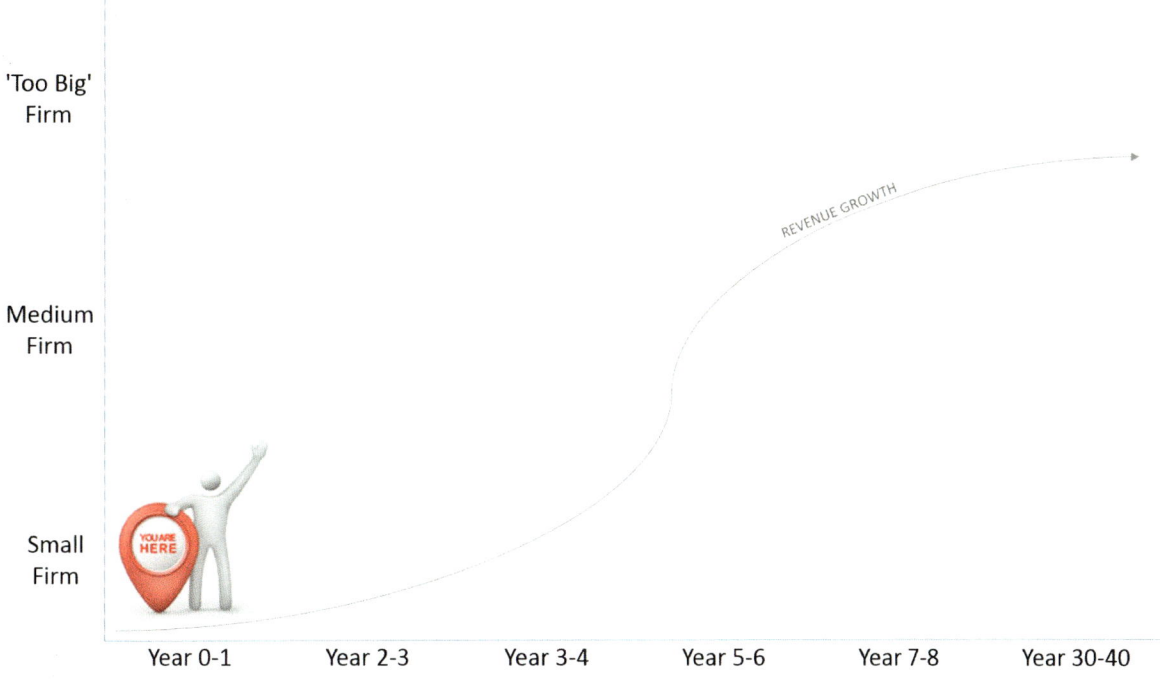

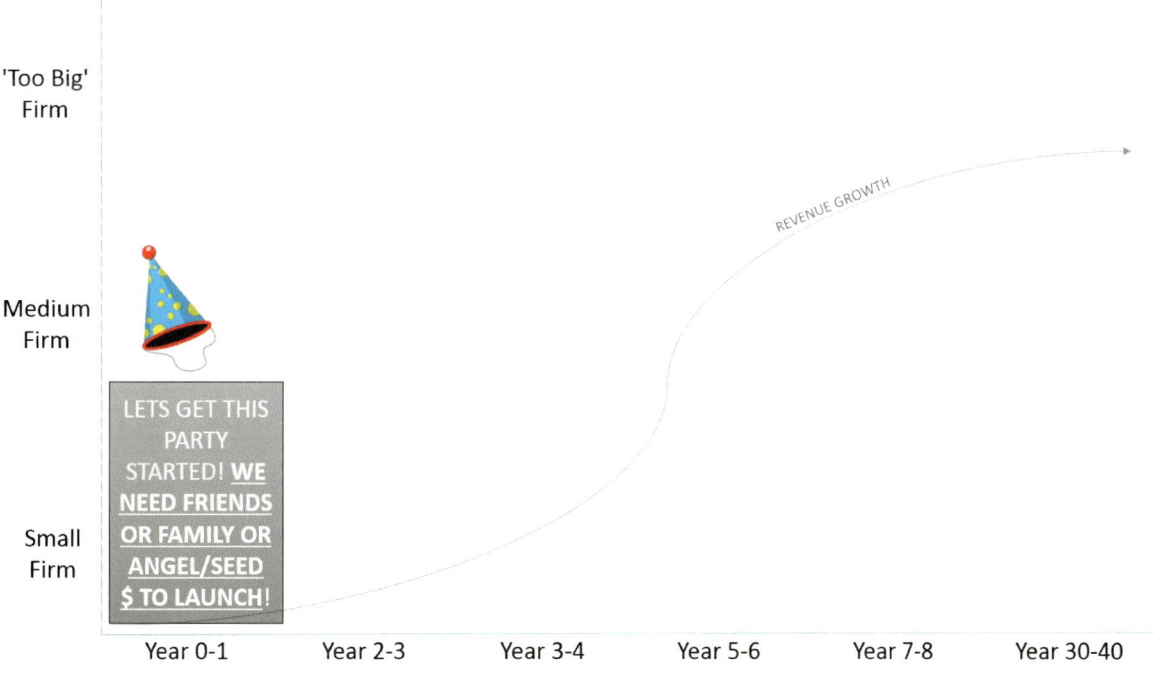

The Ultimate Practical Business Manual

....and we will end here in Chapter 15:

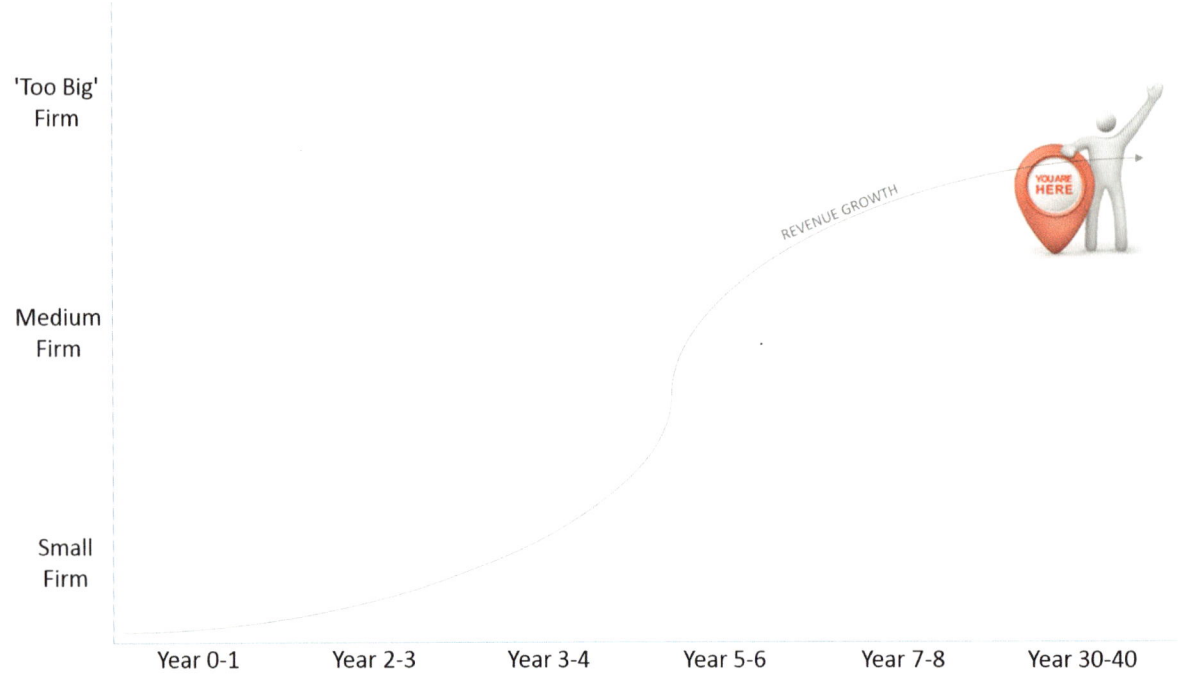

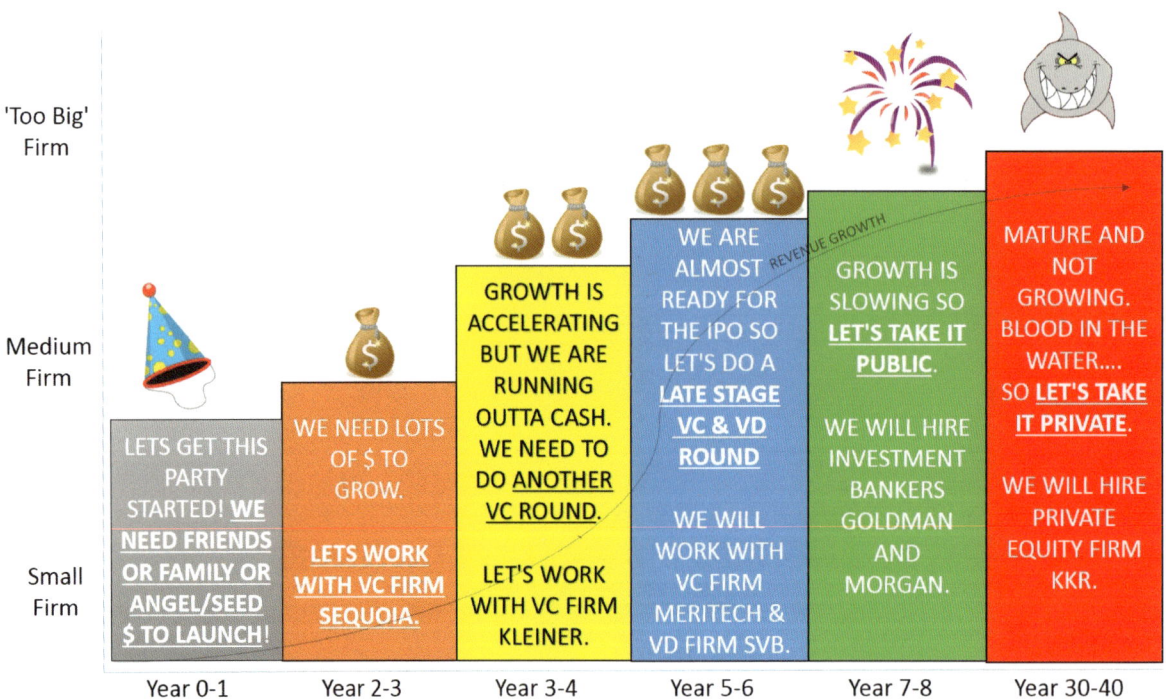

There are 15 chapters in this book as follows:

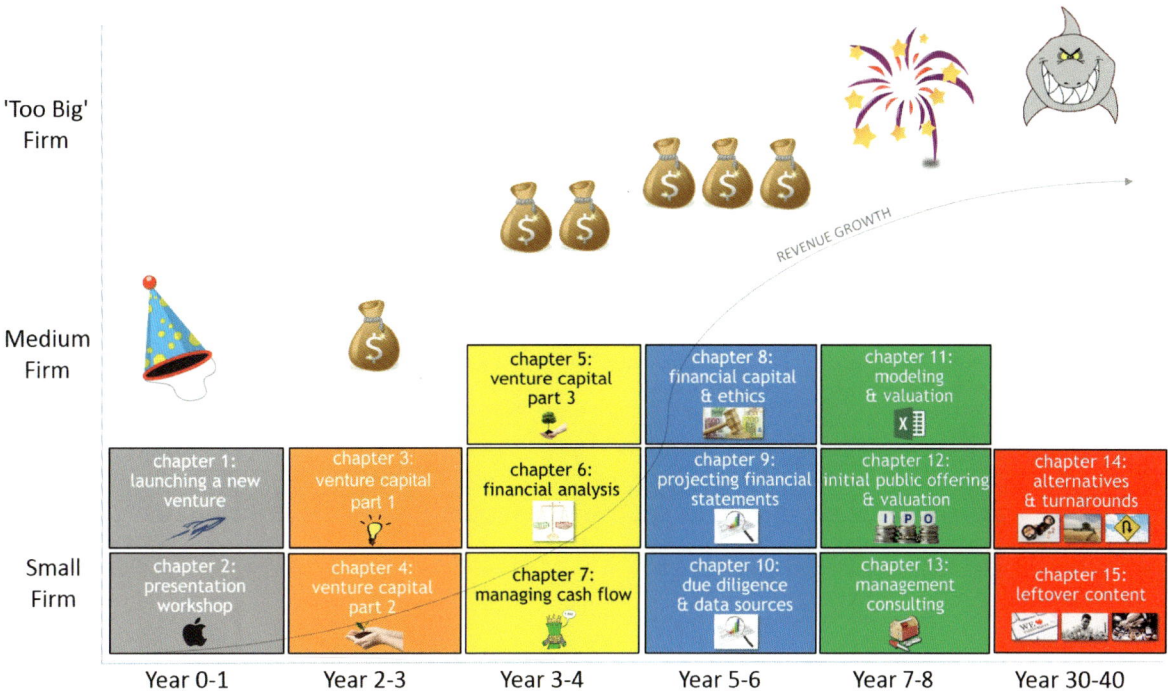

ABOUT THE AUTHOR

Chris Haroun (www.tiny.cc/chris3) is an award winning business school professor, venture capitalist and the author of "*101 Crucial Lessons They Don't Teach You In Business School*", which Forbes magazine calls "*1 of 6 books that all entrepreneurs need to read right now*" (www.tiny.cc/Forbes101) along with Peter Thiel's book and The 7 Habits of Highly Effective People.

Chris is currently a venture capitalist at a prominent San Francisco Bay Area venture capital firm and has previous work experience at Goldman Sachs and several firms that he has founded. He has successfully raised and also has managed over $1bn in his business/finance career. He has an MBA in Finance from Columbia University and a Bachelor of Commerce Degree with a major in Management Information Systems and International Business from McGill University.

Chris is also a frequent guest lecturer at several Bay Area business schools including Berkeley and Stanford. He has written numerous articles and been interviewed in Forbes, VentureBeat, Entrepreneur Magazine, Wired Magazine, AlleyWatch, Pulse as well as an interview on venture capital on Radio Television Hong Kong (RTHK) which is Hong Kong's oldest and sole public service broadcaster. He serves on the boards of several Bay Area technology companies and lives in Hillsborough, California.

Chris Haroun's goal is to "make business education impactful and entertaining with no boring theory!"

Contents

Dedication 3

Please Read This First: Purpose of this Book 4

    We Will Cover the Entire Lifecycle of a Company! 5

About the Author 8

Chapter 1: Launching a New Venture 13

    What Makes a Great Entrepreneur / Leader? 15

    The Most Important Business Skill 16

    The Easy Way to Get Customers or a Job! 16

    Sources of Entrepreneurial Ideas 21

    Ethics 25

    Investment Stages 26

    What Kind of Legal Entity Should I set Up? 27

    What About Taxes? 32

    How Do I Stop Competitors from Illegally Copying My Products? 34

    Chapter Summary: 37

Chapter 2: Presentation Workshop 38

    The Second Most Important Business Skill 40

    How To Create an Impactful Start-Up Presentation 57

    Chapter Summary 59

Chapter 3: Venture Capital Part 1 60

    The Most Important Investment Characteristic Is… 62

    What is Venture Capital? 64

    How do Venture Capital Firms Make Money? 65

    How Do I Raise Money from a VC Firm? 66

    Chapter Summary 67

Chapter 4: Venture Capital Part 2 68

    The Fascinating History of Venture Capital 70

    Chapter Summary 104

Chapter 5: Venture Capital Part 3 105

    How Many Shares Do I Have and How Many Does the VC Have? 107

    Chapter Summary 124

Chapter 6: Financial Analysis 125

    Understanding Financial Statements the Easy Way 127

    Balance Sheet 129

    Income Statement 135

    Cash Flow Statement 138

    Financial Ratios 144

    Income Statement Analysis 147

    Balance Sheet Analysis 148

    Chapter Summary 153

Chapter 7: Managing Cash Flow 154

    Making Forecasts 156

    Chapter Summary 160

Chapter 8: Financial Capital and Securities Laws 161

    Ethics in Finance 163

    Financial Capital 165

    Risk and Return 176

    Cost of Equity Capital 178

    Securities Law and Venture Financing 179

    Chapter Summary 181

Chapter 9: Projecting Financial Statements 182

    Late Stage Investment Round 184

    Chapter Summary 205

Chapter 10: Due Diligence and Data Sources 206
Chapter Summary 217

Chapter 11: Modeling and Valuation 222
Build Financial Models and Value Companies the Easy Way 224
Chapter Summary 271

Chapter 12: Initial Public Offering and Valuation 272
Valuation Drivers 278
Chapter Summary 297

Chapter 13: Management Analytical Frameworks 298
Management Consulting 300
Chapter Summary 319

Chapter 14: Alternatives and Turnarounds 320
What is 'Chapter 11': What is this and Why is it Important to You? 331
Chapter Summary 336

Chapter 15: Leftover Content 337
How Do I Make A Term Sheet? 339
The Most Important Investment You Will Ever Make 342
A Company is Only as Good as Its Customer Service 344
3 Reasons to Be Long-Term Greedy 346
Wealth = Health + Gratitude + Happiness 348
Money Does Not = Happiness 348
Personal Gratitude and Happiness 348
All Your Wealth Can't Buy You Health 349
Turnarounds Don't Work in Tech 350
Success = Apple's Simplicity + Intel's Paranoia 354
Superb Marketing Beats Great Products 356
Less is More in Business 358
Timing is Crucial in Business 359
Frustration is a Good Thing in Business 361

Succeed Like Derek Jeter by Writing these Down 363

Tech Innovation Thrives in the US Due to Youth with Confidence 365

Amazon AWS: This Generation's Berlin Wall Teardown Deflationary Event 367

A Brief History of Silicon Valley, the Region That Revolutionizes How We Do Everything 370

Sputnik, Hippies and the Disruptive Technology of Silicon Valley 372

When a Company Founder Resigns, Investors Should Head for the Exit too 374

You Need Yodas in Order to Succeed in Business and Life 376

When to Change Careers 378

Please Read This Last: Goal Setting Workshop 383

Closing Remarks 384

CHAPTER 1: LAUNCHING A NEW VENTURE

"I've failed over and over and over again in my life and that is why I succeed."

- *Michael Jordan*

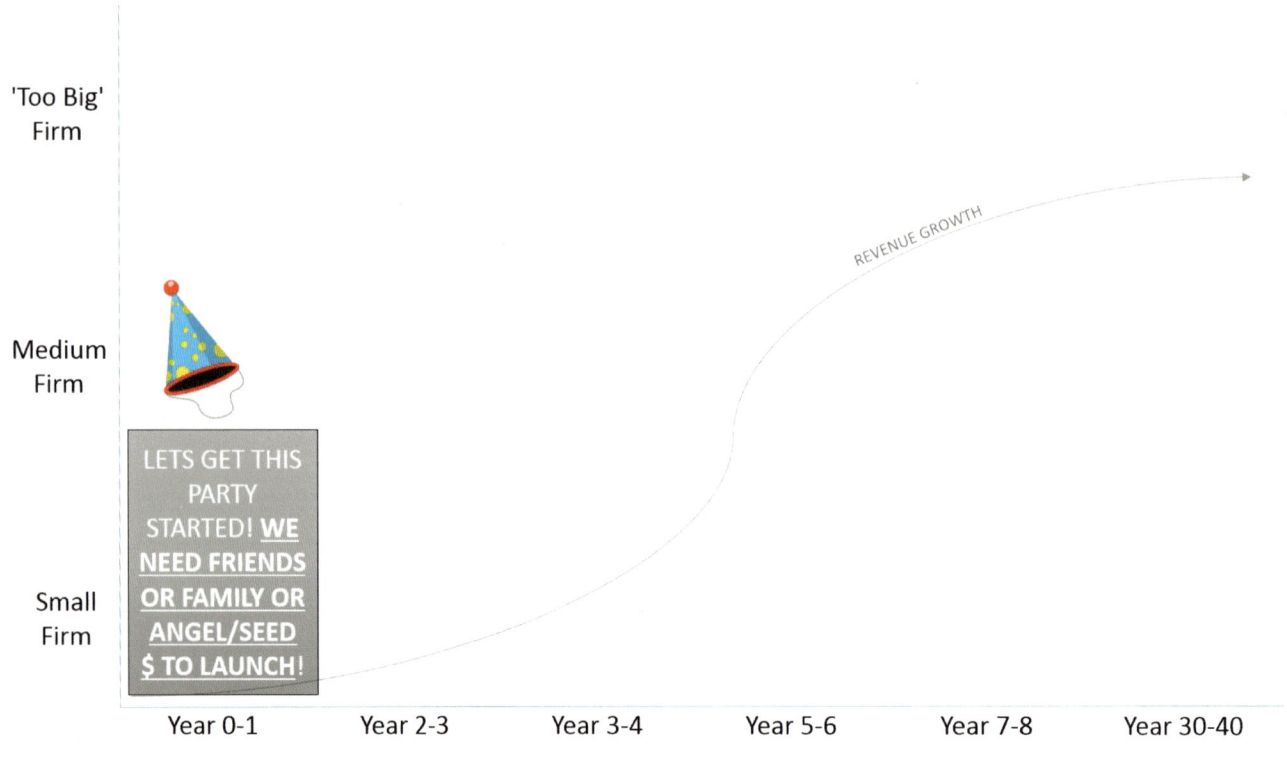

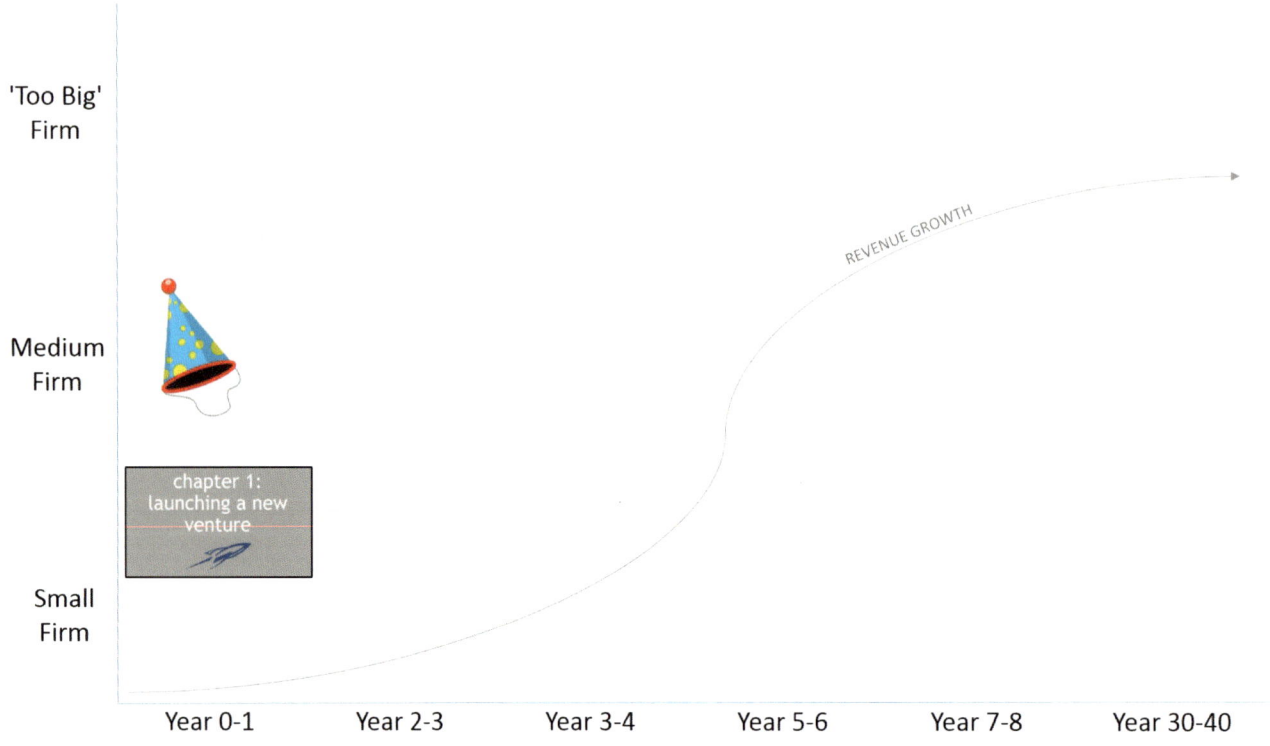

Before we begin, **please** watch this video and believe every damn word of it: www.tiny.cc/chris4 .

WHAT MAKES A GREAT ENTREPRENEUR / LEADER?

You can't successfully launch a new venture unless you and your management team have incredible management qualities. What are some of the qualities that make a great leader or entrepreneur?

- ✓ Passion
- ✓ Optimistic
- ✓ Forward thinking
- ✓ Strategic
- ✓ Determined
- ✓ Team players
- ✓ Long term focused
- ✓ Resilient
- ✓ Great sales skills as all great CEOs and entrepreneurs are superb salespeople.

Wait a minute...what if I don't have any experience at all? Don't worry, investors will take you seriously if, in addition to a great business model, you also have incredible board advisors. In the networking section of this book I will show you how easy this is to do. Mark Zuckerberg is no smarter than you are. Prior to dropping out of school, Mark surrounded himself with incredible advisors, including Peter Thiel (the founder of PayPal) as well as Sean Parker (the founder of Napster) and ~~Justin Timberlake~~...um no not Justin Timberlake, that was in the Social Network movie only!

THE MOST IMPORTANT BUSINESS SKILL

Networking is crucial in business. You can't successfully launch a new venture unless you network. This short video will change your life: www.tiny.cc/chris5 . You need to <u>ask</u> in business.

> networking is key as *relationships are more important than product knowledge*

Many of us use iPhones and iPads and other Apple products because of one simple business and life strategy that Steve Jobs practiced from a very young age: "Ask and you shall receive." Steve Jobs never had issues reaching out and asking for help from strangers. You will be amazed how many people want to help you if you just ask! Fortunately, not many people do this.

When Steve Jobs was only 12 years old he called Bill Hewlett from Hewlett Packard. The young Steve Jobs asked Bill Hewlett if he could give Steve spare parts for a device that he was creating. Hewlett laughed and not only gave him the spare parts, but gave Steve Jobs a job!

Many of us are too shy or we think that it is outside of our comfort zone to ask for help, especially from strangers. Culturally it feels uncomfortable for many people to ask for help or ask strangers for something. You need to do this often.

THE EASY WAY TO GET CUSTOMERS OR A JOB!

So in this day and age of social media, how do we successfully ask for help? It's much easier than you think. In LinkedIn please do an advanced search and find people with something in common with you. If you are from Bombay but live in the United States and live in New York, enter Bombay in LinkedIn and then the zip code that you live in. Then send an "inMail" message in LinkedIn with a very short message as follows:

John,

Hope all is well. I am also from Bombay and I also live in New York. Please let me know if you have time for a coffee in the next few weeks.

Thanks a lot,

Chris

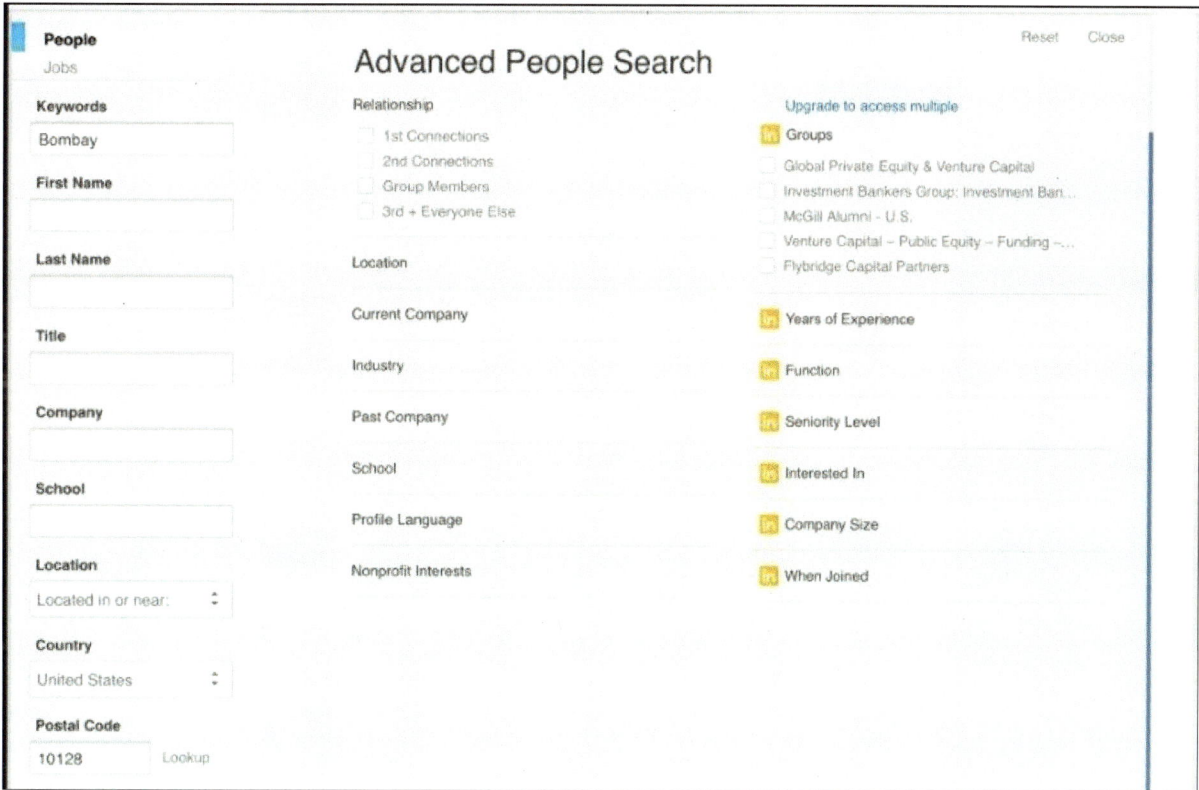

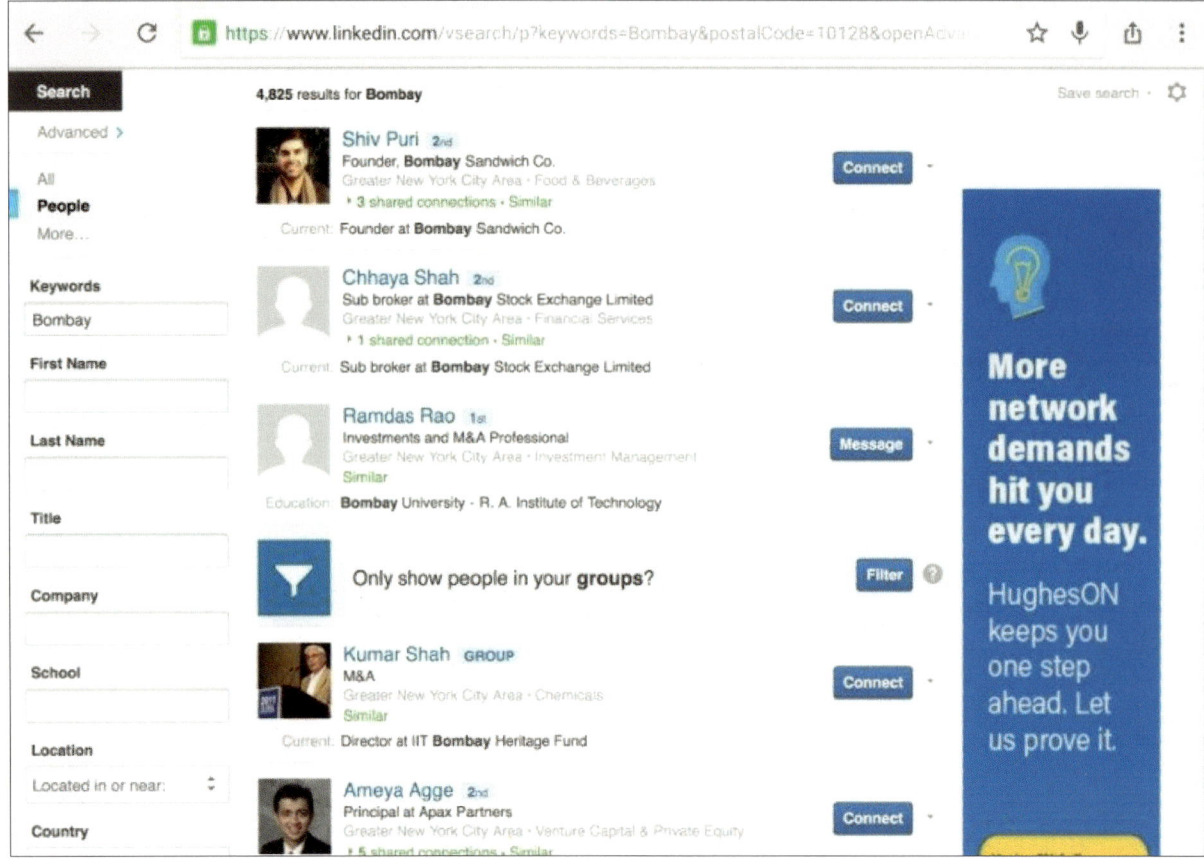

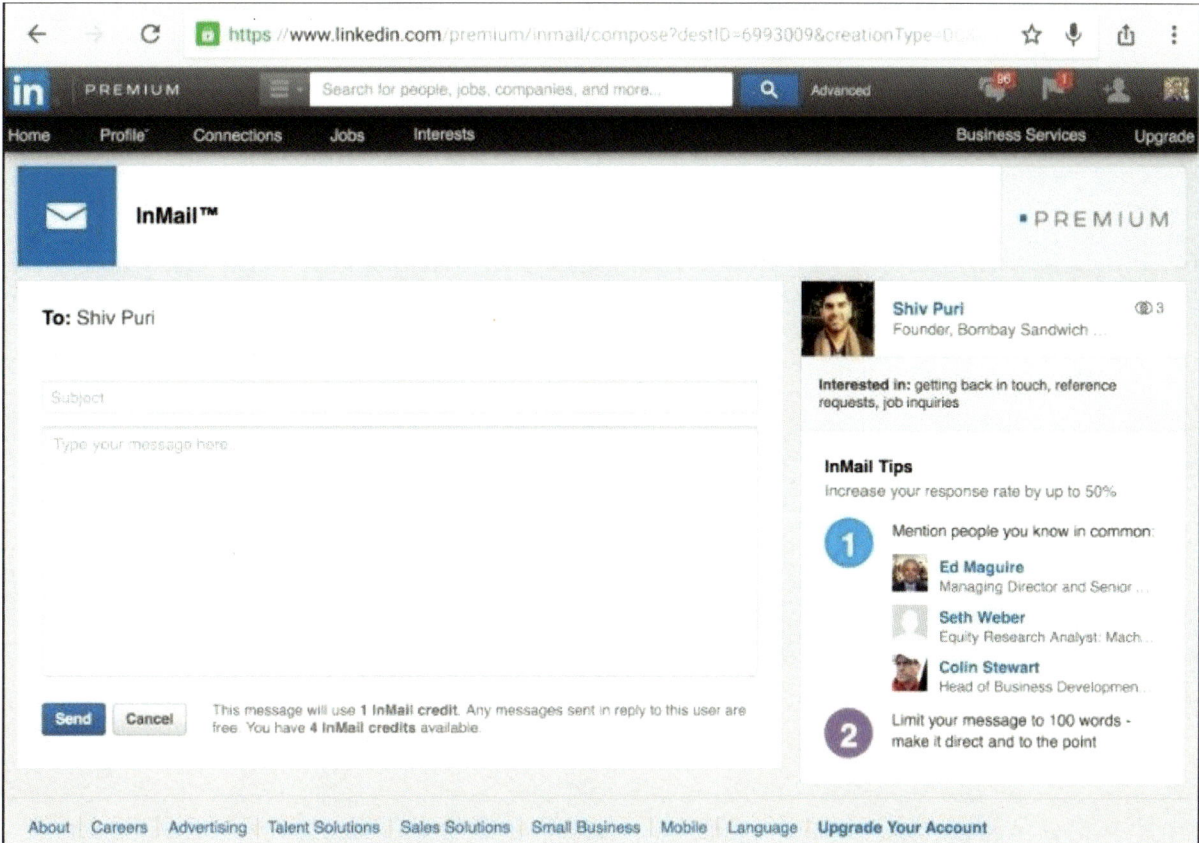

Yes it is that easy! People really do want to help you, especially the farther away you get from the place you grew up in. You can also reach people by leveraging your school as follows:

Matt,

Hope all is well. I also went to McGill University and I also live in the San Francisco Bay Area. Please let me know if you have time for a coffee in the next few weeks.

Thanks a lot,

Chris

Trust me – this works! My success rate on getting meetings with strangers using LinkedIn has always been very high. Why? Because I ask often and most people don't. The key is to find at least one thing you have in common and mention this in your very brief and very polite message. This works exceptionally well. It works because very few people do it. Too many people today use email which is why it is not an effective tool to set up meetings. InMails work. Please try it. I promise you that you will be amazed at the outcome! Relationships are always more important than product knowledge. **People want to help you!** Simply ask and you shall receive :)

If you set up one informational meeting per week with someone that works at a company you want to work at for at least 20 weeks then I guarantee you that you will get an amazing job or customers. Please try it!

Sources of Entrepreneurial Ideas

How do we come up with ideas to launch a company? What are the best sources?

Before coming up with ideas, we must make sure that the size of the Total Addressable Market (or T.A.M.) is massive. Why? Because most start-ups fail and if you are successful, you don't want to get a small piece of a small pie. In venture capital we generally look for the TAM to be at least $20bn. The rationale is that if a company is successful and able to capture 5% of the market then it can achieve an annual revenue target of $1bn (or 5% of $20bn).

Start-up ideas and business themes last longer than we think. The same can be said for business trends. Here is a great example:

Can you believe that the management team below changed the world? Guess who they are: The management team in

this picture saw the cover of a magazine in the 1970s called Popular Electronics on the next page which changed their (and our) lives!

Any idea who they are? It was none other than Bill Gates and his friend Paul Allen who decided in the 1970s that *"one day there would be a computer on every desk and in every home."* This was close to 40 years ago and that investment trend still has legs! Investment trends last much longer than we think they do.

Other investment ideas that are only in the early innings of customer adoption includes the cloud computing paradigm shift where companies and consumers are putting much more data up in the cloud.

Global trends include, the material infrastructure development we see in Dubai or China:

Other trends include the buildout of the Internet, which was initially created in the late 1960s by the US government in case there was a nuclear war and the east coast of the US could not communicate with the west coast.

The 'Internet of things' trend is another one that is in the early innings. We are seeing many startups focused on this area.

Hollywood also has a material impact on investment ideas too! Many great tech products only exist because of Hollywood dreampreneurs that predicted the self-fulfilling way that technology will enhance our lives in the future; the future is now.

Hollywood has always had a fascinating and material impact on consumer technology.

Hollywood is also the place where technology meets the liberal arts. One can argue that we would not have many cool consumer tech products without Hollywood's influence on empowering the empowers to dream in tech. There are so many superb examples of this, including Star Trek's beam me up device, which was the genesis of the flip phone. What is fascinating about Star Trek is that they were on such a tight budget that the only reason that the beam me up device existed was because filming scenes of the Star Trek Enterprise landing on planets was really expensive; as a result, Scotty beamed them up! Without Star Trek we might not have sophisticated space dreampreneurs like Elon Musk.

Other cool Hollywood/media ideas that are now a reality include screen sharing scenes in Avatar that is now Apple's AirPlay, hand based gestures from Minority Report and the voice based operating system from Her; Scarlett Johansson you rock! Even this year's superb Ex Machina movie is now a reality; if you visit the awesome tech entrepreneurial Cuckoo's Nest in Menlo Park you are greeted by robots! Talk about forward thinking! This place is also the intersection of technology and the liberal arts.

Companies that have historically dominated operating systems like Microsoft (Windows), Apple (iOS) and Amazon (AWS) are all aggressively vying to be the market leader in voice based operating systems. You can witness the impact of the media on Microsoft as the company's Cortana voice product was named after a character in Halo; how cool is that! The movie 2001 A Space Odyssey had a chilling voice based operating system called HAL that was the genesis for today's voice based operating system. If you add one letter to H.A.L., you get I.B.M. which is also making progress in the voice market. The movie 2001 A Space Odyssey was released in 1968 while Star Trek was on television; the 1960s was such an incredible decade for tech influence and superb social justice (the two are not mutually exclusive).

Here are links to three movies that have a material impact on Silicon Valley venture capital investments from a graphical user interface perspective:Minority Report: www.tiny.cc/chris7 and the movie Her: www.tiny.cc/chris8

We must keep in mind that start-up ideas are irrelevant if we don't have the right management team.

The best CEOs and entrepreneurs are also superb salespeople. We need to beef up our sales skills in order to create a successful company. When you start a company you are constantly raising money. For more information on how to raise money, please see: www.tiny.cc/chris107 .

> "ideas are commodities. execution is not."
>
> - michael dell

> good entrepreneurs are GREAT salespeople.

ETHICS

All you have in business is your integrity. You might fail one or more times (which is ok) at launching a company, but you can only lose your reputation www.tiny.cc/chris9 .

Transparency builds trust – especially when it comes to crisis management; with crisis comes opportunity. This is precisely what happened in 1994 with Intel. The company noticed a small issue that would result in incorrect calculations for a very small percent of computer users running on Intel's latest Pentium processor. Once CEO Andy Grove found out about the incident he informed the general public about a recall which cost the company close to $500mn.

What Andy Grove didn't realize would happen is that he accidentally created the most important marketing campaign in the history of the semiconductor industry. Many people watching the news that day didn't know what Intel was. By the end of the relatively benign crisis management event, the first impression many consumers had of the Intel brand was that of trust.

Many other technology companies are also incredibly transparent and this creates outstanding brand loyalty and significantly enhances shareholder value. More importantly, it's the right thing to do. Salesforce.com discloses all outages and security issues in real time on this web site: www.tiny.cc/chris10

Google is also incredibly transparent. Google even discloses all Google self-driving car incidents online at this site: : www.tiny.cc/chris11 When companies are transparent, customers and investors are more comfortable doing business with or investing in the underlying company. This often leads to stellar long term revenue growth and in many cases, stock price appreciation. Always be 100% transparent in business, especially with the risks of the product or service you are selling.

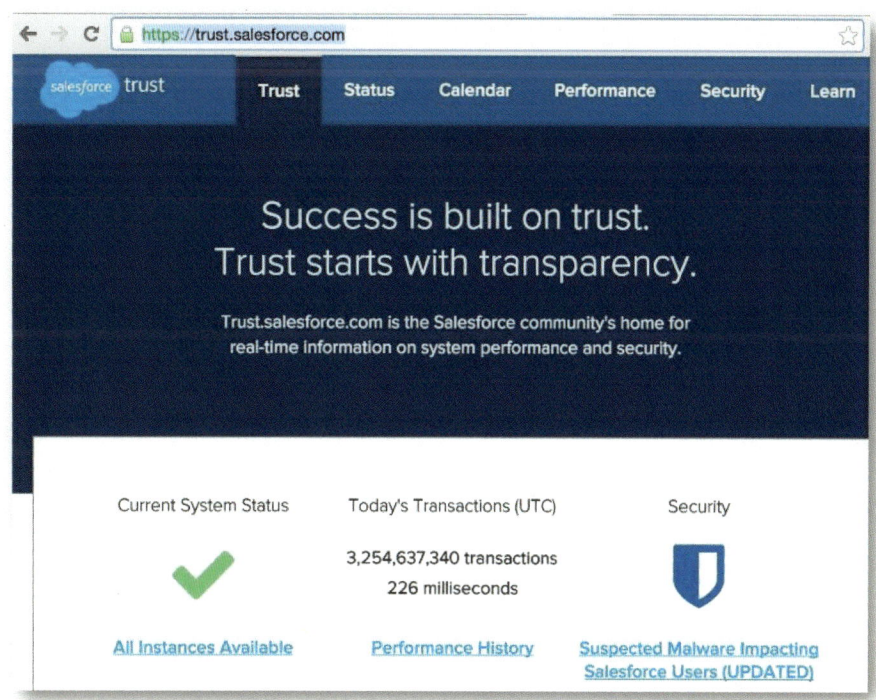

All you have in business is your reputation, which you take with you from one employer or start up to another.

I always feel that it is important to disclose risks within the first 30 minutes of a meeting with a potential or existing client. It's the right and ethical thing to do. It also leads to trust which is of paramount importance in business. It's crucial to disclose all risks to your clients or prospective clients before doing business with them. The only reason you might not offer 100% disclosure is in the rare situation when you can't divulge an issue due to confidentiality reasons. If this is the case and if the investment or product/service has significant risks that outweigh the potential returns, then don't sell the product/service. Life is too short to destroy your or your company's reputation and compromise your values.

I love Warren Buffett's quote of "**It takes 20 years to build a reputation and five minutes to ruin it. If you think about that, you'll do things differently**." Companies like Google, Salesforce and Intel have developed an incredibly loyal following over the years given their intense focus on ethics and transparency. It's not a coincidence that Google, Salesforce and Intel are all the market leaders in their sectors as transparency builds trust.

INVESTMENT STAGES

When you start a company, this is called the "seed stage". During the seed stage you have a concept or an unproven business model. At this stage you might raise money from friends, family or from what are called "seed" or "angel" investors. This is usually a smaller amount ($10,000 to $500,000).

7 or more years later (on average if you are successful) then you go public. This is called an initial public offering which is run by an investment bank. We will cover this topic in detail later in this book.

Quite often, in between the seed stage and the IPO stage you receive funding from either venture capital firms or banks. I strongly recommend never getting bank loans in the first 2 or 3 years of the company's life cycle. The reason is that banks are brutal when it comes to missing just one payment. More often than not, if you miss just one payment to a bank, then your business dies as the banks come after your assets. Brutal! We will cover the different ways to raise money in great detail in a future chapter.

You will find that you are always raising money when you start a company until you are cash flow positive, which can be several years after you launch a company. I don't recommend raising money from friends or families as this can strain your important personal relationships. I also don't recommend using your own money to start a company unless you have a lot of it! Don't ever put your family at risk of losing your house or your lifestyle via debt. Don't worry, we will go into a lot of detail on how to legally protect your family when starting a company and how to raise money from high net worth investors, corporations and venture capital firms.

In this book you will also learn how to present to different types of investors and how to significantly increase your chances of raising money.

What Kind of Legal Entity Should I set Up?

There are many different types of companies that you can set up and each has their pros and cons as follows:

Proprietorship: This is a company registered in one person's name:

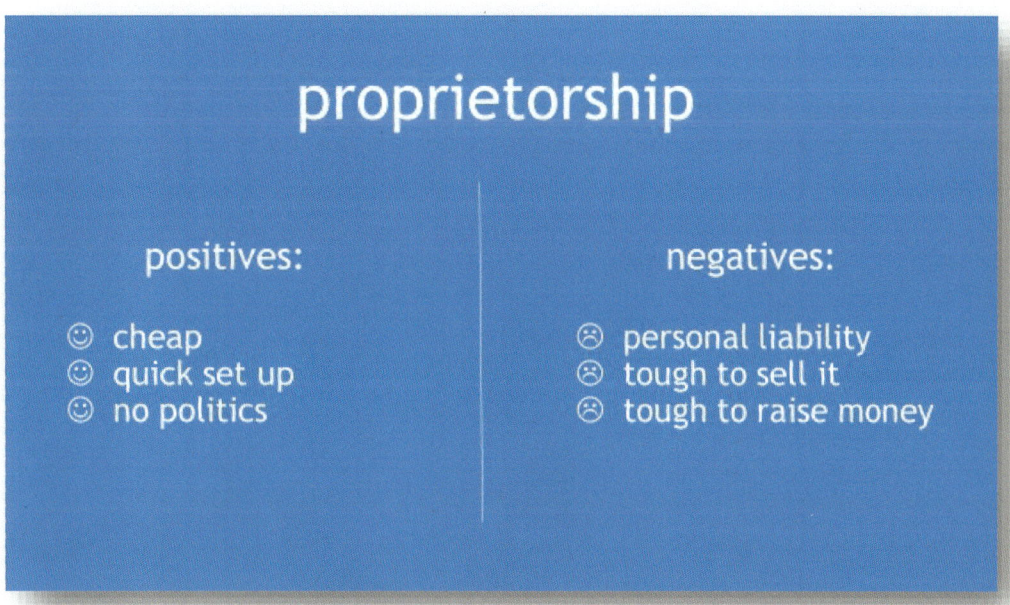

General Partnership: This is a company registered in two or more people's names:

Limited Partnership: This is a company registered where some partners (i.e., investors) are partners in the firm but their influence on the company is limited (they are usually passive investors):

Corporations: This is a company registered usually in many people's names and has a large board of directors and is necessary for an IPO:

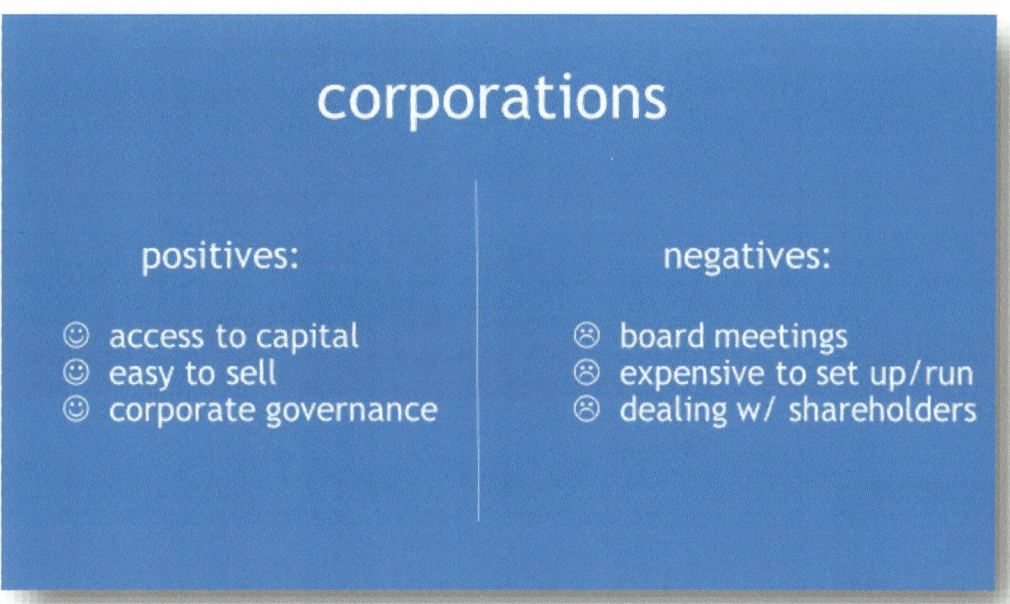

Limited Liability Corporation: My favorite type of legal structure for a new company is the LLC (limited liability corporation) as this type of entity can protect your house and personal assets if your company gets sued:

The annual cost to have a limited liability company is $800 in California, $300 in Delaware and can vary by region. More details are available at www.business.usa.gov. At this website simply search for "register LLC" then select "Start a Business Wizard" or "choose your business structure" or "forming an LLC blog."

Quite often companies choose to register in Delaware as it is more cost effective to do so in this state (among other reasons: www.tiny.cc/chris12). You can register a Delaware based company here: www.tiny.cc/chris13 .

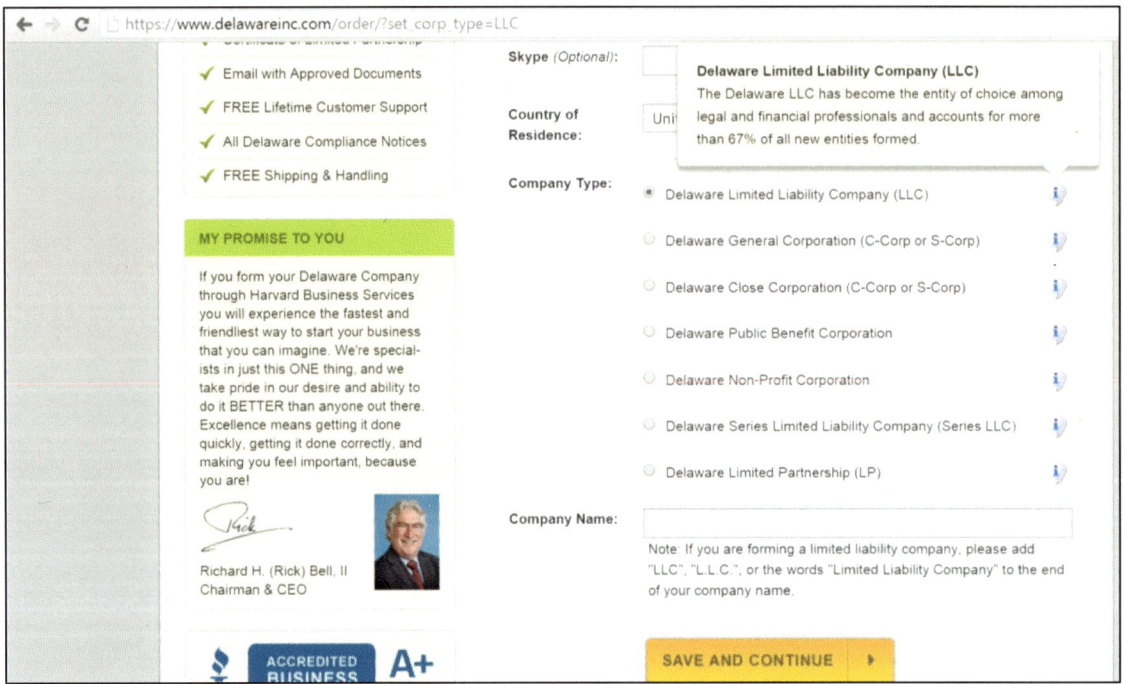

For all other legal startup questions, please visit www.LegalZoom.com which is an incredible resource (and easy to understand)!

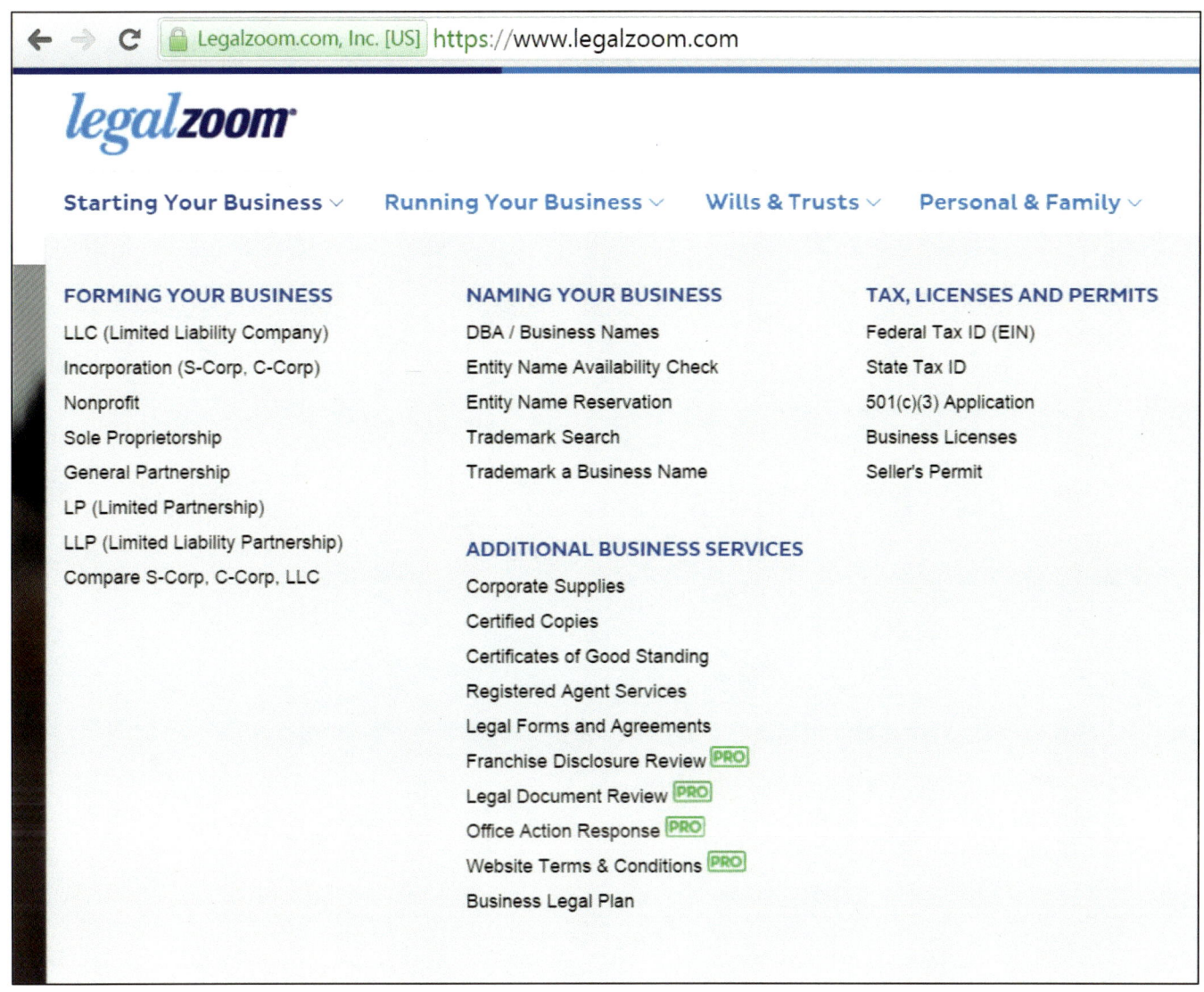

WHAT ABOUT TAXES?

In order to simplify how taxes work for companies or individuals, there are 4 government tax schedules that matter as follows:

Taxes for Single People:

Single:

Taxable Income	Tax Rate
$0 to $9,225	10%
$9,226 to $37,450	$922.50 plus 15% of the amount over $9,225
$37,451 to $90,750	$5,156.25 plus 25% of the amount over $37,450
$90,751 to $189,300	$18,481.25 plus 28% of the amount over $90,750
$189,301 to $411,500	$46,075.25 plus 33% of the amount over $189,300
$411,501 to $413,200	$119,401.25 plus 35% of the amount over $411,500
$413,201 or more	$119,996.25 plus 39.6% of the amount over $413,200

Taxes for Married Couples (filing together):

Married Filing Jointly or Qualifying Widow(er):

Taxable Income	Tax Rate
$0 to $18,450	10%
$18,451 to $74,900	$1,845.00 plus 15% of the amount over $18,450
$74,901 to $151,200	$10,312.50 plus 25% of the amount over $74,900
$151,201 to $230,450	$29,387.50 plus 28% of the amount over $151,200
$230,451 to $411,500	$51,577.50 plus 33% of the amount over $230,450
$411,501 to $464,850	$111,324.00 plus 35% of the amount over $411,500
$464,851 or more	$129,996.50 plus 39.6% of the amount over $464,850

Taxes for Married Couples (filing separately):

Married Filing Separately:

Taxable Income	Tax Rate
$0 to $9,225	10%
$9,226 to $37,450	$922.50 plus 15% of the amount over $9,225
$37,451 to $75,600	$5,156.25 plus 25% of the amount over $37,450
$75,601 to $115,225	$14,693.75 plus 28% of the amount over $75,600
$115,226 to $205,750	$25,788.75 plus 33% of the amount over $115,225
$205,751 to $232,425	$55,662.00 plus 35% of the amount over $205,750
$232,426 or more	$64,998.25 plus 39.6% of the amount over $232,425

Taxes for Companies

Corporate Tax Rate Schedule, 2014

Taxable Income Over	But Not Over	Tax Is		Of the Amount Over
$0	50,000		15%	0
50,000	75,000	$7,500 +	25%	$50,000
75,000	100,000	13,750 +	34%	75,000
100,000	335,000	22,250 +	39%	100,000
335,000	10,000,000	113,900 +	34%	335,000
10,000,000	15,000,000	3,400,000 +	35%	10,000,000
15,000,000	18,333,333	5,150,000 +	38%	15,000,000
18,333,333	—		35%	0

What does all of this mean? Let's look at an example. If a corporation makes $100,000 then how much tax will it have to pay?

Given the fact that we are looking at calculating taxes for a corporation, we have to use the "Taxes for Companies" table. The answer is not 34%. It's not that easy! It's not too hard either. It's just a few steps as follows:

The company pays 15% tax on the first $50,000 that it makes ~ meaning between $0 and $50,000(or $7,500).

The company pays 25% tax on the next $25,000 it makes ~ meaning over $50,000 and $75,000 of income (or $6,250).

The company pays 34% on the next $25,000 it makes ~ meaning between $75,000 and $100,000 (or $8,500).

This means that the total tax paid on $100,000 of corporate income is $7,500 + $6,250 + $8,500 = $22,250 or 22.25%

Now if a company issues dividends, then the recipient has to also pay taxes on the dividends. Hence, we get double taxation with dividends. WTF? Why the face :)

How Do I Stop Competitors from Illegally Copying My Products?

What does that symbol R or TM or C with a circle around it mean? I see that stuff everywhere! Well this is a legal way to protect your stuff. You can also stop your employees from leaking your corporate secrets using an NDA (non-disclosure agreement...more details on this soon).

Patents:

You can legally protect your product from being copied by filing a patent, which usually costs about $1k or much higher for a complex product (Google "hire a patent lawyer" rather than trying to do it yourself: www.tiny.cc/chris14). Once you file the patent, it takes about a year for it to be completed. While you wait to have the patent protected you are basically protected as if the patent had already been granted. This is why you often hear of the term "patent pending".

Trademarks:

How do you protect the name of your company or the name of a brand like Google or Microsoft? You file a trademark. If you want to protect your brand in all states in the United States, then you file a registered trademark, which is an R with a circle around it: ®. If you want to save money on expensive lawyers and just protect your brand in one or a few states (instead of on a federal level), then the trademark is TM with a circle around it: ™.

Copyright:

What if I want to protect something you can't touch like music or software or movies? In this case you can protect it with a copyright, which is a C with a circle around it©. A copyright lasts for 50 years after you die, which is why classical music is cheap to buy! Copyright is very common in the software sector. If you don't file many copyrights in software, you can lose control of protecting your company (www.tiny.cc/chris16)! On your computer in any software program go to the help and then go to "about" (pronounced "abooooot" in my Canadian accent! www.tiny.cc/chris17) and look for ® or © symbols.

Trade Secrets & NDAs:

If I file patents then aren't I giving away my company secrets? Potentially yes. This is why some companies have "trade secrets" and protect their trade secrets by making employees sign complex length contracts. Companies can even get employees to sign NDAs or non-disclosure agreements which means there are legal ramifications to breaking employment contracts www.tiny.cc/chris18 . Be careful with legal contract documents. If they are handed to you, pay a lawyer a few hundred dollars to help you understand what you are signing. Lawyers are a necessary evil. You need to protect your family by seeking their advice whenever you are considering signing an employment or large investment related legal contract.

Questions Based on Chapter 1:

1: T.A.M. stands for

    a) Total Addressable Market
    b) Total Available Market
    c) Total Actual Market
    d) Total Analytical Market

2: Successful founders/entrepreneurs usually have this quality:

    a) They are passionate about their company.
    b) They have great sales skills.
    c) They have an incredibly positive attitude.
    d) All of the above.

3 The benefits of using a Limited Liability Company (LLC) is:

    a) You can protect your family.
    b) You need an LLC structure in order to do an IPO.
    c) There is better corporate governance with an LLC than with a corporation.
    d) All of the above.

4: How do I protect my brand in all states in the US?

    a) You use NDAs.
    b) You use Chapter 11 protection.
    c) You use a registered trademark.
    d) You file a local copyright.

CHAPTER SUMMARY:

Chris Haroun @chris_haroun
entrepreneur qualities (passion, optimism, networking, sales). analyze trends for start-up ideas. company formation legal structures. Intellectual property protection.

CHAPTER 2: PRESENTATION WORKSHOP

"The ultimate measure of a man is not where he stands in moments of comfort and convenience, but where he stands at times of challenge and controversy."

- *Martin Luther King, Jr.*

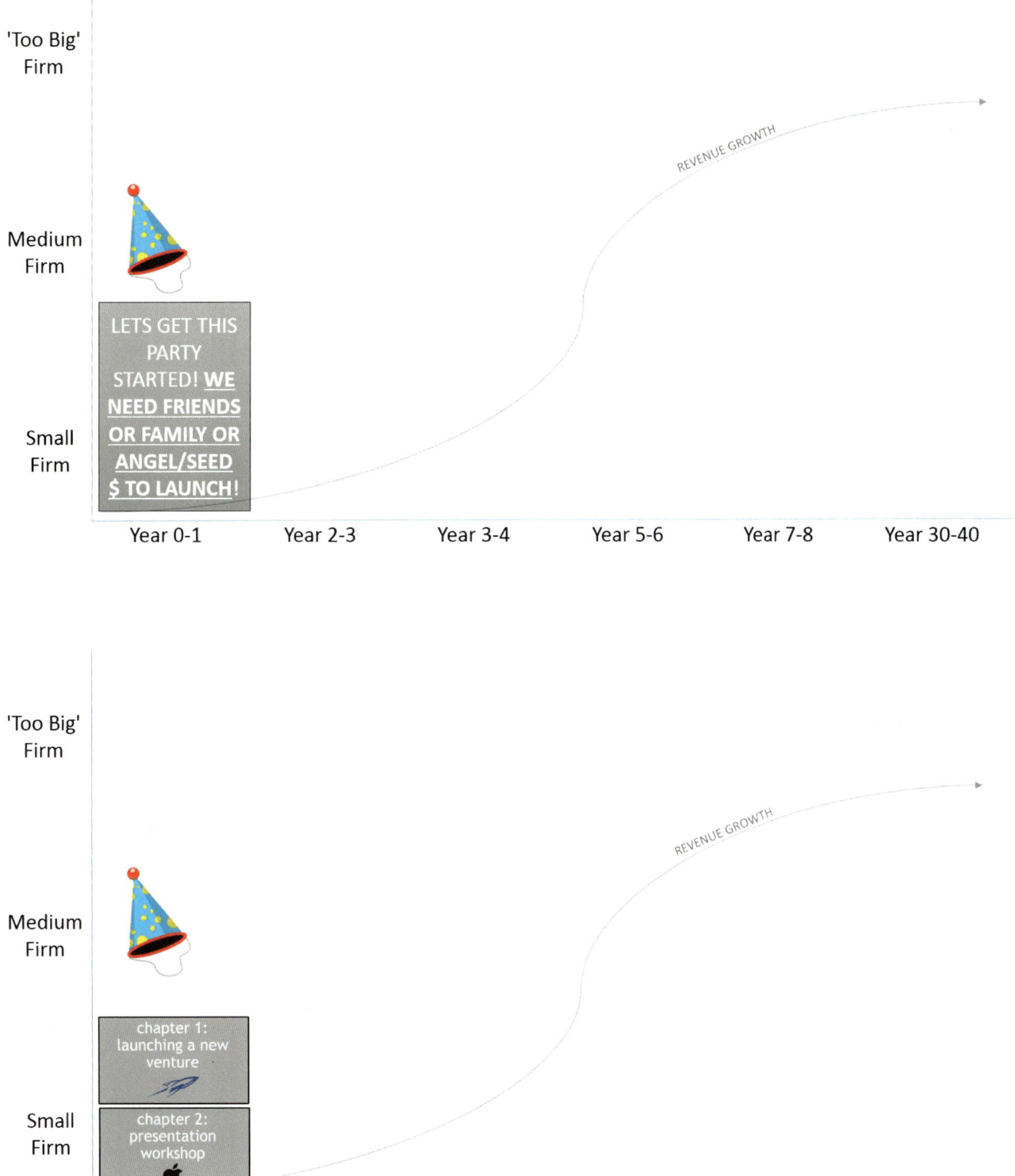

THE SECOND MOST IMPORTANT BUSINESS SKILL

Your ability to present to investors, customers, potential customers and peers is a crucial skill that you can improve at with practice. Please keep in mind that "less is always more" when it comes to presenting. The best CEOs and entrepreneurs often have the best presentation skills. Don't worry as you can improve materially with practice. Steve Jobs is the best presenter in history in my opinion. He didn't start off this way: www.tiny.cc/chris19

Compare and contrast that last video with how Steve Jobs presented later in life. Watch for how easy it is to understand him and how simplistic his slides are (less is more):

www.tiny.cc/chris20

In business presentations there is no need to be nervous. As strange as this might sound, when you present you need to remember that nobody is smarter than you. I am not telling you to be arrogant, just confident and passionate. This video will change your life (repeated on purpose):

www.tiny.cc/chris21

Rather than teach you how to present via boring text, I decided to simply paste presentation slides..less is always more...you can also watch the presentation version of this chapter online at http://tiny.cc/chris108

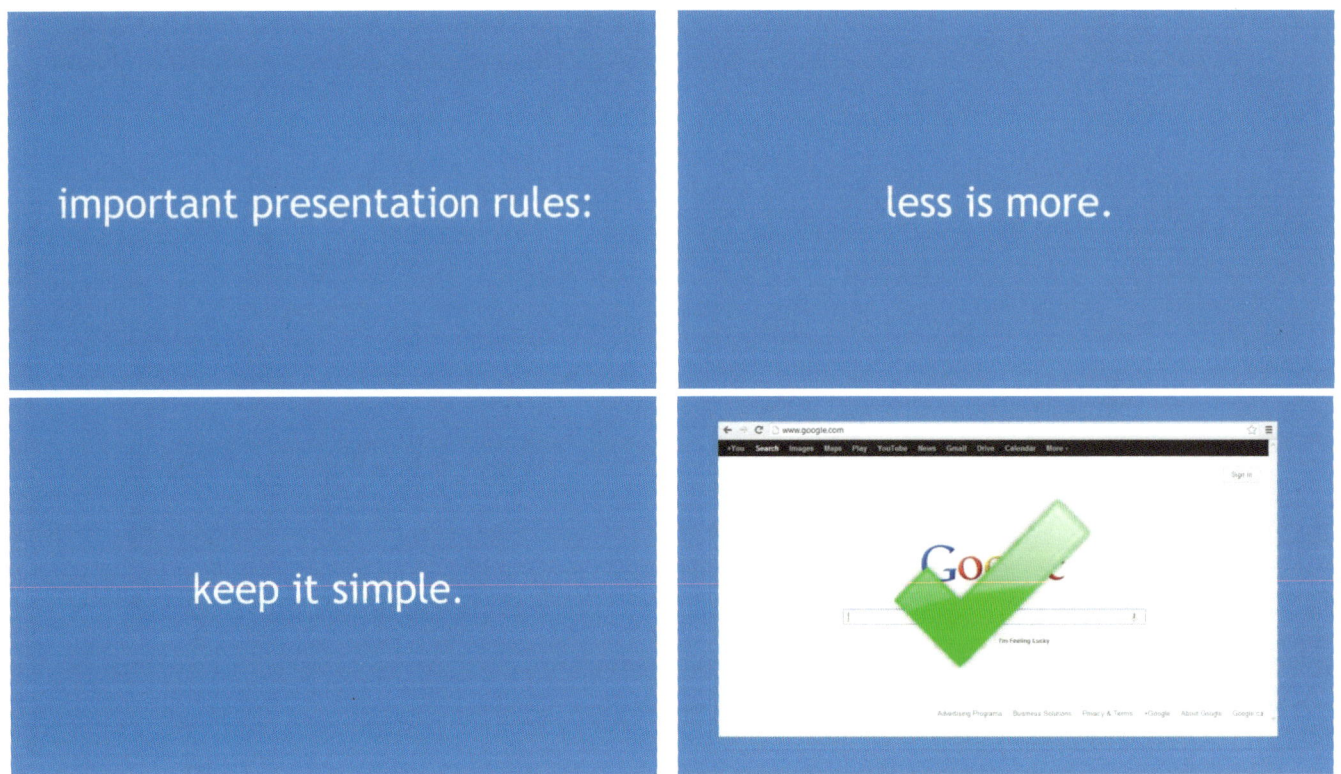

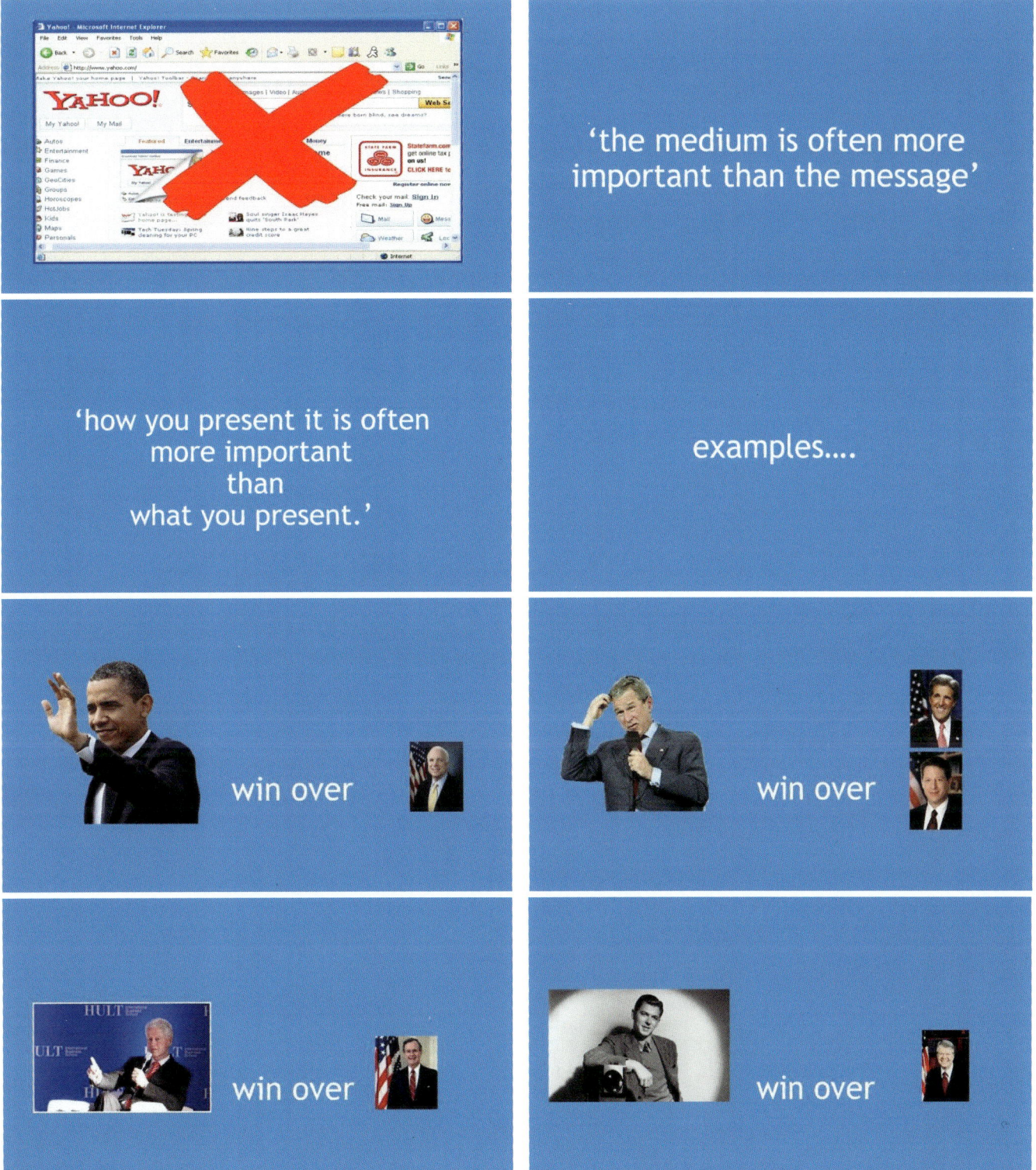

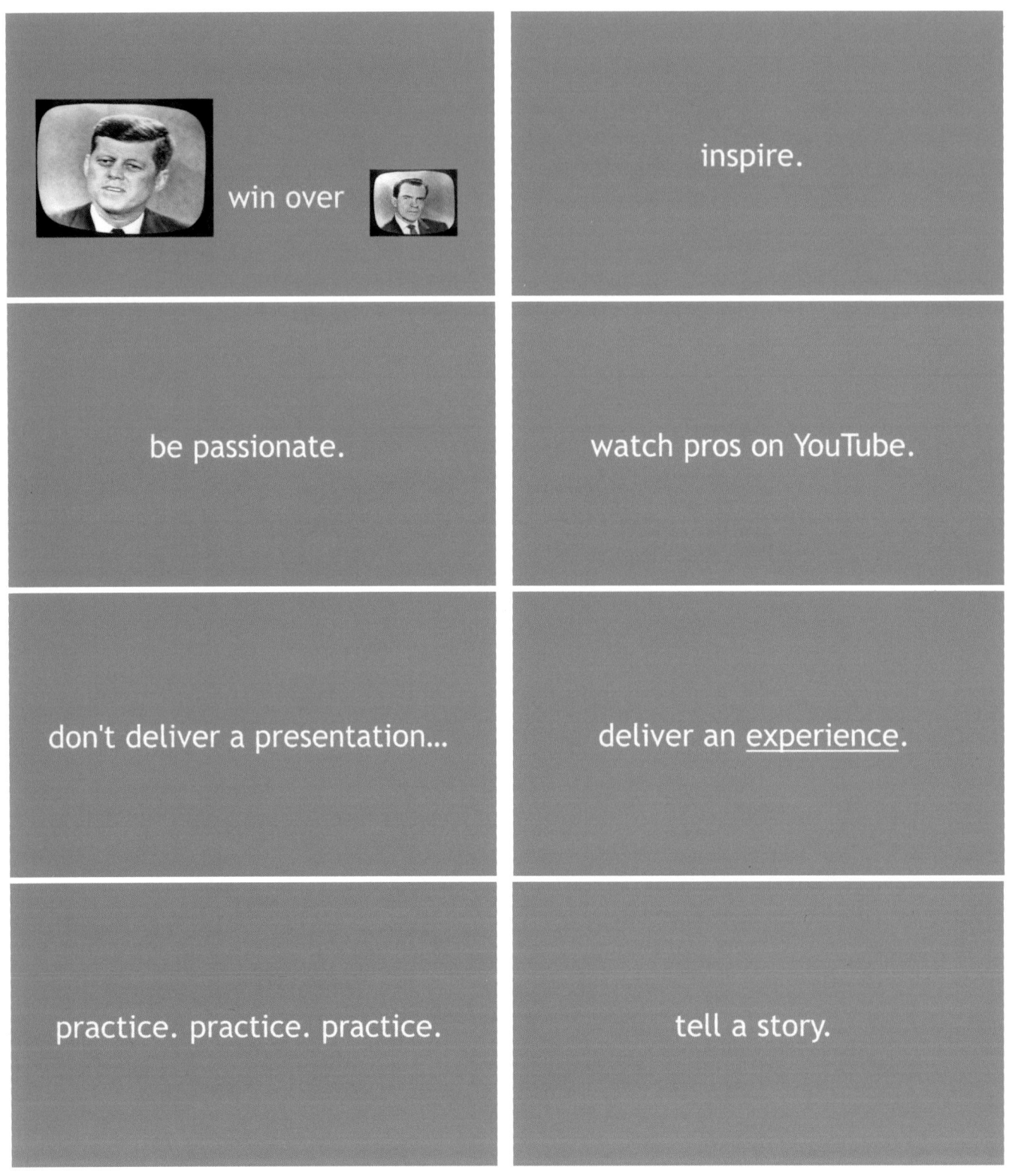

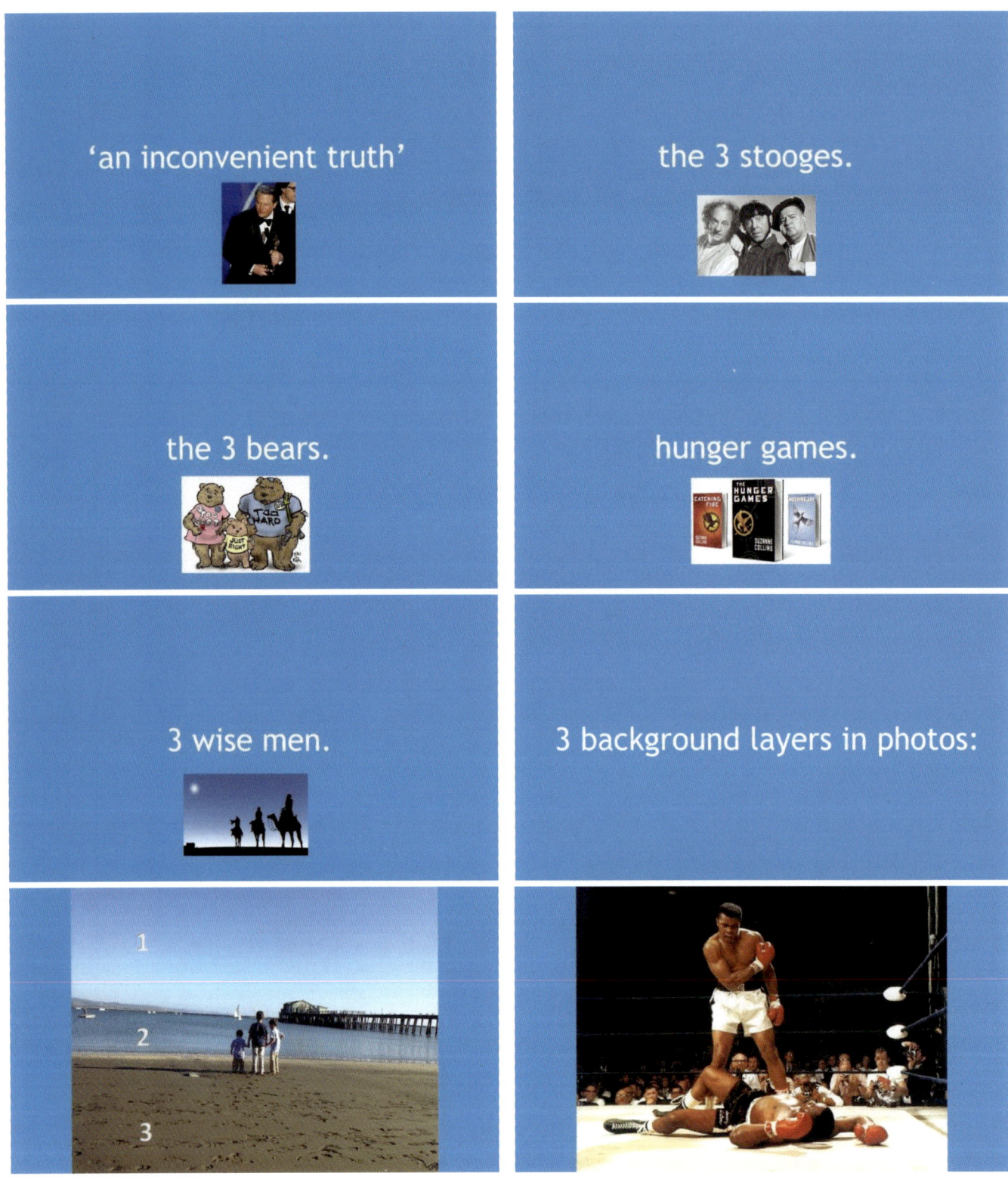

have some fun!	don't be boring.
change the world.	'one more thing'...
marketing is theatre.	~~mission statement~~.
create passion statement.	metaphors work.

The Ultimate Practical Business Manual

'a microprocessor is the brain of the computer'

customer testimonials work.

short video clips work.

props work. 'the product'.

If you don't have passion, you have no energy. If you have no energy, you have nothing.

-donald trump

'It's not about coffee. It's about passion and an experience.'

present with **passion**.

right from the heart.

don't read a script.

Observe how politicians or passionate business leaders like Marc Benioff or Richard Branson present. Also, watch for superb presentations during the annual Oscars award show. Here is an excellent passionate speech right from the heart by Matthew McConaughey: www.tiny.cc/chris109

We can only recall a few items on each slide, so a best practice is always to put as little detail as possible on each slide.

Below are a few examples of brutal slides with waaaaaaay too much information!

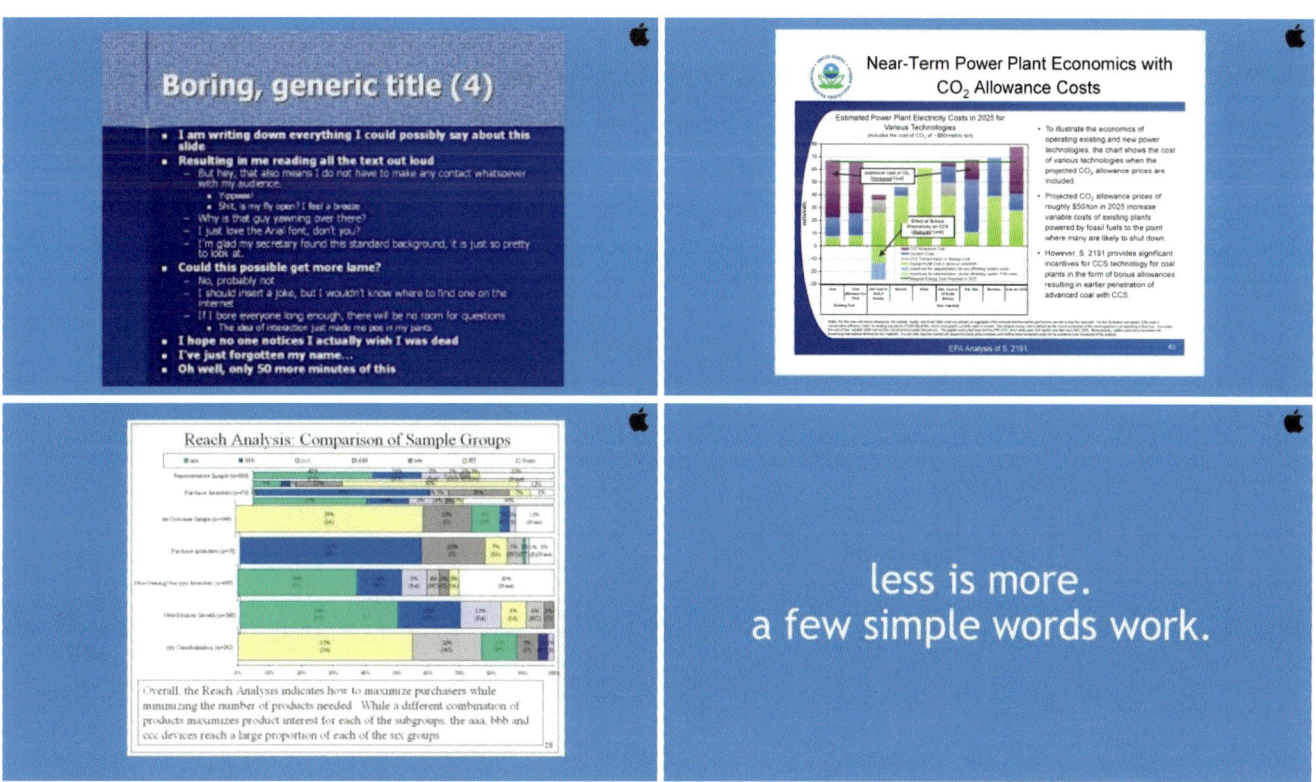

A few simple words can literally change the world. Watch this incredible speech by the late great Ronald Reagan in front of the Berlin Wall. Reagan went off script and created these two brilliant phrases that ended communism: *"Open this gate". "Tear down this wall"*.

www.tiny.cc/chris22

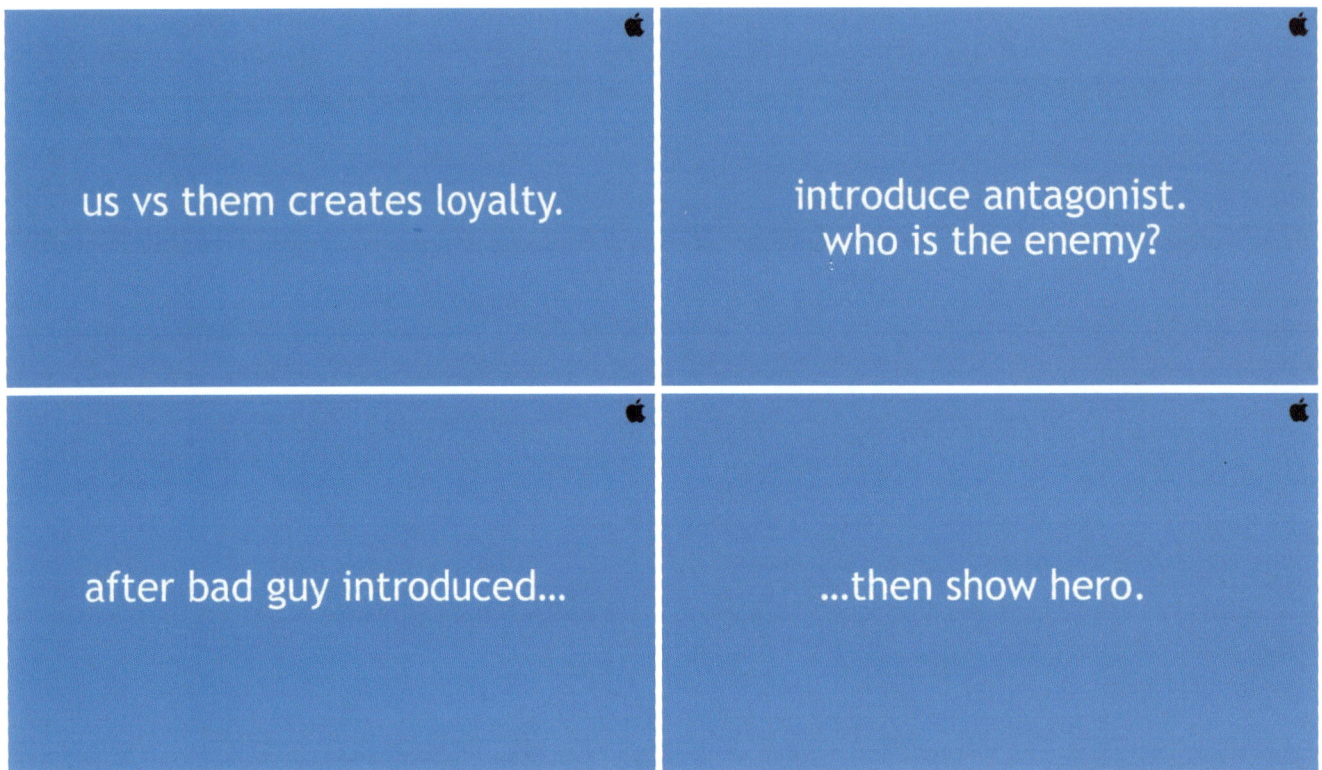

A common enemy is not something that only politicians use. Successful advertising campaigns also highlight who the enemy is. Here is an incredible commercial that Apple aired just one time in 1984 during the super bowl. The athlete represents Apple and every other character represents IBM: www.tiny.cc/chris23

In 2007 Apple used a commensurate strategy using humor to ridicule the competition, which was then Microsoft (the character in this video looks a little bit like Bill Gates): www.tiny.cc/chris25

Here is another sample commercial from Apple:
www.tiny.cc/chris26

> once u understand where pain is, you can define solution.

> clarity is also important...

Meryl Streep is incredibly clear (and humorous) when she presents:

www.tiny.cc/chris27

Conan O'Brien's commencement speech at Dartmouth. He epitomizes how to use humor (especially self-deprecation) when presenting:
www.tiny.cc/chris29

> humor + self 'deprecation' work.
> make eye contact with many:

> continuous presentations
> <
> 10 minutes....

> have breaks via videos etc.

There is a reason that T.E.D. talks are relatively short...people can't pay attention for more than 10-15 minutes without breaks for a short video etc.

Steve Jobs used the phrase 'insanely great' a lot. Always present in layman's or easy to understand terms. Oddly enough, some business executives chose to present at an 8th grade (or lower) vocabulary level in order to reach the widest audience possible. My kids have always been so excited after each Apple keynote presentation as nobody communicates better to the masses than Apple does.

This video from Apple and Steve Jobs on simplicity is incredibly inspiring: www.tiny.cc/chris30

George Bush gave the best speech of his presidency at ground zero when he went off script and spoke right from his heart: www.tiny.cc/chris31

use your hands.

Your audience will pay more attention to you if you use your hands often as this makes you present in a much more passionate and engaging way.

If you try your best to make eye contact with as many people as possible when you are presenting, then most people will pay attention as they feel that you are communicating directly with them.

make eye contact with everyone.

use dramatic pauses.

When you say something prophetic in a speech or somewhat confrontational, pause for about 2 seconds. Then resume your presentation. This dramatic pause is incredibly effective. The next time you see a politician like Barrack Obama on television, watch how he uses dramatic pauses.

Speak honestly from your heart and don't memorize speeches or use cue cards. If you speak from the heart you will come across as incredibly engaging and sincere.

be honest and sincere.

It's a cliché, but every battle is won before it has been fought. You can become literally the best presenter in the world (yes) if you practice a lot. I sometimes record myself with my iPhone and I watch for my bad habits, which includes the words "um", "ah", etc… I also try to watch that my voice isn't too monotone. I practice in front of my wife and friends often before presenting to a large audience.

Malcolm Gladwell coined the term "the 10,000 rule" in his book called Outliers. Each of the stars above practiced for literally 10,000 before they became the best in their game. See if you can name them all! The same can be said for Steve Jobs.

As a proud Canadian, I will be incredibly insulted if you don't recognize the "great one" in the black and white photo above :)

Let's revisit Steve Jobs' first television appearance: www.tiny.cc/chris32

"If you're not comfortable with public speaking - and nobody starts out comfortable; you have to learn how to be comfortable - practice. I cannot overstate the importance of practicing. Get some close friends or family members to help evaluate you, or somebody at work that you trust." - Hillary Clinton

[Slide: workshop.]

For the presentation workshop portion of this chapter, please see the rules on the next few slides and practice in front of your peers, family, friends etc. If you are not in a group setting, you can upload a video to YouTube and email me at charoun@gmail.com I will gladly give you my feedback! For this exercise, your only source of content for your presentation is Wikipedia.com .

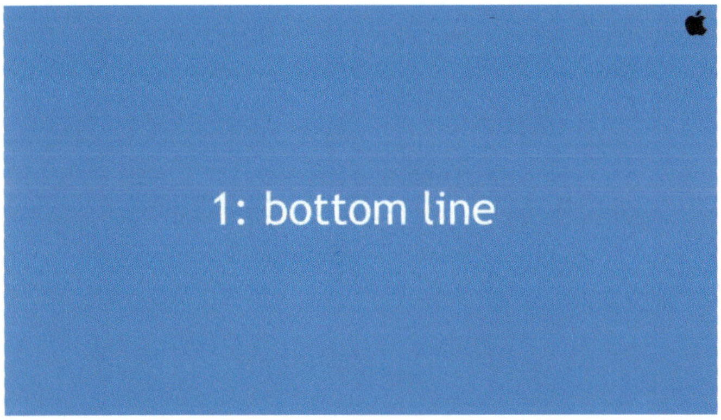

[Slide: source: wikipedia only.]

[Slide: 3 things to focus on...]

[Slide: 1: bottom line]

[Slide: 2: passion / delivery]

[Slide: 3: content]

After each bullet point you put on a slide (or after any sentence you ever write in business), ask yourself "so what?" Also, make sure that you reach a conclusion or bottom line in your presentation.

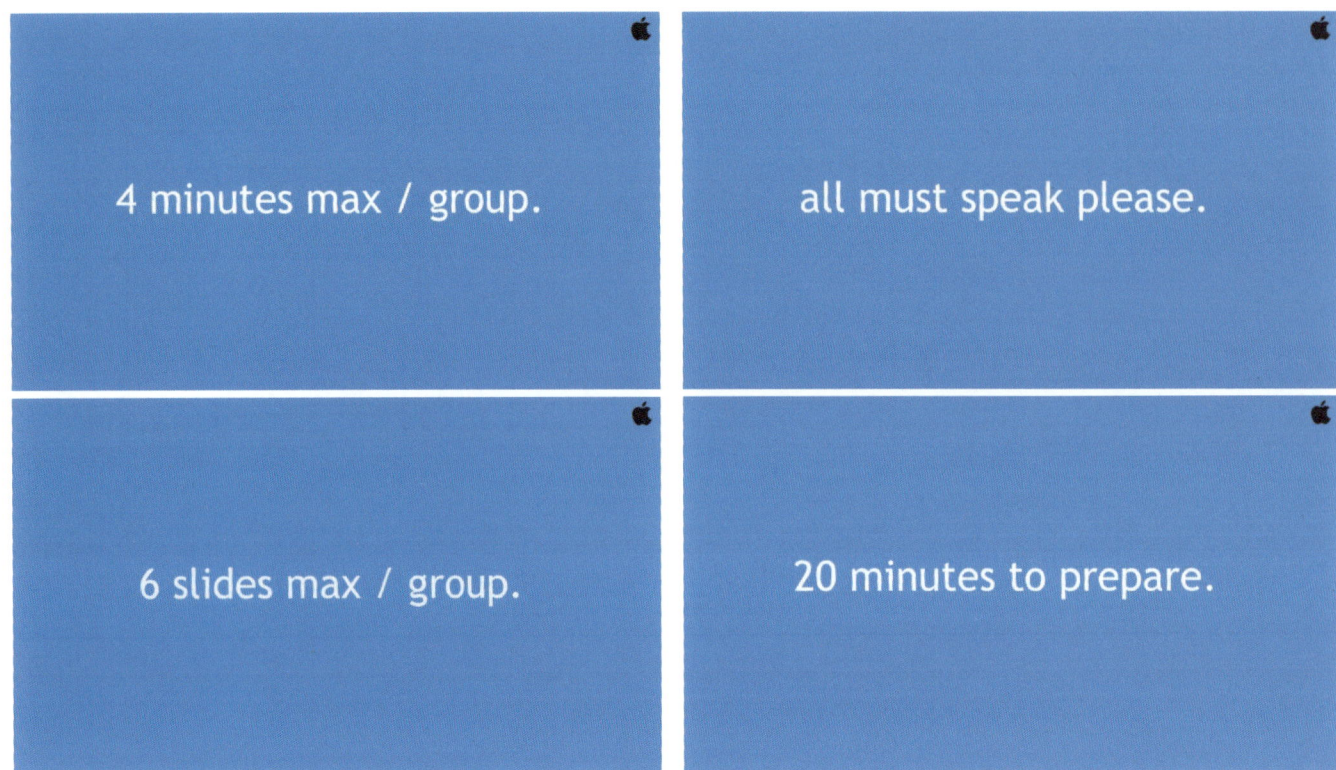

If you are doing this workshop with friends or work / school colleagues, please make sure everybody speaks. Have fun doing this! :) Each group should chose only 1 topic from the list of logos below. If more than 1 group is presenting, then each group should select a different logo. Again, have fun with this!

Let's end this section with the most empowering speech of Barrack Obama's career from 2004. Regardless of our political affiliation, you have to admire his ability to present in front of large groups of people. Watch for how he uses his hands, how he pauses, how he makes eye contact with as many people as possible and how he speaks right from his heart: www.tiny.cc/chris33

HOW TO CREATE AN IMPACTFUL START-UP PRESENTATION

Below is a rudimentary template to use for presenting a business model to potential investors (especially for very early stage companies). Remember that less is more. The goal of this presentation template is simply to impress your audience with the clarity and simplicity of your message so that you get a 2nd meeting.

less is more. keep it simple. 10 slides or less.	Company Name / Logo.
140 characters or less of what your company does. Picture of product.	Management team and advisors (if available).
Problem your company addresses.	Solution (how your company solves this problem).

Size of the market ("total addressable market").	Competition (and their weaknesses).
Basic annual financials (5-10 year revenue and earnings estimates).	Your contact details

Questions Based on Chapter 2:

1: When presenting, the best practices that you should keep in mind are:

    a) Present with passion.
    b) Less is more.
    c) Deliver an entertaining experience.
    d) All of the above.

2: Which of the following physical characteristics are important when presenting?

    a) Use your hands.
    b) Make eye contact with everyone.
    c) Move/walk on the stage if you can during the presentation.
    d) All of the above.

3: When making a presentation, each slide should have:

    a) More than 10 bullet points.
    b) Many small pictures.

c) About 3 bullet points max.
d) None of the above.

CHAPTER SUMMARY

Chris Haroun @chris_haroun
presentation rules: pls keep it simple. less = more. b passionate. c experts on youtube. video yourself. practice more than you need to :)

For more details on how to present and how to raise money, please see my Udemy courses:

Give Amazing Presentations & Enjoy Public Speaking!

www.tiny.cc/chris34

Fundraising: Raise Money from Anyone & from Venture Capital:

www.tiny.cc/chris35

Chapter 3: Venture Capital Part 1

"Ideas are commodities. Execution is not."

- *Michael Dell*

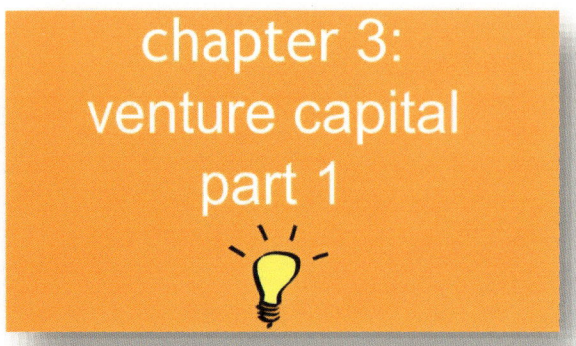

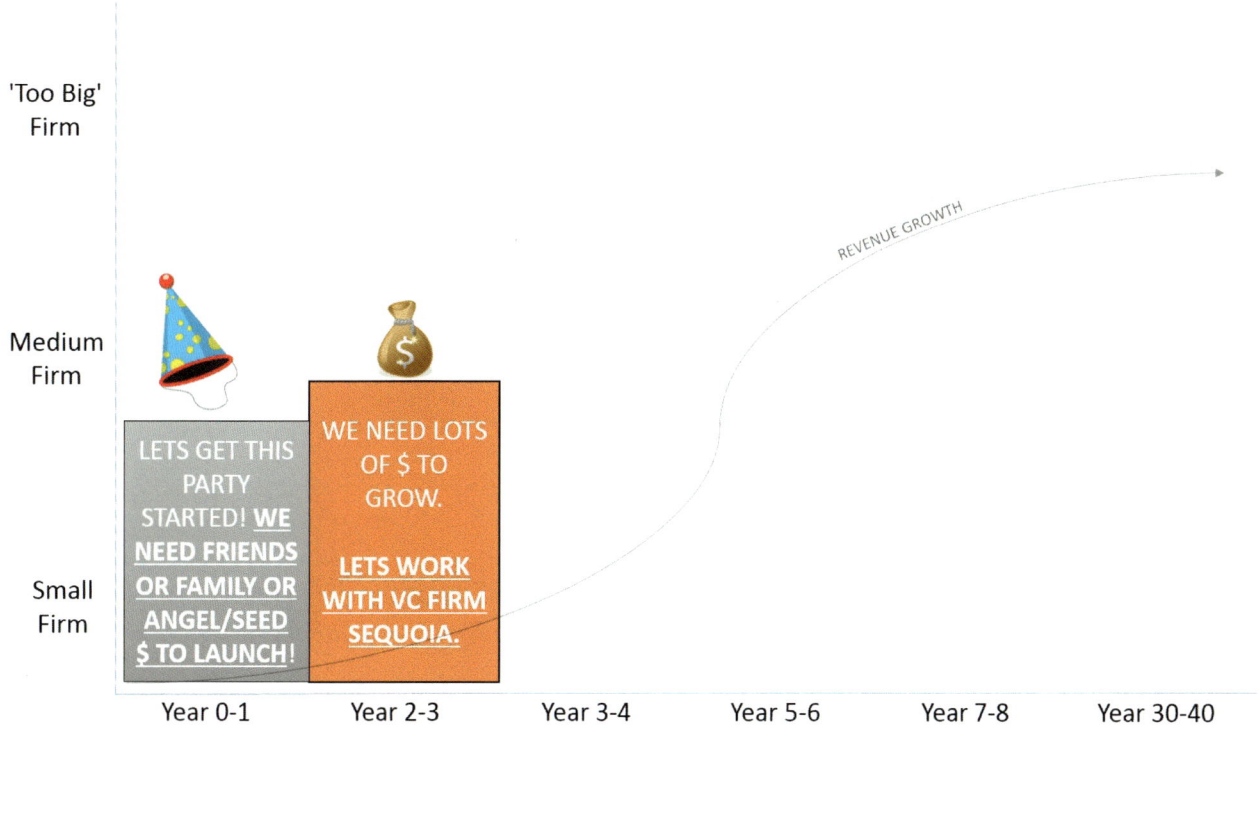
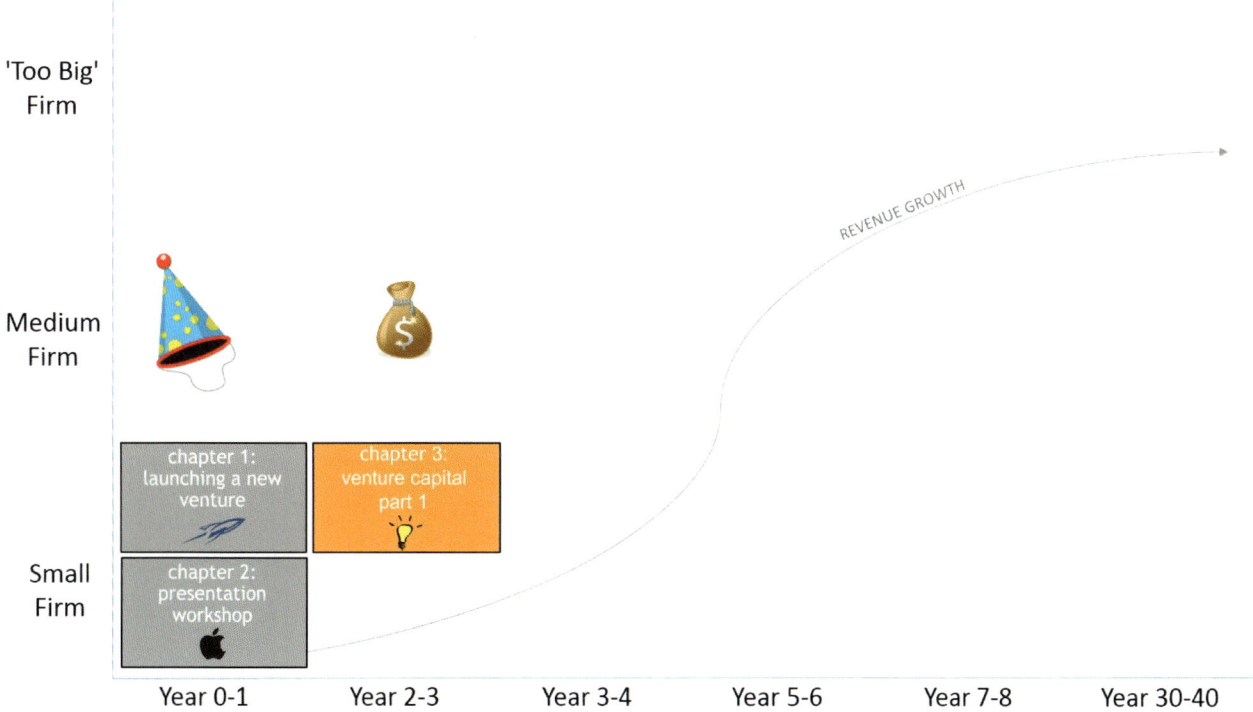

Why do we spend so much time on venture capital in this book? The reason is that you always want to use other people's money when starting a company (unless you are loaded). I don't want you to put your family at risk by over leveraging yourself. I don't want you to ever get bank loans either as banks will panic and make you pay back every penny if you are late on just one loan payment (and maybe come after your house...always put your family first)! Instead, I want you to sell part of your company (unless you are loaded) to an equity investor, including high net worths, companies or venture capital firms. It is so incredibly hard to get funded by a top venture capital firm. If a top venture capital firm funds you, then your chances of being successful rises materially. As such, we need to understand what these top venture capital firms look for in a company they are considering investing in! We also need to understand the fascinating history of the venture industry too (which we will do in another chapter...observe how the greatest entrepreneurs did it).

THE MOST IMPORTANT INVESTMENT CHARACTERISTIC IS....

Venture capital firms focus primarily on having a superb management team unlike this dude presenting to a potential investor and also to venture capitalists. Pay **very** close attention to what not to do in this video:

www.tiny.cc/chris36

:)

There is nothing more important with an investment that finding the right management team. The jockey is always more important than the horse.

Ideas are commodities. Execution is not. The most important critical success factor in business is investing in the right management team and not investing in the right idea. Why is it that most business schools don't dedicate any time to assessing the quality of a company's management team? Shouldn't this be the most important thing to consider before making an investment in a company? We spend far too much time  analyzing business models, markets and financial statements and we often overlook the most important investment quality, which is who is running the company and are they the right choice?

This is especially true in the money management or venture capital industry where the most important success factor in any investment is making sure that you have the right management team in place. The right management team can pivot, adapt and react to a material crisis or constantly changing end markets. The right management team can effectively market elegant products to their customers with the simplicity of Apple's Steve Jobs and with the healthy paranoia of Intel's Andy Grove.

Past performance is indicative of future performance if you have the right CEO and the right management team. Yes that was a very controversial statement, but I believe that if you bet on a management team that has been extraordinarily successful in the past, then your chance of success betting on this management team in the future is materially higher than it is betting on a B or a C management team.

The best CEOs and entrepreneurs don't have a job; they have a passion. Superb examples of passionate CEOs and entrepreneurs include Richard Branson of Virgin, Marc Benioff of Salesforce, Christian Chabot of Tableau and Godfrey Sullivan of Splunk. The best CEOs and businesspeople in the world are passionate salespeople with unbelievably positive attitudes. Their positive attitudes lead to an incredibly positive corporate culture. Fly on Virgin America or Virgin Atlantic and you will understand why Virgin is an exceptional brand. Virgin employees are so happy that they don't appear to have a job! Rather, they have a passion. Watch an interview with Richard Branson and you will understand why.

Similarly, employees of technology company Splunk are incredibly positive people and this might be due, in part, to the incredible leadership of their CEO Godfrey Sullivan whose genius is that he praises often in public and only offers constructive feedback in private. The result is a relentless, positive 'can-do' attitude that resonates throughout the entire company. This has led to the creation of one of the best corporate cultures in the history of the technology sector.

How do we assess if a CEO or an entrepreneur is worth backing? We can use www.Glassdoor.com and read reviews of the management team written by employees. Godfrey Sullivan from Splunk and Marc Benioff from Salesforce both have 96% approval ratings according to Glassdoor.com from employees and Christian Chabot from Tableau has a 100% approval rating!

How do we do additional background checks on a CEO before deciding to invest in the company? Never call references that the CEO provides as nobody would ever provide a reference list of people that wouldn't say something positive! Rather, use LinkedIn and find contacts that you (or your friends/colleagues) have that know the CEO or people that work at the CEO's company. Then simply call these contacts and ask for feedback on whether or not the CEO is an effective salesperson and leader.

For private companies, read about the background of the management team on the company's website. For publically traded companies, you can read the annual reports, which all have descriptions of the background experience of the executive team. You can find a wealth of information online at www.sec.gov.

The productivity of employees of a company with a passionate, visionary leader is materially higher than the competition. More productive employees leads to enhanced shareholder value over time. We will all be much better investors if we spent a lot more time analyzing management teams. Only after we feel comfortable backing the right management teams should we start doing due diligence on the business model or the total addressable market.

Ideas are commodities. Execution is not. Always bet on the jockey and not on the horse.

WHAT IS VENTURE CAPITAL?

When you start a company you raise money from friends or family members or high net worth individuals (if you can, avoid soliciting money from family and friends). All of these investors in an early stage company are referred to as "seed" or "angel" investors:

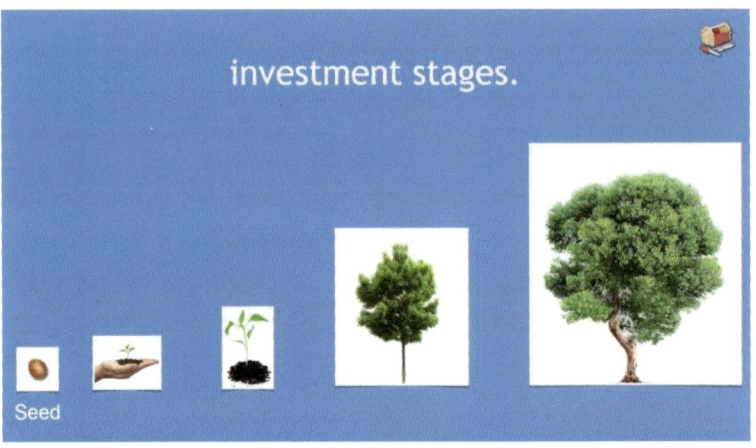

Then once your company is huge and usually at least 7 or 8 years old and growth is positive but slowing, then a company goes public through an IPO (initial public offering):

Everything in between the Seed investment and the IPO is what we refer to as venture capital:

Venture capital is usually raised when a firm has been around for more than one year and the company needs access to larger pools of capital to grow. The first time a company raises money from a venture capital firm it is called "The A Round". Then 1 or 2 years later when a start-up needs even more capital to grow then they raise even more money from another venture capital firm in what is called "The B Round". Then in another 1-2 years when the firm needs even more capital to grow, then there is "The C Round". Quite often companies do a D or E round and then they go public. 6 months after the IPO then the venture capital firms are allowed to sell their stake in the company and "harvest" their investment.

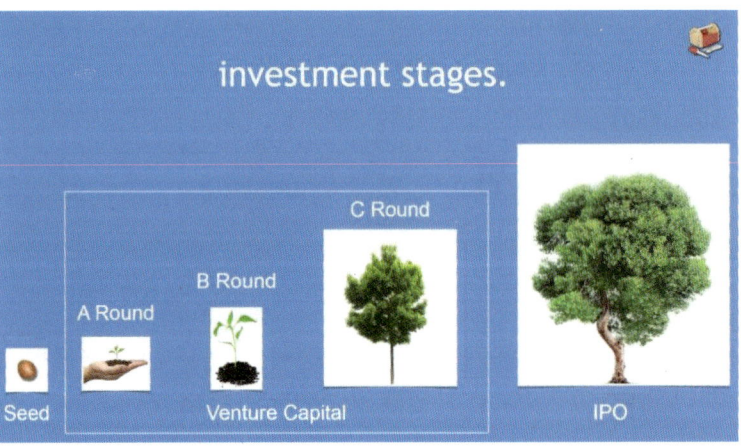

About 50% of all venture capital in the United States is based in the San Francisco Bay Area given the plethora of high quality technology engineers, of which more than 60% were born overseas.

There has been a lot of recent interest in the venture capital from institutional investment firms that have historically focused on public only investments. Many publicly focused mutual fund companies are now also investing in the venture capital sector as they are realizing that technology companies are staying private much longer. Many technology companies are staying private much longer as they know that large cap technology companies like Cisco or HP or Oracle no longer have great organic growth prospects (given their size and the law of large numbers). The aforementioned companies have also realized that it makes more sense for them to acquire innovation instead of innovating internally. As a result, valuation has become a bit of an issue in venture capital lately.

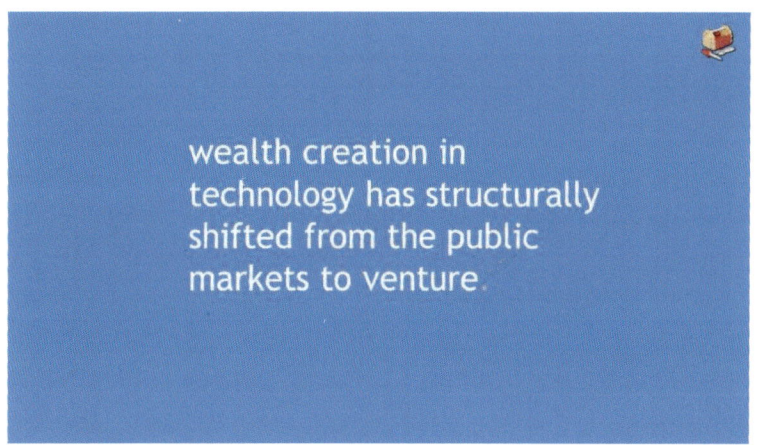

HOW DO VENTURE CAPITAL FIRMS MAKE MONEY?

Venture firms charge an annual 2% management fee that covers their labor and infrastructure overhead.

Venture firms charge a 20% fee on investments that have been harvested through either an IPO or a sale to another company. For example, if you invested $100 in a venture capital fund for 5 years that had a 10x return profile, then you would make $790 as follows

- Management fee = $2 annual management fee x's 5 years = $10 in management fees over 5 years
- Fund carry (or 'incentive') fee of 20% + management fee= $100*10x return *0.20 fee minus the $10 management fees over 5 years = $210 fee for the venture capital firm over 10 years
- Profit for the investor on a $100 investment = 100x10 -210 = $790

Venture capital firms typically look to make 5x's their money in 5 or so years on each company that they invest in. They call this "a 5 by 5". The reason that they have to focus on significant returns is that most of their investments end up not making any money. For every Facebook, there are countless thousands of investments that run out of money and go belly up.

How Do I Raise Money from a VC Firm?

In the previous section we covered the basics of presenting to potential investors. That was part of the 30 minute first meeting with a VC firm. You need to also have a condensed 30 second "tweet pitch" which is also referred to as an elevator pitch. This 30 second pitch is crucial as you need it to get your first meeting with a venture capital firm.

Once you get your first meeting with a venture capital firm, you need to sell yourself. They will be assessing you more so than your business model. Give them every reason to believe that you are a superb salesperson and the right passionate leader for your company. If you don't have enough experience, then make sure that your board of advisors do! For more details on how to put together a board of advisors please refer to the networking section of this book. If you are building a tech company, then use your LinkedIn networking skills to get employees of Apple or Google or Facebook, for example, on your board. All you have to do is ask (that's right). Investors will take you more seriously if you have a seriously awesome board.

Make sure to keep your pitch to no more than 10 slides and dumb it down a lot as your investors are not as sophisticated as you think they are. Keep everything in easy to understand language like Steve Jobs did when pitching the iPhone or iPod or iPad to customers. I have a friend in Boston named Rubin Gruber from McGill University who has founded many incredibly successful companies, including Sonus Networks. Before starting any company, he flies up to Montreal and has dinner with his 90 year old mother who is also his best advisor. If he has trouble pitching the idea to his mom, then he either changes his approach or he decides not to launch that company.

Make sure that you are an expert in the market that you are participating in when presenting to venture capital firms. You need to be able to discuss the total addressable market size, your anticipated market share and who your partners, investors and advisors are (name drop if you can). You also need very basic annual revenue and expense line items for at least 5 years.

Show the product by the second slide of the presentation. You will be amazed how many people pitch business models without ever showing the product! By showing the product early in your presentation, your potential investors will have no problem paying attention or understanding your business model. If you confuse them in the first few minutes of a presentation, then you have lost them for good. Why? Because they won't have confidence that you can sell to potential customers! Remember that the best founders and CEOs are incredible sales people like Marc Benioff from cloud company pioneer Salesforce, which is now the largest employer in San Francisco.

Make sure that your pitch and slides are simplistic, elegant and be somewhat entertaining too. Be passionate about the company when presenting. You want to let them know that this is not a job for you. Rather, it is a passion. Keep it simple; less is always more!

Questions Based on Chapter 3:

1: The seed or angel stage comes after venture capital stages.

> True   or   False

2: Venture capital firms have a very short-term investment time horizon.

> True   or   False

3: The quality of the business model is much more important than the quality of the management team.

> True   or   False

CHAPTER SUMMARY

Chris Haroun @chris_haroun

vc overview. importance of having a strong management team. how to pitch to VC. BE PASSIONATE WHEN PRESENTING!

CHAPTER 4: VENTURE CAPITAL PART 2

"Only those who dare to fail greatly can ever achieve greatly."

- *Robert Kennedy*

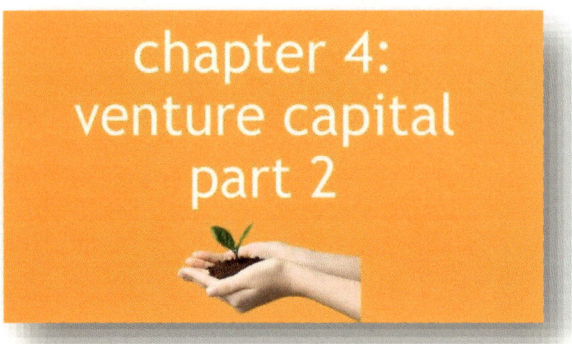

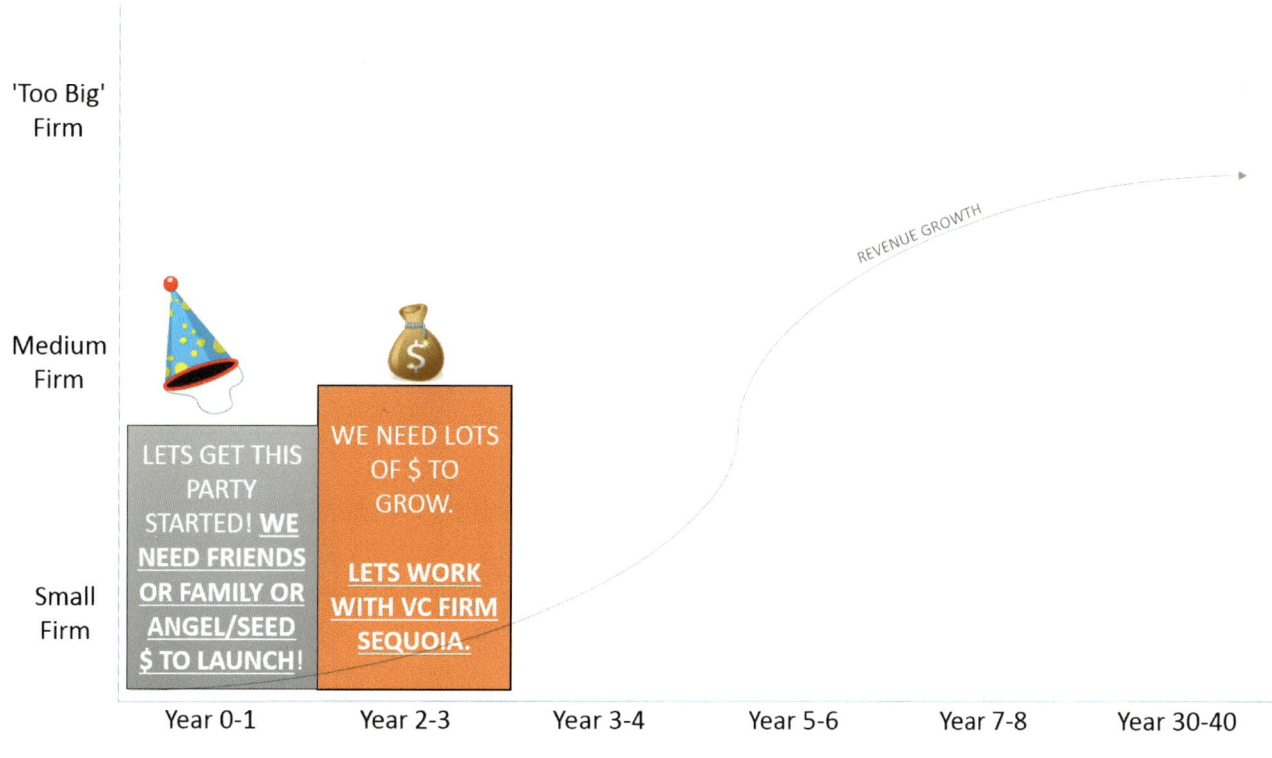
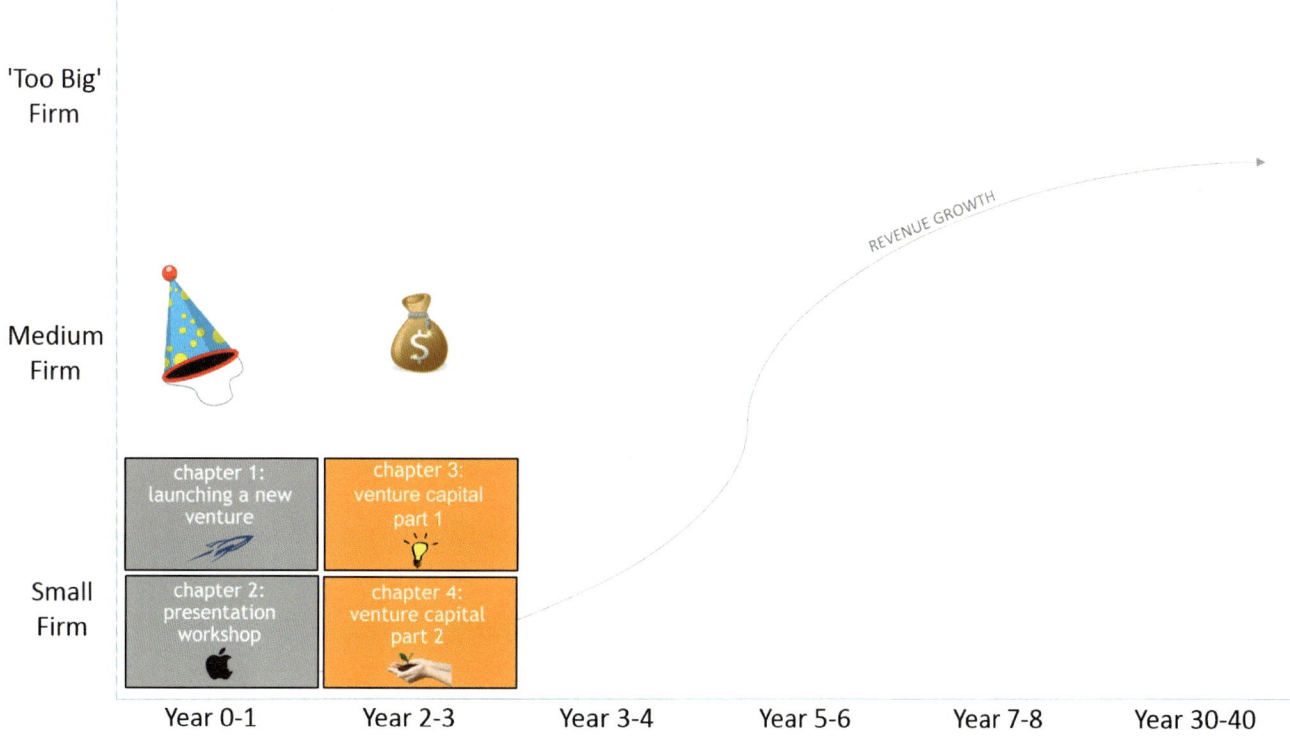

THE FASCINATING HISTORY OF VENTURE CAPITAL

In order to understand the brilliant minds of commerce, including Steve Jobs, Andy Grove, John Doer, Bill Gates, Mark Zuckerberg, Larry Ellison, Marc Benioff, Doug Leone, Andy Bechtolsheim, and other Silicon Valley legends, we need to understand why Silicon Valley is the birthplace of so many incredible companies. Why is it relevant? Shouldn't Boston be more relevant with MIT, Harvard and other great schools? Shouldn't London be more relevant given Oxford, Cambridge and other great schools? What is it about Silicon Valley that makes brilliant drop outs like Steve Jobs and Mark Zuckerberg so successful?

We need to do a deep dive on the genesis of Silicon Valley to really understand what drives entrepreneurs in this region and what we can learn from them. This chapter and Silicon Valley is where *technology meets the liberal arts…*

The most successful people in business think different. They challenge conventional wisdom and authority and the way things are done. They don't care what others think about them. They are pioneers. They are passionate. They are positive and often criticized; they believe that unjustified criticism is a disguised complement…and so they welcome criticism and thrive on it…..I love that! They are my business heroes and we will learn about what drove/drives them in this chapter.

This will be a highly entertaining chapter. A video version of this chapter can be accessed online at www.tiny.cc/chris37 .

Silicon Valley is relevant today because of many different 1960's conflicts, including the following:

- ❏ The conflict between the USSR and the USA.
- ❏ The conflict between those in favor of and those against the war in Vietnam.
- ❏ The conflict between those over 30 and those under 30. A popular hippie saying then was "don't trust anyone over 30".
- ❏ Those in favor of drug use and those against drug use.
- ❏ Those in favor of free love and those against it.

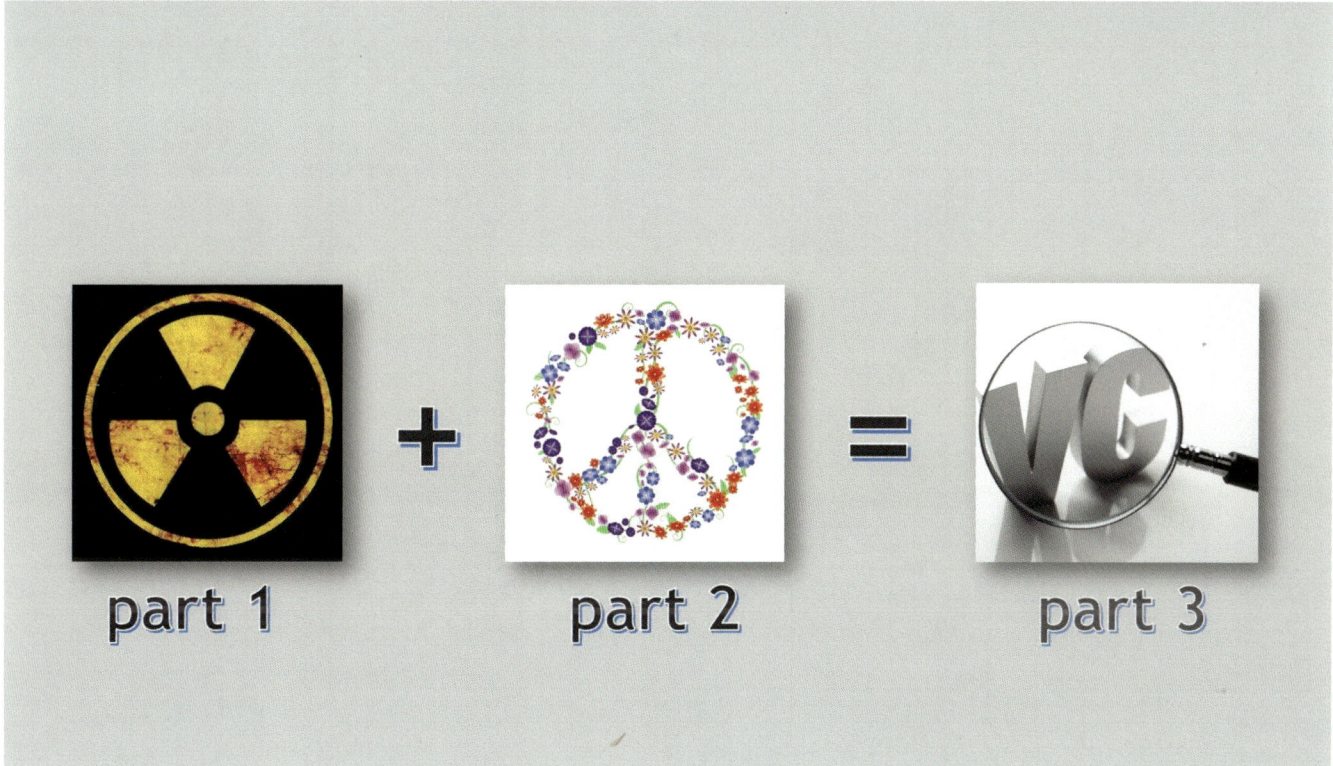

There are 3 parts to this historical chapter on venture capital. We will start with War (Part 1).

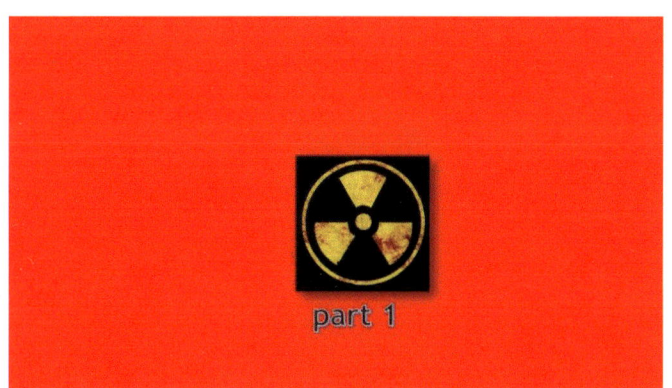

The Ultimate Practical Business Manual

yes...american fear of russia is the only reason the vc industry exists.

the post ww2 catalyst that created vc was both:

war & peace

the post ww2 catalyst that created vc was both:

 &

是. competing with russia is the only reason the vc industry exists.

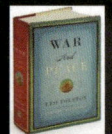

fear and the cold war led to the creation of the internet.

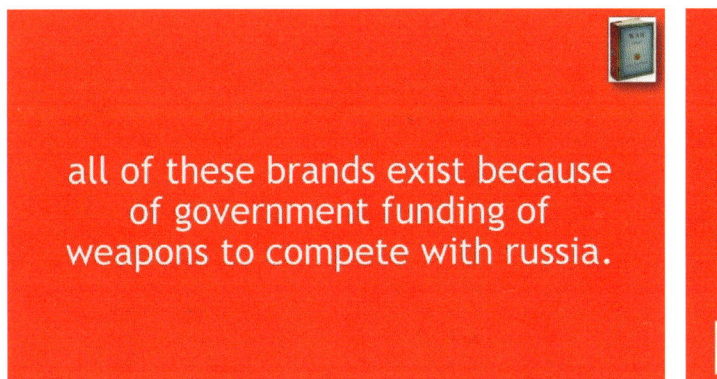

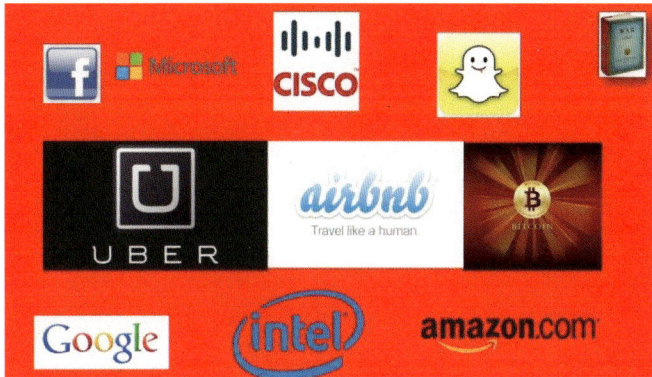

all of these brands exist because
of government funding of
weapons to compete with russia.

Microsoft
CISCO
UBER
airbnb
Travel like a human.
Google
intel
amazon.com

The underlying technology behind all of the aforementioned brands was based on government funding of military based technology research projects.

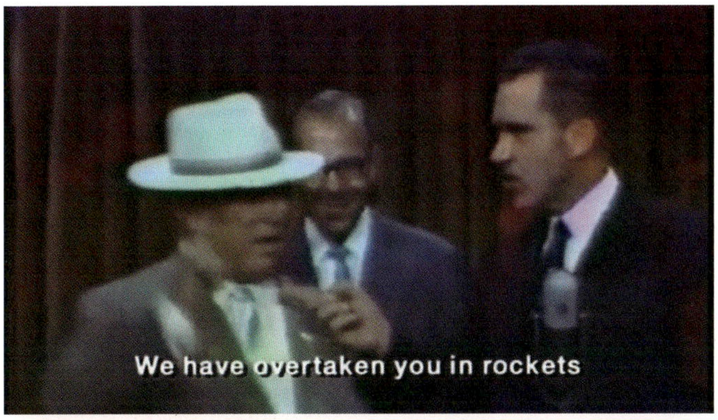
We have overtaken you in rockets

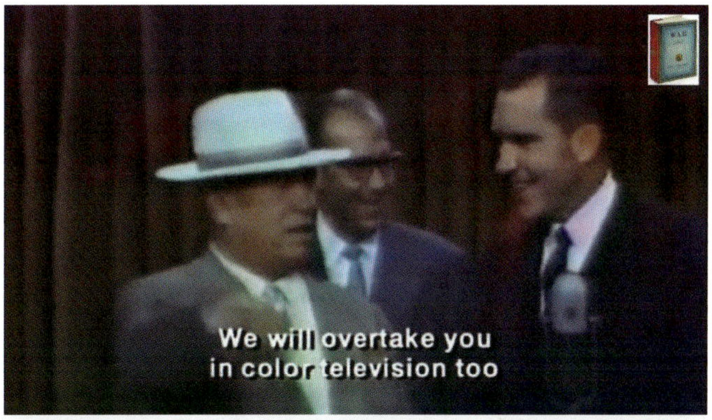
We will overtake you
in color television too

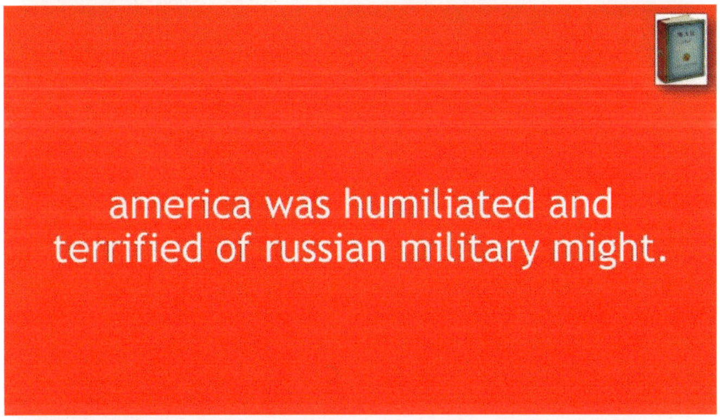
america was humiliated and
terrified of russian military might.

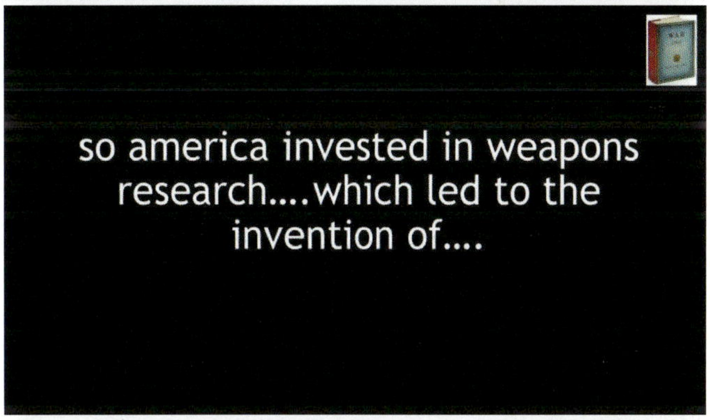
so america invested in weapons
research....which led to the
invention of....

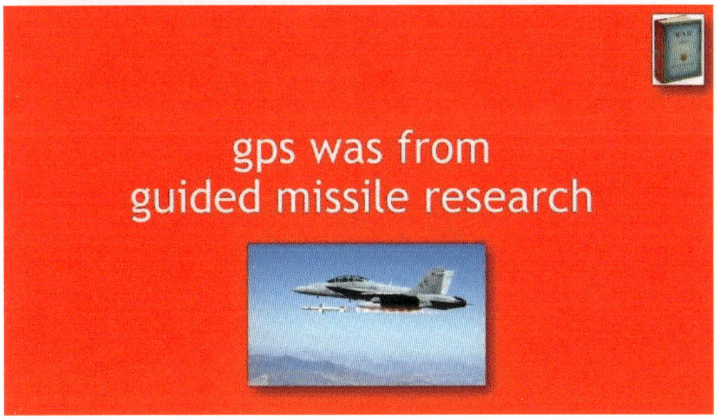
gps was from
guided missile research

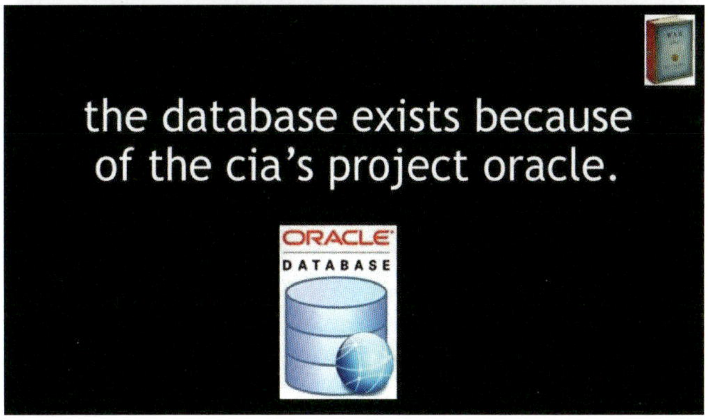
the database exists because
of the cia's project oracle.
ORACLE
DATABASE

Most people don't realize that the largest employer today in Palo Alto is not Facebook. Palantir (www.tiny.cc/chris39)is now the largest Palo Alto based employer. Palantir makes an extremely sophisticated software program that solves many of the world's most complex problems. In fact, a significant reason that the Obama administration was able to find Osama bin Laden was because of the use of Palantir.

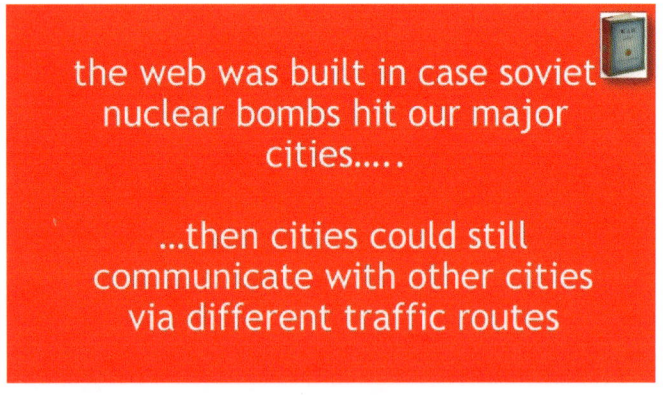

Russia put weapons in Cuba and almost started World War 3. Khrushchev told America we will bury you. www.tiny.cc/chris38

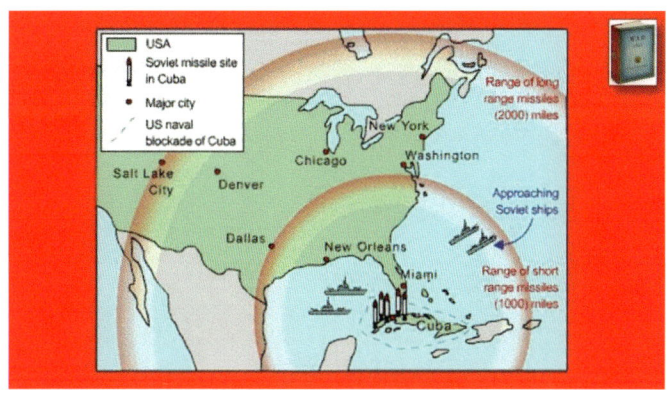 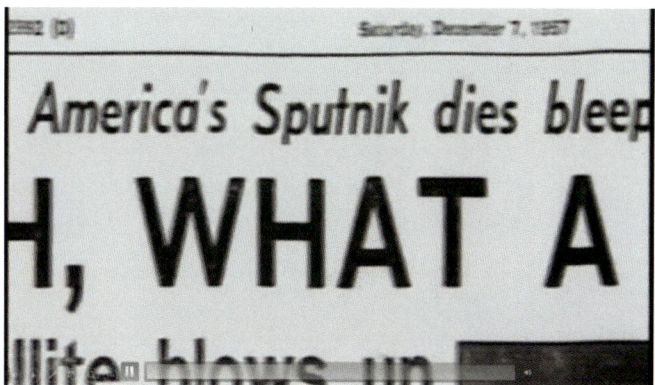

America was worried about the Soviet Union's superior rocket technologies and military might. Russia's 'Sputnik' rocket beat America's rockets to space. National pride was a significant issue in the 1960s for America for so many reasons, including the cold war, many assassinations etc. America needed to get a person on the moon before The Soviet Union.

 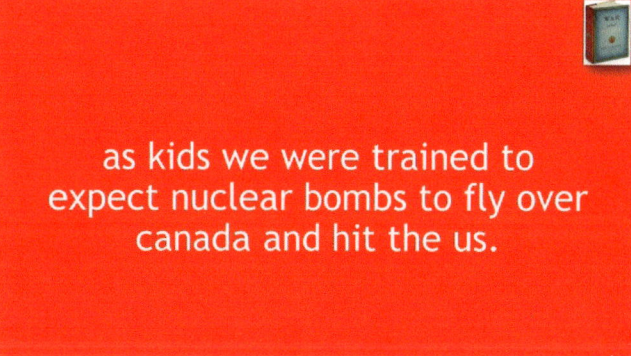

Growing up in Canada we were warned that Soviet nuclear missiles would fly over Alaska and Canada en route to America. The media was in on it too.

My mom told me they saw "duck and cover" commercials on television when they were children like the absolutely ridiculous one listed above: www.tiny.cc/chris41

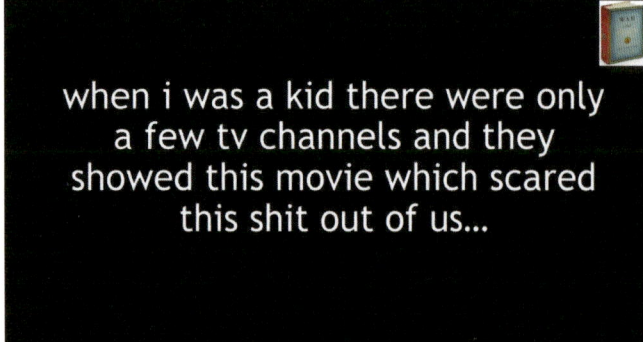 

Our teachers sent letters home to our parents in Canada warning us of the movie that was going to air on our networks: www.tiny.cc/chris42

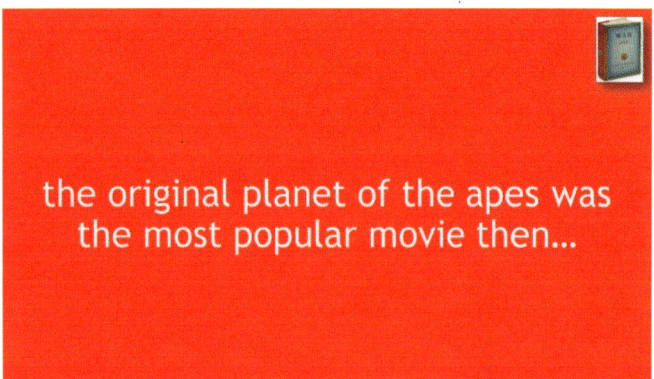 

During the peak of the cold war in the late 1960s, a post nuclear America was the most popular movie…..the end scene was epic and frightening: www.tiny.cc/chris43

part 2

Peace (part 2). Fortunately, the hippie movement in the San Francisco Bay Area influenced the rest of the nation to embrace peace instead of war: www.tiny.cc/chris44

in the late 60s an amazing thing happened...

youth in san francisco rebelled.

they chanted make love not war

The 'summer of love' had a profound impact on those coming of age in the 1960s, including Steve Jobs and many other tech sector legends. www.tiny.cc/chris45

Berkeley's hippies changed America and the world. www.tiny.cc/chris46

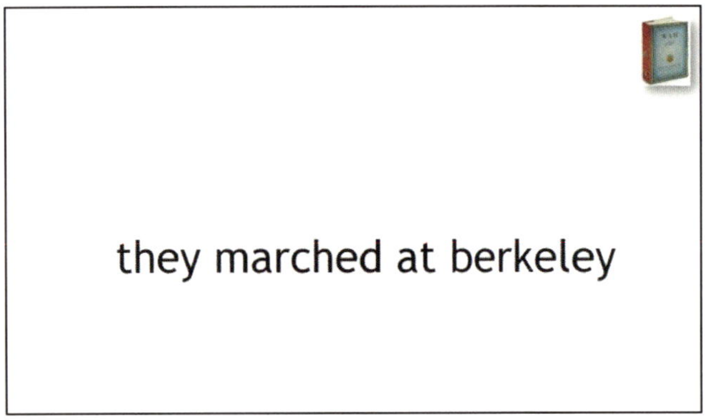

they marched at berkeley

Riots spread across America as the clash between those in favor of conflict and those that didn't reached an all-time high: www.tiny.cc/chris47

they marched at stanford

they held peace events in sf at telegraph tower

they shared everything.

shareable open source software was born.

stanford got rid of all government weapons research on campus (which was 50%+ of their r&d budget at the time)

even universities like stanford let their students and teachers share ideas and make money from it.

the counter culture movement was born.

The Ultimate Practical Business Manual

they experimented with drugs

which led to the invention of the personal computer.

they didn't trust anyone over 30

they hated the war focused movement of the day.

their family and friends were dying in vietnam fighting a bullshit war they couldn't win or understand.

inspired by music

music inspired entrepreneurs

The Ultimate Practical Business Manual

these entrepreneurs were former hippies and they thought differently from their parents.

they thought differently and embraced change (thank God)

inter racial marriage was illegal in 13 states in the 60s. WTF!

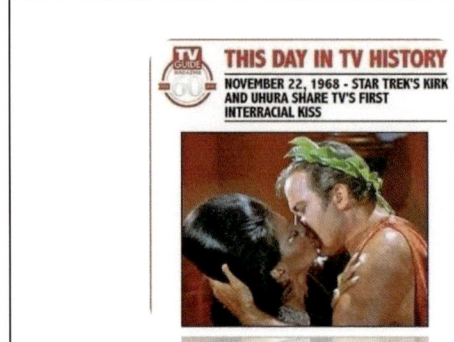

these heroes were ready to share ideas and change the world.

on the 'left' coast they thought "hey man, it's cool to fail... just keep trying"

here it's cool to be and think different as all ideas are accepted here.

a fertile tigris and euphrates technology crescent was born out of evolution and revolution.

these big bang unique events haven't occurred anywhere else in the world yet….

and only took place because america is a country of extremes

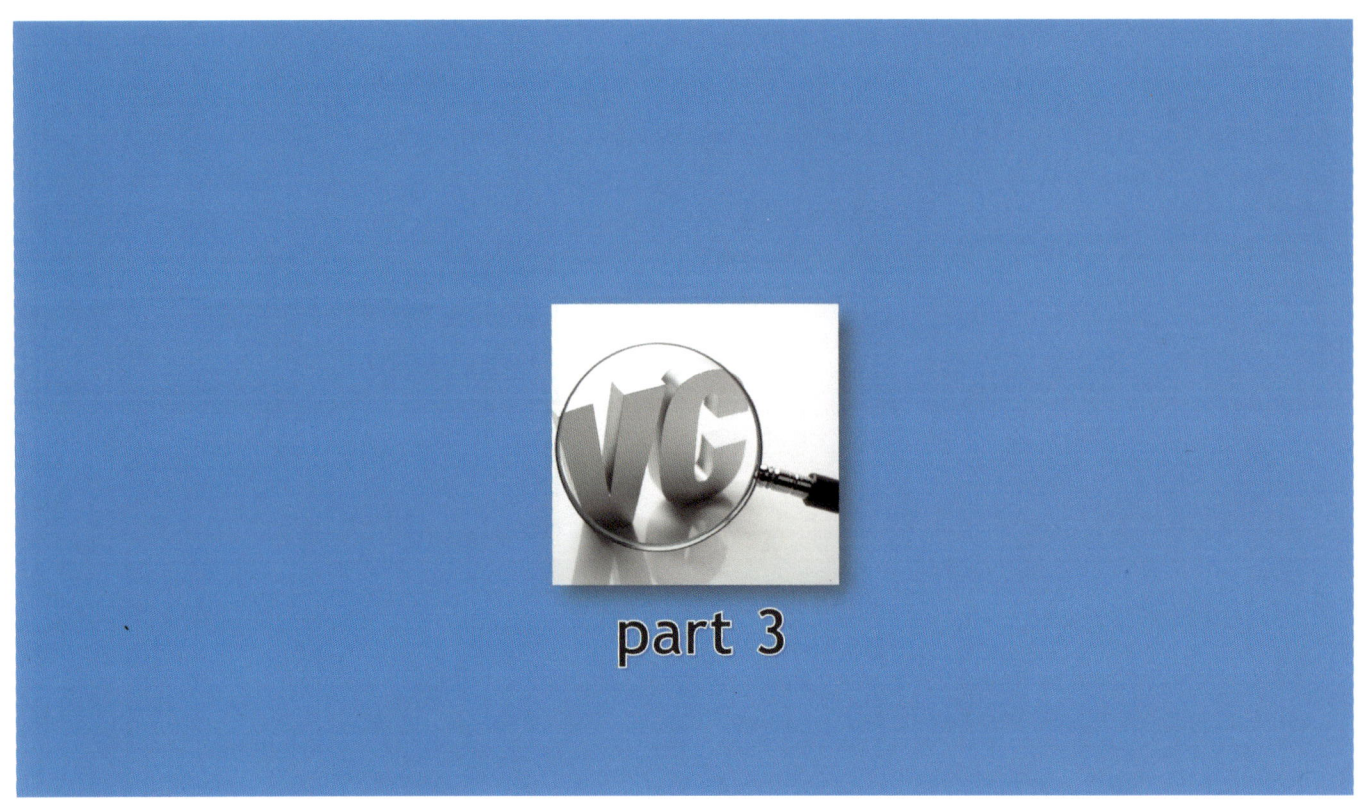

the richest* family in america...

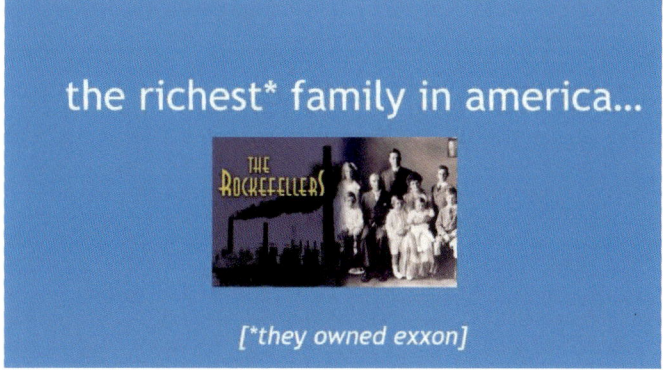

[*they owned exxon]

they have a vc division called:

venrock invested in fairchild semiconductor

The government created NASA with the intent of putting the first person on the moon. They couldn't do so as they needed to fit many transistors in the fuselage or top portion of a rocket. Fairchild Semiconductor was the Bay Area start-up that was successful in building these chips!

these 8 folks are called "the traitorous 8" and they founded Fairchild semiconductor and CHANGED THE FN' WORLD!

the company got too big!!!!

As with all great technology companies, eventually they get bloated and bureaucratic. As a result, they can no longer innovate (especially if the founders resign).

and therefore couldn't innovate!

and so many quit….

so many "fairchildren" were born:

"fairchildren" were backed by VCs

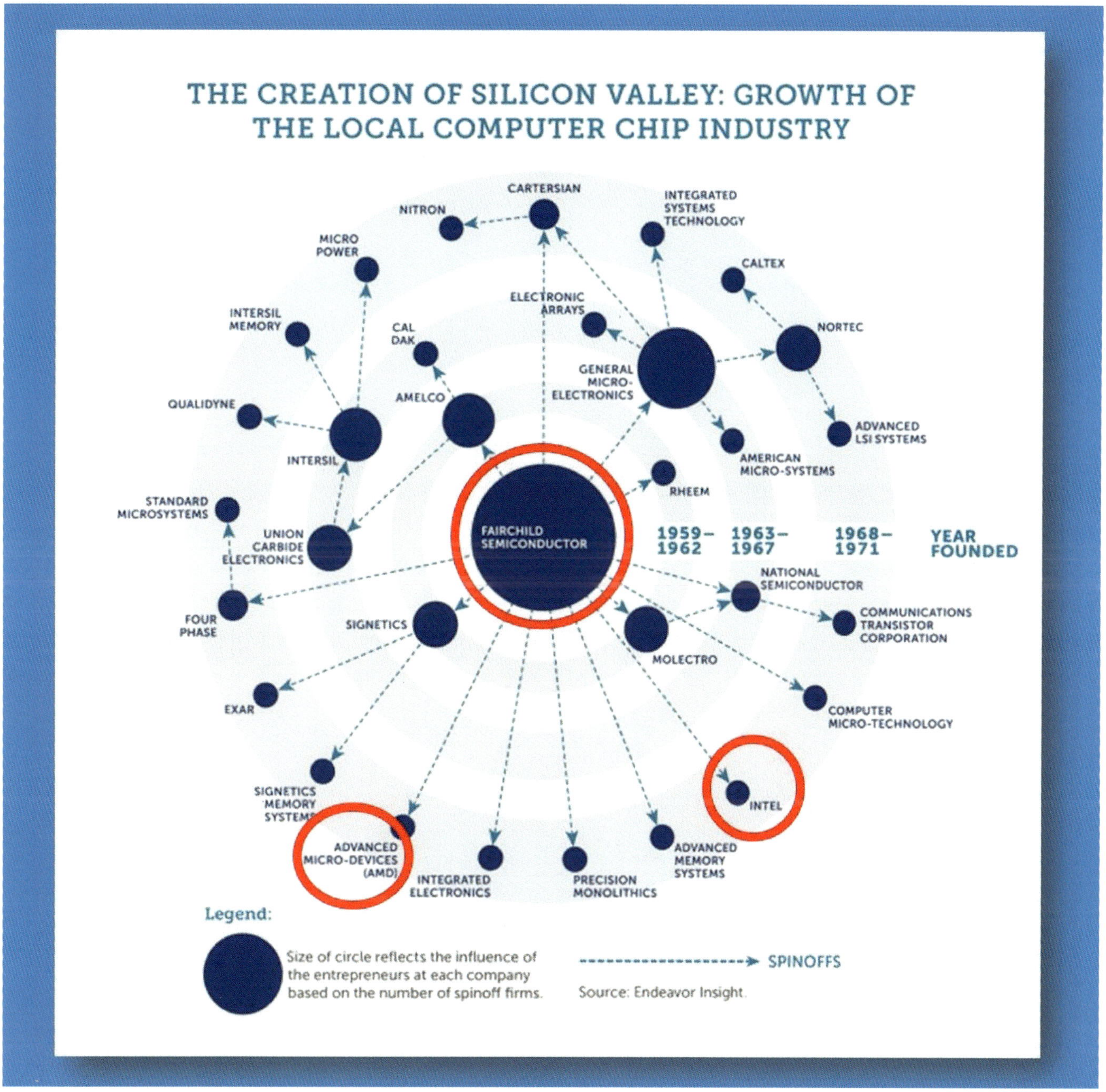

Fairchildren companies include Intel, AMD and NVIDIA.

in the internet space, VCs backed the paypal mafia!

PayPal is the most important technology company to go public in the past 20 years because out of PayPal came many incredible companies. Including the founders of YouTube, Yelp, Tesla, SpaceX and many more. Similar to the 1960s hippie heroes, Peter Thiel (the cofounder of PayPal along with Elon Musk) believes in decreasing government authority. His libertarian political views via PayPal intended to disintermediate government authority by creating a form of payment that governments could not regulate. Take away a government's ability to alter monetary policy, and take away its most important weapon (the ability to print money in order to fund government projects or to stabilize economies etc.).

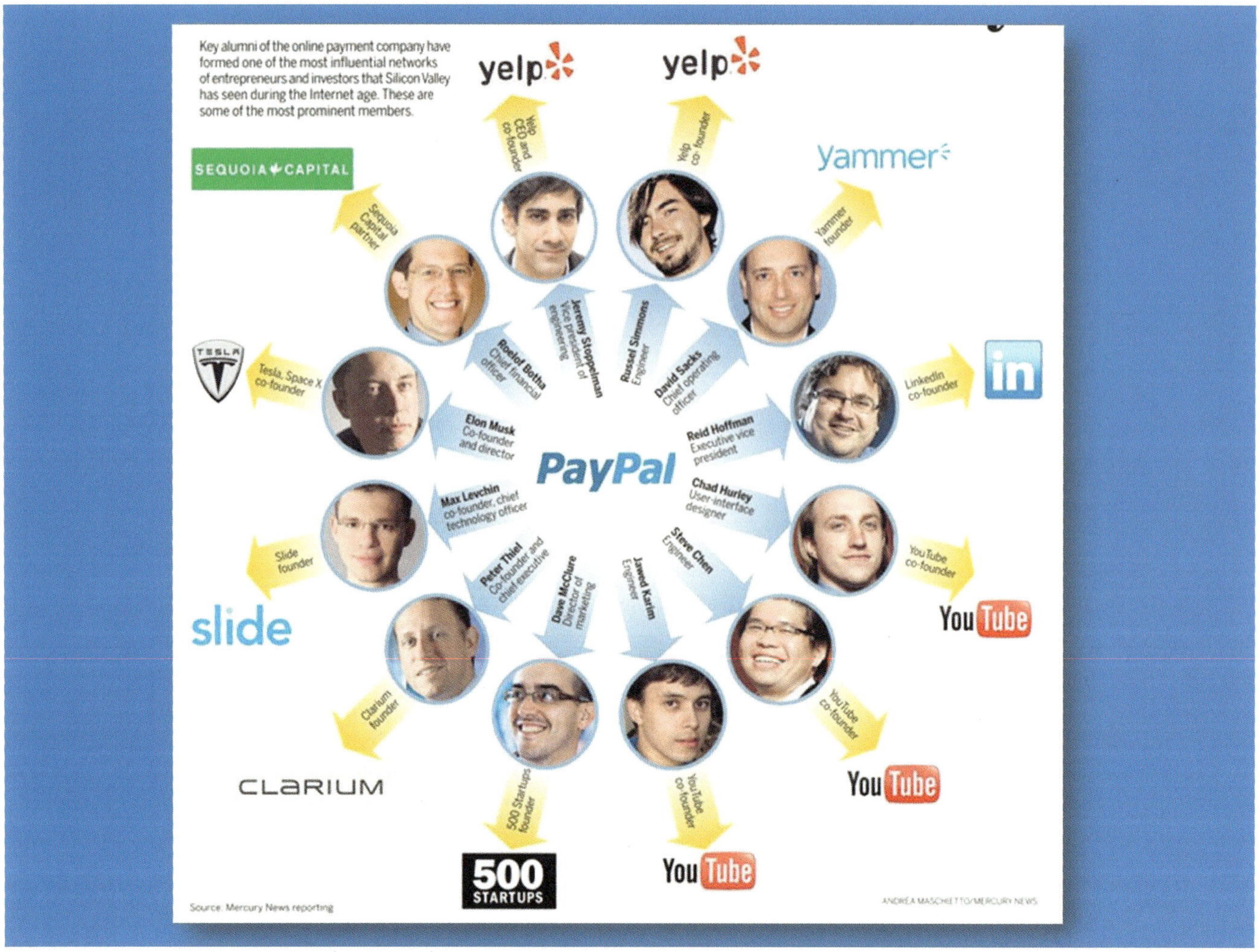

> vc firms love backing the same executives again...

In the public markets, there is a notion that 'past performance is not indicative of future performance.' In the private markets it is though - if you have an incredible management team. A founder that has started and sold multiple successful start-ups has a much higher probability of being successful in the future. As a result, venture capitalists prefer to invest in solid management teams (ahead of solid ideas). For some reason, public market investors don't spend enough time analyzing management teams. The jockey is always way more important than the horse with <u>all</u> investments.

The top venture firms continually get access to the best deals. In the next few pages are websites and corresponding venture capital investments for these top vc firms. We will kick it off with Kleiner Perkins:

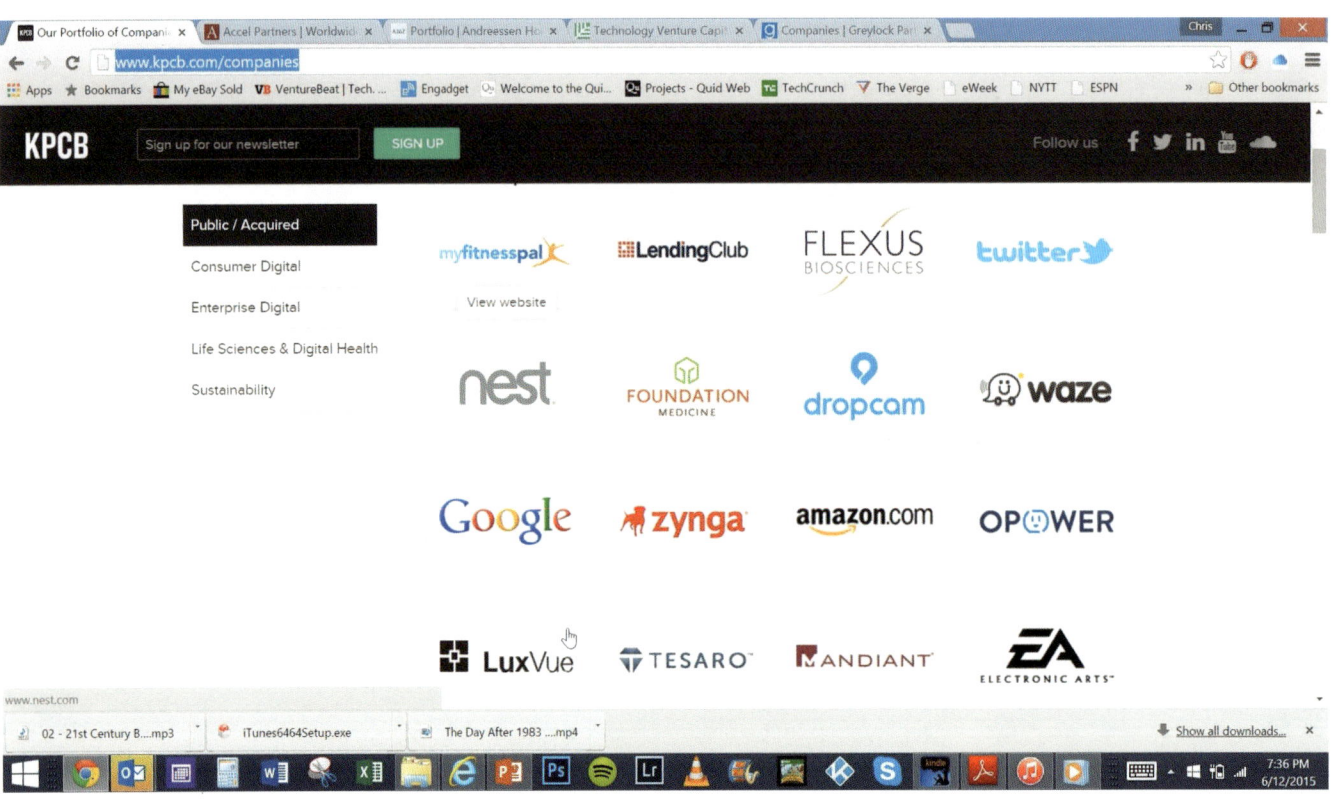

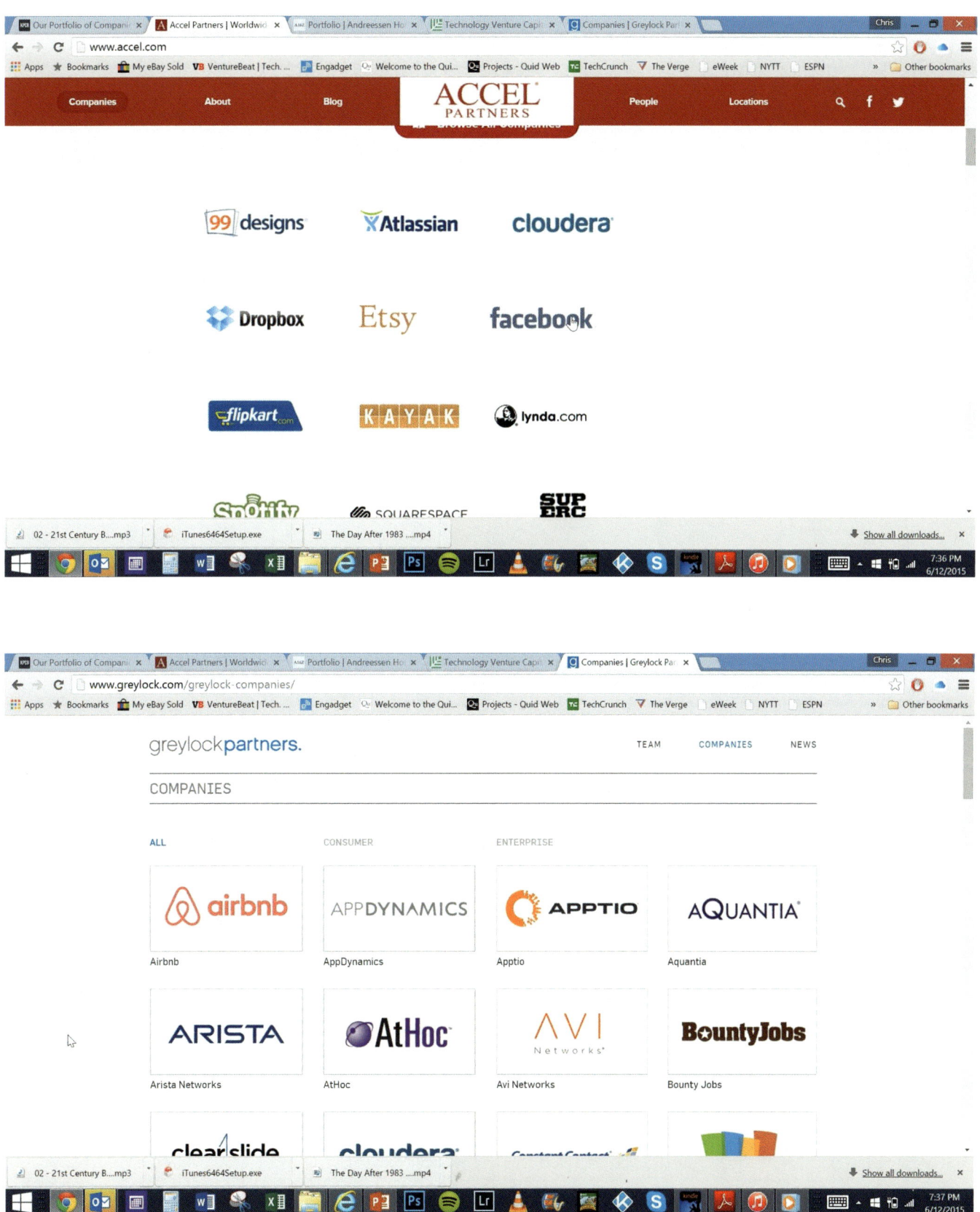

ideas are commodities but execution is not

see how sequoia highlights the founders and not the companies as much?

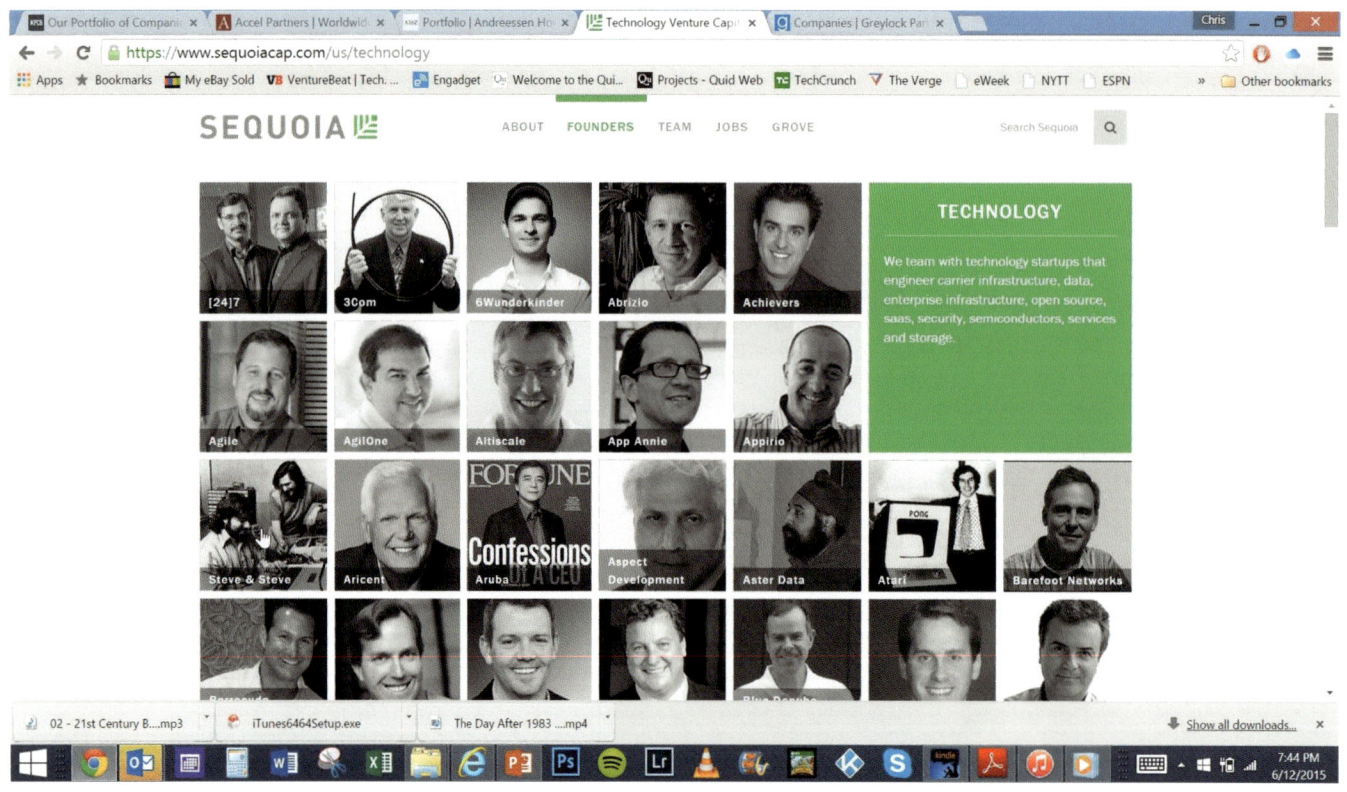

most vc in america is in the bay area	
the industry is highly cyclical	external events = bubbles burst
60% of engineers in the valley are born overseas.	no limits to what they (you) can achieve here.
dream.	

Valuations are lofty for many venture backed companies today, but not nearly as egregious as what we saw when the last VC cycle peaked shortly after 1999 when Pets.com was still in business. When rates rise (and they will) then investors will likely invest in other asset classes. That being said, the best investors have a very long term investment time horizon and aren't easily influenced by long term economic cycles.

What Buffett is saying is common sense of course…but being a contrarian in the investment industry always pays off.

> **worth repeating!**
>
> "be fearful when others are greedy and greedy when others are fearful."
>
> -warren buffet

If you are looking for your company to get funded by a venture capital firm, it is imperative that you pick the right VC firm to partner with, otherwise you cannot be successful. Make sure the VC firm is early stage if your business is too. If you raised seed money and you are now looking for an A Round VC investor, then target a superb earlier stage VC firm like Sequoia or Kleiner. If you are closer to your initial public offering (IPO) and you want to do one more late stage D or E round, then try to work with the best late stage venture firms like Meritech, who have a great reputation and are fantastic trustworthy people too.

> **what vc should you target?**
> ✓ know their stage focus
> ✓ know their sector focus
> ✓ know their reputation
> ✓ know their target return date

> **what vc should you target?**
> ✓ are they founder friendly?
> ✓ are they growth or value?
> ✓ do you enjoy their company?
> ✓ do you trust them?

To state the obvious, don't approach venture capital firms or partners at these firms that don't cover the market that your company operates in. Also, make sure the VC firm that you partner with has an impeccable reputation of helping founders grow their company (instead of being activist disturbers in board meetings…. "lead, follow or get out of the way" to quote Ted Turner).

Make sure the venture firm that is going to finance your company's growth has a similar view on their target return on investment period. If your business won't likely do an IPO in 7-10 years, then make sure you pick a patient, long-term focused VC firm to work with.

If your gut tells you not to trust them (even after a brief first meeting), then chose to partner with another venture firm. Your gut impression is right more often than not, when it comes to who to partner with in business.

Make sure the VC firm is growth oriented (most are) instead of value focused if your firm isn't going to be profitable for many years. There is nothing more stressful than having differing expectations of business goals than your investors do.

Most venture capital firms charge their investors a 2% annual management fee (to pay for salaries, rent etc.). Venture firms make most of their money, though, through a 20% incentive fee that they collect after they are profitable (as we covered in more detail earlier in this book). The "2 and 20" economics of the VC sector is commensurate with how the hedge fund industry works. The difference between

> **how does investing in vc work?**
> ✓ capital calls
> ✓ 20% left over to avoid dilution

the two sectors is that the hedge fund market is incredibly short-term focused and the venture capital sector is incredibly long-term focused.

When you invest your money in a venture capital firm, you don't give your entire agreed upon investment amount to the firm right away. Instead, they call you and ask for the capital as they need it. This is called "a capital call." Venture firms will call you when they need to deploy the capital. Let's look at an example. Let's assume you are an "accredited investor", meaning you have a very large liquid net worth and are allowed to invest in a venture capital firm. You agree to invest $100,000. The hypothetical venture capital firm you are investing in has a risk management policy of never investing more than 10% of their fund in any one particular company. Then one month after you agree to invest your $100,000 in the venture firm their CFO calls you and informs you that they are making a 10% (of their fund) investment in a company. They call you and ask for you to wire them $10,000 of your $100,000 investment. They will keep calling you and asking for money until about 80% or 90% of your capital has been invested or called for. The 10%-20% of your money that has not been called for is left over in case another venture capital firm invests in a company the VC firm you invested in at a future round. This is to offset your percent ownership in a company from being diluted. This process is called "pro rata."

What does this mean? Let's assume that 10% of a $100mn venture capital firm that you invested in was put in Facebook in say 2005 in the first VC funded round, called the A round. That means $10mn of the fund was invested in Facebook at a valuation of say $1bn. The CFO of the VC firm called you and asked for $10k from you for an investment in Facebook. Then in 2006 (1 year later) another venture capital firm invests in Facebook at a valuation of $2bn. Since Facebook is a great company and since the VC firm that you invested in doesn't want their percent ownership of Facebook to be diluted, then they will call all of their investors and ask them to invest in Facebook again so that the amount they own of Facebook remains the same percent wise. This is called "pro rata". You contribute more money (or your "pro rata") to offset dilution. This is why VC firms typically only invest 80%-90% of your investment as they leave 10% to 20% left over in case there are "pro rata" investment follow-on opportunities.

We know that networking is the most important skill that we can learn in business. Venture capital firms get access to the best deals by networking aggressively. Your success in business will be predicated on the strength of your network, so make sure to connect with everyone you have ever met with using LinkedIn.

> **how do vc firms get deals?**
> ✓ network network network
> ✓ past investments
> ✓ other vc introduce firms to vc
> ✓ "why am i so luck to see this..."
> ✓ universities (goog example)

Venture firms love to invest in the same entrepreneurs over and over again (of course assuming the executives they are investing in have had a successful exit in the past). Venture firms also work with competing venture firms by introducing them to their portfolio companies so that other VC firms can lead future rounds. Co-opetition in the venture industry makes it incredibly unique compared to other roles in financial services industries. You usually need to fight to get access to the best investments in VC though. If you are introduced to a potential investment by another VC firm or from a friend, always ask yourself "why am I so lucky to be seeing this investment opportunity?" Unfortunately the reason can sometimes be that nobody else wants to invest. Venture capitalists also love to spend time walking up and down the halls of the best universities in search of the next Google!

Since venture capital firms often become "stuck holders" or long term shareholders in illiquid investments, they have to do an enormous amount of due diligence before deciding whether or not to invest in a company. Venture capital employees will leverage LinkedIn and find contacts of theirs (or their friends) that know the management team of a start-up they are considering investing in when doing background checks.

how vcs do due diligence

Venture firms will also study the competition at length and often interview them as well. I found from working in the hedge fund industry years ago that meeting with competitors and asking them what the weaknesses are of their competitors really helps you to find gaps in an underlying company's business model (of course assuming that you are not compromising your integrity by discussing confidential information with those not privy to this information).

Venture firms will also analyze in great detail what the size is of a particular market they are considering investing in. Quite often they won't invest in a company that has a T.A.M. or total addressable market of less than $20bn. Why? Because they want the company they are investing in to get at least 5% market share of this market in the very long run, which equates to $1bn+ in annual revenue. Venture firms have to aim high as many of their investments will lose money. Often all you need is a handful of investments in a given fund to make money for the fund to be incredibly profitable.

I know that the end markets or business models of many companies that VC firms invest in will change materially in the long run. As such, it is always prudent to invest in industry veterans that have been successful pivoting or changing their business models in the past.

Each venture capital round has a different venture capital firm leading the investment round. Investors in earlier rounds usually invest again as well so as not to get diluted (we covered this in the pro forma explanation). Most venture backed investor rounds have several different venture capital investors for risk management purposes. The same thing happens with IPOs and investment banks, which will cover

vc lead investor

&

deal composition

later in this book. Several investment firms working together is called an 'investment syndicate'. Why does this happen? Because the investment rounds are enormous. Ask yourself "would I ever only get loans many years from now when my business is massive from just one bank?" Heck no! You need to diversify by doing business with several banks so they will compete for your business and give you the best terms.

So what is a good blueprint to use for a successful venture capital investment? Here is a model that works (for VC and other investments):

1)   Make sure the management team is strong and with a deep bench (if it is a later stage investment). It is ok if the management team has failed in the past….but make sure they learned a lot from this failure and that they have had multiple successes (past exits) as well. Chances are if they have made other investors money in the past, then they will make you money as well (or at least have a higher probability of making you money). If the management team has no experience or if they are just out of school, make sure they have a solid board of advisors.

> **who do we back?**
> ✓ strong management team (ok if they have failed before…)
> ✓ huge tam
> ✓ strong syndicate
> ✓ disruptive business model

2)   As mentioned earlier, you need to invest in companies that compete in markets with enormous TAMs as you want to get paid huge if they make it big!

3)   If this is a later stage investment, it is more often than not prudent to make sure that the previous investors have great reputations for returning a very high return on investment to their investors over the years. The same can be said for an investment in anything!

4)   Lastly (yes I know it's bizarre that I list this one last….) we need to make sure that the company has an incredibly disruptive business model. Can they do to the industry that they participate in what Airbnb has done to the hotel sector? What is unique and proprietary about their value proposition? Is the market too crowded? Is it scalable (meaning can revenue growth massively accelerate with little additional investment capital and labor)?

I will keep saying this: 'ideas are commodities, but execution is not'. Start always with a solid management team. If you aren't thoroughly impressed by the management team's ability to get you excited about their business prospects, then pass on this investment. Make sure that the founder(s) is not running the business to make money. Make sure that they are so incredibly driven that they want their company to literally change the world. Otherwise, this founder might look to sell the company at a very low return on investment. They need to convince you like you are a customer. They need to sincerely convince you that the reason that they were put on this earth was to make their company bigger and better than Apple, Inc.

Attitude is everything.

preferred shares & harvest

There are many different legal structures for ownership of investment vehicles. We will only cover the most common ones and we will do so in easy to understand terms (my boss at hedge fund Citadel used to tell me that if I can't explain it, then I don't understand it)!

security structures:

You are done if you don't lawyer up when starting a company! www.tiny.cc/chris49 . As painful as it may seem, you need to hire a lawyer to help you with the legal paperwork of protecting you and your company and your company if you are accepting investments from anyone, including a venture capital firm. If it's costly, don't worry as you can bill this to your company. In fact, after you raise money from investors, you can bill your company for this. I used to amortize my legal set up fees for my companies over 60 moths (or 5 years), which is allowed under US corporate accounting laws.

You wouldn't operate on yourself if you needed surgery. Why? Because doctors spend 4-5+ years in medical school learnings how to not kill patients! The same can be said for lawyers, who spend 3+ years learning how to not kill your career, business and life. If you work for someone else, you need to hire a lawyer for $500+ to quickly review the contract you are signing so you can protect your family and your assets. Your employer is likely cool but her or his lawyer is never looking in the best interests of your family.

Your employer did not write the legal employment documents; Rather, her or his lawyer did…..so please lawyer up like Peter Parker did in that movie clip you just watched. ;)

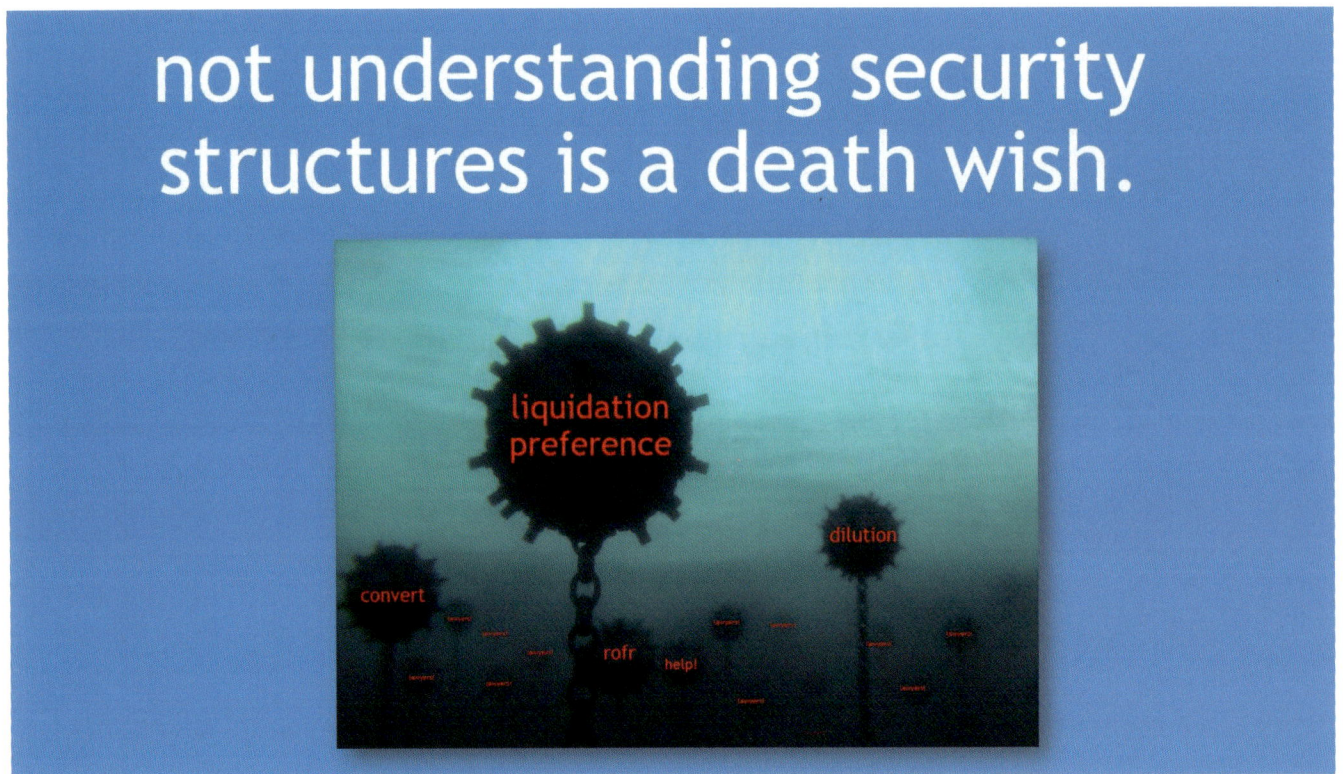

If a company goes belly up and there is a little bit of money left over then the first to get their money back are the banks or people that loaned the company money. The last class of investors to get paid back are the common stock holders. Employees of a firm that is VC backed usually get common stock. The VC investors usually get shares that are better, or preferred. Not surprisingly, they are called preferred shares.

Why would anyone want to own common stock then? Because they are very easy to buy and sell. Most stocks on the stock exchanges are common stock.

convertible preferred

- ✓ at IPO preferred shares convert to common shares
- ✓ when you buy stocks in US markets they are common shares
- ✓ sometimes convert = 2:1 ratio

Don't ever value your company too high when dealing with investors. I know that this sounds strange. If you raise multiple investment rounds, existing investors usually only agree to let you raise more money if it is done at a much higher valuation. Why? Because they want their shares to be worth more! If you raise more money at the same valuation as the previous investment round, then new investors have to be given new shares, which dilutes existing investors' ownership stake in the company. Keep valuations low enough so that you have the luxury of being able to raise more money at a higher valuation in the future. A "down round" can destroy a company as existing investors and current employees will be upset that their investment is now worth less!

down round?	up round?
✓ if you price the series a too high	✓ if you price the series 'a' low enough (this is smart)
✓ price of new shares (b) is lower	✓ series b is higher valuation
✓ everyone is angry at the ceo	✓ vc from a round does 'pro rata'
✓ anti dilution clause protection	✓ therefore no dilution

It is always prudent to price the company during the A Round low enough so that you can do the B Round at a higher valuation.

i don't get it. show me an example

- ok I will! assume you are sequoia
- you led the series 'a'
- you own 10% at a valuation of $1m
- you own $100k worth and 100k shrs

i don't get it. show me an example

- now kleiner does series b at a $2mn valuation and new shares are created because employees and sequoia aren't selling their shares!
- so now you own <10%... you got diluted!
- why? because 500k shares were created for kp
- $2mn/1.5m shares = $1.33/sh.

i don't get it. show me an example

- i'm only a bit upset..100k sh * $1.33 = 33% return
- i now own 6.6%
- not fair....
- i should own 10% darn it!
- i have rights!

i don't get it. show me an example

- but wait as i have legal protections
- per the legal docs, 'pro rata'
- 10% of $2mn = $200k
- if i buy ~50k more shares then no dilution for me
- solution.....kleiner only gets to buy 450k shares

---

sequoia owns preferred shares so they had the right to invest a pro rata amount of $67k to offset dilution!

this is why vc firms only invest 75% - 90% of a fund.

'capital call'

convertible debt

- this is a debt instrument and hence has senior debt claims over preferred shareholders
- if the firm can't pay the debt, then the convertible debt holders take your stuff (cars, factory etc)

> **convertible debt**
> - government tax incentive not to pay debt on interest for start ups
> - [side note on nol's startup tax benefit]
> - in between a and b round many startups do a 20% discount convert

Sometimes start-ups plan on doing the B round, for example, about 2 years after the A round. However, in this hypothetical scenario, the start-up unexpectedly immediately runs out of money 1.5 years after the A round. As a result, the start-up needs to raise money right away. The start-up was planning on raising a large amount in 6 months anyway….but needs a small amount of capital to make sure they can make payroll before doing the Series B in 6 months (which is 2 years after the Series A). The start-up can raise debt from an investor (or venture debt investor like Silicon Valley Bank – also called SVB). This debt can be at an annual interest rate of say 8% and will convert into shares (or equity) once the B round is done at a 20% discount to the Series B valuation.

Warrants can be granted to service providers like legal or debt firms that do business with a start-up. It is just another way to give financing flexibility to a start-up.

> **warrants**
> - a startup can incentivize investors when they invest by giving them warrants ('an option to get new shares later for free')
> - options are shares that exist (from the options pool). by contrast, warrants are worth less than options as they are new shares.

Options are granted to employees slowly over a long period of time. An option is the right to buy or receive shares in a company in the future at a certain price. They are slowly granted over time or else employees might quit after receiving them. They are given usually over 4 years so that 25% of the options realize their true value (or "vest") every year for 4 years. After two years this employee in this hypothetical example is "50% vested" and then "100% vested over 4 years". CEOs of publically traded companies and many employees also receive stock options that "vest" over time. Vesting is also known as "golden handcuffs" for employees to make sure that they remain loyal and don't leave for another company.

> **options**
> - why do we grant options?
> - call option = the right to buy shares at a specific price in the future

Questions Based on Chapter 4:

1: Who has the highest claim on a company?

 a) Common Shareholder
 b) Option Holder
 c) Preferred Shareholder
 d) Debt holder

2: VC firms prefer backing founders that they have successfully invested in in the past.

   True   or   False

3: Investors in VC firms have the right to invest in future rounds and this is called their "pro rata" rights.

   True   or   False

CHAPTER SUMMARY

Chris Haroun @chris_haroun
history of vc is important to understand. term sheets. security structures. 'be greedy when others are fearful…& vv' 'you better lawyer up #%@*&%$'!

We covered a lot in this chapter. We even watched a clip from an awesome 1960s cold war movie called Planet of the Apes. Let's end this chapter with this… www.tiny.cc/chris48   ;)

Chapter 5: Venture Capital Part 3

"Success is stumbling from failure to failure with no loss of enthusiasm."

- *Winston Churchill*

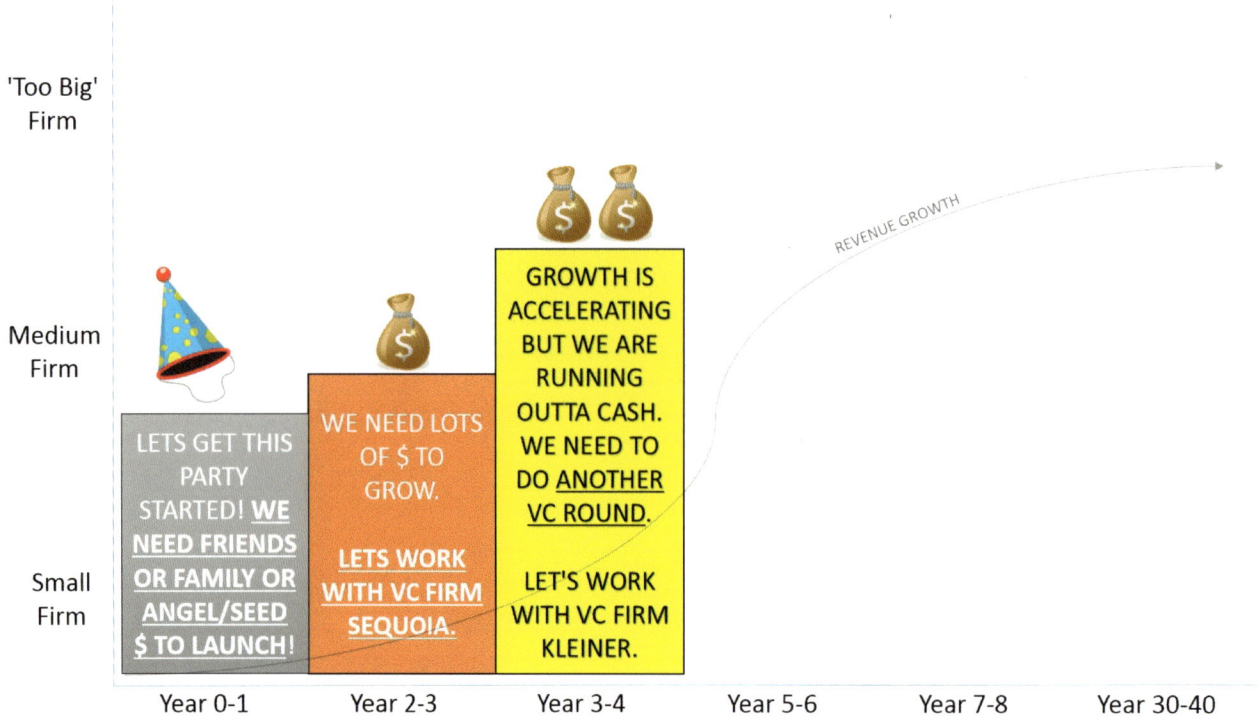

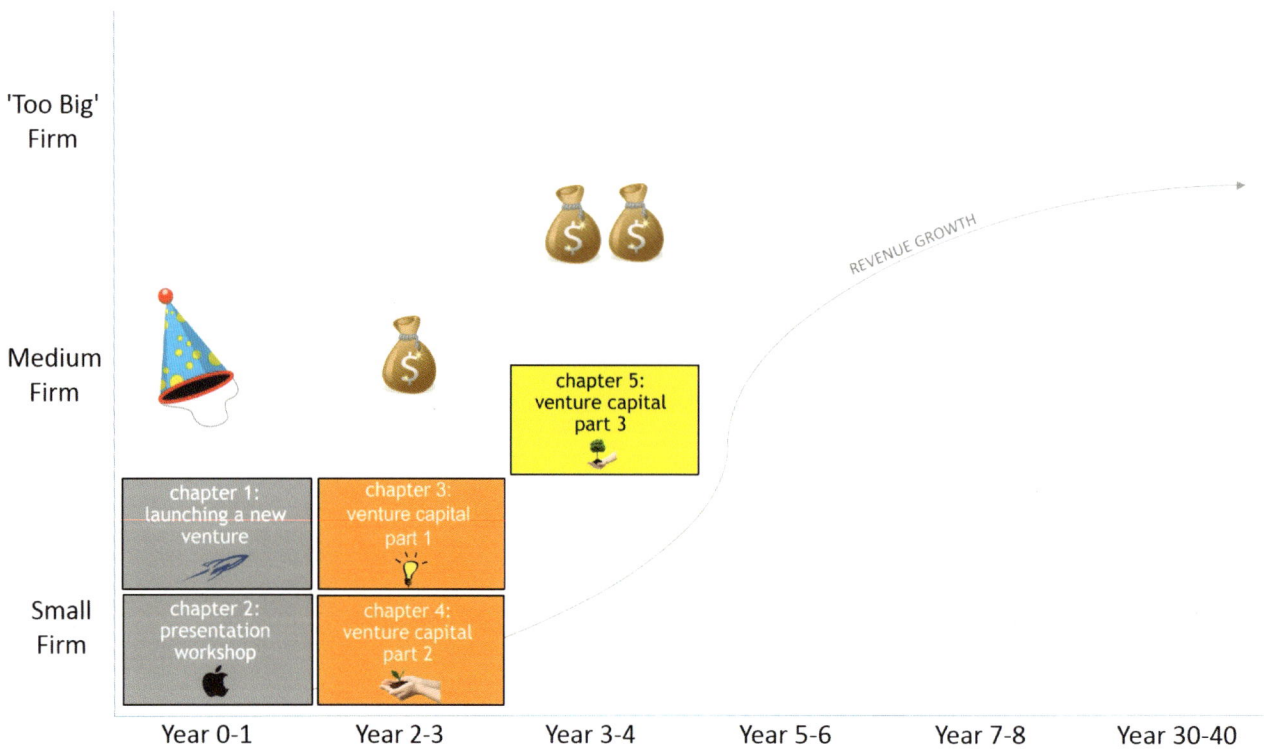

If you get out of bed in the morning and tell yourself that you are going to work, then you are doing it wrong. You need to keep changing careers until you find your passion. Find out what is the reason you were put on this earth to accomplish professionally. www.tiny.cc/chris50

> find your passion

> the jockey is more important than the horse.
>
> vc firms bet on the best athlete

I repeat the most important themes in the book often, like finding your passion or the importance of networking and, of course, the importance of investing in the right people, which is more important than investing in the right business model. VC firms love investing in the best athlete.

How Many Shares Do I Have and How Many Does the VC Have?

I love baseball so this chapter we will use the best athlete analogy in venture by investing in the best athlete in baseball, who in my humble opinion is Giancarlo Stanton: www.tiny.cc/chris51

In our hypothetical example, let's assume that Giancarlo started a cool payments company similar to Square and that he was also a founder of PayPal, which he took public and then sold to eBay. So yes

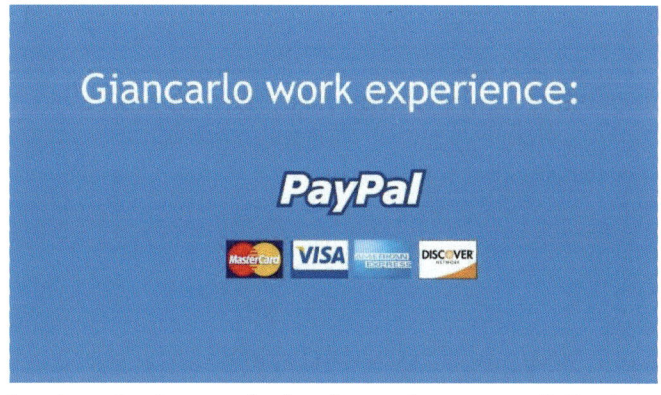

he has had an exit (and not just out of Dodger stadium)!

Giancarlo designed a prototype or a P.O.C. (proof of concept) device that is a P.O.S. (ahem....a point of sale product that is). The P.O.C. was created using angel or seed money he raised from his a few high net worth investors.

> he designed a p.o.c. revolutionary payment terminal

he needs a $1mn to build a non prototype version

Now Giancarlo needs to raise $1mn in an A Round. Since he has had an exit and he is the best athlete, naturally the best venture capital firm, Sequoia will lead the Series A. Sequoia thinks they will make a 50% annual return for 5 years (yes they are that good).

SEQUOIA CAPITAL
THE ENTREPRENEURS BEHIND THE ENTREPRENEURS

wants to back him.

they think they will make 50% return / year

As a side note, the best VC firms in the world have 1% of their portfolios in 'unicorns', which means companies that have a valuation above $1bn. Sequoia has 5% of their portfolio in unicorns!

Sequoia did a deep due diligence dive on the company and they think that the P.O.S. company will make $1mn in net income in 5 years.

> he and sequoia agree that in 5 years his company will make $1mn in net income.

Giancarlo decided to launch the firm with an arbitrary 2mn shares. Don't overthink this – it's always a random number and results in a random share price at launch   …usually well under $1 per share. We will do a lot of math in the next few pages that will determine Giancarlo's ownership in the firm….but the original price per share and the number of shares is always given and not calculated.

> when he launched his payment company last year he had $10,000 in equity capital.
>
> he decided to launch then with 2,000,000 shares.
>
> he needs to negotiate with sequoia on how many shares they get.

Awesome! One of Giancarlo's competitors did an IPO at a price / earnings multiple of $20mn divided by $2mn in net income of a P/E or price to earnings multiple of 10 times! Hmm – ok this means that in 5 years when Giancarlo's company makes $1mn in net income, then he and Sequoia agree that their P.O.S. firm will be worth the same 10x multiple or 10 x's $1mn or $10mn! Sweet!

> a competitor of his just went public at a $20mn valuation with $2mn in net income
>
> p/e = $20mn/$2mn = 10x
>
> in 5 years we want to go public at a $10mn (half the n.i.)

> what is his firm worth today?

If the firm is worth $10mn in 5 years then what is the firm worth today? Well Sequoia expects to make 50% annually on this investment. So if we know that the company is worth $10mn in 5 years (which is 10x's $1mn in net income), then what is $10mn in 5 years worth today? We need to discount $10mn over 5 years assuming that it will be worth 50% more annually each year for 5 years.

> **sequoia expects to make 50% per year**
>
> we need to calculate what his company in 5 years is worth today
>
> $10mn / (1+ 50\%)^5$
>
> = $1,316,872

The math is calculated as follows (I will use another example first): if I tell you that you have an investment in a hypothetical company that will go up 50% in one year to be worth $1mn, then today your investment is worth $1mn / 1+50% = 1,000,000/1.5 = $666,667.

Ok now if I tell you that if you invested a certain amount of money for 2 years and each year you would make a 50% return and that the value of your investment is $1mn in 2 years, then how much would you need to invest today? In this example we need to discount the $1mn over 2 years as follows: $1,000,000/(1+50\%)^2$ = $444,444.

Ok so if Sequoia expects to make 50% per year for 5 years, then $10,000,000 in 5 years is worth what today? $10,000,000 / (1.5)^5 = $1,316,872 today. Or $1,316,872 that appreciates 50% annually for 5 years = $1,316,872 *1.5^5 = $10,000,000.. Recall that Giancarlo wants to raise $1mn from Sequoia so he can build his P.O.S.. So what percent of the firm does Sequoia own today? The firm is worth $1,316,872 today, so Sequoia owns $1,000,000 / $1,316,872 or 76% of the company, leaving Giancarlo owning 24% of the firm. Per the next image, we already know that Giancarlo owns 2mn shares, so we can calculate how many shares Sequoia owns.

> **the value today is $1,316,872**
>
> **sequoia owns $1mn/$1.32mn = 76%**
>
> **he owns 24% and has 2m shares**
>
> **total shares = 2m/.24 = 8.3m shares**
>
> **sequoia owns 6.3m shares**

Cool. So Sequoia owns 6.3mn shares, and $1mn of these shares.

what is the share price?

$1mn / 6.3mn shares

15.8c per share

how much does he own?

2mn shares * 15.8c per share

= $316k...called "pre $ valuation"

= $316k...called "**pre $ valuation**"

total valuation
= 8.3m shares * 15.8c
= $1.31m

the "**post $ valuation**"
= $1.31m

in 5 years:

pre $ valuation = 24% x $10mn
(his ownership) = $2.4mn

post $ valuation = 100% x $10mn
(his ownership + sequoia) = $10mn

notice how we didn't do any income statement or cash flow projections to get to that valuation?

Don't worry, we will go over the easy way to create financial models and value companies in a future chapter using Microsoft Excel. The fun thing about finance and math is that there are multiple ways to value companies and model companies. More on that later. Finance isn't hard when you slowly build on basic math and layer more stuff on it over time....you'll see.

what sequoia just did was they led the "a round" or first round

Oh no. We have an unfortunate set back with our company….don't worry as Giancarlo will be 100% ok:
www.tiny.cc/chris52

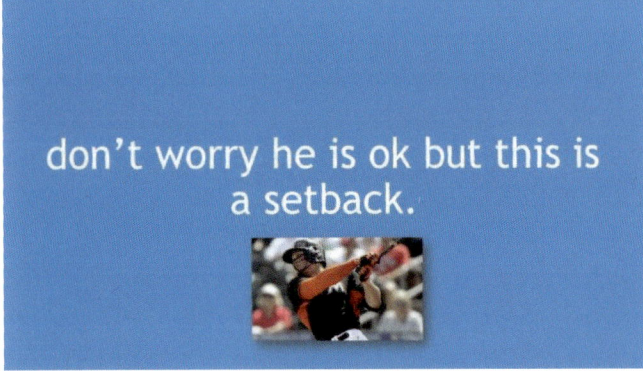

Companies tend to overestimate what they can accomplish in a year but they underestimate what they can accomplish in a decade. We always know in venture capital that the companies that we invest in are often dramatically different by the time we harvest the investment. This is why we invest in superb managers/athletes. Giancarlo is the best athlete for our hypothetical P.O.S. company.

We went through a set back and unfortunately we need to raise more money way sooner than we expected. **Remember that cash is always 'king'!**

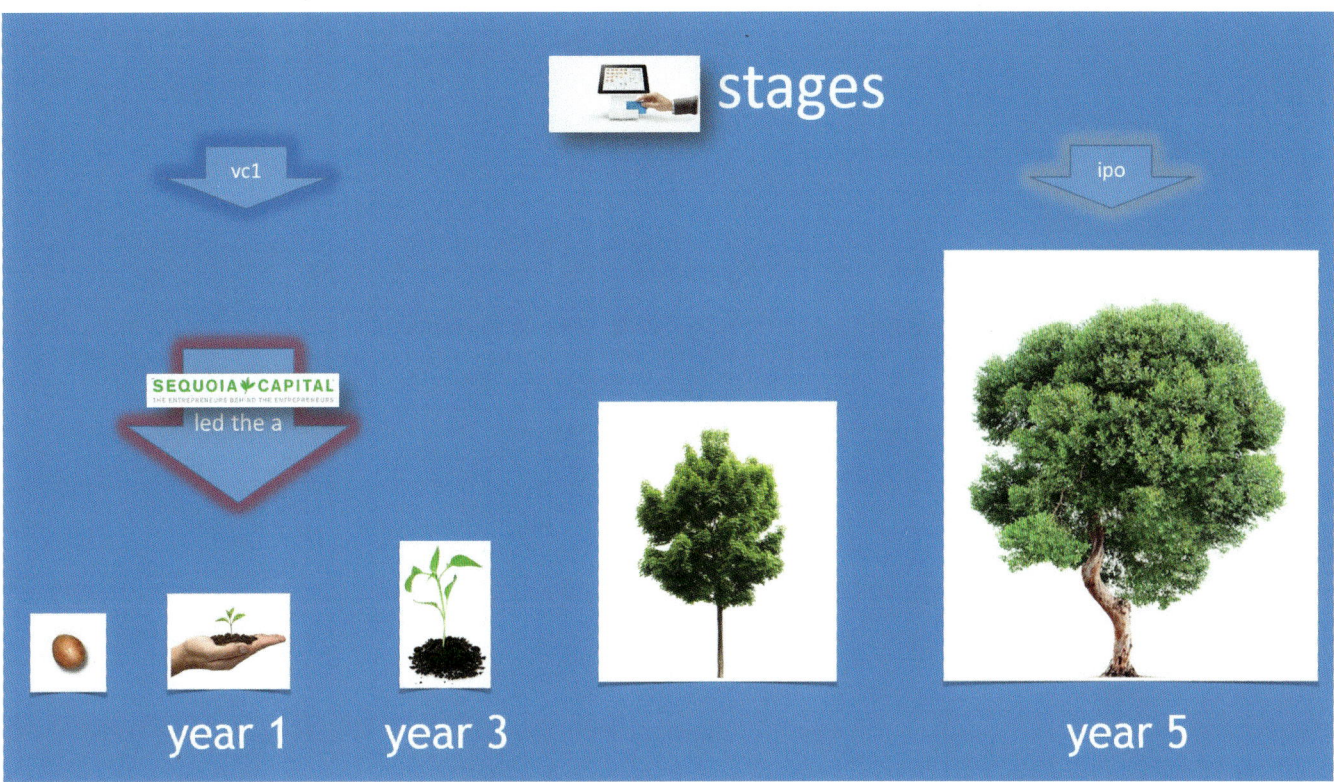

When Giancarlo did the A round with Sequoia he was so confident in his P.O.S. company that he made the terrible mistake of assuming that he would never need to raise money again until the IPO in 5 years. To make matters even worse, Giancarlo never consulted a lawyer when he registered his company! His fiancé Sue Yoo is a prominent lawyer and told him time and time again that he needed to lawyer up. Even his best friend Benjamin Dover who is also a lawyer warned him many times. Unfortunately Giancarlo will get diluted….and it's not any venture capital's fault. It is 100% Giancarlo's fault for not lawyering up.

www.tiny.cc/chris53

Giancarlo got lucky as another amazing venture capital firm wants to invest. Sequoia led the A round and Kleiner Perkins will lead the B. How awesome is Kleiner's reputation? Legend has it that John Doer from Kleiner who led an early venture capital round in Amazon.com has never sold a share of AMZN and his return on investment is literally 55,000%!

The Ultimate Practical Business Manual

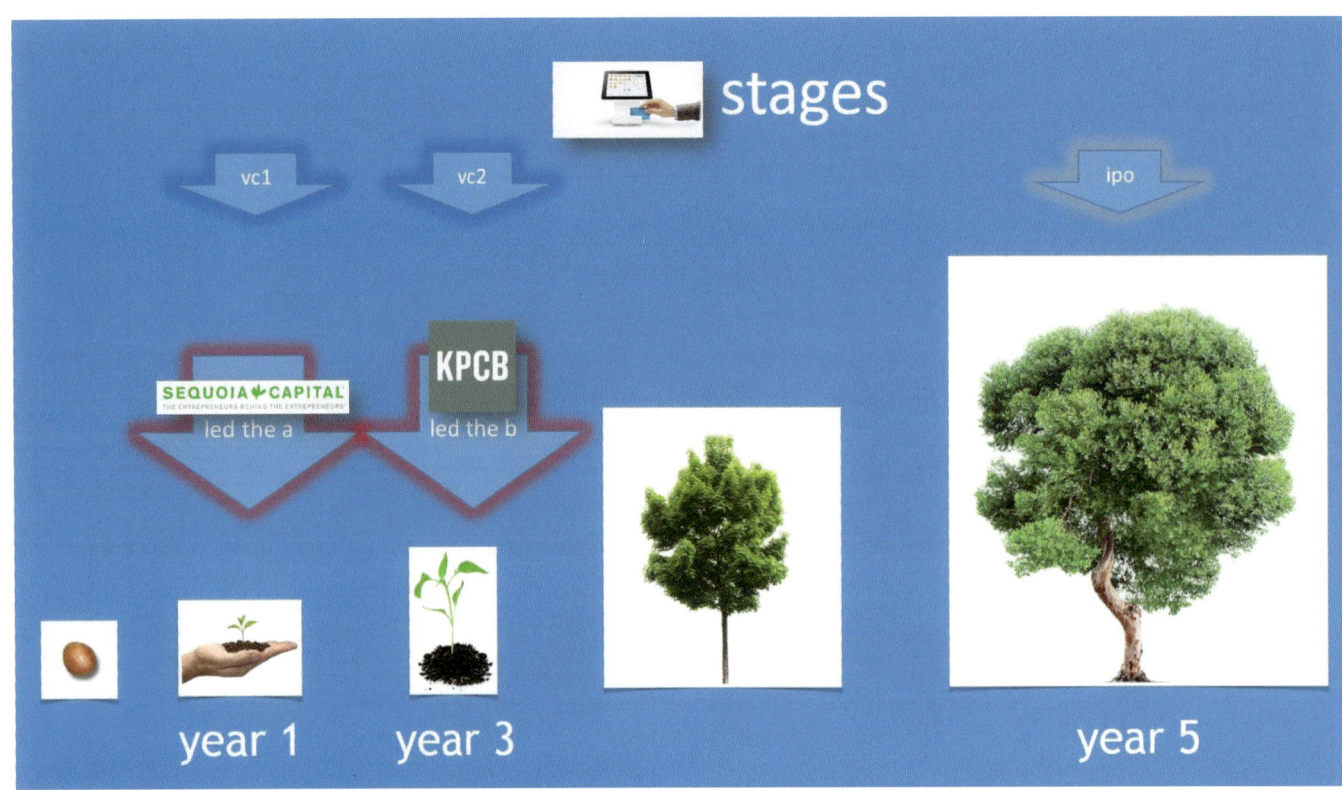

in year 3 we need another $1mn

Ok so we are now in year 3 and Giancarlo needs to raise another $1mn.

Giancarlo is a machine – he still expects to go public in year 5 at a $10mn valuation!

we still expect to go public in year 5 at a $10mn valuation

here comes the dilution...

damn lawyers!

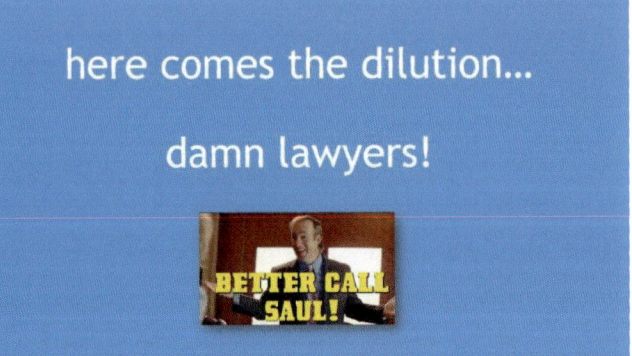

Eesh – too bad Giancarlo didn't talk to Sue Yoo or Benjamin Dover. He is going to get diluted. I want to stress that it is his fault entirely.

The Ultimate Practical Business Manual

> **kleiner expects a 25% return for the next 2 years.**
>
> **sequoia still expects a 50% annual return**
>
> **unfortunately the founder gets all of the dilution.**

Sequoia is not going to get diluted and nor should they as they had a law firm do the paperwork on their end. It's ok because Giancarlo will still make a lot of money but unfortunately the only way he could get another investor to take a risk and invest was if he gave up more of his equity.

Later stage investments usually have lower return profiles as they are usually closer to going public. Kleiner expects to make 25% annually for the next 2 years (when the P.O.S. firm will go public). Kleiner will put in $1mn and in 2 years expects to have $1mn * (1+25%)^2 = $1.5625mn

> **kleiner's expected return:**
>
> = $1mn *(1.25)^2 = $1.5625m

> **kleiner's ownership:**
>
> $1.5625m / $10mn = 15.625%

So Kleiner will do the deal with Giancarlo if their $1mn buys them $15.625%. Giancarlo does the deal despite the dilution. He is so passionate about the P.O.S. market that the dilution doesn't bother him too much. He isn't in this for the money. He wants to put a dent in the P.O.S. market!

> **sequoia's ownership:**
>
> remains at 75.94%

> **our ownership goes from**
>
> 100% - 75.93% = 24.07%
>
> to
>
> 24.07% - 15.625% = 8.4%

Giancarlo's ownership was 24.07% and now that he has given 15.625% of his stake to Kleiner, he now owns 8.4% of the company.

how many shares now?

2mn / 8.4%
=
23.7mn

share [new] history:

a round we issued:
23.7mn * 75.9% to sequoia
=
18mn shares

He still wants to keep his 2mn shares….so there are now 23.7mn shares.

share history:

b round we issued:
23.7mn * 15.6% to kleiner
=
3.7mn shares

it gets worse as we forgot about employee ownership via stock options…..

let's analyze the pie chart

before the dilution we owned 24% in the a

after the b we own 8.4%

My kids told me not to put this in the book. I presented to 2 Stanford MBA classes recently and only a few students in one of the classes politely laughed at this pie chart. Come on I thought this was a bit funny!

Ok hopefully you laughed a bit there! Back to our math...employees need to be incentivized to stay at Giancarlo's awesome P.O.S. firm!

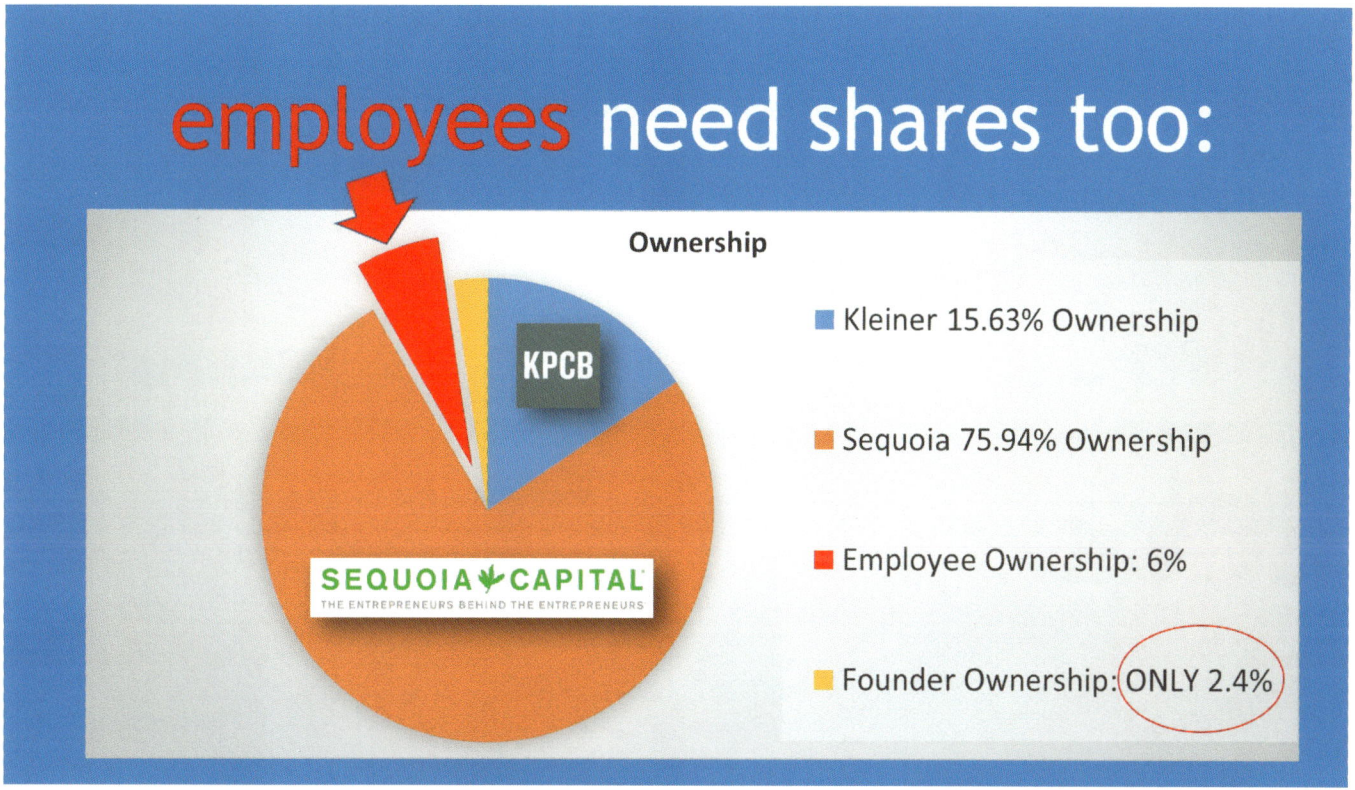

Unfortunately Giancarlo never hired a lawyer and forgot to given then options.....

Well unfortunately Giancarlo will get diluted for a 3rd time now! He needs to give 6% of the firm to his employees to keep them hanging around. They are worried as the firm almost ran out of money. He is in good company as this has happened to many amazing firms, including Oracle in the early 90s! Ok now Giancarlo only has 2.4% ownership!

why do we issue stock options? cheaper than paying a salary motivates all to work as a team **vesting.**	**now that we only own 2.4375% of the company. how many shares are there?** 2,000,000 / 2.4375% = 82mn shares options = 82mn *6% = 4.92m shares
oh man...we got diluted by 90%!	**outside (venture) investors are protected against dilution.** because they own 'preferred shares' we get diluted as we own 'common shares'
founders need to understand dilution before dealing with venture capital firms.	**it's not all bad as founders can also get HUGE option grants and hit the ball out of the park (especially if the $10mn IPO is a huge success)!**

Giancarlo is now on top of the world again as his company went public at $10mn and was a 10 bagger in the first year post IPO and a 10 bagger again in the next year and YES a 10 bagger again in the 3rd year! There is a reason Sequoia and Kleiner backed him! Giancarlo did such an amazing job that the board even granted him lots and lots of options. The firm is worth $10bn and Giancarlo owns 10% of it! A happy ending as he knocked it out of the park! www.tiny.cc/chris54 CURTAIN CALL!!!!

why do a 'b' round?

if we were tracking to $10mn in net income by year 5 instead of $1mn...

and we wanted to accelerate growth...

then we can raise $x at a $100mn series b round valuation

more vc return terminology

unicorns. $1bn+ valuation. pr <0.07%

In VC, a unicorn is a VC backed company that has a private or public market valuation of at least $1bn. The probability of this occurring is <0.07%. Most VC investments are black holes or fims that are walking dead.

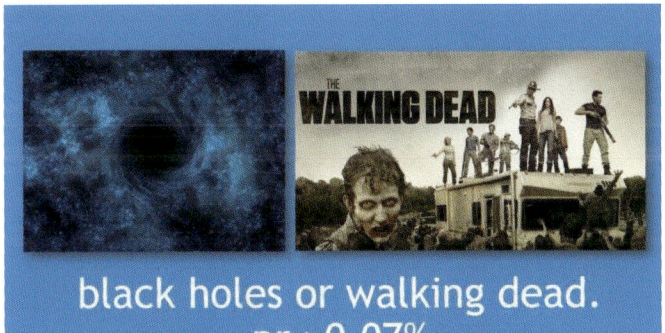

black holes or walking dead. pr >0.07%

1 / 1538 is the odds of a VC backed investment becoming a unicorn.

in order to return just the capital on a $400mn fund you need to own 20% of 2 unicorns.

that's how hard vc is!

there are ~40 unicorns that have been born since 2003

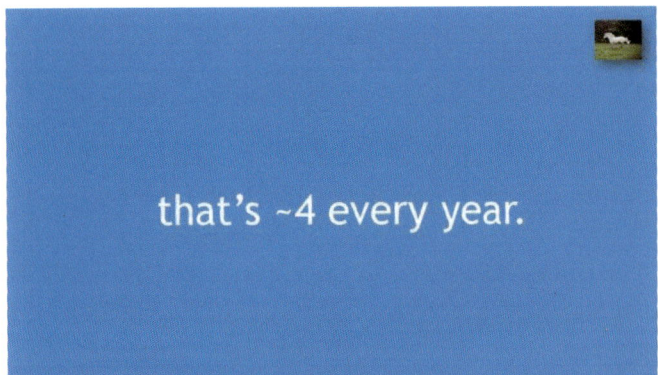

that's ~4 every year.

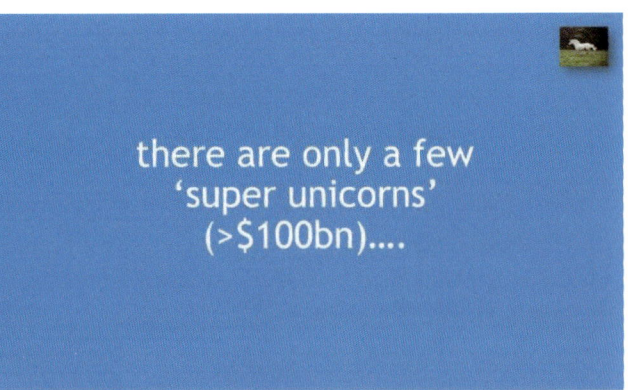

there are only a few 'super unicorns' (>$100bn)....

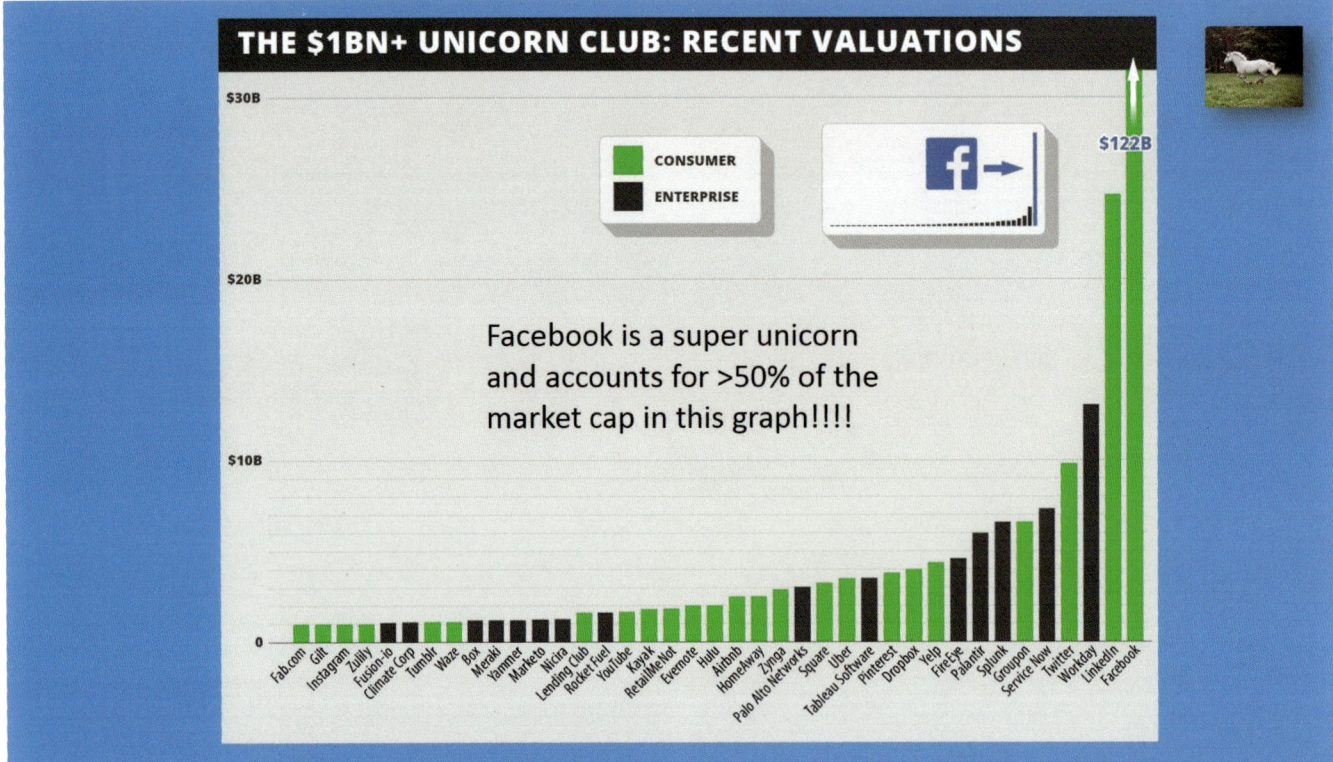

it takes 7 years on average from founding to IPO.

the average founder age is 34

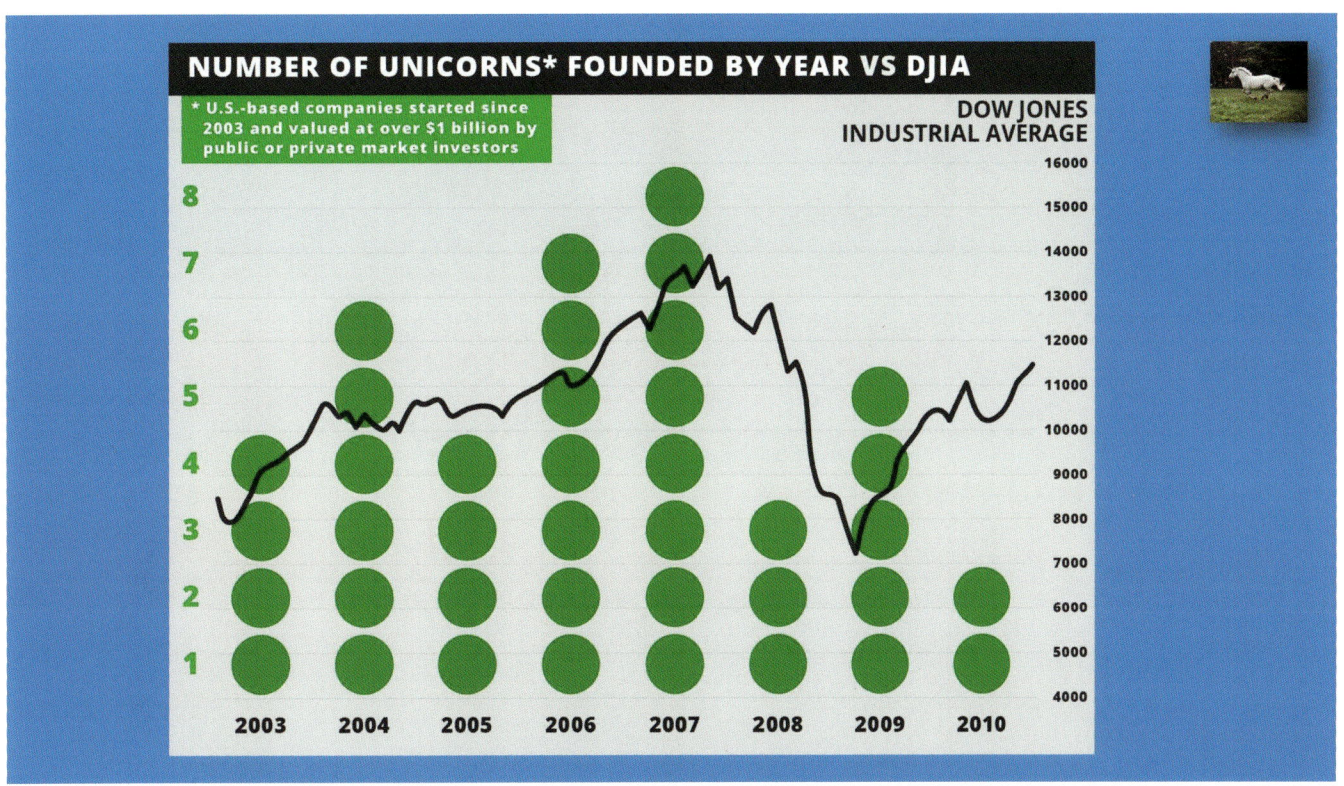
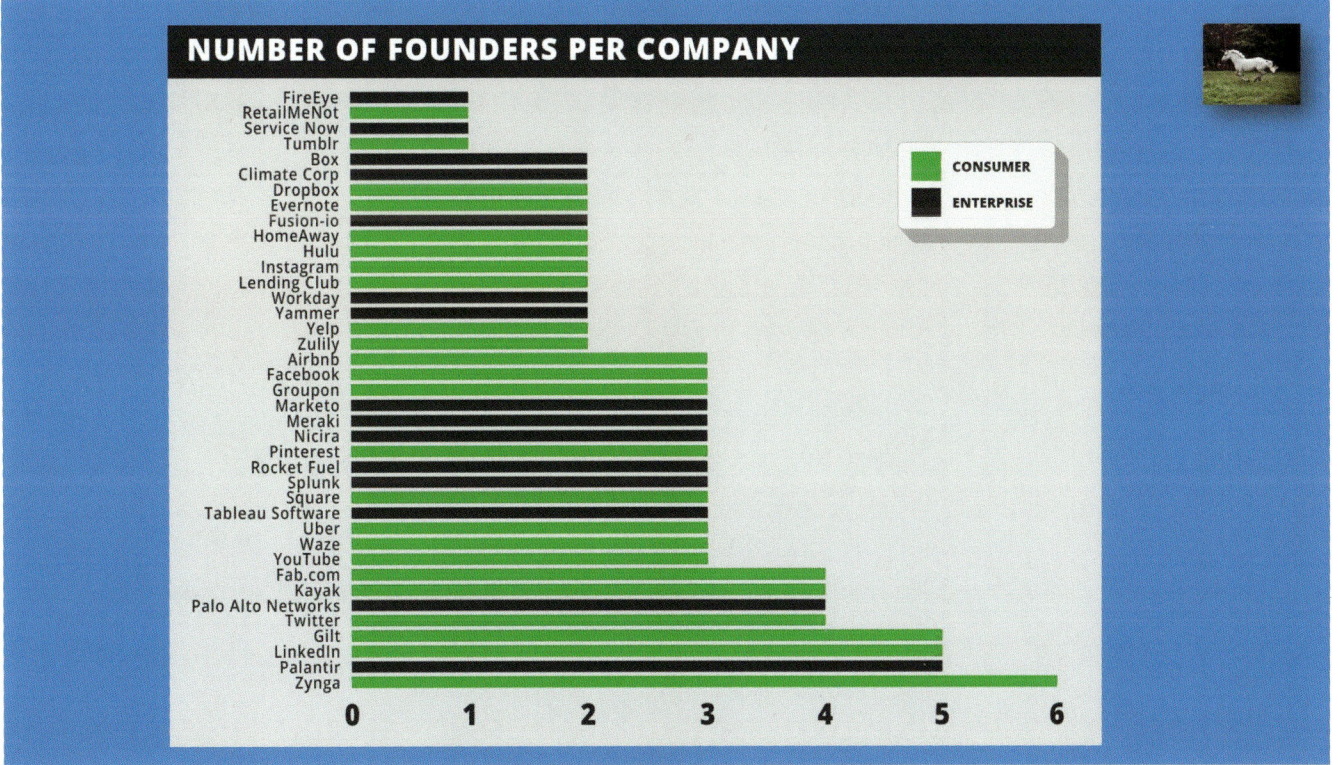

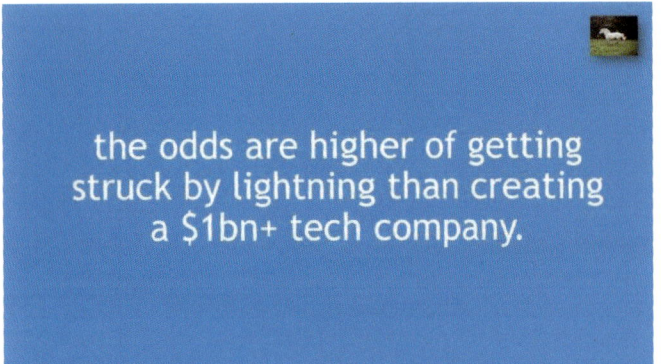 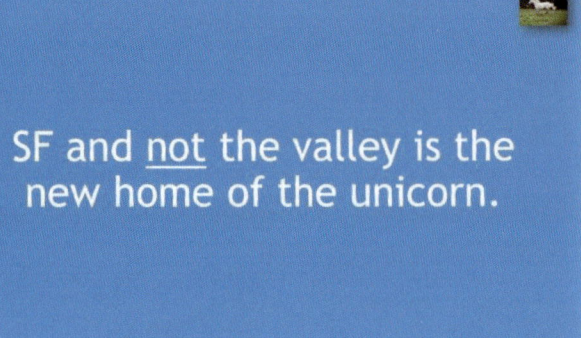

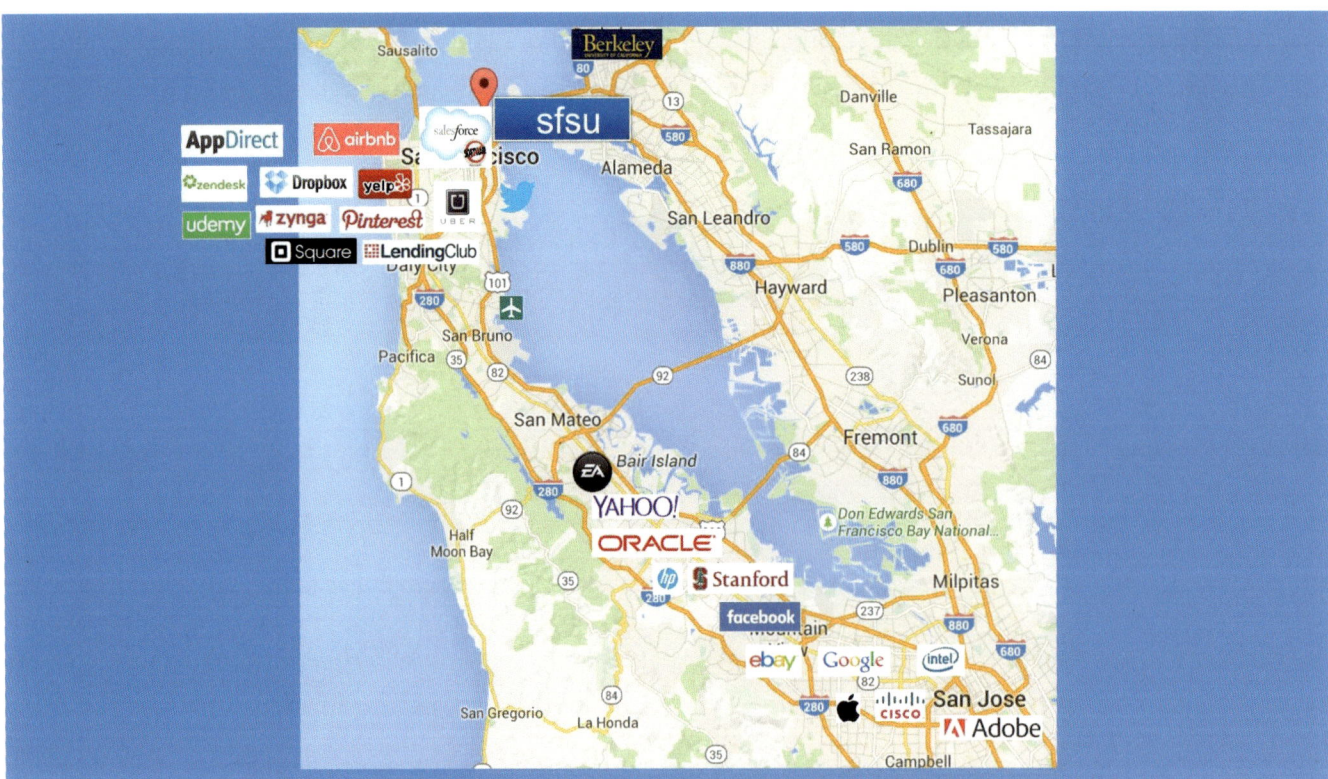

A lot of the cool new tech companies are being founded in San Francisco (north of the airport icon in the previous image) and not in the valley anymore (the valley is south of the airport icon).

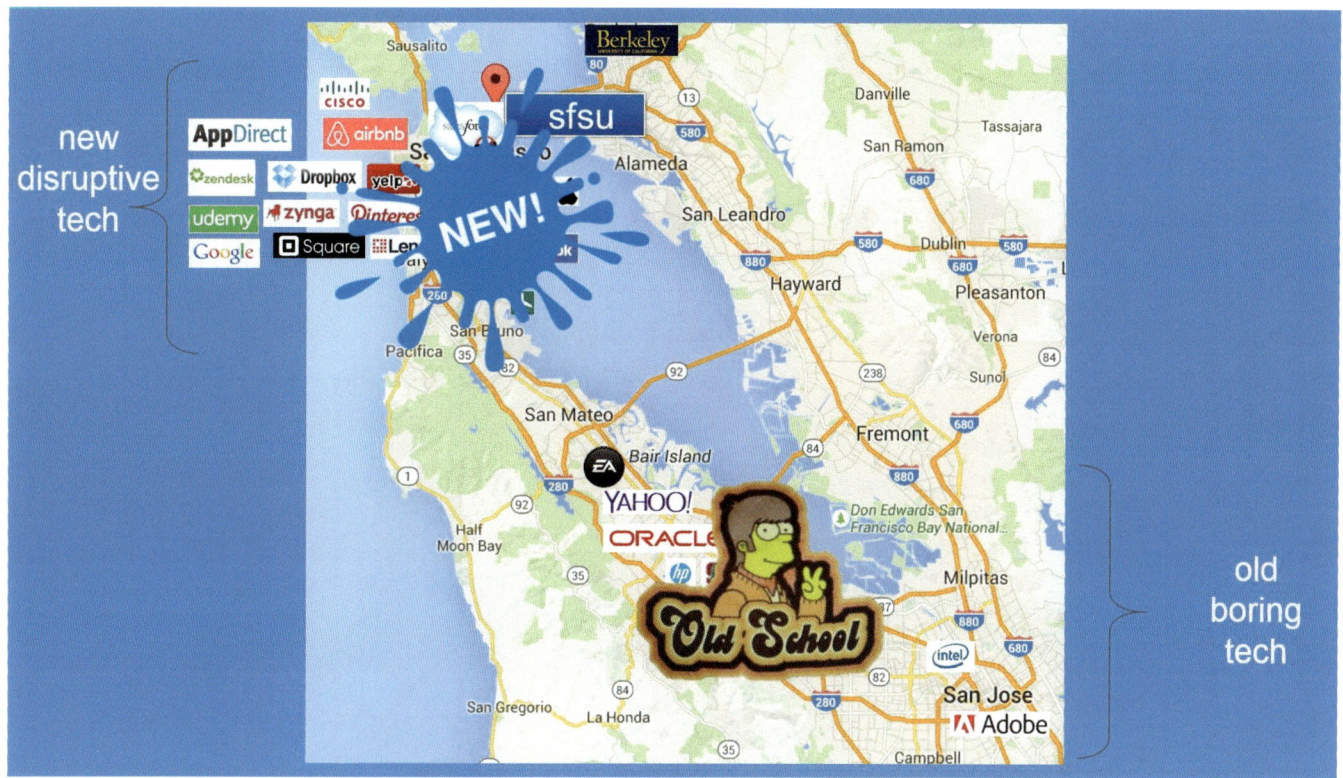

The largest employer in San Francisco is now Salesforce.com. Salesforce Tower will be completed very soon and it will tower way way way above every SF building and create a beautiful new skyline in San Francisco: www.tiny.cc/chris55

Questions Based on Chapter 5:

1: It makes more sense to get a loan rather than an investment from a VC or angel investor when you start a company.

    True or False

2: It makes sense to hire a lawyer only when dealing with banks.

    True or False

3: Hiring a lawyer makes sense when dealing with investors so you protect yourself from getting too diluted.

    True or False

CHAPTER SUMMARY

Chris Haroun @chris_haroun
we also discussed first round ('a') round valuation and dilution. b round. option pools. importance of contracts. vc sector return metrics. Unicorns.

CHAPTER 6: FINANCIAL ANALYSIS

"The biggest risk is not taking any risk... in a world that is changing really quickly, the only strategy that is guaranteed to fail is not taking risks."

- *Mark Zuckerberg*

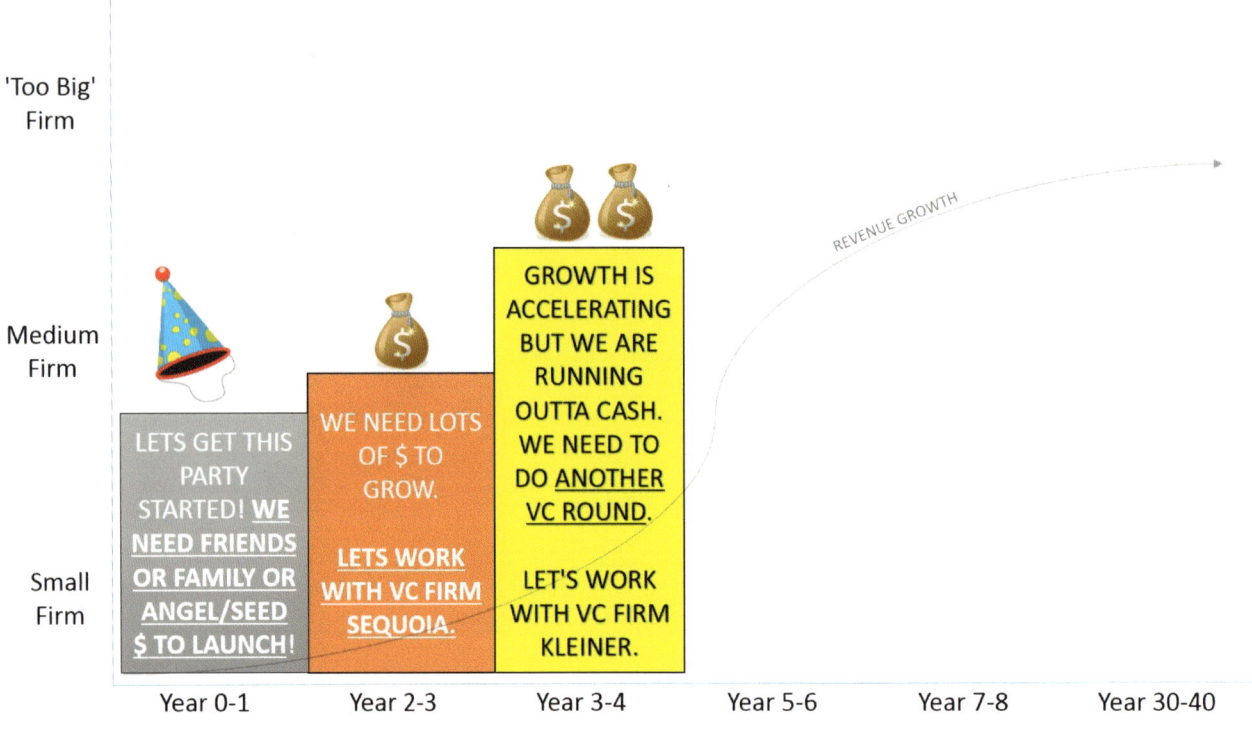

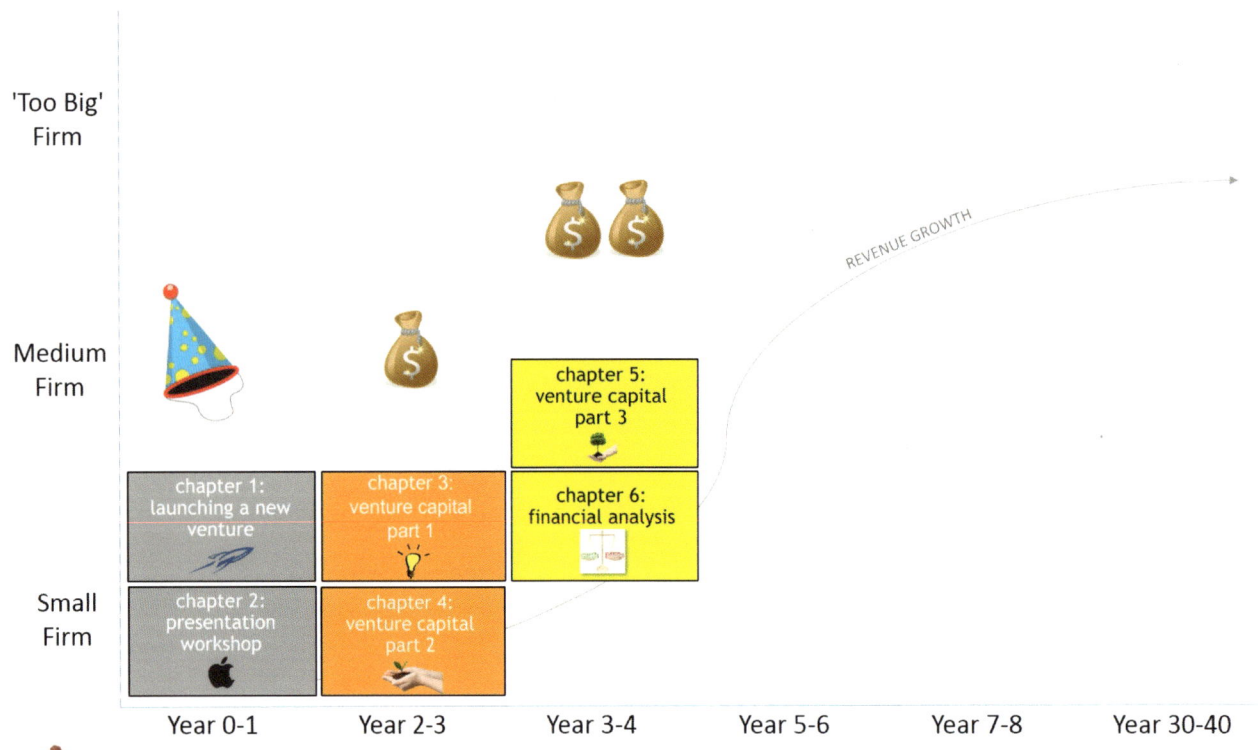

The most successful entrepreneurs are exceptionally confident. They didn't always start out this way, but over time they learned to develop confidence and eventually learned how to stay in this peak mental confident state, especially when presenting in business.

Whether or not you think you can do it, you are right! www.tiny.cc/chris56

Understanding Financial Statements the Easy Way

Ok. Next topic we will discuss is financial analysis and accounting.

The first time I took accounting during my undergraduate business degree at McGill University, I got a D and I had to retake the course. Why did I get a D? Because I was fresh out of high school and I did well in high school because I memorized stuff. In university and in business, you need to *understand* concepts, not memorize them. As such, I want you to understand finance and accounting concepts. Understand why math formulas are the way they are in finance and accounting and I promise you that you will excel and enjoy the finance and accounting process.

Your company is getting closer to an IPO. In addition to Point of Sale Terminals you decide to start also selling watches. "Banana Watch" is your product. You want to sell them in all 50 states in the US.

www.tiny.cc/chris57

introducing banana watch

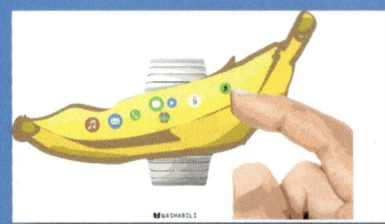

There are 3 financial statements we need to understand. Don't worry, we won't go into too much detail. Why? Because we use software in this century to actually create financial statements for us! That's right the Internet and software programs do accounting stuff for us. Heck if we don't call taxis to pick us up this century but we use Uber, then why can't we also simplify the accounting process? We will. In fact, I don't want you to create financial statements ever again after reading this book. Instead, find your favorite software package like QuickBooks from Intuit and just insert "money spent" and "money not spent" into those programs! I told you this is a modern business book!

As with all concepts in business, understand why they are called what they are called! Say what Chris? There are 3 financial statements we will learn aboooot (my Canadian again for about). They are as follows:

1: '**Balance Sheet**': think of an old scale that balances stuff….this tells you what you own and who owns that stuff (you, your investors or a bank).

2: '**Income Statement**': this tells you how much money or income you make after you subtract the money it cost you to sell a product or service.

3: '**Cash Flow Statement**': for some reason the income statement records expenses that you deduct that aren't cash out of your pocket expenses. Why? It's cool because it does this to make sure you pay less taxes. Huh? Well if you buy a car and it starts getting old, then you can 'depreciate' it so you can deduct part of the wear and tear of the car to reduce how much tax you have to pay. Don't worry, we will cover all this stuff in a bit more detail.

BALANCE SHEET

Why is it called a balance sheet again? Because stuff you own is owned by you, an investor in your company or a bank. Why do I even need to care about the balance sheet anyway? Because it tells you exactly what you own and who else owns your stuff. The left side of the balance scale must equal the right side of the balance scale. Why? Because someone owns all of the stuff in your company – it's either you or your investors or a bank. The balance sheet keeps track of who owns stuff!

 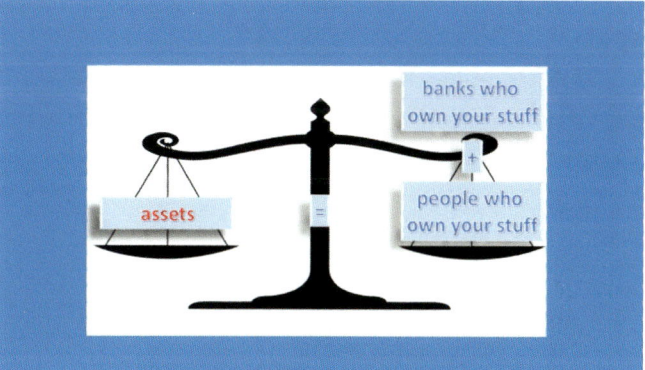

On the right side of the scale or balance sheet is the offsetting or balancing side. The right side is just telling you who owns your stuff….it can be you or other people (including yourself) or banks/companies that lend you money like credit card companies etc.

There is a left side and a right side of the balance sheet. The left side is stuff you own. This is called 'assets'. Capiche?

On the right side of the balance sheet you have 2 claims or 2 groups that claim they own your assets. The first group is called liabilities or banks (and other groups) that you owe money too. So liabilities is people you owe money to and includes your employees or credit card companies etc.

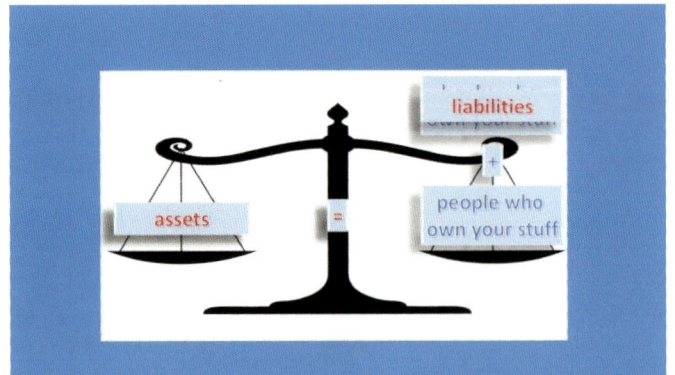

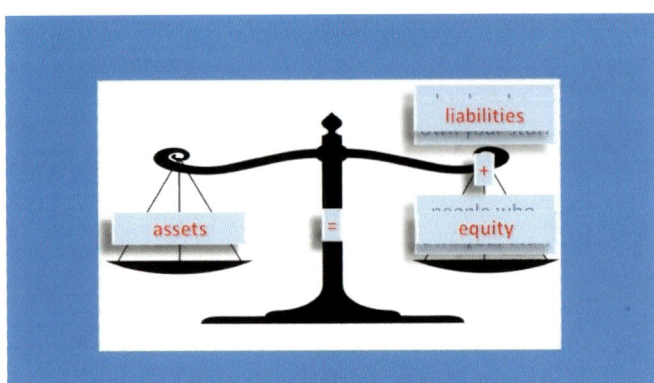

Well the banks don't own all of your stuff. Credit card companies don't own all of your stuff either. Say you buy a car for $10k with a $10k bank loan. The $10k car is an asset which you put on the left side of the scale. Then in order to make sure the scale remains balanced, then on the right side you include the bank loan for the car. The scale always has to be balanced because all of your stuff is either owned by people you owe money to or people that own your company (including you). Chris why is this statement even necessary? Because you will forget who you owe money to if you don't have a balance sheet.

Assets		Liabilities and Equity	
Cash +Stuff We Can Turn to $<1y	$60k	Bills we have to Pay	$20k
Stuff Owed to Us	$0k	Wages We Have to Pay	$0k
Inventory	$20k	Loans due in <1 year	$0k
		Other Current Liabilities	$0k
Total Current Assets	$80k	Total Current Liabilities	$20k
Equipment	$40k	Debt owed in >1 year	$20k
Less: Wear and Tear on it	$0k	Leases (equipment rented)	$0k
Equipment minus wear and tear	$40k	Total Long Term Liabilities	$20k
Building	$0k		
Other Long-Term Assets	$0k	Equity ($ of company we own)	$80k
Total Assets	$120k	Total Liabilities + Equity	$120k

See how the left side (assets) has to equal the right side (liabilities + equity)?

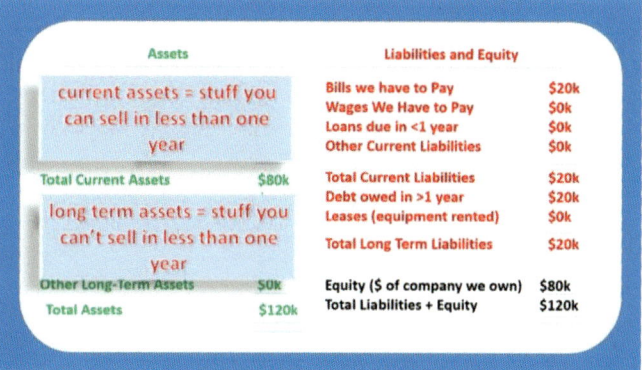

Let's build on this concept. Current assets are assets you can sell or liquidate in less than a year like cash or bonds you own.

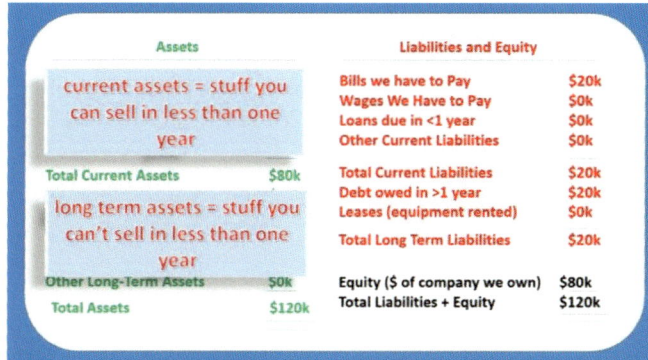
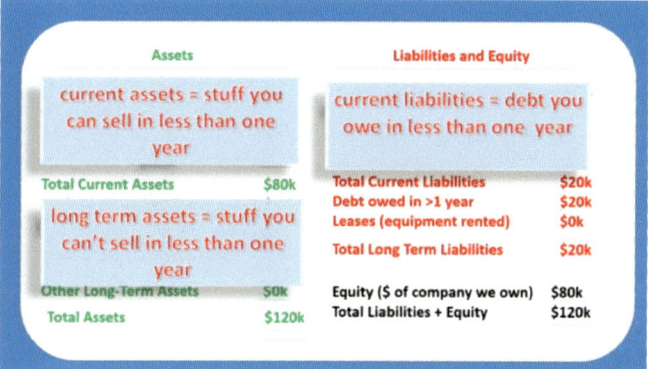

Stuff that likely takes you more than a year to sell is called long term assets, like a building which can take >1 year to sell. Similarly, stuff you owe in under a year like credit cards or short term loans are called current liabilities.

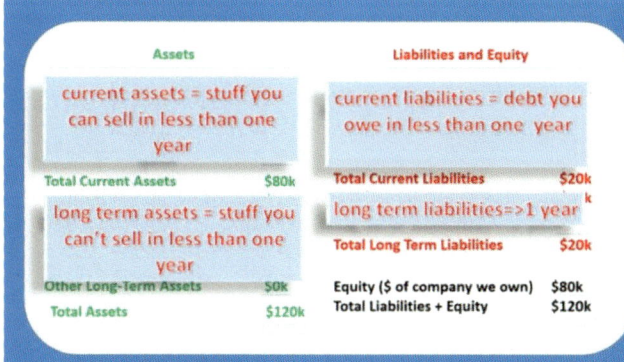
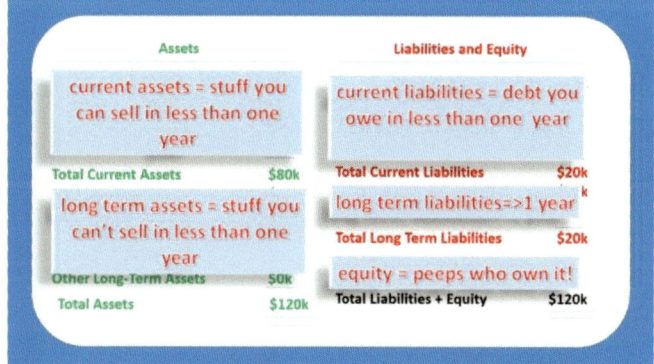

Long term liabilities are debts that you owe in greater than 1 year like a long term loan that is not due for a few years. Equity is just people that own your company including you!

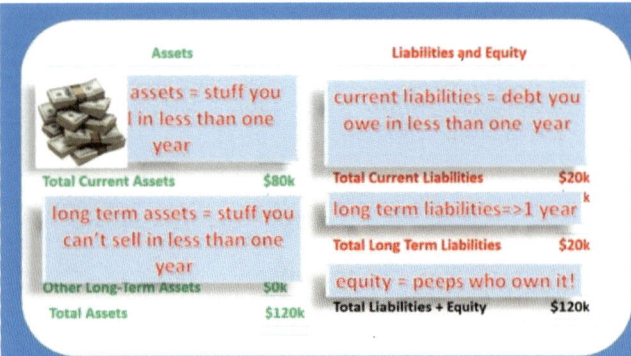
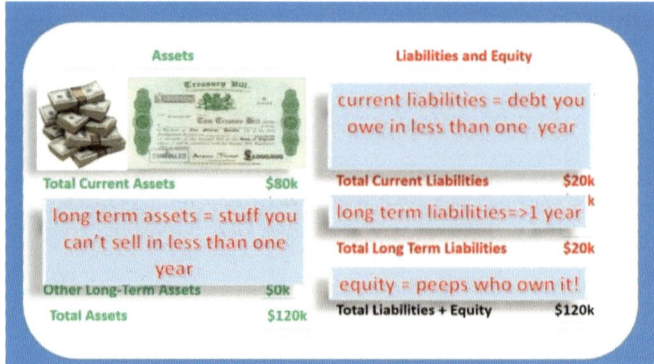

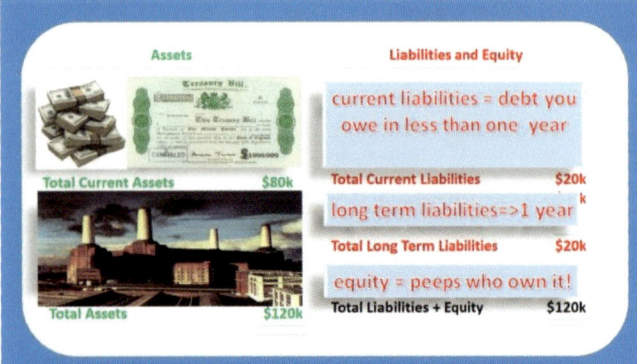

Long term assets includes factories. If you can tell me what album cover is showed above in long term assets I will be very impressed!

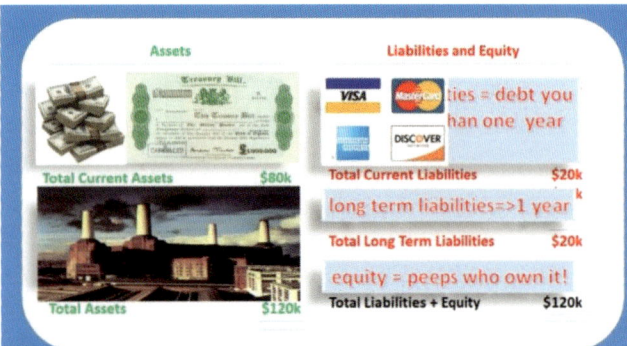

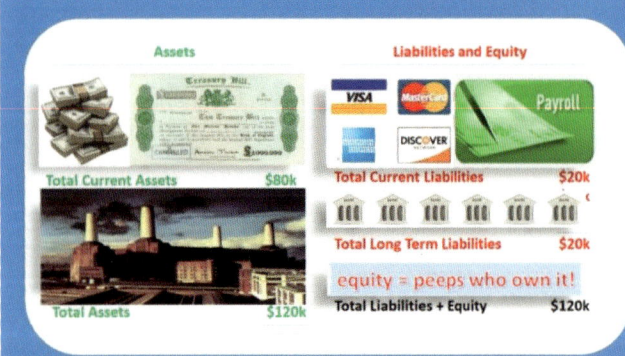

Notice how I included many banks in the long term section. I am not encouraging you to take on too much debt. Rather, if you have to work with banks when your company is mature, then please work with a few so that you can make them compete to give you the best rates.

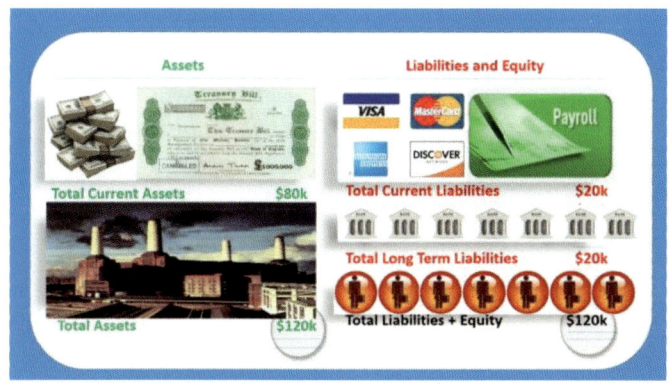

Please don't forget that the left side of the Balance Sheet (Assets) must always equal the right side of the Balance Sheet (Liabilities + Equity)

Assets		Liabilities and Equity	
Cash + marketable Securities	$60k	Accounts payable	$20k
Accounts receivable	$0k	Accrued wages	$0k
Inventory	$20k	Short Terms Loans	$0k
		Other Current Liabilities	$0k
Total Current Assets	$80k	Total Current Liabilities	$20k
Equipment	$40k	Long Term Loans	$20k
Less: Accumulated Depreciation	$0k	Leases	$0k
Net Equipment	$40k	Total Long Term Liabilities	$20k
Building	$0k		
Other Long-Term Assets	$0k	Equity ($ of company we own)	$80k
Total Assets	$120k	Total Liabilities + Equity	$120k

how do we order bs items?

You order stuff on a balance sheet in the order of liquidity. Say what? This means the stuff that you can convert to cash first is listed first and the stuff you can convert to cash last you list last.

In the next image of assets, obviously the first thing you would list is cash. Notice the kids playing hockey on the back of the $5 Canadian bill? How awesome is that!

Similarly, order liabilities on the balance sheet in the order that you have to pay them back. Credit cards go first as well as salaries payable.

What the heck is this lease stuff? I don't get it.

You lease something for accounting reasons. Huh? Well think of it like renting a machine. If you don't have enough money to buy a machine then you can lease or rent it.

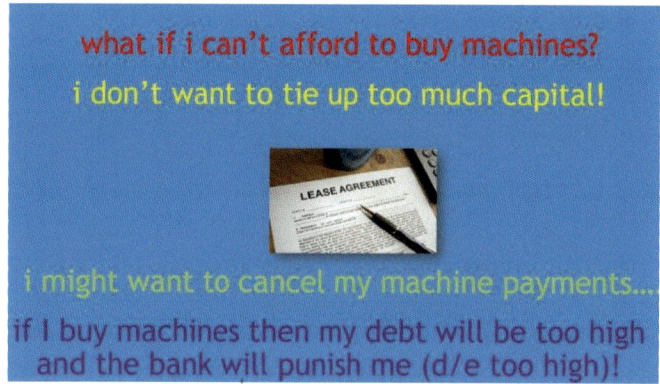

INCOME STATEMENT

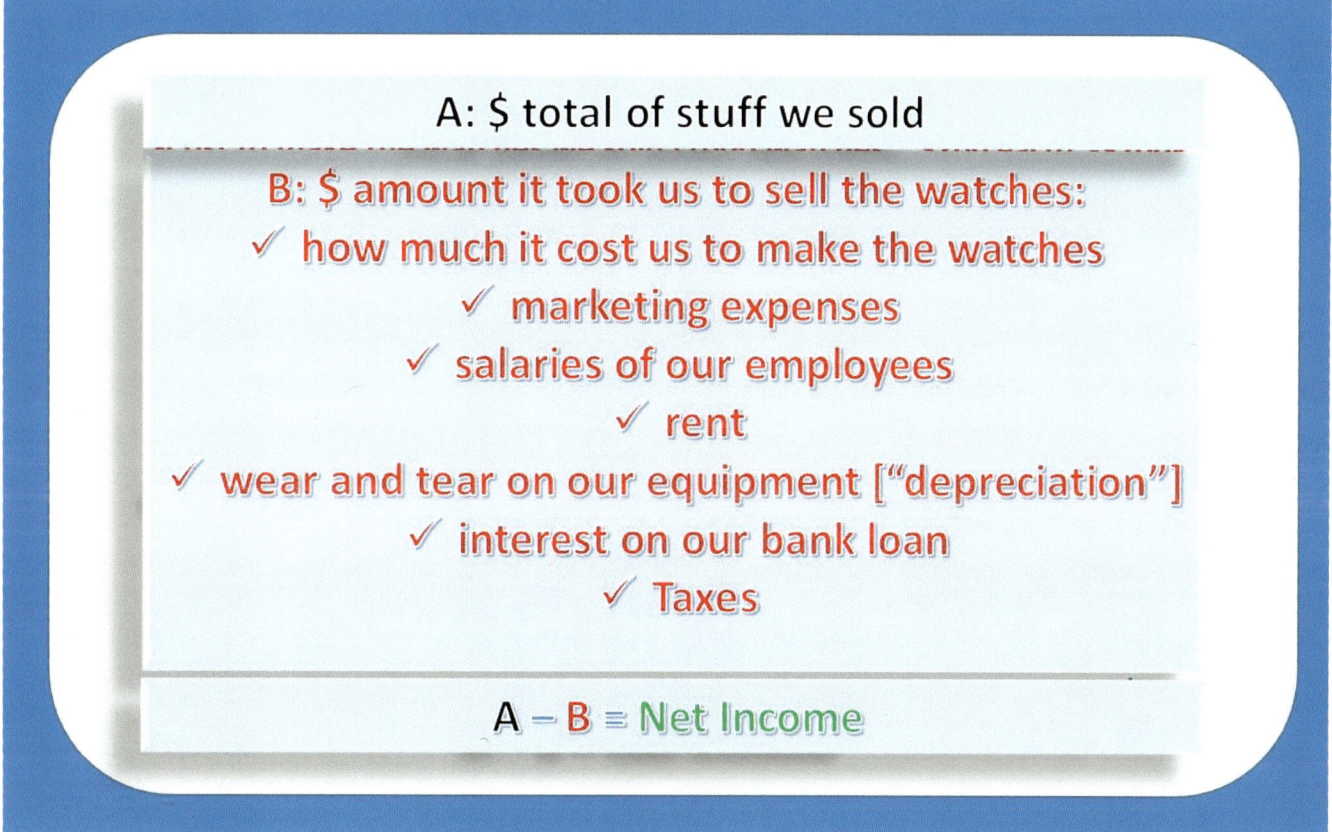

Recall that a balance sheet just tells you who owns your stuff (a bank or people that own part of your company., including you). How do I keep track of how much money I make and how much I need to pay in taxes? The answer is through the income statement…..the statement that explains to you how much income you make (and how we can pay as little tax as possible….great now the IRS is going to fn audit me)!

The income statement has 2 sections: A and B. A is the amount we sold our banana watches for. B is the cost to sell those bad ass watches! A – B = our Net Income.

Sales [1000 watches sold for $300 each]	**$300k**
-Cost to make the watches we sold [1000 watches * $200 each]	-$200k
Gross profit	=$100k
-Marketing expenses	-$10k
-Employee expenses	-$30k
-Rent expense	-$17k
-Depreciation (wear and tear on our equipment]	-$2k
Earnings before interest and taxes ["E.B.I.T."]	=$41k
-Interest	-$1k
Earnings before taxes	=$40k
-Taxes [the tax rate is 25%]	-$10k
Net Income	=$30k

Let's walk through an income statement. At the top is <u>always</u> sales (which is the same thing as revenue). Accounting and finance nerds call this the 'top line'. They say stuff like "what is my top line growth". This means how fast is my revenue (or sales…same thing) growing. Then the bottom of the income statement is called net income or 'the bottom line' [of the income statement]. Accounting and finance nerds will say "what is my bottom line growth" which just means how much is my net income or profit (same thing) growing. The top line is at the top and the bottom line is at the bottom. Easy.

Sales minus the cost to make that product is called "Gross Profit" as dumb as that sounds. So with our banana watch, the cost to make that product includes the cost of all the little components inside of the watch.

Hold on a second. How do we 'account' for other expenses in our company like salaries and rent etc.? Well this is recorded after 'Gross Profit'. The cost of paying employees or research and development or rent or other stuff are the expenses you have associated with 'operating' your business. Ok so we will call these expenses 'operating expenses'. If you deduct the cost to operate your business from Gross Profit, then this is called 'Operating Profit' or E.B.I.T. EBIT stands for earnings before interest and taxes.

Why the heck do we have to learn about EBIT? This sucks. Why don't you just look at net income? Because all companies pay a different tax rate and have different interest amounts. Therefore we might want to compare our company to our competition or other companies that are similar. We know that their expenses are similar but their tax or interest they pay are all massively different. Huh? Well we have a few competitors in Switzerland that claim that they make better watches than we do (what the heck do the Swiss know abooot watches anyway?). The tax rate is way different in Switzerland. We have a potential investor in our company that is also an investor in a few Swiss watch companies. He is looking at our financial statements now and he wants an "apples to apples" comparison of our company to the Swiss companies. Ok cool – he will compare the EBIT of those companies to our EBIT because the tax rates are wildly different for different companies.

For some dumb reason, expenses below EBIT (also called Operating Profit) are called 'below the line items'. These items include taxes or interest. Once you deduct taxes and interest payments (or interest income) from Operating Profit (also called EBIT), then you get the bottom line, which is called Net Income or Net Profit…..think if this as Profit or Income 'net of all expenses.'

Cool. I get it. So I see that our net income is $30k.

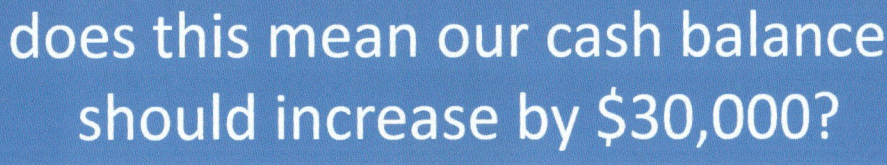

No our cash balance doesn't go up by $30k. But Chris you said our net income was $30k so of course I have $30k more now right? No you might have more than this (or less)!!!! How awesome. Pennies from heaven!

www.tiny.cc/chris58

On our income statement there is $2k in 'depreciation' (also called wear and tear) that we paid….but wait we didn't actually pay. So we have more than $30k? Maybe…

CASH FLOW STATEMENT

All we really care about is cash in my hand and cash out of my hand….heck let's just let software figure this out for us. We will….but I want you to understand accounting and finance with our very last financial statement, called 'The Cash Flow Statement'.

Cool. Ok so the $30k in our income statement isn't our new cash balance? No. Let's start the Cash Flow Statement by trying to find out what our cash balance should be. Actually there are 3 sections to our Cash Flow Statement. Let's start with understanding how much cash we made or lost while 'operating' our business. Let's add back or deduct cash items that helped or hurt our operations. Let's call this section "Cash Flow from Operations." At the top of this section we always put in net income.

Let's add back the wear and tear on our equipment that we deducted in our income statement. This is called depreciation and we get to add it back to our cash flow statement because we never paid $2k out of our pocket! Why did we deduct it then in our income statement? Because the government wants you to invest in your company through having the most bad ass and newest equipment. The government incentivizes you by letting you deduct the wear and tear from your pre-tax income so you pay less tax!

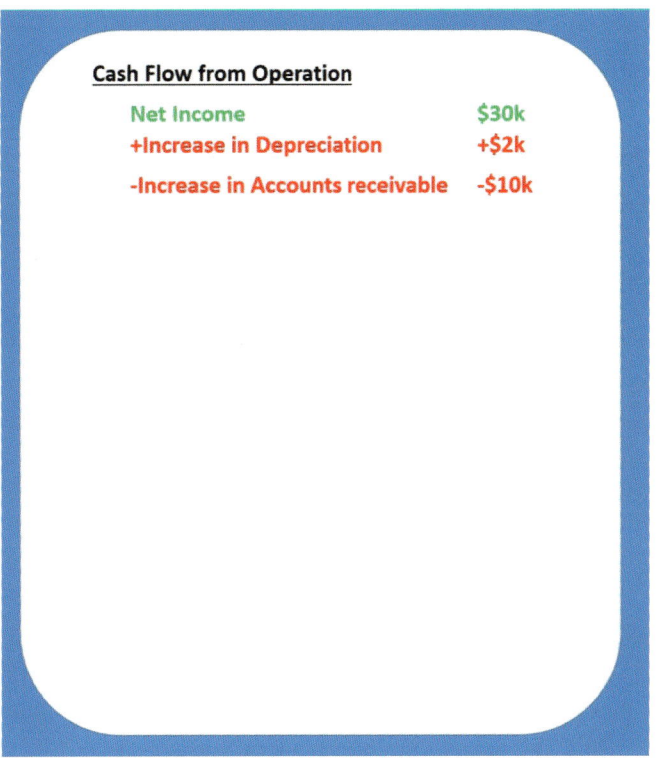

From the assets section of the balance sheet we saw an item called 'accounts receivable', which is accounting nerd talk for money that is owed to us….think of it like money owed to us by a customer. Sometimes we sell stuff and we tell the customer, just pay us later or within 30 days (we are desperate to sell stuff sometimes). Well we didn't get that money yet so we need to deduct it from our net income (or what we think we have for cash on hand).

From the liabilities section of the balance sheet we saw an item called 'accounts payable'. This means money we haven't paid yet to (for example) a credit card company or employees. Since we haven't paid for this item yet but we accounted for it, we add it back to our cash balance.

Cash Flow from Operation

Net Income	$30k
+Increase in Depreciation	+$2k
-Increase in Accounts receivable	-$10k
+Increase in Accounts payable	+$20k

In fact, you always want to pay back debts as late as you can (assuming you don't get penalized through interest payments). Why? Because in accounting everyone thinks of people they do business with as banks.

Everyone wants to pay everyone else back as late as possible without incurring late expenses as this is always economically beneficial (you earn a bit of interest in the bank if you pay bills right before they are due).

Cash Flow from Operation
Net Income	$30k
+Increase in Depreciation	+$2k
-Increase in Accounts receivable	-$10k
+Increase in Accounts payable	+$20k
A=Net cash flow from operations	=+$42k

Cool. Ok so instead of making $30k in net income we actually made $42k from operating our business; this cash flow statement stuff rocks! You are thinking that you actually hate accounting a little bit less now (just a little bit).....but wait, there's more!!!!

We invested in buying equipment to make our watches faster. This cost us $40k in cash.

Cash Flow from Operation
Net Income	$30k
+Increase in Depreciation	+$2k
-Increase in Accounts receivable	-$10k
+Increase in Accounts payable	+$20k
A=Net cash flow from operations	=+$42k

Cash Flow from Investing
-Increase in equipment	-$40k
B=Net cash flow from investing	=-$40k

We also got a loan this month so add $20k

Cash Flow from Operation
- Net Income — $30k
- +Increase in Depreciation — +$2k
- -Increase in Accounts receivable — -$10k
- +Increase in Accounts payable — +$20k
- A=Net cash flow from operations — =+$42k

Cash Flow from Investing
- -Increase in equipment — -$40k
- B=Net cash flow from investing — =-$40k

Cash Flow from Investing
- +Increase in Loans — +$20k
- C=Net cash flow from financing — =+$20k

A+B+C=TOTAL net change in cash — =+$22k

Cash Flow from Operation
- Net Income — $30k
- +Increase in Depreciation — +$2k
- -Increase in Accounts receivable — -$10k
- +Increase in Accounts payable — +$20k
- A=Net cash flow from operations — =+$42k

Cash Flow from Investing
- -Increase in equipment — -$40k
- B=Net cash flow from investing — =-$40k

Cash Flow from Investing
- +Increase in Loans — +$20k
- C=Net cash flow from financing — =+$20k

A+B+C=TOTAL net change in cash — =+$22k
+Beginning cash balance — +$60k

Ok so we actually make $22k in net cash.

Cash Flow from Operation

Net Income	**$30k**
+Increase in Depreciation	+$2k
-Increase in Accounts receivable	-$10k
+Increase in Accounts payable	+$20k
A=Net cash flow from operations	=+$42k

Cash Flow from Investing

-Increase in equipment	-$40k
B=Net cash flow from investing	=-$40k

Cash Flow from Investing

+Increase in Loans	+$20k
C=Net cash flow from financing	=+$20k
A+B+C=TOTAL net change in cash	=+$22k
+Beginning cash balance	**+$60k**
=Ending cash balance	=+$82k

The balance sheet told us that we already had $60k….no we now have $82k in cash!

There is a link between the 3 financial statements as show in the previous graphic. The income statement talks to the balance sheet because net income is also in the balance sheet's equity section. The balance sheet talks to the cash flow statement as beginning cash is on both statements. The cash flow statement talks to the income statement as both have net income reflected.

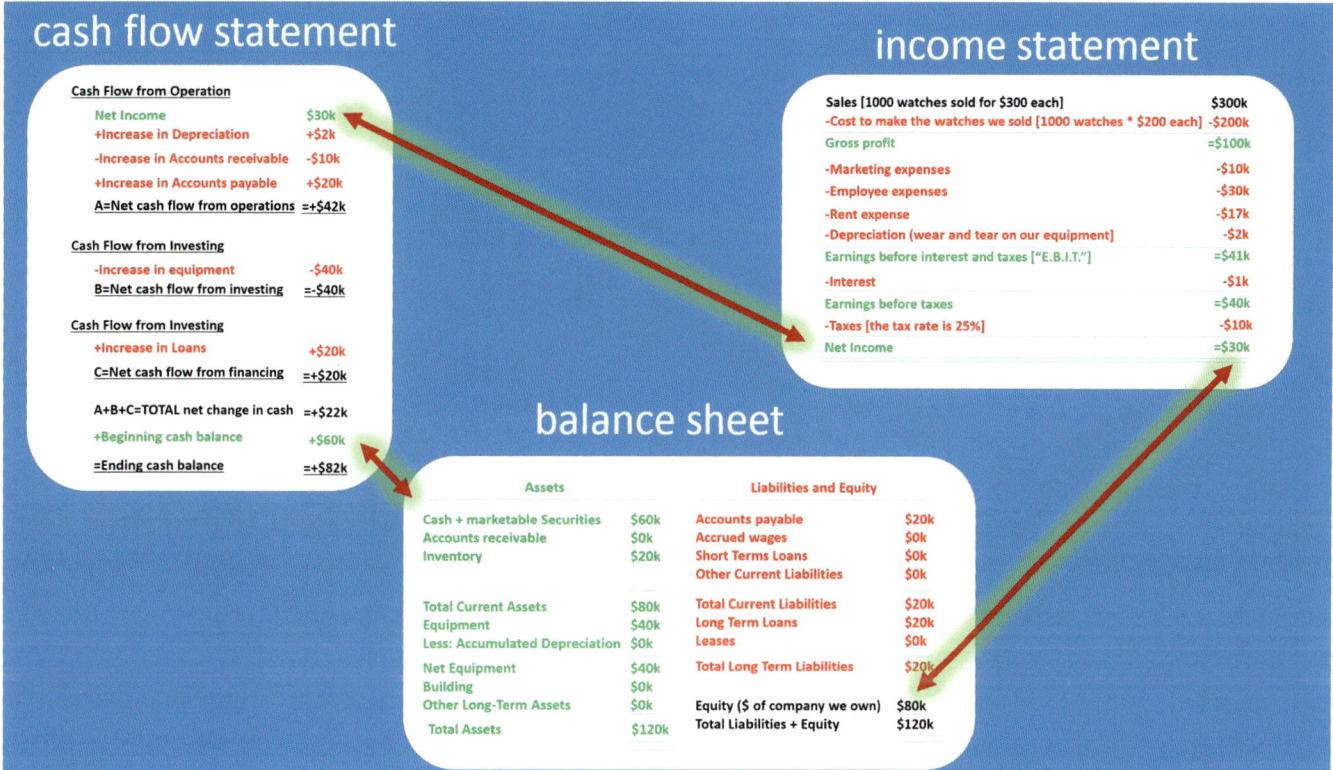

Ok no more financial statement talk! (Yay!)

In reality you use software to do all that accounting stuff for you. If you are a small firm, I recommend and have used QuickBooks a lot. It is so awesome as all you do is enter in money made and money owed and QuickBooks makes a gazillion financial statements for you! I even had QuickBooks automatically pay my employees and automatically

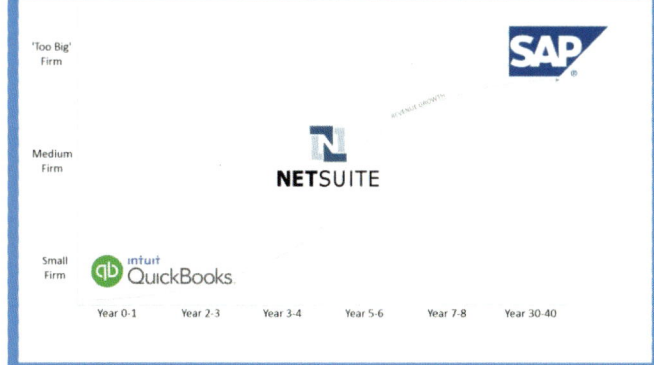

send taxes when due at both the state and federal level! When you have a firm with a few hundred employees then you graduate from using QuickBooks to using NetSuite which is all cloud based. Then when you are a massive 'too big' firm, you use accounting software from a bigger firm like SAP or Oracle.

FINANCIAL RATIOS

financial ratios
(understanding them…not memorizing them)

Understand financial ratios and never memorize them or you will be bored to tears learning this stuff. www.tiny.cc/chris59 **…..please don't be stubborn…take time to understand financial ratios :)**

why do we care about financial ratios?

3 reasons

1: so **equity** investors can decide to invest or they can assess investment performance

2: so **lenders** can decide to lend or they can assess loan performance

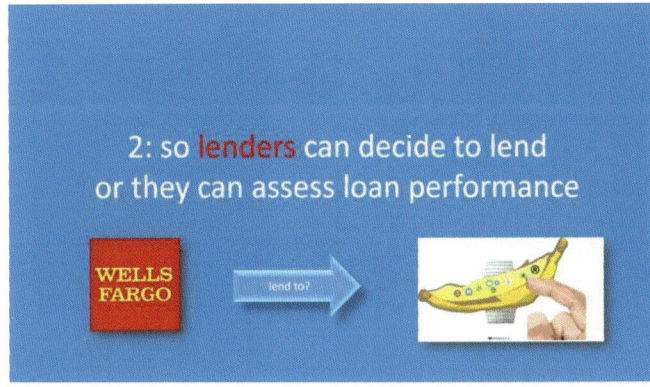

3: so business owners can track performance

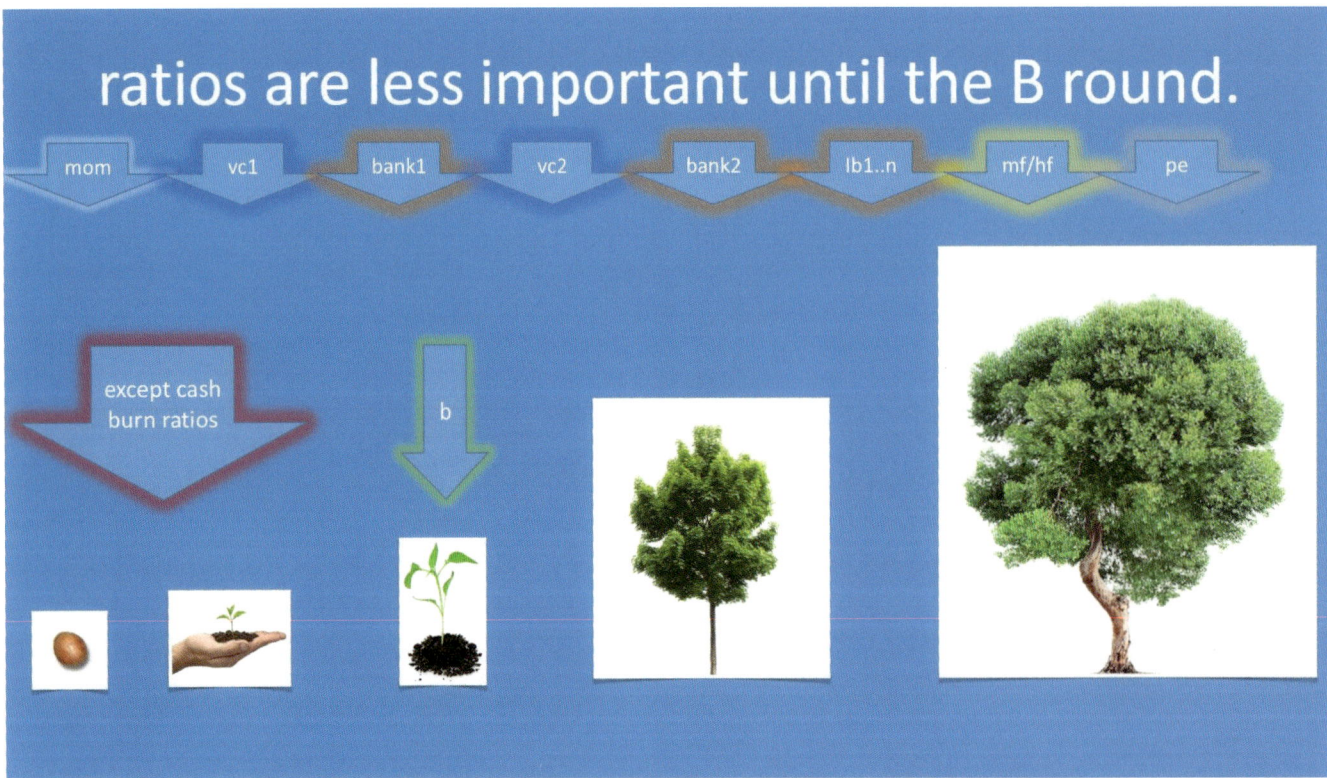

The only ratio we really care about when we start a company is the monthly cash burn rate....or how much cash we spend each month. Then closer to the B venture capital round when we are actually selling our product, then we have more financial data to analyze and apply ratio analytics to.

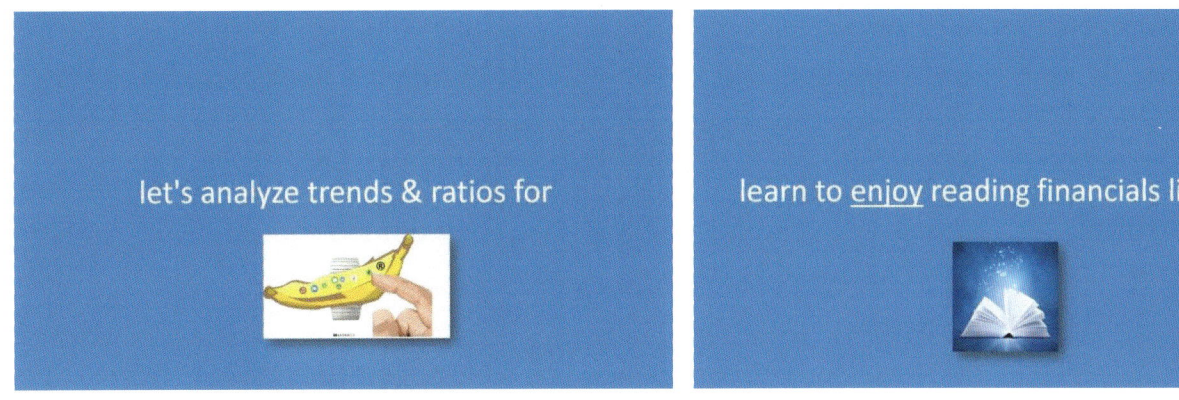

I know it sounds nerdy, but learn to enjoy reading financials like a good book. Looks for trends in the data. One data point does not make a trend, but multiple data points do...this is what Wall Street Analysts do! They look for trends! Fun!

INCOME STATEMENT ANALYSIS

	Year 1		Year 2
Sales	$800k	25% yoy growth	$1000K
-Cost of goods sold	-$520k		-$660k
Gross profit	=$280k	35% of sales to 34%	=$340k
-Marketing expenses	-$80k	10% of sales to 11%	-$110k
-Employee expenses	-$58k	7.3% of sales to 6.8%	-$68k
-Rent expense	-$36k	4.5% of sales to 4.7%	-$47k
-Depreciation	-$26k	3.2% of sales to 2.9%	-$29k
E.B.I.T.	=$80k	10% of sales to 8.6%	=$86k
-Interest	-$22k	2.7% of sales to 3.4%	-$34k
Earnings before taxes	=$58k	7.3% of sales to 5.2%	=$52k
-Taxes [the tax rate is 30%]	-$18k		-$16k
Net Income	=$41k	5.1% sales to 3.6%	=$36k

Cool. Let's look for trends in our income statement. It looks like revenue is growing at a healthy 25% rate YoY (year over year). Let's look at everything on this income statement as a percent of revenue. In fact, the most important thing to keep in mind is analyzing everything in finance as a percent of revenue (much more on that later).

Aha! We found a number of red flags or problems with our company. Our gross profit as a percent of revenue was 35% last year and it is only 34% now. Ouch – our profitability on selling our stuff is going down as a percent of revenue. Many line items as a percent of revenue are rising. I see a lot of red flags here.

BALANCE SHEET ANALYSIS

Assets	Year 1	Year 2	
Cash + marketable Securities	$60k	$40k	-$20mn…deadly… what is happening?
Accounts receivable	$0k	$0k	
Inventory	$20k	$130k	+$110mn…why is inventory up?
Total Current Assets	$80k	$170k	
Equipment	$40k	$50k	
Less: Accumulated Depreciation	$0k	$10k	
Net Equipment	$40k	$40k	
Building	$0k	$0k	
Other Long-Term Assets	$0k	$0k	
Total Assets	$120k	$210k	
Liabilities and Equity			
Accounts payable	$20k	$20k	
Accrued wages	$0k	$0k	
Short Terms Loans	$0k	$20k	+$20mn…looks like loans are
Other Current Liabilities	$0k	$0k	financing the inventory (bad)
Total Current Liabilities	$20k	$40k	
Long Term Loans	$20k	$60k	+$40mn….loans financing inventory
Leases	$0k	$0k	spike and not net income (bad)
Total Long Term Liabilities	$20k	$60k	
Equity ($ of company we own)	$80k	$110k	+$30mn: note that we had $30mn in…
Total Liabilities + Equity	$120k	$210k	…net income on our income statement

Oh no….there are many issues with our balance sheet. Cash is down $20 but our inventory is up $110! So our assets are up $90 but due to an inventory spike? Recall that Assets = Liabilities + Equity. So what went up $90 in the Liabilities and Equity section? Well it looks like we are financing our $90 increase through a combination of short term loans ($20) + long terms loans ($40) + our $30 in net income. Disaster. We are burning through too much cash!!!!

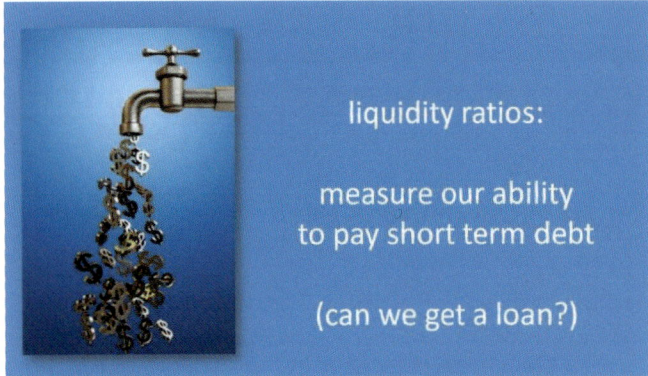

Liquidity is a term that means how fast can we turn our stuff into cash...or how liquid we are. Banks and investors analyze liquidity ratios a lot to determine whether or not they will finance or lend us money.

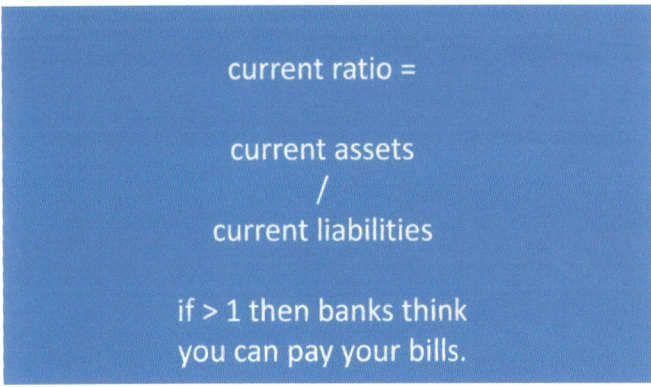

Recall that current assets are stuff we can convert to cash in less than 1 year and current liabilities are debt due in less than a year. Banks love looking at the current ratio...or the ratio of current assets to current liabilities. If the number is >1 then they feel that you can pay back your debts. Don't memorize this...understand it.

However, if your company has inventory (unsold products) then it's not fair to look at the current ratio. Why? Because current assets includes inventory. Why should we benefit in the current ratio from a high current assets amount if our inventory levels are too high?

a massive recall was just announced on our banana watch as it doesn't work when it is over 70% outside and if it is under 60% outside!

....this is a HUGE problem for us as the current ratio uses current assets (which includes inventory) in its calculation!

Shute. The banana watches we just made have a massive recall! The watches don't work if the temperature is above 70 degrees or under 60 degrees. Damnit we forgot to account for this when we made the watches! We thought people only use watches inside...

The bank now thinks that the current ratio is misleading because of our massive inventory position given the recall. Well how can the bank assess our company now that the previous ratio is useless?

> **solution?**
> the "quick ratio" is like the current ratio...
> ....except it ignores inventory if needed!
> quick ratio =
> (current assets – inventory) / current liabilities
> is not > 1 (oh no!)

> "when you combine ignorance and leverage, you get some pretty interesting results."
>
> - warren buffet

Oh boy, we are in BIG trouble now as the quick ratio is not more than 1. Oh no are we in trouble???? www.tiny.cc/chris60 .

> **debt to total assets**
> = debt / assets

Banks will analyze your business by looking at the ratio of how much debt you have to your assets.

> **other ratios**
> ROA = net income / assets
> ROE = net income / equity

> **interest coverage**
> = EBITDA / interest

Lenders also want to make sure that you have enough operating profit (also called EBIT or EBITDA) to cover your interest payments. Lenders want you to be able to make enough money to cover your interest payments many times over. EBITDA is just like EBIT but it stands for Earnings Before I Tricked Dumb Accountant. Kidding of course. It actually stands for Earnings Before Interest, Depreciation and Amortization. The A in EBITDA accounts for when you overpay for an acquisition (for example) and you want to depreciate it like you depreciate equipment.

Questions Based on Chapter 6:

1: On the balance sheet:

    a) Assets + Liabilities = Equity
    b) Assets + Long Term Debt = Equity
    <u>c)</u> Assets = Liabilities + Equity
    d) Assets + Equity = Liabilities

2: On the income statement:

    a) Sales – Expenses = Assets
    b) Sales – Assets = Equity
    <u>c)</u> Sales – Expenses = Net Income
    d) Sales – Depreciation = Liabilities

3: On the cash flow statement:

    a) Depreciation is subtracted from net income.
    b) Depreciation is added to net income.
    <u>c)</u> The net income is not the same as net income on the income statement.
    d) The net income is always the same as the current assets balance.

4: The current ratio is:

    <u>a)</u> Current assets / current liabilities
    b) Current liabilities / current assets
    c) Current assets – inventory / current liabilities
    d) Current liabilities – inventory / current assets

5: The interest coverage ratio:

    a) Measures how many times your EBITDA (also called operating profit) can cover or pay your accounts payable.
    b) Measures how many times your EBITDA (also called operating profit) can cover or pay your interest expense.
    c) Measures how many times your net income (also called operating profit) can cover or pay your interest expense.

Measures how many times your net income (also called operating profit) can cover or pay your accounts payable.

Chapter Summary

Chris Haroun @chris_haroun
don't memorize accounting; understand it! all 3 financial statements are related but most importantly, cash is king. ratios help investors and entrepreneurs understand trends.

CHAPTER 7: MANAGING CASH FLOW

"I have pledged… to always run Berkshire with more than ample cash… I will not trade even a night's sleep for the chance of extra profits."

- *Warren Buffett*

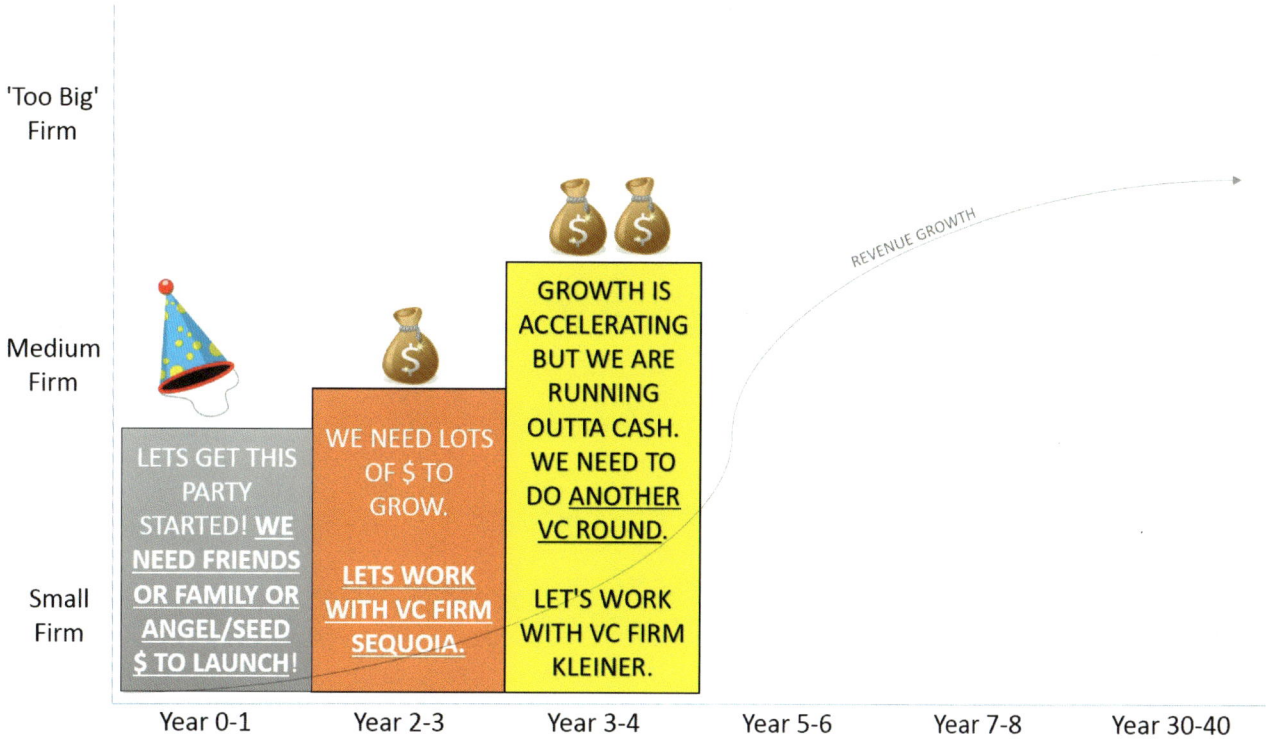

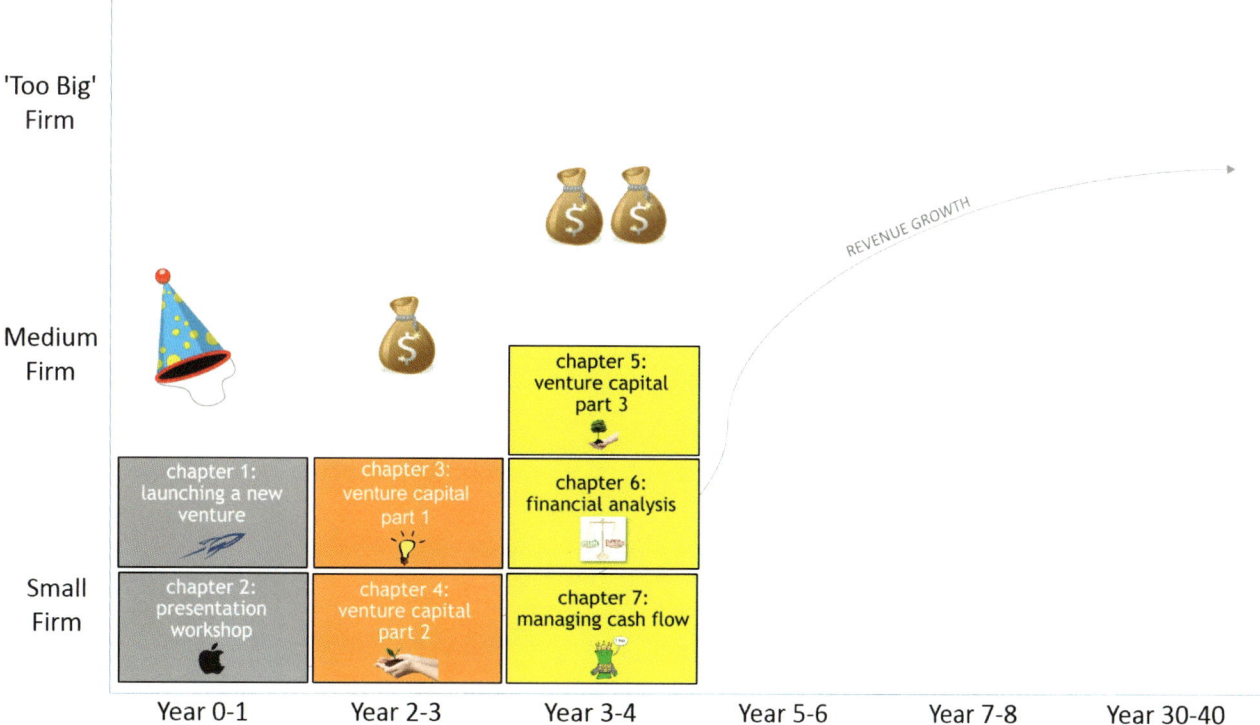

MAKING FORECASTS

www.tiny.cc/chris62

how do companies make budgets?	forecasting is not hard.
all forecasts are based on % of sales	then you make assumptions…
forecasts are never 100% accurate	forecasting is easy. forecast sales and then the rest of the model is simple.

Percent of sales analysis is the most important quantitative concept in business.

We will go through this in great detail soon.

> public companies forecast quarterly.
>
> start-ups forecast monthly.

> why?
>
> because survival is the goal.

> all successful entities have budget forecasts

Every company, successful business person or even countries has to make budgets: www.tiny.cc/chris61

Most companies end their accounting or 'fiscal' year on December 31st. However, some companies end their fiscal years at different times. Why? Because some companies started their companies in the summer. As a result, they start their accounting years then, like Microsoft and Oracle, whose accounting years end and begin in the summer.

> seasonality & fy end
>
>

Interestingly enough, retail companies have their fiscal years ending in January and not December. Why? Because they make most of their money in the holiday shopping season. This is why they call it 'Black Friday'…because they go from losing money (in the red) to making money every year by black Friday where they are 'in the black'.

We need to understand seasonality too when making forecasts. Most companies have their best quarter of the year in calendar Q4 (October through December) and their lowest in calendar Q1 or during the summer (especially in Europe where business can grind to a halt there in the summer).

different countries and fy end

Japanese companies almost always end their fiscal years in March.

When making business forecasts, I can almost guarantee that you will come across people that fudge or make up numbers. Please be careful of liars in business: www.tiny.cc/chris63 .

ethics.

you might one day work with people that lie about financials.

please always be <u>conservative</u> & <u>honest</u> with forecasts.

how can we measure how long it takes for assets and liabilities to turn into cash?

"cash conversion period ratios"

if we have $5000 of inventory and the average daily COGS is $100 then we have 50 days of COGS in inventory.

Cash conversion ratios tell us how many days it takes to convert something into cash.

COGS stands for the cost of goods sold.

another way to think about it is...

If we put another $1 into inventory, it won't be converted into cash (or COGS) for another 50 days.

inventory issues can destroy a company.

Inventory to sale conversion period
=
average inventories
/
COGS
/365

The inventory to sale conversion period tells us how many days it takes to convert inventory into a sale. Understand this equation. Please don't memorize it.

if we sell our product on credit...can we track how long it takes us to collect cash?

sale to cash conversion period
=
average receivables
/
sales/365

The sale to cash conversion period tells us how many days it takes to convert sales into cash!

it is good practice to pay bills as late as you can (without incurring fees or upsetting your business partners).

how can we measure this?

If you replace 365 with 90 then grab the latest quarterly average payable and average accrued liabilities numbers to calculate quarterly ratios instead of annual ratios.

purchase to payment conversion period
=
average payables + average accrued liabilities
/
cogs/365

Questions Based on Chapter 7:

1: The most important forecasting rule is:

    <u>a)</u> Most forecasts are based on a percent of revenue.
    b) Most forecasts are based on a percent of income.
    c) Most forecasts are based on a percent of revenue.
    d) Most forecasts are based on a percent of equity.

2: Early stage start-ups are more likely to forecast revenue:

    a) On a yearly basis
    b) On a decade basis
    <u>c)</u> On a monthly basis
    d) On a quarterly basis

3: Fiscal and calendar years are always the same for every company.

    True or <u>False</u>

CHAPTER SUMMARY

Chris Haroun @chris_haroun
short term forecasting is primarily about cash flow estimates. many assumptions are made and many are based on a % of sales. cash conversion ratios tell us # days to convert.

Since I am Canadian, I have to end this chapter with the funniest Canadian ever! www.tiny.cc/chris64   :)

Chapter 8: Financial Capital and Securities Laws

"It takes 20 years to build a reputation and five minutes to ruin it. If you think about that, you'll do things differently."

- *Warren Buffett*

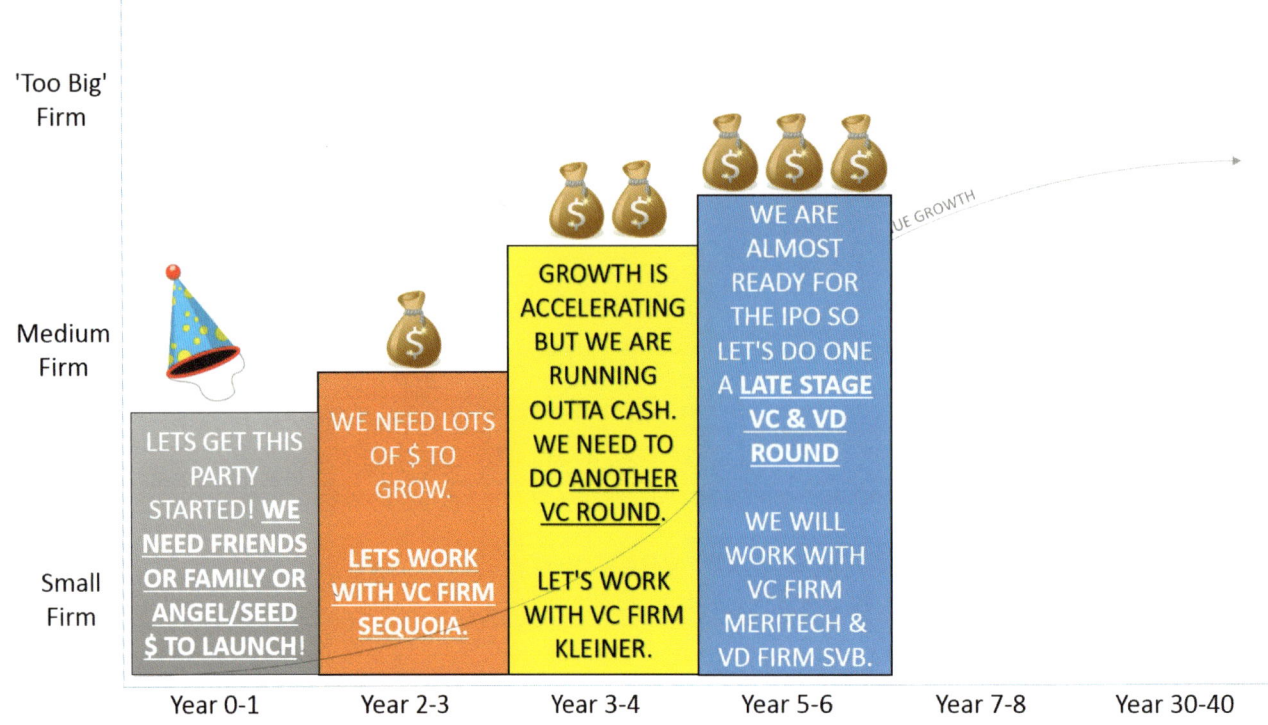
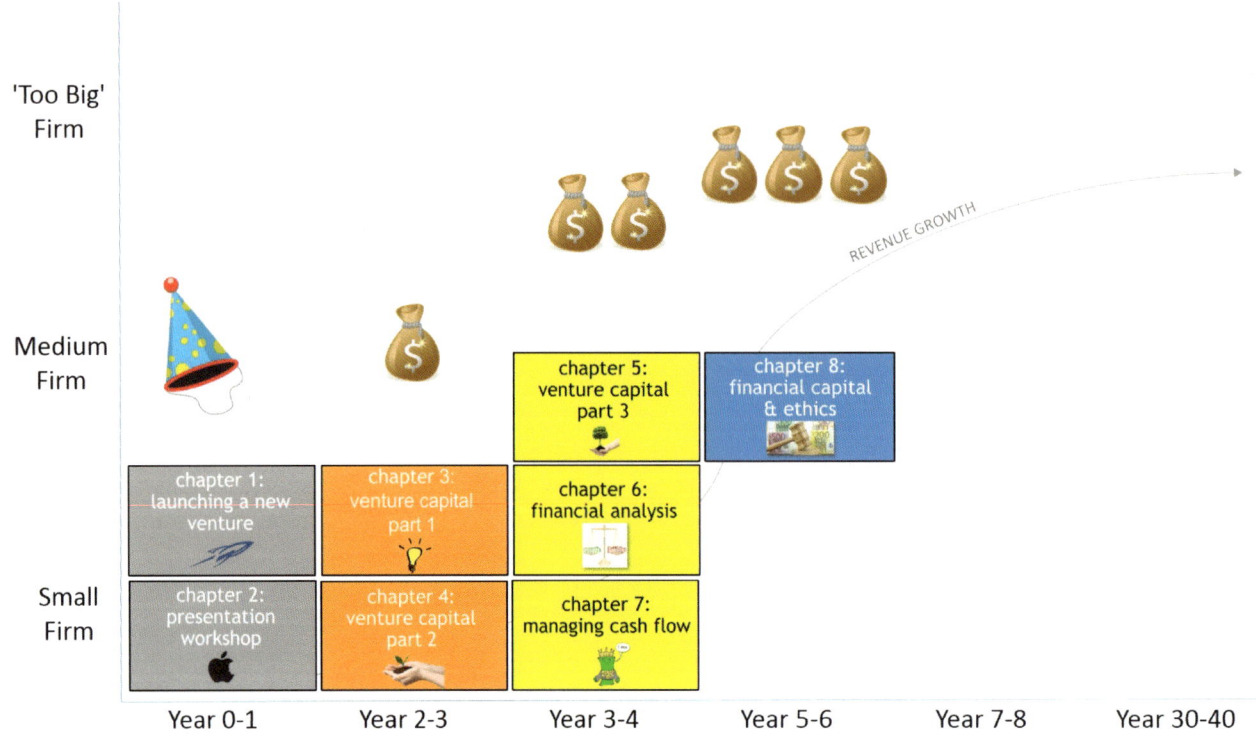

> be passionate about your work….set high standards for yourself…

> find your passion and you will never have a job.

Please set very high standards for your work and only do what you are most passionate about in business and in life. www.tiny.cc/chris65

ETHICS IN FINANCE

It is so easy to break the law in finance. A short quick buck is never worth it in the long run. www.tiny.cc/chris66

I have a lot of respect for Goldman Sachs, where I worked for 5 years. I will never forget my first day of work there. They told us "Welcome to Goldman Sachs. You have a greater chance of causing harm than good to this company. Don't ever do anything that can get you or this firm on the front page of the Wall Street Journal." Then they fingerprinted us.

If you think someone is unethical in business, avoid them at all costs. www.tiny.cc/chris67 . Raj Rajaratnam started a hedge fund called Galleon and he is in jail today. He is in jail because of greed and a lack of business ethics. He broke many securities laws and the FBI raided his company.

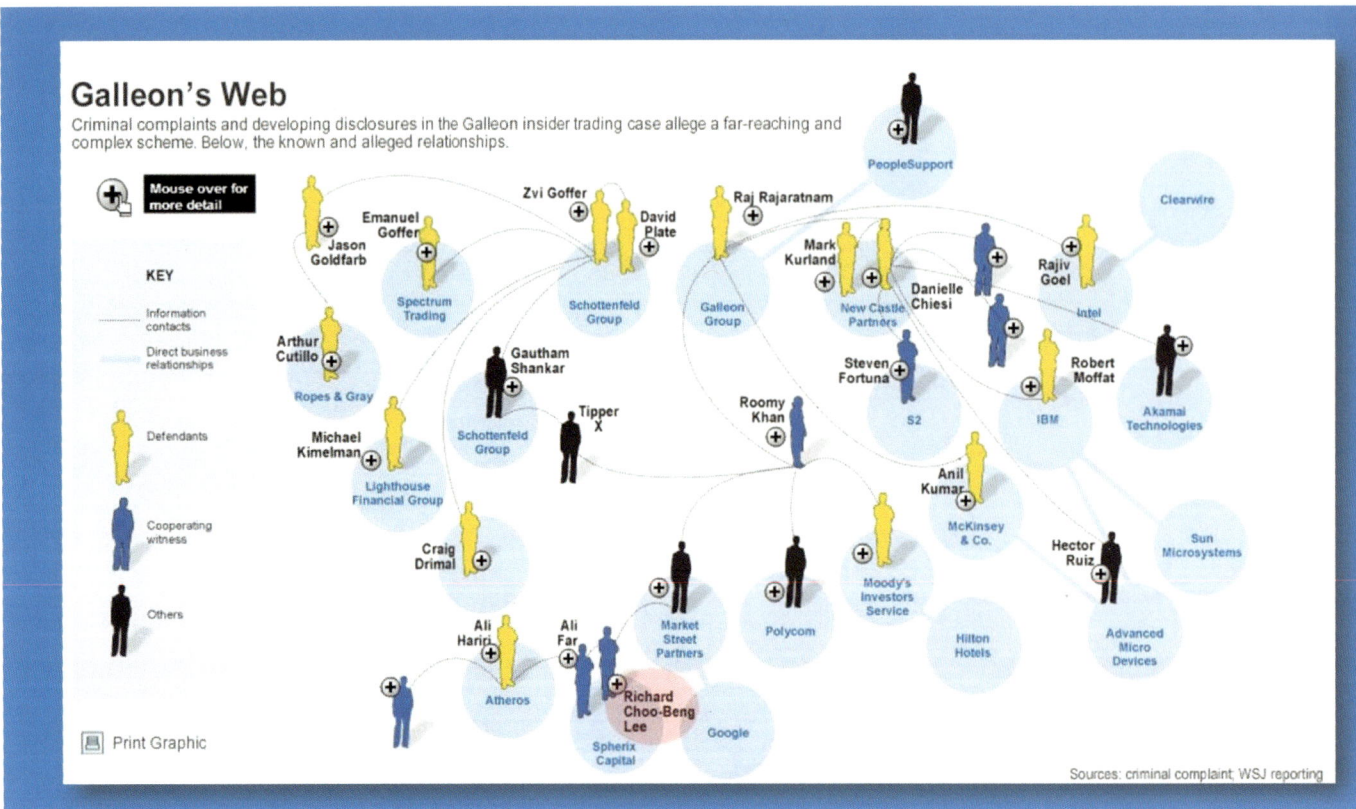

Many people were tied up in the Galleon scandal on Wall Street and Silicon Valley. Don't ever compromise your integrity in business. If you think someone might be unethical, again please avoid them at all costs.

email & phone calls are 4 ever

Assume that every email and every call that you conduct in business is recorded.

FINANCIAL CAPITAL

There is a big difference between finance and accounting.

finance & accounting differences

accounting is more focused on accrued revs & expenses

Accounting is more focused on recording revenue that you recognized ('accrued') or expenses that have taken place.

finance is more focused on cash revs & expenses

finance is more focused on the cost of capital

In finance we focus a bit more on projections and real cash earnings and real expenses.

Accounting is a science. Finance is a science and an art. Accounting is quantitative. Finance is quantitative and qualitative.

Let's analyze the differences between early stage companies ('seed') and late stage companies (ones that might be publicly traded on the stock market). The x axis is t=time:

The cost to raise money (i=interest) is always lower for a company that is mature and has been in business for a long time (common sense I know).

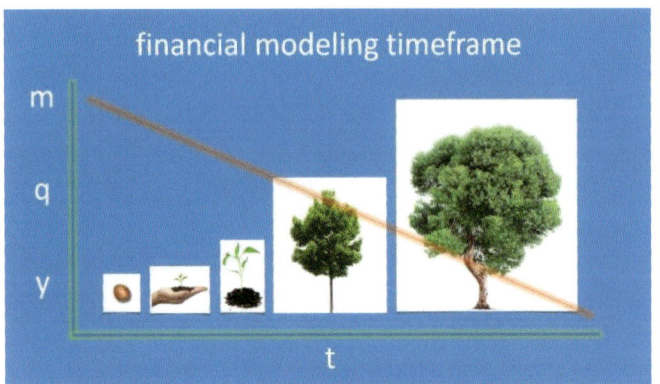

Earlier stage companies tend to look at cash flow on a monthly basis. Companies that have been in business for a few years look a bit more at quarterly cash flow. Companies that have been in business for a long time often look at annual cash flow metrics.

To state the obvious, earlier stage companies have much more risk than companies that have been in business for years.

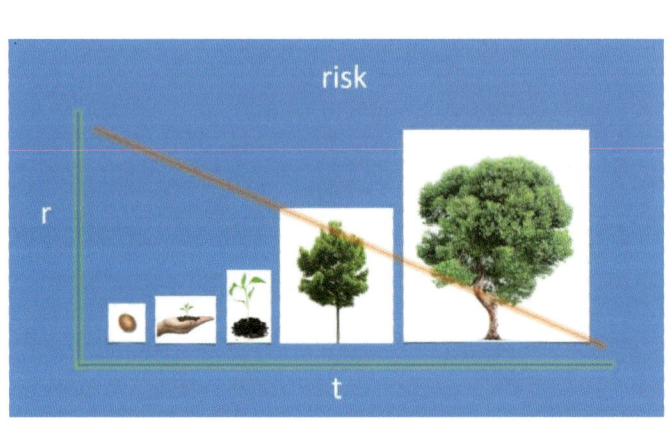

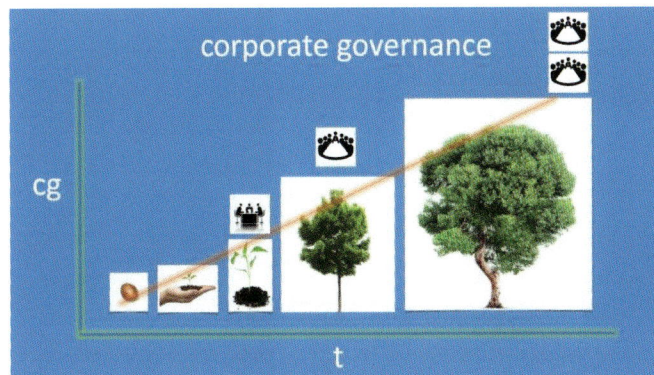

Older companies have much more corporate governance than earlier stage companies. This means that they have more checks and balances in place like a larger board of directors who have a fiduciary duty or a fiscal responsibility to their shareholders.

Older companies usually also have many more patents to protect their intellectual property.

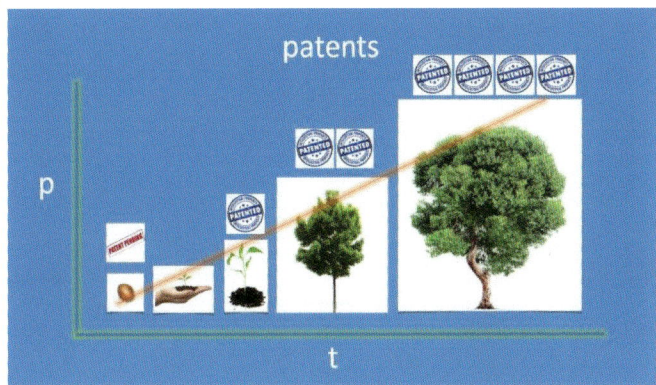

Early stage companies should NEVER use debt to grow. Why? Because if you miss just one payment, the banks don't give a damn and they could make your business go belly up.

debt.

The interest rate for companies that are more seasoned and want to get a loan is determined by analyzing liquidity risk, inflation risk, default risk and maturity (time) risk.

nominal interest rate

=

interest rate of a bank loan

what about:

☑ liquidity risk
☑ inflation risk
☑ default risk
☑ maturity (time) risk

cost of debt =

a) ☑ liquidity risk
b) ☑ inflation risk
c) ☑ default risk
d) ☑ maturity (time) risk

cost of debt =

a) + b) + c) + d)

+ the real interest rate

what is the lowest risk interest rate?

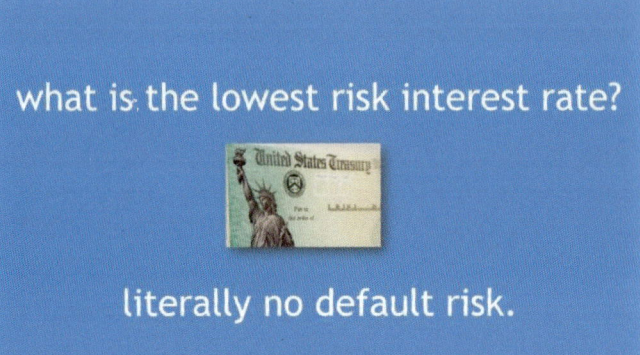

literally no default risk.

The lowest interest rate is usually the rate on US government as this entity has the lowest risk of defaulting.

risk free rate
=
real rate of interest
+
inflation premium

what the heck is a yield curve and why does it matter?

A yield curve is a chart that shows you what the interest rate is over time. Let's build one from scratch: www.tiny.cc/chris68

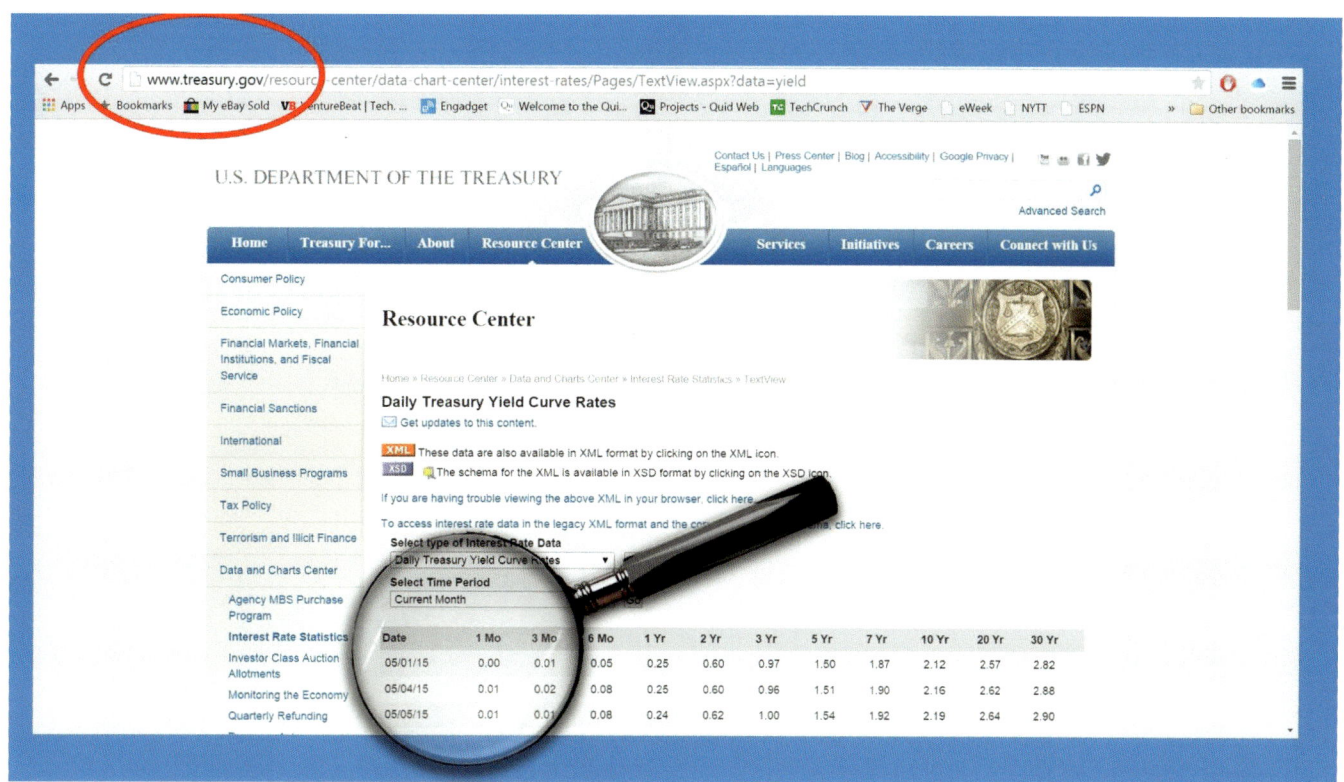

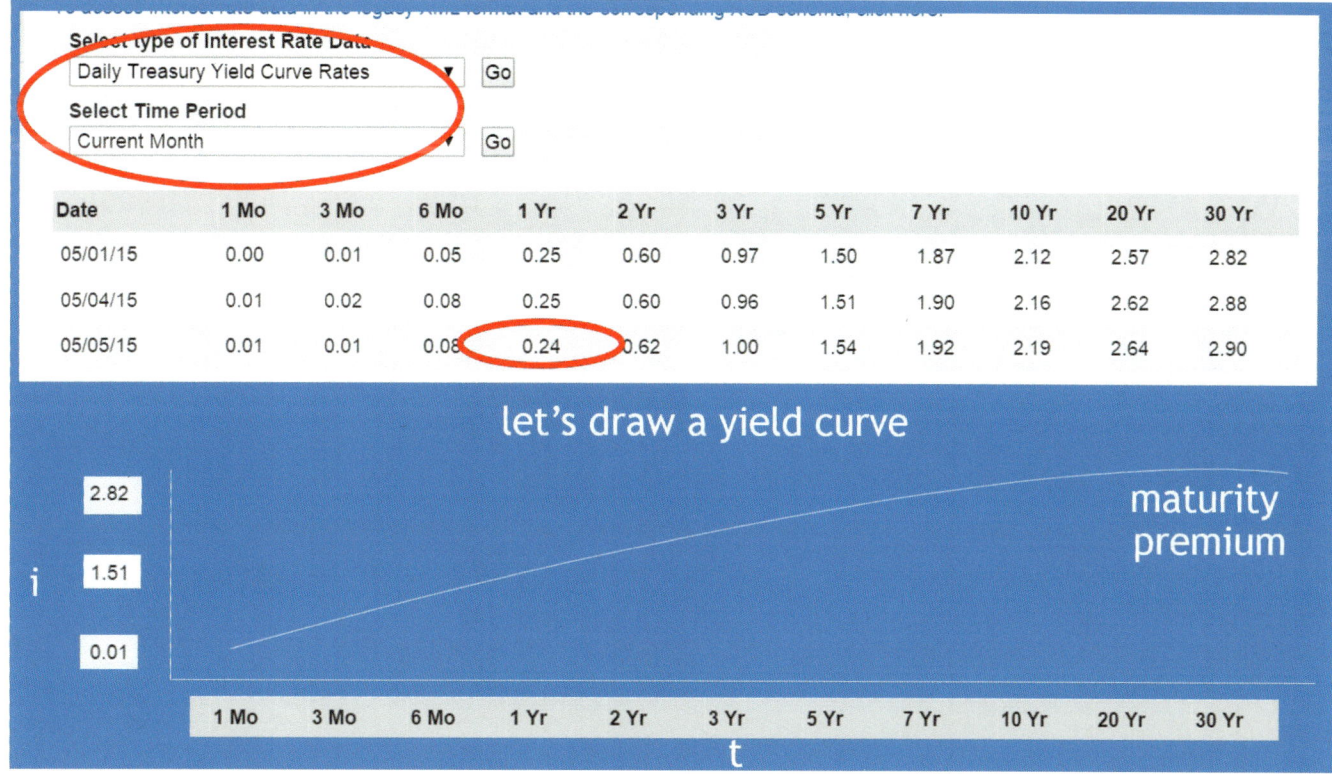

Great. Now we know how to calculate what government interest rates will be over time. What about inflation? We can calculate it online:

www.tiny.cc/chris69

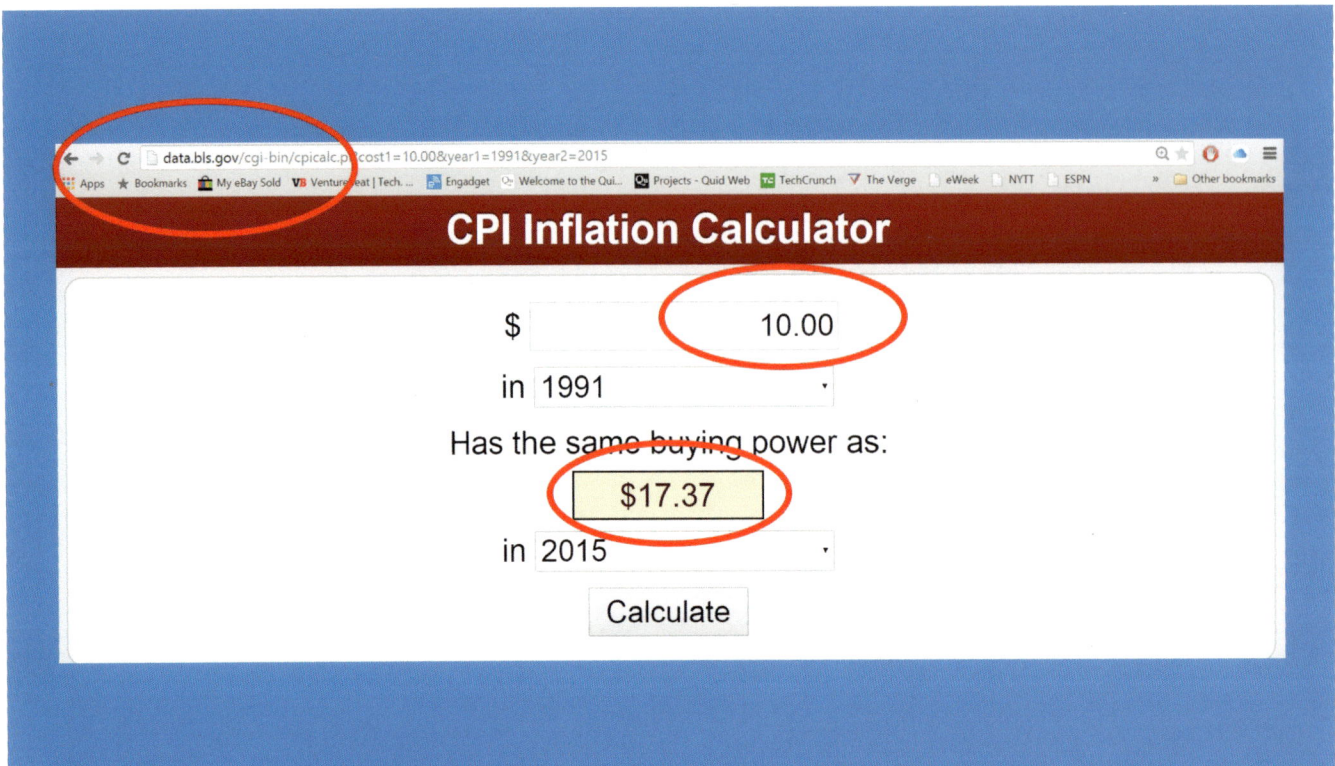

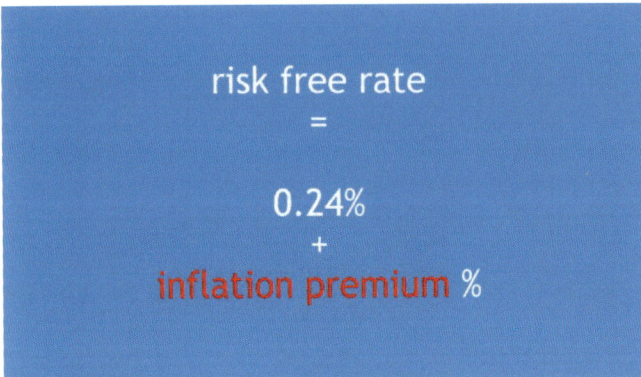

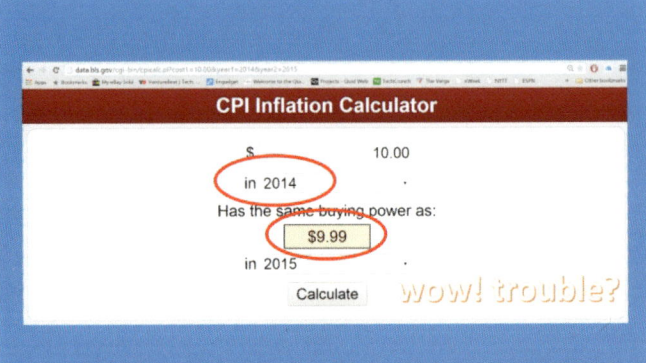

In 2014 per the previous image, I saw that we were temporarily in a deflationary environment. Wow! This is a big deal. Why? Because governments only raise interest rates if the economy is doing well. In fact, until recently interest rates had not increased for literally 9 years! From 2006 until 2015 rates were declining and near zero as the global economy had anemic growth.

Why does this matter? Because you need to understand global macroeconomics in order to understand what interest rate you will be getting. If the economy sucks, rates are usually low. Why? Because the government wants to encourage economic growth by having low rates so companies will borrow and invest in growing their company.

When the economy is doing incredibly well, then demand for goods and services is high and, as a result, prices go up. This is called inflation. In an effort to cool down the economy, the government likes to raise rates so that prices don't go up much. They raise rates so that they can later cut rates if the economy is not doing well.

What does raising rates really mean? Well the government raises interest rates by selling bonds to the public. By selling bonds to the public the public gives the government money, in exchange for a piece of paper saying that the government owes the buyer the money back plus interest. The government then takes this money <u>out of circulation</u>. If there is less money out there, then demand for money goes up (or the money supply goes down), which means the interest rates banks charge for borrowing money goes up. This is called supply and demand. I won't nerd out on economic stuff, but just keep in mind that if there is a scarcity of a product like diamonds, then the price of that product goes up. Just like with money. If there is less money in circulation, then the price of money goes up. This means demand for money goes up as the supply decreases and, hence, the interest rate rises for borrowing money.

You need to understand these concepts because one day you might borrow money to buy a house or to expand your business empire. **Let's talk about what happened in 2008. We were literally 24 hours away from bank machines not working then!**

> too big to fail?
>
> why rates are still low...
>
> ....2008 crisis explained

I recommend that you all watch the movie "Too Big to Fail".

www.tiny.cc/chris70

www.tiny.cc/chris71

Fortunately, reckless unethical business practices that pushed us into the "great recession" in 2008 will never occur again.

> nobody could get loans then...
>
> ...we were within 24 hours of
>
> <u>all</u>
>
> ATMs not working

Up until recently, deflation was flat or even slightly negative!

> risk free rate
> =
> 0.24%
> +
> -0.001 %

> however, that inflation rate was for today. we all know inflation will be higher in the future and we all know that nobody will lend to us at that rate.
>
> we live in interesting times…..

> no wonder venture capital and real estate and the stock market are in a bubble!

Because rates are so incredibly low, housing prices are high. Why? Because you pay next to nothing for a loan. The government tried to save the economy by making rates (or the cost of capital) very low. As a result, people borrow money to invest in houses or less liquid venture capital investments etc.

Business is highly cyclical. Once rates rise a bunch (and they will one day), then people will prefer to keep money in the bank as rates are higher and they can make money on the interest rate that the bank is providing them. As a result, fewer people will buy houses or invest in illiquid investments when rates go up a bunch.

Recall that we calculated using the yield curve that the cost of capital (or interest rate) is about 0.24%. This doesn't mean that you can borrow from the bank or the government at only 0.24%. Why? Because the lender needs to account for the risks associated with lending to you or to a company by looking as various risk factors, including liquidity risk, inflation risk, default risk and maturity (or time) risk.

> does this mean I can borrow for just under 0.24% per year?
>
> heck no!

> heck no because of:
>
> ☑ liquidity risk
> ☑ inflation risk
> ☑ default risk
> ☑ maturity (time) risk

> cost of debt =
>
> a) + b) + c) + d)
>
> + the real interest rate

This is all a bit complex and theoretical. Don't worry, you don't need to memorize all of this. Give me a few slides to explain why.

IBM is a mature company with a long history and a decent balance sheet. They are fiscally conservative. How can we tell what interest rate they should pay?

> a mature, cash rich company would pay a lower cost of debt

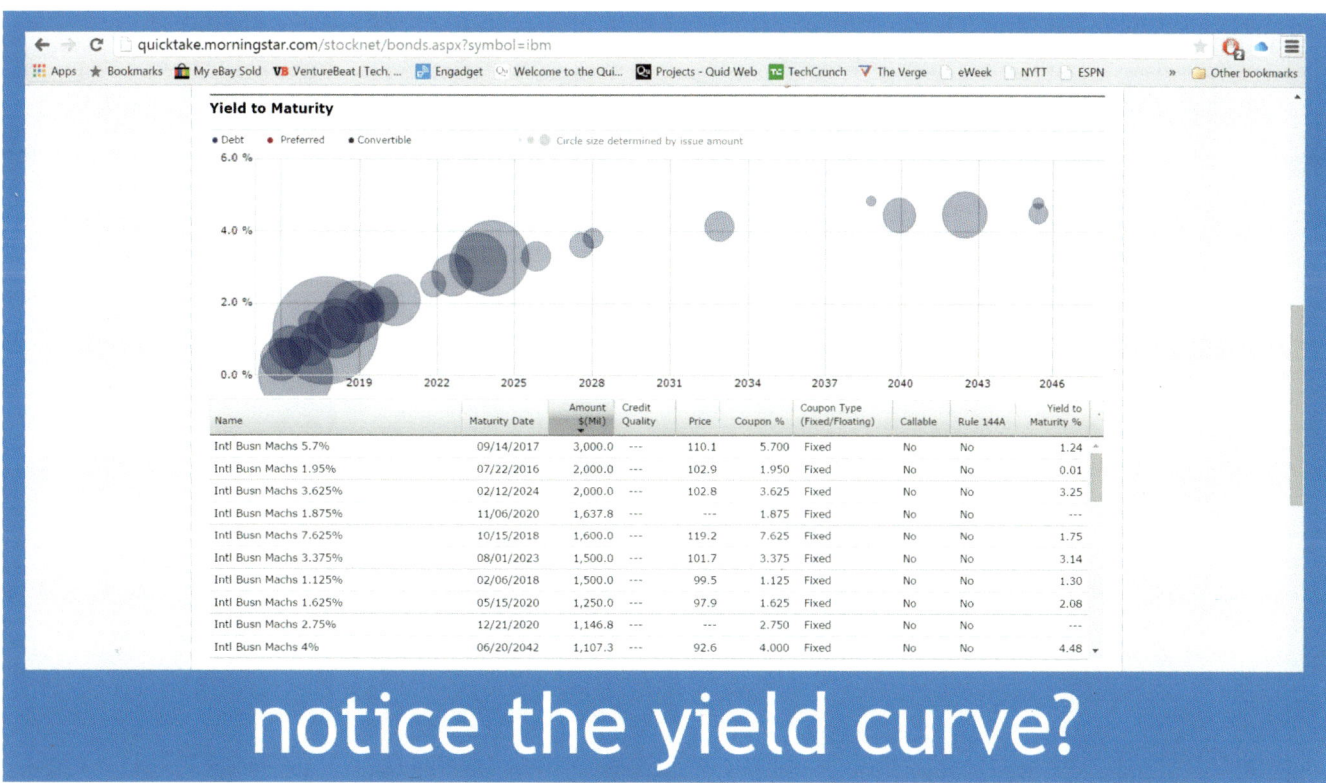

> notice the yield curve?

Well we can look at IBM's yield curve! We can even buy bonds from IBM and they will pay you an interest rate in return that is higher than the US government's rate as IBM has a higher risk of defaulting than the US government does.

let's just keep it simple...

we all just refer to banks lending at the "prime" rate for their best customers and "prime plus X" for higher risk customers.

in the real world all this default risk math is a waste of time....

....because we all just rely on ratings agencies like s&p and moody's

aaa is the best rating....

then aa

a

bbb

bb

b

ccc...etc

bbb and higher
=
investment grade

anything lower =
junk bond
or
"high yield"

investment grade means the DRP (default risk premium) is <1% above us treasuries rate.

The Ultimate Practical Business Manual

- the DRP on junk bonds is 5% above treasury rates.

- early stage companies pay junk bond rates....hence their preference for equity/vc financing

- when interest rates are low many companies are born.

- if inflation is high (as in the early 80s), startups aren't born.

1990s

In the 1990s an amazing thing happened. We had amazing economic growth and interest rates were low! Why? Because even though demand for goods and services were high, inflation was low! Why? Because in the late 1980s the Berlin Wall fell and all of this awesome cheap and brilliant Eastern European labor moved west into first world countries. As a result, the cost of labor didn't rise much. Labor is the biggest input in inflation statistics. For more information on this topics, please see the Berlin Wall section in the last chapter of this book.

> if debt is secured via access to assets upon default, then this is called senior debt...

> if not, then it is called subordinated debt

Wow this chapter is heavy! www.tiny.cc/chris72

RISK AND RETURN

> risk adverse lenders prefer to lend to the investment with the lower standard deviation.

Remember all that standard deviation statistics crap you learned but never thought you would ever apply in real life? Well now we can! Lenders like to lend to firms that have lower risk or have a lower standard deviation. When we look at stocks and we calculate what they might make us, we call this the 'expected return' which is the return % we expect to receive.

However, when we analyze a lot of data, we find that some stocks go up and down a lot more than others. This up and down movement is called volatility and the standard deviation measures the magnitude of this up and down behavior!

Again, this up and down behavior is a measure of risk.

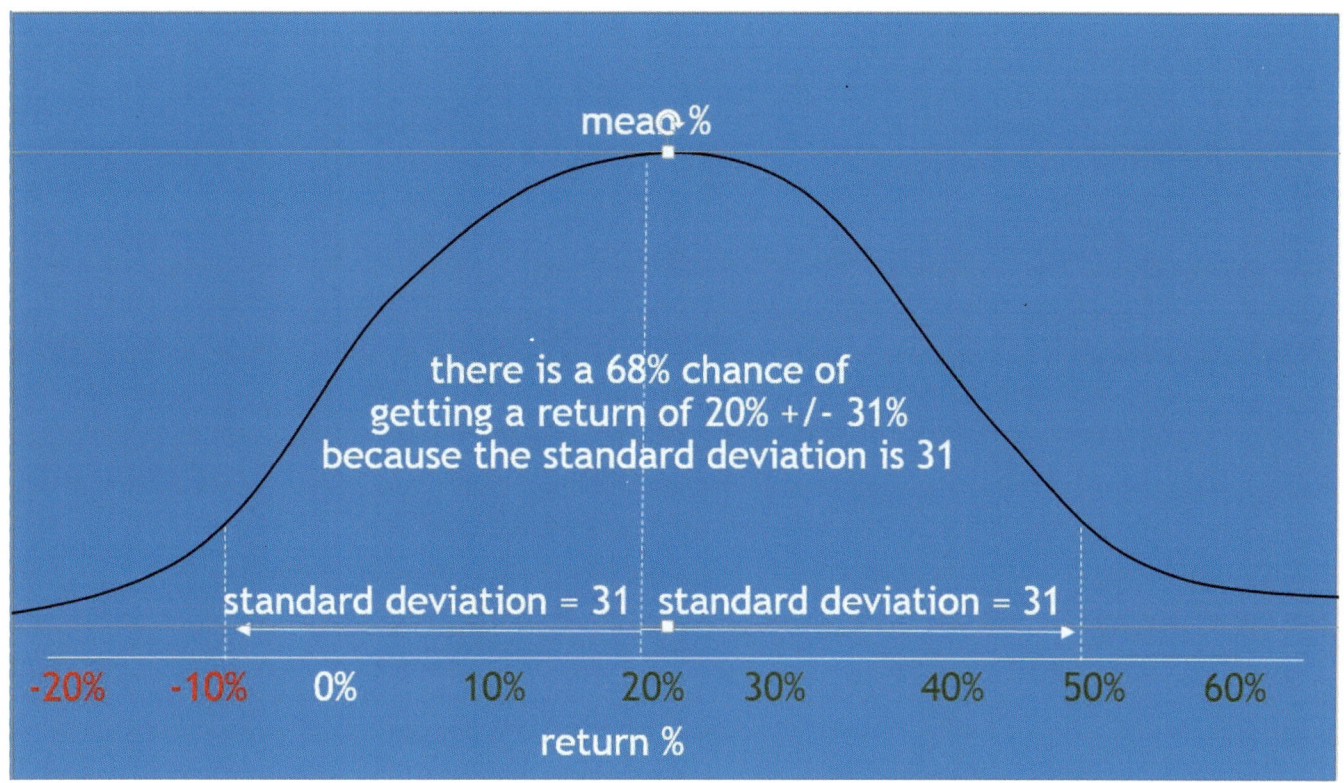

If I tell you that a stock has an average or 'mean' return to investors of 20% with a standard deviation of 31, then this means that 68% of the potential returns on investment in this stock will be 20% plus or minus 31%. So the stock that returns 20% has a risk or 1 standard deviation probability of making you 51% or losing you 11%. One standard deviation means 68% of all data points are within the average plus one standard deviation. Now 2 standard deviations means that 98% of your data points will lie within 2 standard deviations. This means that 98% of our investment scenarios will return up 20% +/- 62 (or 31 times2). You always want the standard deviation (which measures risk) to be as low as possible.

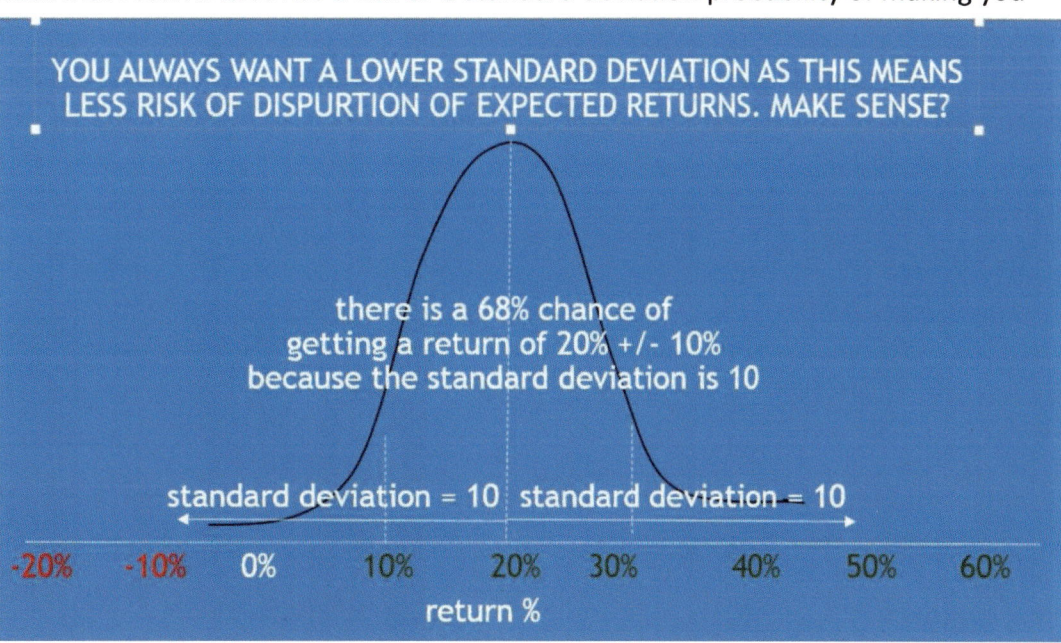

> ok i understand that standard deviation means how spread out returns are....but is there a formula to measure risk and returns?

> yes!
>
> standard deviation / expected return = how much risk i am taking on per unit of return!

COST OF EQUITY CAPITAL

> we expect public equity returns to =
>
> the risk free rate (includes inflation)
>
> +
>
> the volatility of the company versus the market
>
> x
>
> how much we expect stocks to outperform government bonds

> we expect equity returns to =
>
> the risk free rate (includes inflation)
>
> +
>
> ß
>
> x
>
> how much we expect stocks to outperform government bonds

The beta means how volatile a stock is relative to the market. We will cover this later in this book in much more detail.

> how do we calculate the cost of capital if we use equity AND debt?

> wacc = weighted average cost of capital

I am not going to go into too much detail on this concept yet because reality is much different. As most investors calculate the interest rate in debt instruments using 3rd party companies like Moody's or Standard and Poors. When it comes to equity investment returns, many venture capital firms look for a 5 x 5., which means that they would like the underlying investment to return 500% within 5 years. Why so high? Because many venture capital investments go to zero.

> reality can be much different from the last few pages.....
>
> vc expects 5x5
>
> debt uses moody's
>
> equity pm's look at portfolio construction

SECURITIES LAW AND VENTURE FINANCING

If you end up starting an investment firm (or working for one) you need to understand the rules. You can take government sponsored exams to help you with understanding the rules, like the Series 7 exam. www.tiny.cc/chris73

> it's not hard to break the law by accident....

> ....if you do, your sentence could be the same as the sentence of a murderer. no joke....as insane as that sounds.

ignorance of the [securities] law is no excuse.

www.tiny.cc/chris74

securities laws:

1: prospective investors must receive all relevant information before investing. [S1 etc.]

2: if you have been defrauded, you should receive compensation. [class action lawsuits]

3: insider information for publicly traded stocks is illegal and results in prison. [no excuses]

securities act of 1933

created as the stock market crash in the 20s created the great depression

laws set by act are governed by the sec

laws haven't really changed since then

securities exchange act of 1934

laws on inside information

investment company act of 1940

regulates pools of capital including vc....although vc firms aren't that regulated by the sec and neither are hedge funds.

investment advisor act of 1940

laws for brokers and banks

Questions Based on Chapter 8:

1: A mature company has a higher cost of capital:

True or <u>False</u>

2: Early stage investments are more risky than later stage investments.

<u>True</u> or False

3: Corporate governance is usually superior at later stage companies than early stage companies.

True or False

4: The lowest risk interest rate is usually:

a) IBM's bonds
b) Facebook's bonds
c) Goldman's bonds
d) US Treasury securities

5: Yield curves include information on:

a) Equity volatility
b) Corporate governance metrics
c) Standard deviation risk metrics
d) Interest rates

CHAPTER SUMMARY

Chris Haroun @chris_haroun
mature firms have many financing options. start-ups do not. we learned about expected debt and equity returns and risk metrics. ignorance of sec laws = no excuse. ethics.

Chapter 9: Projecting Financial Statements

"The longer the view, the wiser the intention."

- *Warren Buffett*

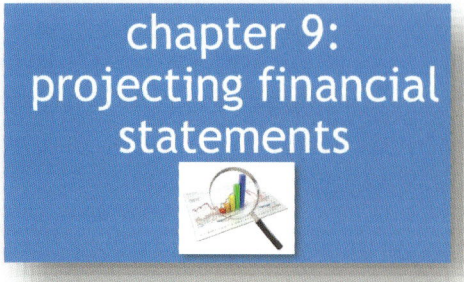

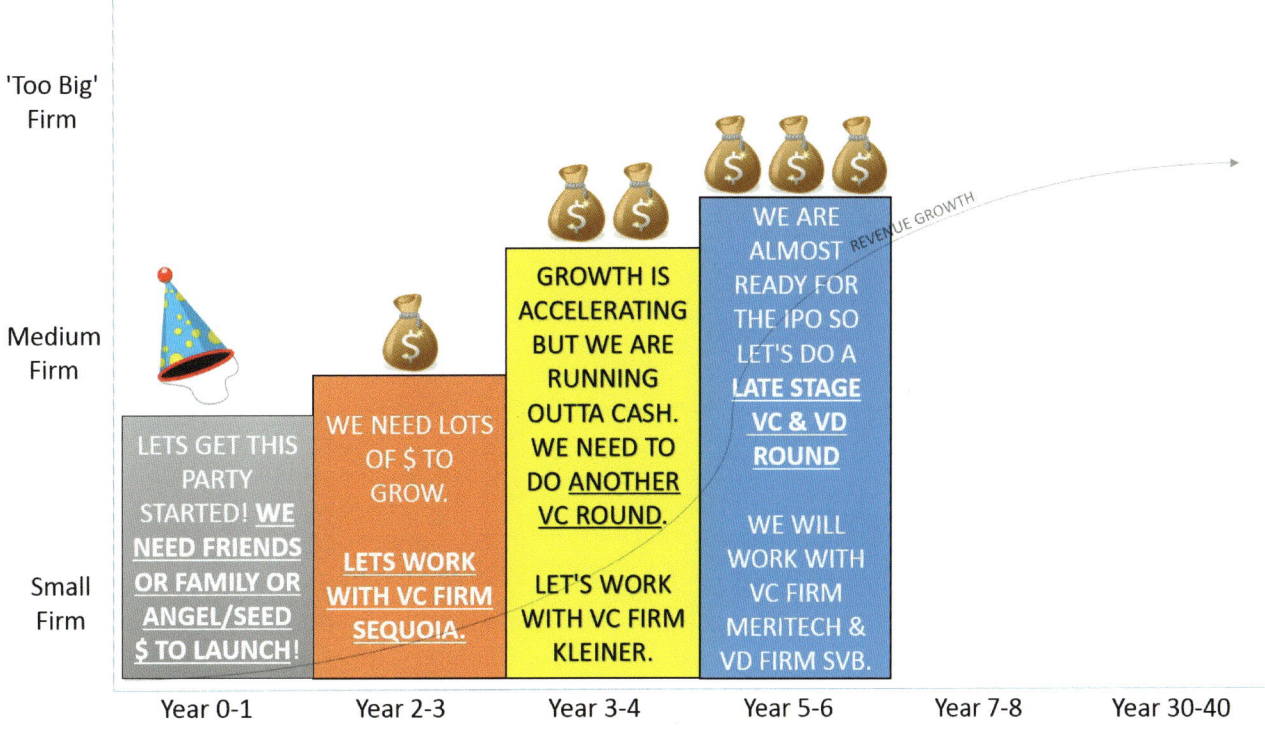

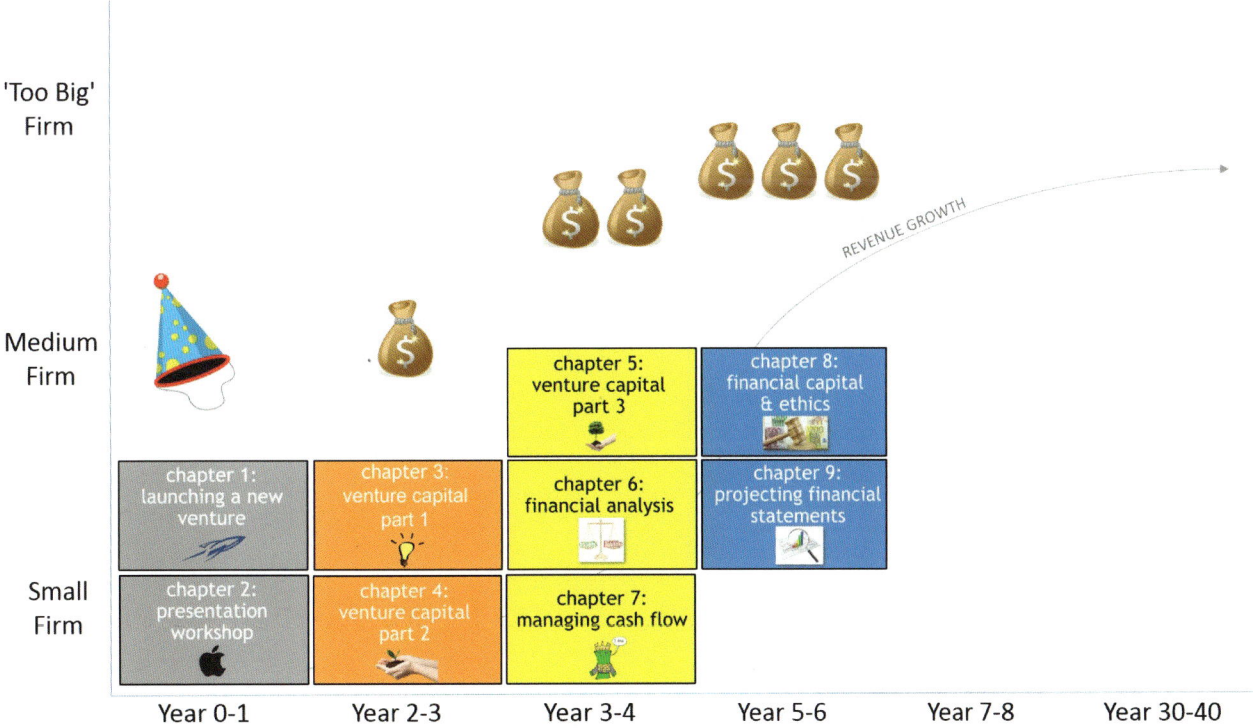

LATE STAGE INVESTMENT ROUND

We are going to do our last venture capital round now before our IPO. We will work with a late stage company and eventually a venture debt company. Prior to our IPO and last round though, we should complete a detailed model on our company and come up with an appropriate valuation. We re-engineered our product so we are now selling supercomputers and not P.O.S. or banana watches anymore (remember our awful recall issues)! These computers will sell for close to an ASP (average selling price) of $100k each. The software that runs on these bad boys is off the charts awesome! This last pre IPO VC round valuation might be around $350mn….we are <u>close to signing</u> a term sheet with a superb late stage VC firm. Fingers crossed…!

> project at least 3-5 years.

> always start with sales projections

We need to project our financial model for 3-5 years. Creating financial forecasts is a lot of fun and it was easier than you think! Wall Street analysts call projections "pro forma".

> "pro forma" = projections

> what is the most important thing to assess for a potential investment in a start-up?

> ideas are commodities.
>
> execution is not.

That's right – ideas are commodities and there is no point ever making a model if you don't have the right management team to invest in. As a result, all financial modeling done in this book assumes that you are happy first of all with the management team that you are investing in.

Fortunately our management team is off the charts awesome! The company is relatively new but they are already on a run rate to make $1mn in revenue this year.

In the previous company that our founder founded, he got the company from founding to $300mn+ in revenue in 3 years! He is a rock star! He thinks that he can get to $500mn in revenue in 3 years with this company.

is the TAM big enough?	$50bn.

Recall that the T.A.M. stands for the total addressable market. We will never invest in a company that doesn't have a T.A.M. of at least $20bn. Fortunately the T.A.M. of this company is $50bn!

10% of TAM in 10 years.	The founder tells us that he thinks the company can get 10% market share in 10 years or $5bn in revenue in 10 years. Wow!
ok let's do a long term model	start with the TAM.

> then what percent of TAM can you own within 10 years.

> then list assumptions.

> then build the model starting with sales.

We always start our financial models with sales. Remember that modeling is easy as everything becomes a percent of revenue (remember that sales is the same thing as revenue)

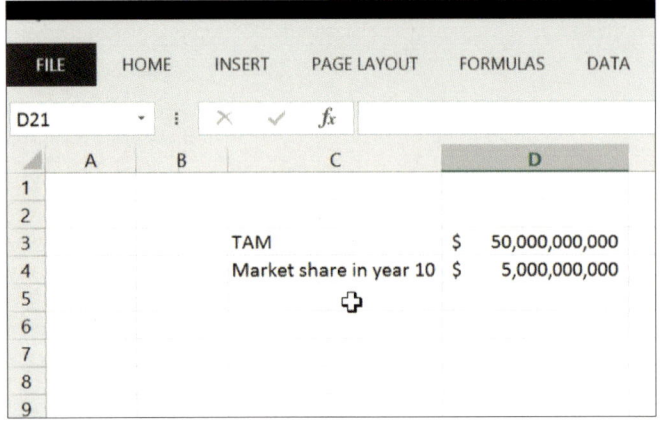

The market size is $50bn and our guy thinks he will get 10% of this market in 10 years.

The average selling price (ASP) of the product is $100k. Revenue divided by the ASP = 50k units sold in year 10. Remember we are spending the bulk of our modeling time on figuring out what revenue will be. Then almost every other line item in the model becomes a percent of revenue.

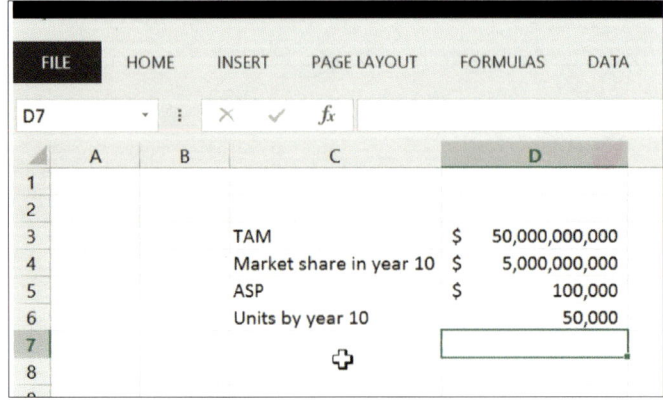

	C		E	F	G	H	I	J
fx	.....ok in year 3 he said he can get to 500mn in revenue							
	TAM	$	50,000,000,000					
	Market share in year 10	$	5,000,000,000					
	ASP	$	100,000					
	Units by year 10		50,000					
	Units expected in year 1		20					
	Units year 2		200					
	Units year 3		4,000	.....ok in year 3 he said he can get to 500mn in revenue				
	Units year 4							
	Units year 5							
	Units year 6							
	Units year 7							
	Units year 8							
	Units year 9							
	Units year 10		50,000					

His forecast of $500mn in revenue in year 3 seems too high to me; let's haircut it and assume it is $400mn.

E11 fx =E10-0.2

	A	B	C	D	E
1					
2					
3			TAM	$ 50,000,000,000	
4			Market share in year 10	$ 5,000,000,000	
5			ASP	$ 100,000	
6			Units by year 10	50,000	YoY Growth
7			Units expected in year 1	20	
8			Units year 2	200	900%
9			Units year 3	4,000	1900%
10			Units year 4	10,000	250%
11			Units year 5	23,000	230%
12			Units year 6	48,300	210%
13			Units year 7	91,770	190%
14			Units year 8	156,009	170%
15			Units year 9	234,014	150%
16			Units year 10	50,000	50%

> …..ok in year 3 he said he can get to 500mn in revenue   hmm…pretty aggressive….let's assume 400mn
> …hmm this growth is pretty high…let's assume it slows a lot in future years due to the law of large numbers
>
> 50 % unit growth in year 10….still seems high.
>
> my numbers are way too big….ok lets harcut them a lot
>
> ok….but the increase between year 2 and 3 seems nutty high
> I don't think 10% share in 10 years can be done…..i mean there will be a recession at some point and these growth rates seem too high….
>
> ok fine let's assume this is our UBER OPTIMISTIC scenario…..as companies don't grow triple digit that many uears

Spend a lot of time on forecasting revenue. I often spend a whole day doing this….then I sleep on it and revisit my model the next morning.

YEAR				YoY Growth	REVENUE	
	TAM	$	50,000,000,000			
	Market share in year 10	$	5,000,000,000			
	ASP	$	100,000			
	Units by year 10		50,000			
2015	Units expected in year 1		20		$ 2,000,000	
2016	Units year 2		200	900%	$ 20,000,000	
2017	Units year 3		4,000	1900%	$ 400,000,000	…..ok in year 3 he said he
2018	Units year 4		8,400	210%	$ 840,000,000	…hmm this growth is pret
2019	Units year 5		15,540	185%	$ 1,554,000,000	
2020	Units year 6		26,418	170%	$ 2,641,800,000	
2021	Units year 7		35,664	135%	$ 3,566,430,000	
2022	Units year 8		44,580	125%	$ 4,458,037,500	
2023	Units year 9		49,038	110%	$ 4,903,841,250	
2024	Units year 10		51,490	105%	$ 5,149,033,313	**Christopher Haroun:** assumes 10 percent of the $50b

ok….but the increase betw

When we create financial models, we make many assumptions. Please document all of them per the images in this chapter. You can enter comments in each cell (the yellow boxes) or you can just type your assumptions in your spreadsheet. If you are working in groups modeling a company (which happens often in the asset management and investment banking business), make sure to enter your name at the beginning of each cell comment. When I used to be a software engineer, I would add many comments to my code…this helps a lot when you revisit your model or code in the future.

there must be competition at some point.....so we have to hair cut the average selling price
let's assume compeitition enters the market in 3 years and hence the price drops.

fx =D10*(D5*.9)

B	C	D	E	F
	TAM	$ 50,000,000,000		
	Market share in year 10	$ 5,000,000,000		
	ASP	$ 100,000		
YEAR	Units by year 10	50,000	YoY Growth	REVENUE
2015	Units expected in year 1	20		$ 2,000,000
2016	Units year 2	200	900%	$ 20,000,000
2017	Units year 3	4,000	1900%	$ 400,000,000
2018	Units year 4	8,400	210%	=D10*(D5*.9)
2019	Units year 5	15,540	185%	$ 1,554,000,000
2020	Units year 6	26,418	170%	$ 2,641,800,000
2021	Units year 7	35,664	135%	$ 3,566,430,000
2022	Units year 8	44,580	125%	$ 4,458,037,500
2023	Units year 9	49,038	110%	$ 4,903,841,250
2024	Units year 10	51,490	105%	$ 5,149,033,313

	TAM	$ 50,000,000,000		
	Market share in year 10	$ 5,000,000,000		
	ASP	$ 100,000		
YEAR	Units by year 10	50,000	YoY Growth	REVENUE
2015	Units expected in year 1	20		$ 2,000,000
2016	Units year 2	200	900%	$ 20,000,000
2017	Units year 3	4,000	1900%	$ 400,000,000
2018	Units year 4	8,400	210%	$ 756,000,000
2019	Units year 5	15,540	185%	$ 1,554,000,000
2020	Units year 6	26,418	170%	$ 2,641,800,000
2021	Units year 7	35,664	135%	$ 3,566,430,000
2022	Units year 8	44,580	125%	$ 4,458,037,500
2023	Units year 9	49,038	110%	$ 4,903,841,250
2024	Units year 10	51,490	105%	$ 5,149,033,313

Christopher Haroun: 10 percent price drop

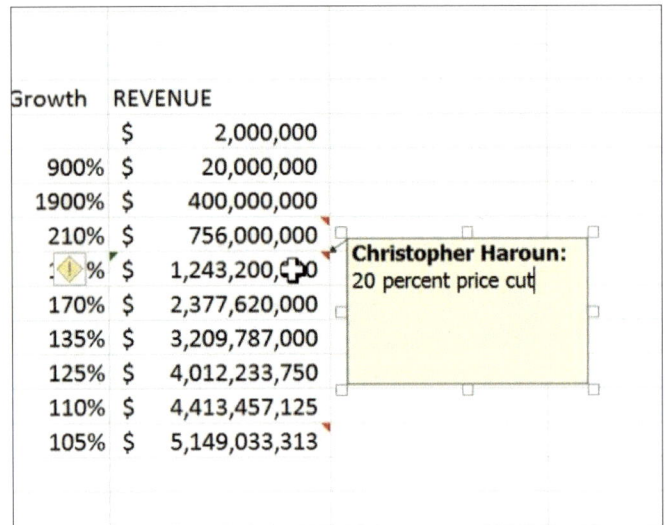

Growth	REVENUE
	$ 2,000,000
900%	$ 20,000,000
1900%	$ 400,000,000
210%	$ 756,000,000
185%	$ 1,243,200,000
170%	$ 2,377,620,000
135%	$ 3,209,787,000
125%	$ 4,012,233,750
110%	$ 4,413,457,125
105%	$ 5,149,033,313

Christopher Haroun: 20 percent price cut

YoY Growth	REVENUE
	$ 2,000,000
900%	$ 20,000,000
1900%	$ 400,000,000
210%	$ 756,000,000
185%	$ 1,243,200,000
170%	$ 2,113,440,000
135%	$ 2,853,144,000
125%	$ 3,120,626,250
110%	$ 4,413,457,125
105%	$ 5,149,033,313

Christopher Haroun: 20 percent price cut....especially since component costs are always dropping

	TAM	$ 50,000,000,000			
	Market share in year 10	$ 5,000,000,000			
	ASP	$ 100,000			
YEAR	Units by year 10	50,000	YoY Growth	REVENUE	
2015	Units expected in year 1	20		$	2,000,000
2016	Units year 2	200	900%	$	20,000,000
2017	Units year 3	4,000	1900%	$	400,000,000
2018	Units year 4	8,400	210%	$	756,000,000
2019	Units year 5	15,540	185%	$	1,243,200,000
2020	Units year 6	26,418	170%	$	2,113,440,000
2021	Units year 7	35,664	135%	$	2,853,144,000
2022	Units year 8	44,580	125%	$	3,120,626,250
2023	Units year 9	49,038	110%	$	2,942,304,750
2024	Units year 10	51,490	105%	$	3,089,419,988

there must be competition at some point.....so we have to hair cut the average selling price let's assume compeitition enters the market in 3 years and hence the price drops. ok....now I am second guessing my unit estimates......let me hair cut them

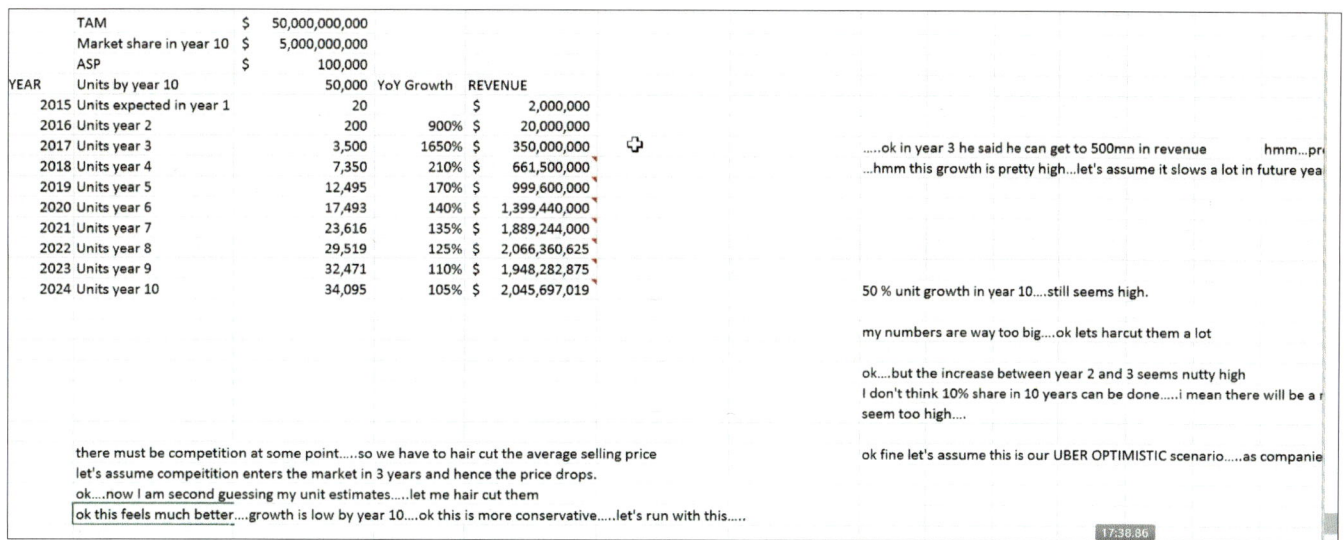

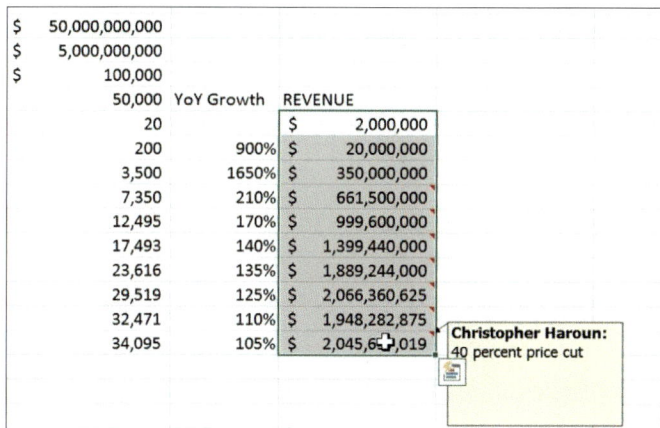

Ok this feels much better. Growth has slowed a lot by year ten. Ok let's use this for revenue. Now the easy part…

Cool. Ok let's copy our revenue column and past special and transpose it to a revenue row in a new tab in our spreadsheet.

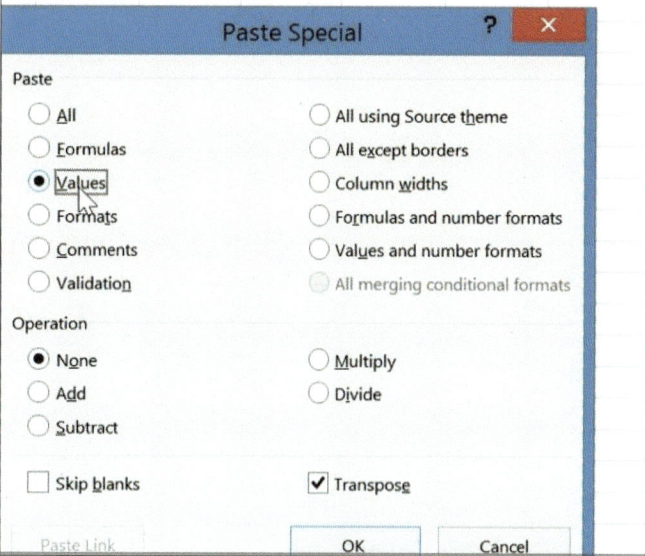

	2015	2016	2017	2018	2019
Revenue	$2,000,000	$20,000,000	$350,000,000		0,000

Christopher Haroun: company thinks they can do $500mn here….i think $350mn is more appropriate

Again, remember to add many comments to your spreadsheet. The comment above reminds us that we think that $350mn is more accurate for our revenue estimate in year 3.

Wow – lots going on here….let's take a break and watch this incredibly important video: www.tiny.cc/chris75

Recall that COGS is the cost of goods sold. You can ask the founder or their CFO to help you construct the expense line items. Alternatively, you can go to www.sec.gov and find financial statements for companies that are similar to this company and find out what the percent of revenue was for each line item in the early years for their company.

	2015	2016	2017	2018	2019
Revenue	$ 2,000,000	$20,000,000	$350,000,000	$661,500,000	$999,
COGS	$ 1,800,000	$16,000,000	$175,000,000	$264,600,000	$299,
GM pct	10%	20%	50%	60%	
Gross Profit	$ 200,000	$ 4,000,000	$175,000,000	$396,900,000	$699

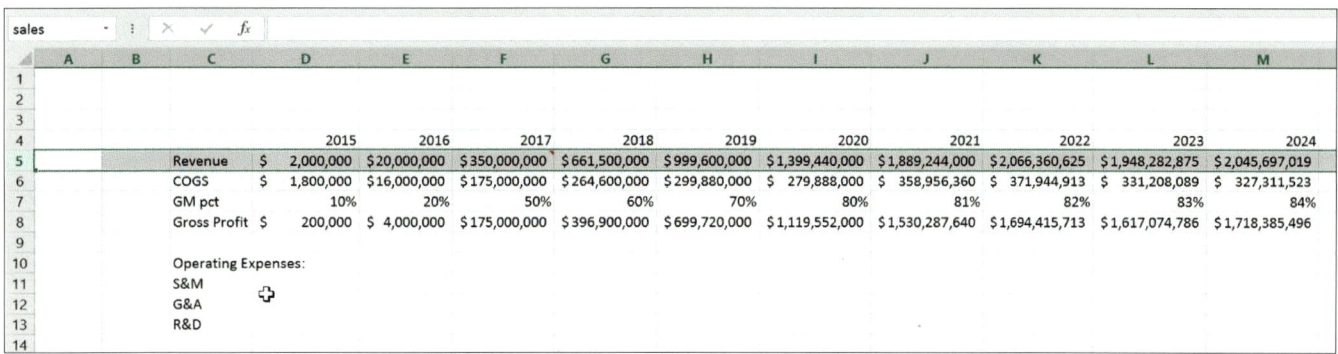

This modeling trick will save you a lot of time: highlight the sales or revenue row and then rename it 'sales', which you can see in the top left hand corner of the previous image. Going forward, don't worry about referring to row 5....just call it sales in your formulas!

Cool beans! We are making progress. See how S&M (sales and marketing) is 25% of revenue and improving to 20% the next year?

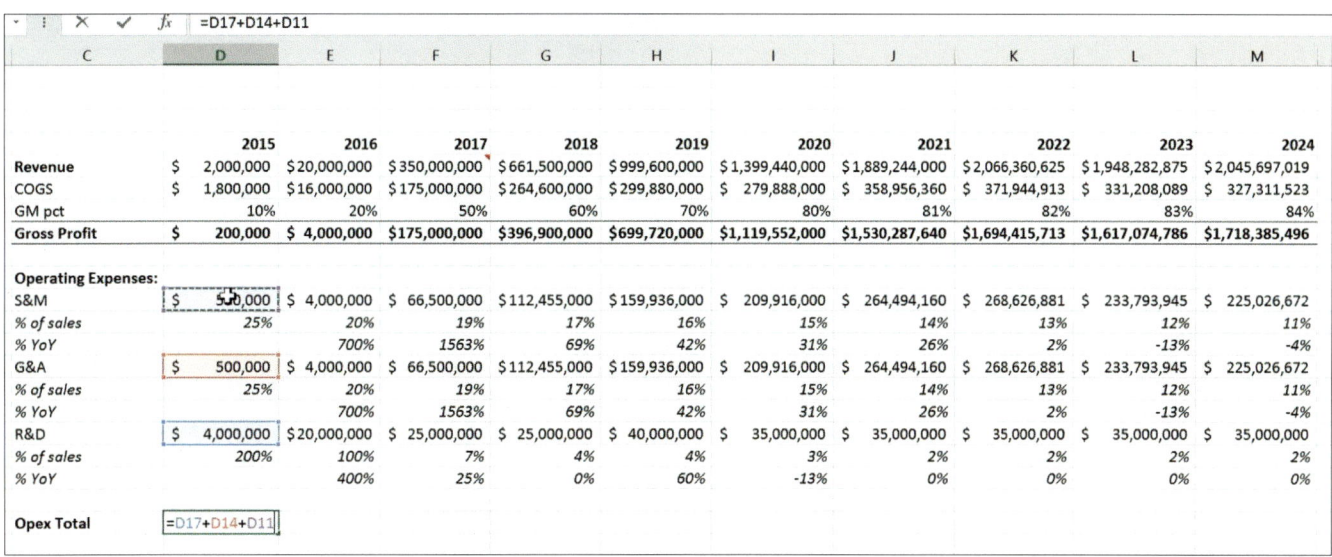

	2015	2016	2017	2018	2019	2020	2021	2022	2023	2024
Revenue	$ 2,000,000	$ 20,000,000	$ 350,000,000	$ 661,500,000	$ 999,600,000	$ 1,399,440,000	$ 1,889,244,000	$ 2,066,360,625	$ 1,948,282,875	$ 2,045,697,019
COGS	$ 1,800,000	$ 16,000,000	$ 175,000,000	$ 264,600,000	$ 299,880,000	$ 279,888,000	$ 358,956,360	$ 371,944,913	$ 331,208,089	$ 327,311,523
GM pct	10%	20%	50%	60%	70%	80%	81%	82%	83%	84%
Gross Profit	$ 200,000	$ 4,000,000	$175,000,000	$396,900,000	$699,720,000	$1,119,552,000	$1,530,287,640	$1,694,415,713	$1,617,074,786	$1,718,385,496
Operating Expenses:										
S&M	$ 500,000	$ 4,000,000	$ 66,500,000	$112,455,000	$159,936,000	$ 209,916,000	$ 264,494,160	$ 268,626,881	$ 233,793,945	$ 225,026,672
% of sales	25%	20%	19%	17%	16%	15%	14%	13%	12%	11%
% YoY		700%	1563%	69%	42%	31%	26%	2%	-13%	-4%
G&A	$ 500,000	$ 4,000,000	$ 66,500,000	$112,455,000	$159,936,000	$ 209,916,000	$ 264,494,160	$ 268,626,881	$ 233,793,945	$ 225,026,672
% of sales	25%	20%	19%	17%	16%	15%	14%	13%	12%	11%
% YoY		700%	1563%	69%	42%	31%	26%	2%	-13%	-4%
R&D	$ 4,000,000	$ 20,000,000	$ 25,000,000	$ 25,000,000	$ 40,000,000	$ 35,000,000	$ 35,000,000	$ 35,000,000	$ 35,000,000	$ 35,000,000
% of sales	200%	100%	7%	4%	4%	3%	2%	2%	2%	2%
% YoY		400%	25%	0%	60%	-13%	0%	0%	0%	0%
Opex Total	$ 5,000,000	$ 28,000,000	$158,000,000	$249,910,000	$359,872,000	$ 454,832,000	$ 563,988,320	$ 572,253,763	$ 502,587,890	$ 485,053,344
Operating Profit (EBIT)	$ (4,800,000)	$(24,000,000)	$ 17,000,000	$146,990,000	$339,848,000	$ 664,720,000	$ 966,299,320	$1,122,161,950	$1,114,486,896	$1,233,332,152
% of sales	-240%	-120%	5%	22%	34%	47%	51%	54%	57%	60%

Alrighty then we are getting there. Let's now do the '**below the line**' items

	2015	2016	2017	2018
Revenue	$ 2,000,000	$ 20,000,000	$ 350,000,000	$ 661,500,000
COGS	$ 1,800,000	$ 16,000,000	$ 175,000,000	$ 264,600,000
GM pct		10%	20%	50%
Gross Profit	$ 200,000	$ 4,000,000	$175,000,000	$396,900,000
Operating Expenses:				
S&M	$ 500,000	$ 4,000,000	$ 66,500,000	$112,455,000
% of sales		25%	20%	19%
% YoY			700%	1563%
G&A	$ 500,000	$ 4,000,000	$ 66,500,000	$112,455,000
% of sales		25%	20%	19%
% YoY			700%	1563%
R&D	$ 4,000,000	$ 20,000,000	$ 25,000,000	$ 25,000,000
% of sales		200%	100%	7%
% YoY			400%	25%
Opex Total	$ 5,000,000	$ 28,000,000	$158,000,000	$249,910,000
Operating Profit (EBIT)	$ (4,800,000)	$(24,000,000)	$ 17,000,000	$146,990,000
% of sales		-240%	-120%	5%
Interest	$ -	$ -	$ 85,000	

> **Christopher Haroun:** assume half of ebit at a 1% annual interest rate

	2015	2016	2017
Revenue	$ 2,000,000	$ 20,000,000	$ 350,000,000
COGS	$ 1,800,000	$ 16,000,000	$ 175,000,000
GM pct	10%	20%	50%
Gross Profit	$ 200,000	$ 4,000,000	$ 175,000,000
Operating Expenses:			
S&M	$ 500,000	$ 4,000,000	$ 66,500,000
% of sales	25%	20%	19%
% YoY		700%	1563%
G&A	$ 500,000	$ 4,000,000	$ 66,500,000
% of sales	25%	20%	19%
% YoY		700%	1563%
R&D	$ 4,000,000	$ 20,000,000	$ 25,000,000
% of sales	200%	100%	7%
% YoY		400%	25%
Opex Total	$ 5,000,000	$ 28,000,000	$ 158,000,000
Operating Profit (EBIT)	$ (4,800,000)	$(24,000,000)	$ 17,000,000
% of sales	-240%	-120%	5%
Interest	$ -	$ -	$ 85,000
Tax	$ -	$ -	$ 4,250,000
% of EBIT	0%	0%	25%
Net Income	$ (4,800,000)	$(24,000,000)	$ 12,835,000
% of sales	-240%	-120%	4%

Sweet nectar we are done! Note that we are not paying any tax in the first few years as we are not yet profitable.

See how easy the rest of this income statement was!

> all based on a percent of sales.

> is our $350mn valuation attractive or not?

Now that we are done with the model we can ask ourselves if the $350mn valuation of the private company we just invested in is attractive or not?

> stock market paying 10x's revs. (for <u>growth</u> investors)

Since the stock market is valuing similar companies to ours that go public at close to 10x's revenue, then is our company cheap or expensive at a valuation of $350mn? I would argue that it is a damn bargain as we will go public in a few years when revenue is higher than $400mn annually….. which means that 10x's revenue over $400mn implies an IPO valuation of way over $4bn, which means that we have more than a 10 bagger here!

Woohoo! Yeah! Can you feel that!!!!!! www.tiny.cc/chris76

> stock market paying 10x's eps. (for <u>value</u> investors)

Value investors suck at tech so we will only stick with appeasing our growth investors. You are either a growth investor (meaning you don't mind paying high perceived near term valuations as a company will be uber profitable in the future…like Amazon or LinkedIn)…..or you are a value investor and you like companies that have low price to earnings ratios, of which there are relatively few that are relevant in tech.

ok let's assume an IPO in 5 years

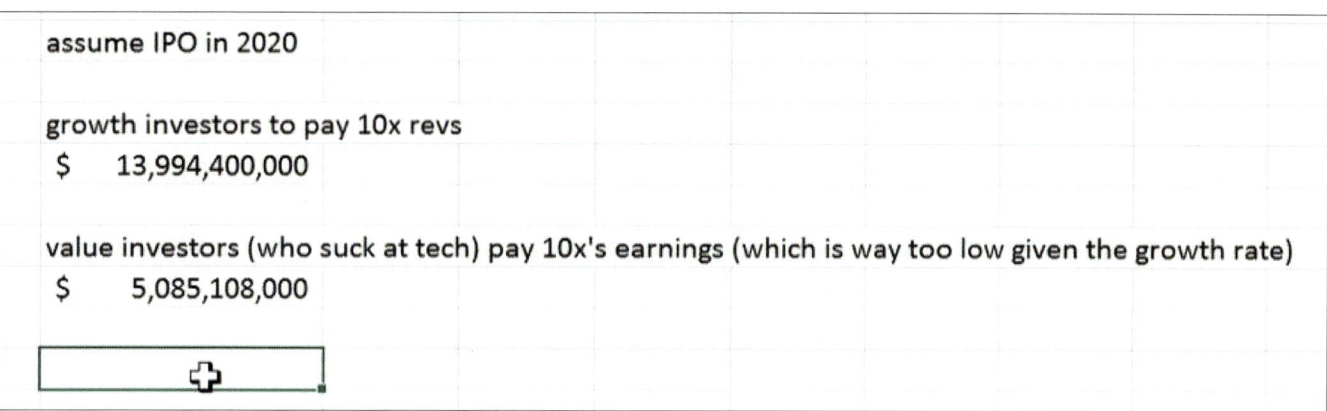

Assume we are in 2015 today and we will go public in 2020. Assume that the market will pay 10x's revenue for a high growth company like ours. Cool as this means that our company can be valued at almost a $14bn market cap by then. Value investors (who again suck at tech investing) will argue that they should pay 10 times earnings on our earnings estimate in 5 years. We think we can make about $500mn in net income in 5 years to those investors would pay 10 times' earnings or about $5bn. Either way, we are looking to make a damn impressive return on investment in our company!

Wait a second…..10x's revenue is what investors pay in a bull (or great) stock market environment. Ok let's be conservative and haircut our target price for both methodologies by say 25%. Let's be even more conservative by taking an average valuation of the growth investor's math and the value investor's math. This very conservatively values our company at over $4.8bn, which is still a hefty 14 bagger return given our $350mn investment.

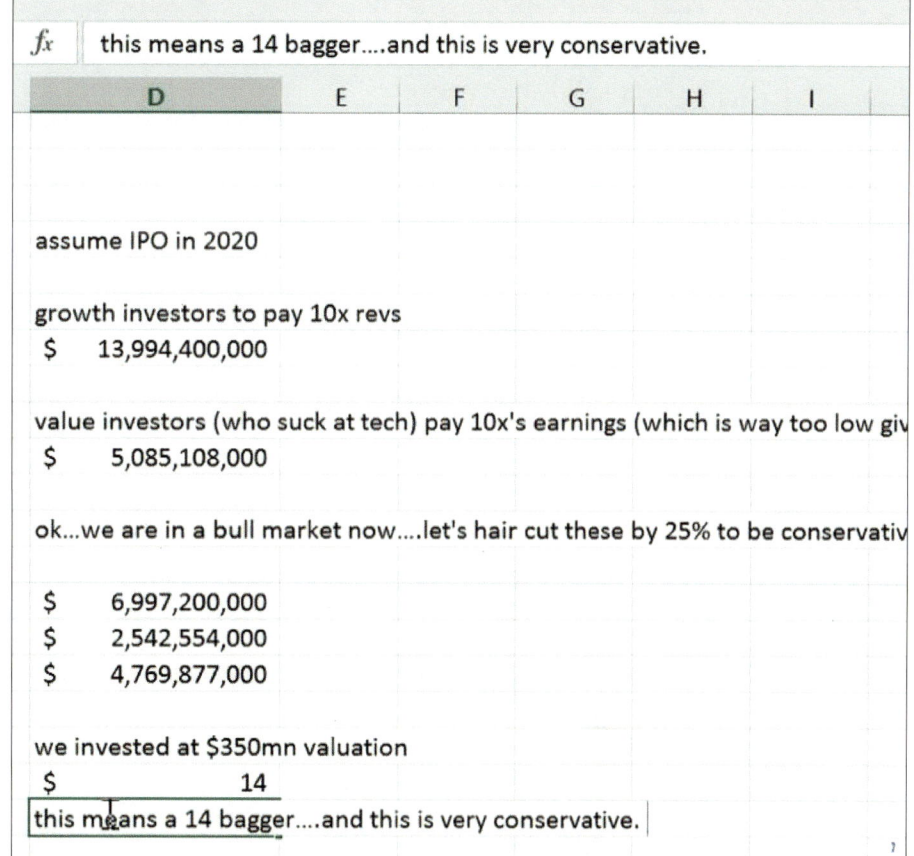

Wait a second. Is our revenue multiple estimate too high? Well we can compare our company to other amazing high growth tech companies to compare for a sanity check.

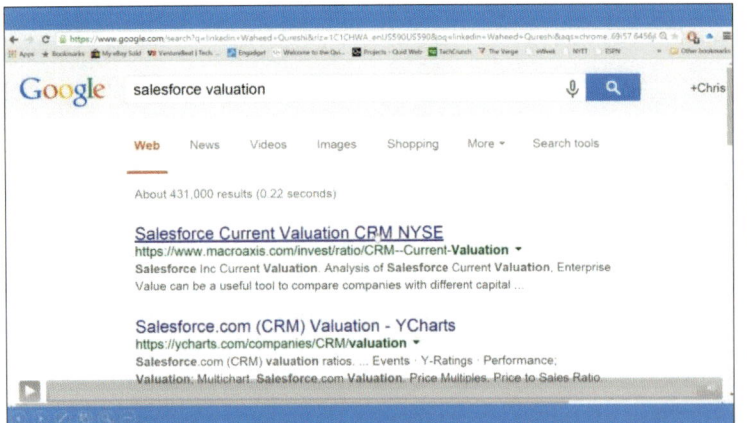

We see that Salesforce is trading at close to 9x's revenue and its growth rate is way lower than our firm. Even if you think Salesforce is overvalued, you likely see tremendous value in our investment (there is a cloud software component to our business model too which is why we compare it to Salesforce's valuation).

```
assume IPO in 2020

growth investors to pay 10x revs
$   13,994,400,000

value investors (who suck at tech) pay 10x's earnings (which is way too low given the growth rate)
$    5,085,108,000

ok...we are in a bull market now....let's hair cut these by 25% to be conservative and assume we could be in a bear market then

$    6,997,200,000
$    2,542,554,000
$    4,769,877,000

we invested at $350mn valuation
$         13.63
this means a 14 bagger....and this is very conservative.
what does a mature large cap growth company like salesforce trade at?

wow 9x revenue for salesforce.....and growth is way slower for them....
this $350mn valuation is a bargain!
```

Heck our growth rate in 2020 is 40% which is likely at least 2x's higher than Salesforce's growth in 2020. So if we apply a 9x's revenue multiple on 2020 revenue, then our return on our $350mn investment is off the charts!

	2019	2020	
	$999,600,000	$1,399,440,000	$
	51%	40%	
	$299,880,000	$ 279,888,000	$
	70%	80%	
	$699,720,000	$1,119,552,000	$1

what is their sustainable growth rate in 2020 when they ipo?

sustainable growth =

what is the maximum growth rate they can achieve without additional equity or debt financing

sustainable growth =

(ending equity - beginning equity)
/
beginning equity

retained earnings is part of equity....which is how much profits we have derived over the years.

> let's checkout our sustainable growth rate in 2020 - the year of our IPO
> (assume no dividends)

sustainable growth		
beginning equity	$	351,597,690
ending equity	$	860,108,490
		145%

so the most we can grow in 2020 is 145%......let's make sure we are below this metric...

2020 growth= 98%

we are growing at a rate below our sustainable growth rate. All good!

> if we were growing above the sustainable growth rate we would need to raise money (equity sale or debt).

sustainable growth = 145%
and we are at 98%

but if an activist investor like carl icon pressures us to issue a dividend of say 40%....

then you simply multiply the sustainable growth rate by 1-d.

145% * (1-0.40) = 87%

---

sustainable growth =

net income
/
beginning equity
*
retention rate

---

sustainable growth =

net income
/
beginning equity
*
retention rate

← this is ending equity MINUS beginning equity (points to net income)

← this is 1 MINUS the dividend rate (points to retention rate)

Heavy chapter! Another break time: www.tiny.cc/chris77

---

let's manipulate that last formula and have some fun with math so we can better understand how to manipulate our financials to meet our sustainable growth targets.

---

net income
/
equity

=

return on equity (or ROE)

$NI/E =$ ROE (or sustainable growth)

ROE = NI/E

ROE = NI/E * 1 * 1

ROE = NI/E * S/S * A/A

ROE = NI/S * S/A * A/E

G = NI/S * S/A * A/E

G = NI/S * S/A * A/E

G = Net Profit Margin * Asset Turnover * Equity Multiplier

G = NI/S * S/A * A/E

G = Net Profit Margin * Asset Turnover * Equity Multiplier

I can increase my sustainable growth using one of those 3 equations

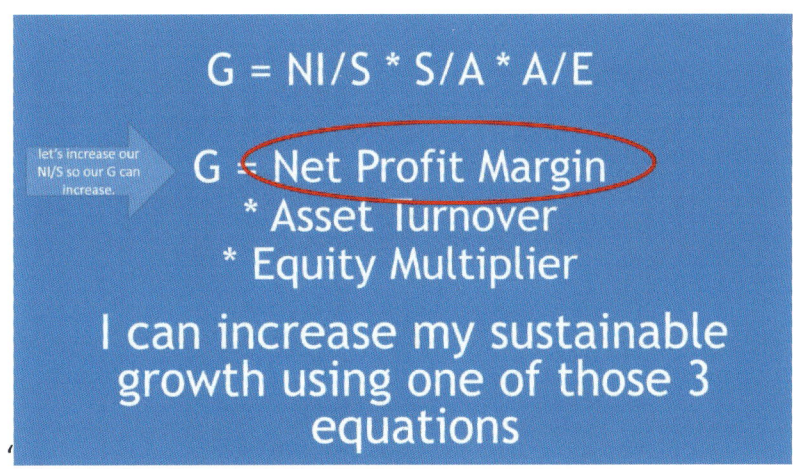

Cool. So let's increase our sustainable growth rate by increasing our net profit margin, which is currently 98%:

C	I
	2020
Revenue	$1,399,440,000
% YoY	40%
COGS	$ 279,888,000
GM pct	80%
Gross Profit	**$1,119,552,000**
Operating Expenses:	
S&M	$ 209,916,000
% of sales	15%
% YoY	31%
G&A	$ 209,916,000
% of sales	15%
% YoY	31%
R&D	$ 35,000,000
% of sales	3%
% YoY	-13%
Opex Total	**$ 454,832,000**
Operating Profit (EBIT)	**$ 664,720,000**
% of sales	47%
Interest	$ 9,970,800
Tax	$ 166,180,000
% of EBIT	25%
Net Income	**$ 508,510,800**
% of sales	36%
% YoY	98%
assumptions and revenue	

Ok note how Sales and Marketing (S&M) as a percent of revenue is 15%? Let's decrease this to 14% and see what happens to our YoY (year over year) net income growth. It should increase from 98%.to….

	2020
Revenue	$1,399,440,000
% YoY	40%
COGS	$ 279,888,000
GM pct	80%
Gross Profit	**$1,119,552,000**
Operating Expenses:	
S&M	$ 195,921,600
% of sales	14%
% YoY	~~23%~~
G&A	$ 167,932,800
% of sales	12%
% YoY	5%
R&D	$ 35,000,000
% of sales	3%
% YoY	-13%
Opex Total	$ 398,854,400
Operating Profit (EBIT)	$ 720,697,600
% of sales	51%
Interest	$ 10,810,464
Tax	$ 180,174,400
% of EBIT	25%
	wow nice leverage!!
Net Income	**$ 551,333,664**
% of sales	39%
% YoY	115%

Holy leverage! Wow – our net income growth increased from 98% to 115% year over year by tweaking our Sales and Marketing as a percent of revenue from 15% to 14%!!!! Leverage is a beautiful thing.

Questions Based on Chapter 9:

1: When creating models and valuing private companies, we can focus on the TAM metric to help us determine our revenue metric.

    True or False

2: It is crucial that you add many comments to your model.

True   or   False

3: Growth investors only invest in companies that have very low price to earnings ratios in year 1.

True   or   False

CHAPTER SUMMARY

Chris Haroun @chris_haroun
longer term forecasts are annual estimates. % of sales is the most important part of financial modelling. expenses are easy to tweak. spend most of your time on revenue.

Chapter 10: Due Diligence and Data Sources

"What gets measured gets managed."

- *Peter Drucker*

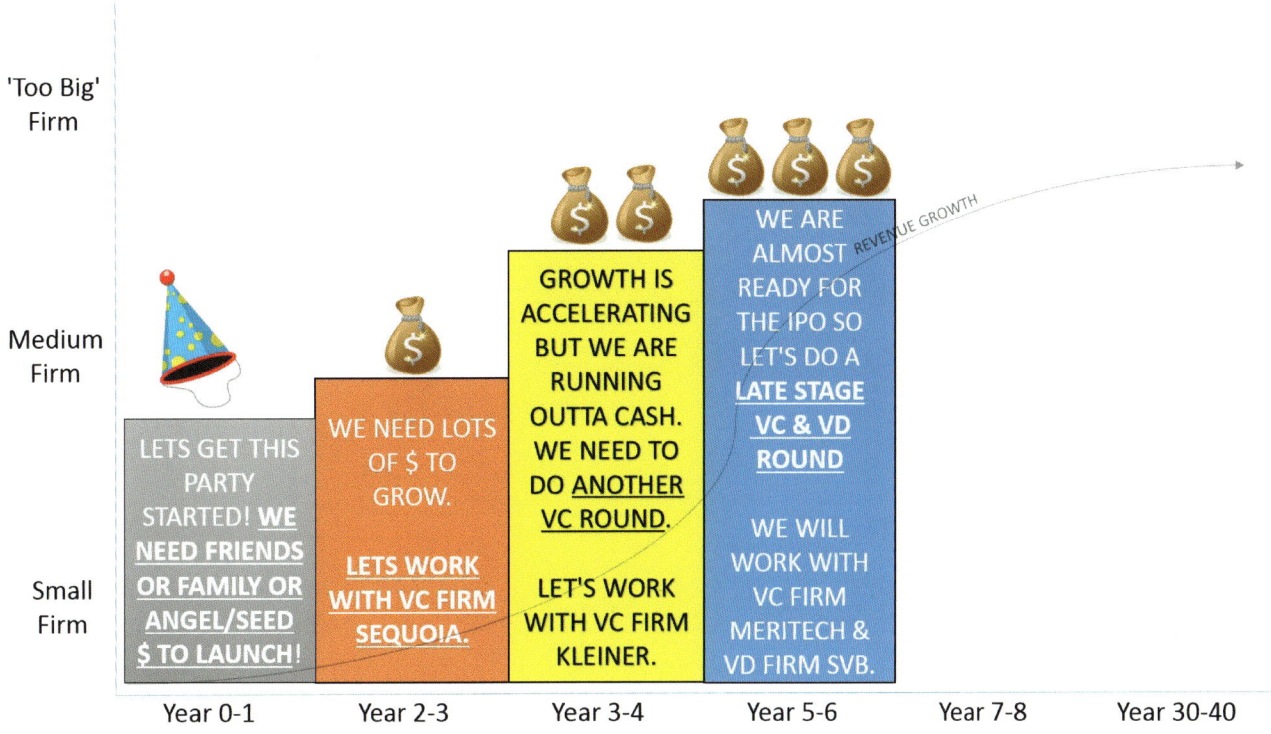

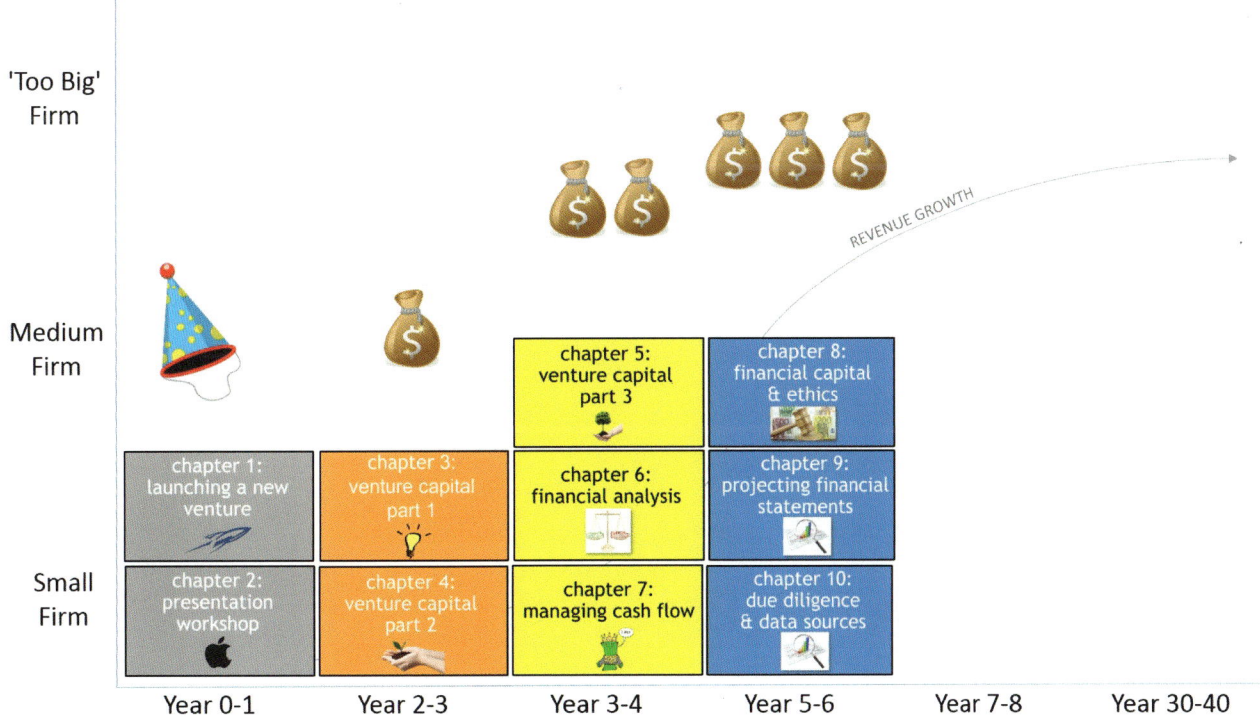

Always do your own research. Always do your own due diligence. Everyone else has a bias and they want to influence your opinion. Please please please don't let anyone rent space in your head. Do your own work.

great financial analysts...

form their <u>own</u> opinions.

others have hidden agendas...

...but most are wrong.

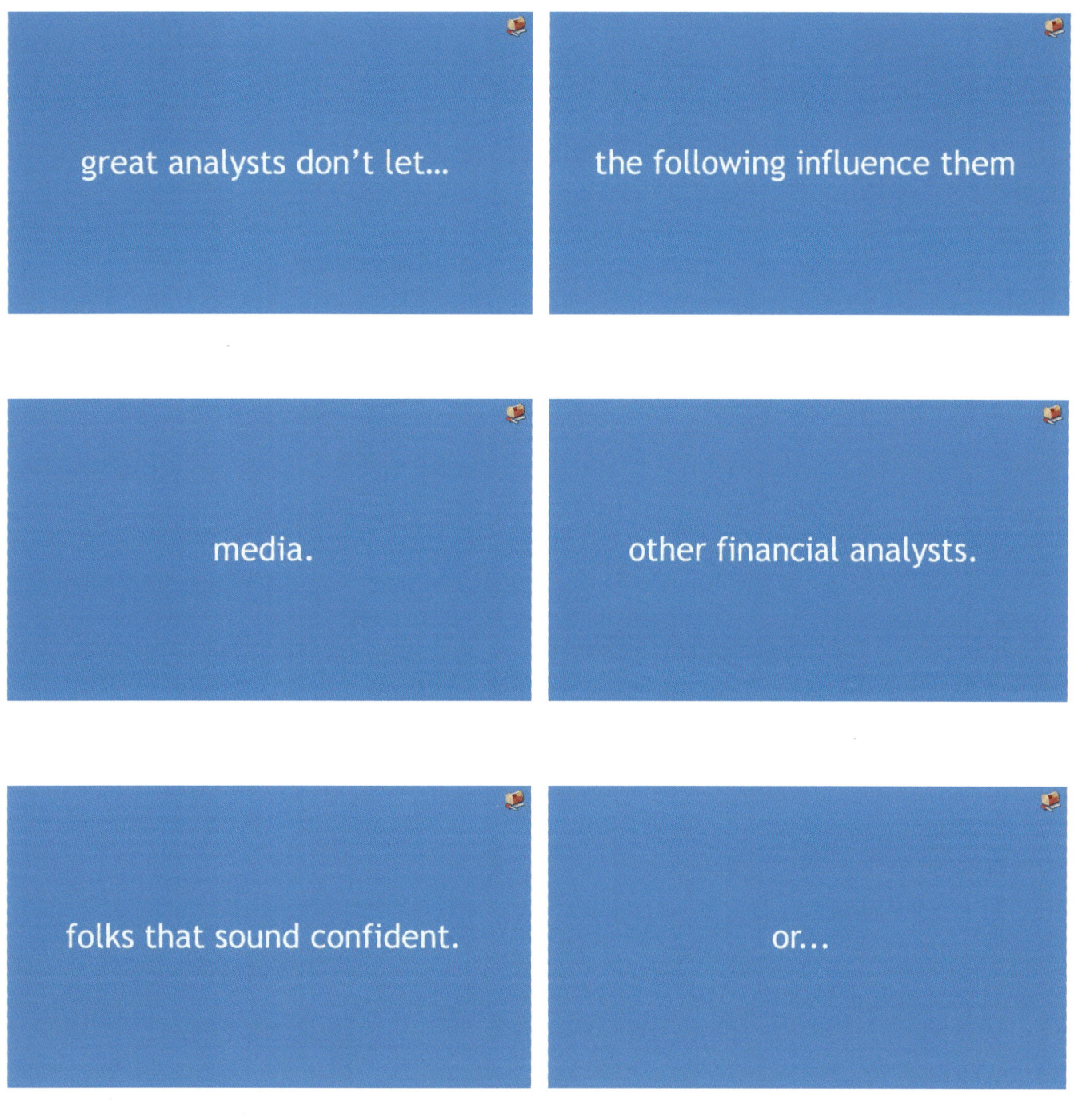

politicians.

:)

in finance, please remember

confidence does not =

competence.

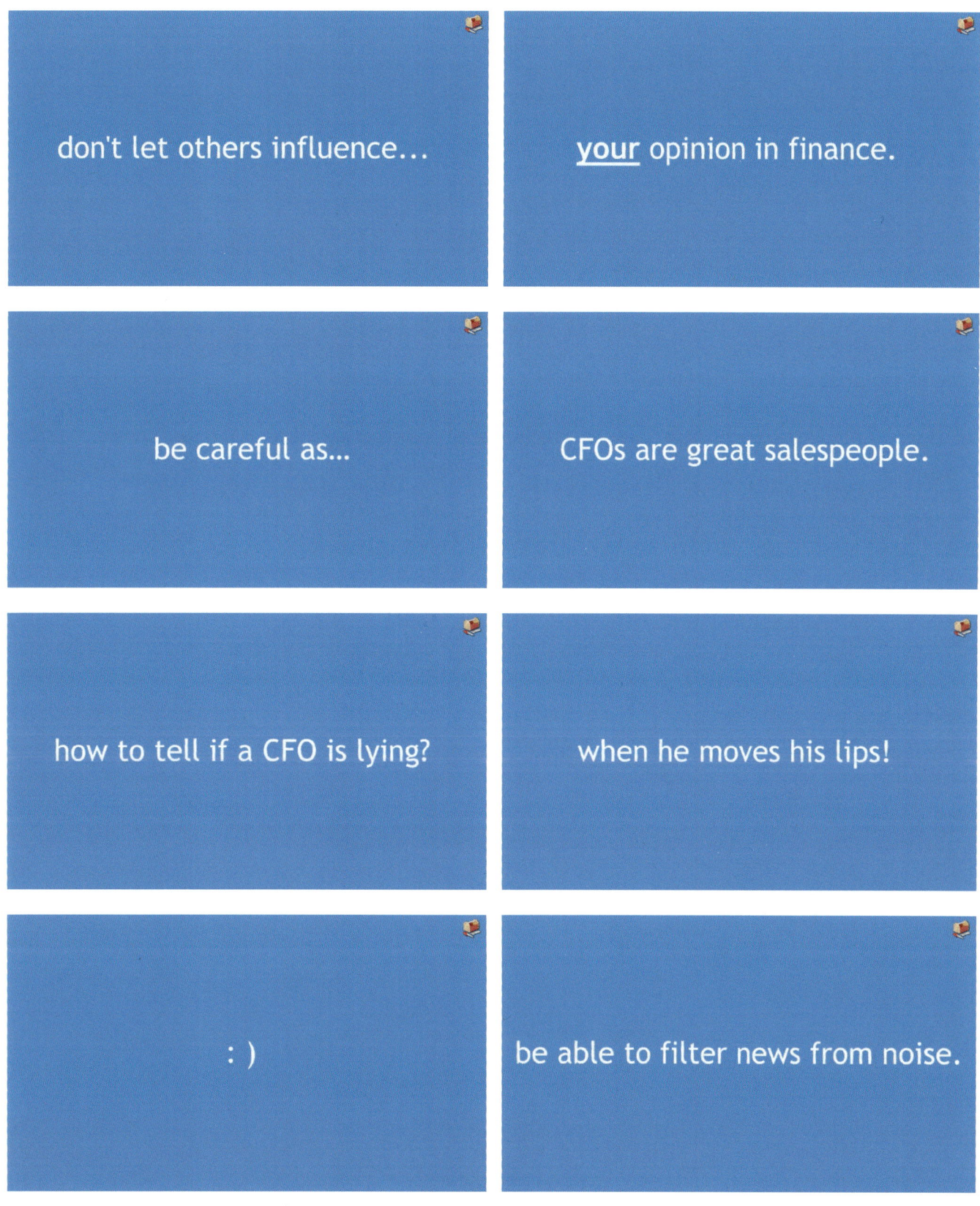

www.tiny.cc/chris78 :)

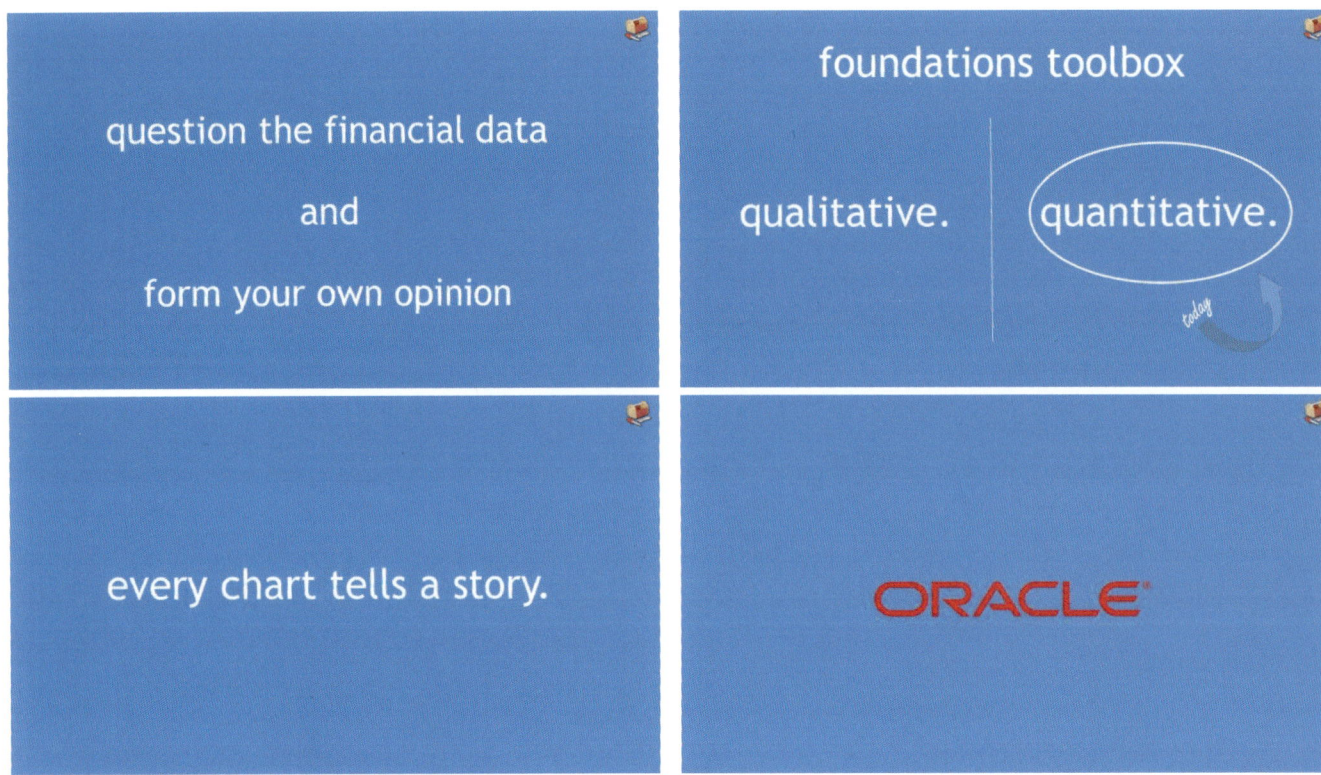

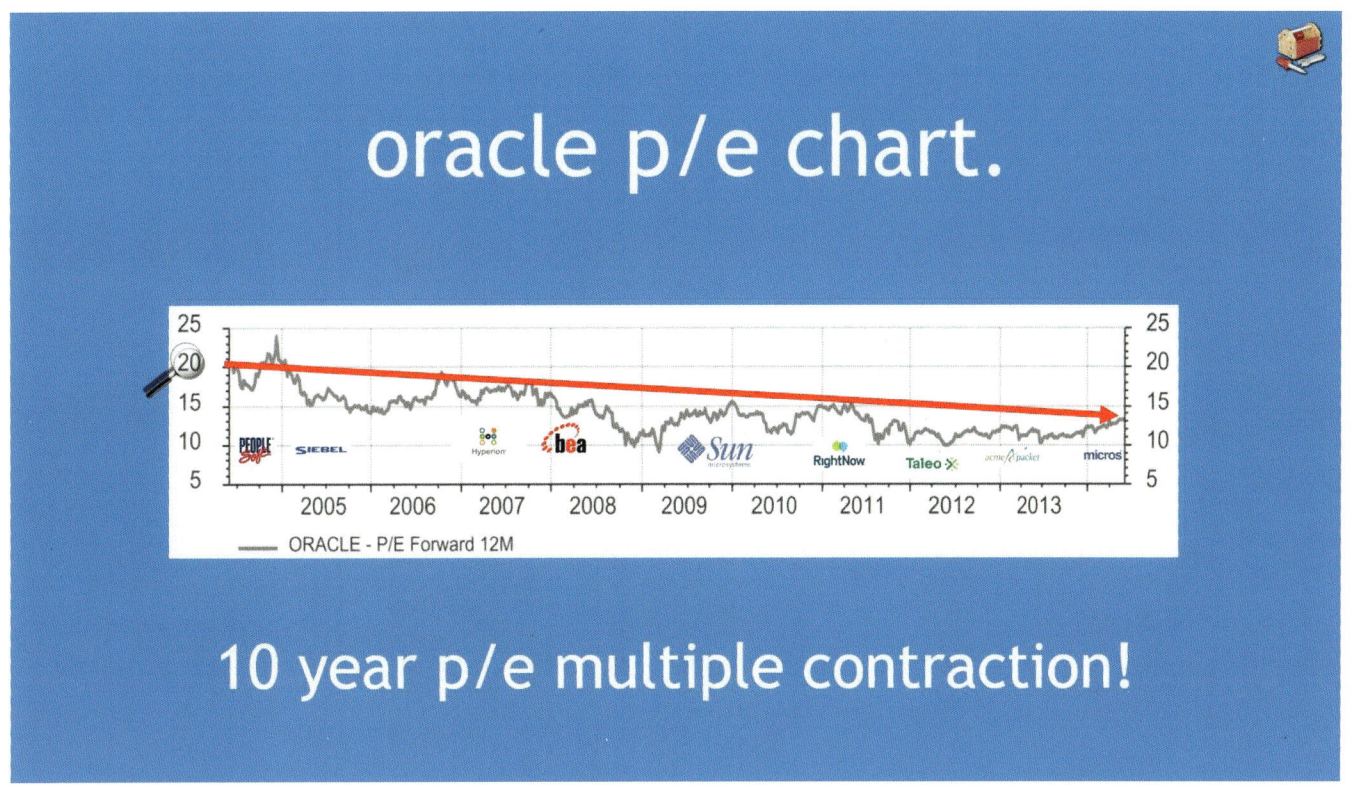

You need to understand why companies do what they do ('market signals'). Why is Oracle buying a massive tech company every year? Because the company is so big that organic revenue (its core competency) is actually contracting! Others will tell you otherwise. Just do your own research.

Don't rely on people that seem to speak gooder than you do :)

Every financial model that you create when analyzing a company is different as different companies have different revenue drivers for your model.

tech model i.s. **drivers**.

✓ subscribers or license revenues

✓ bookings

✓ operating and gross margin trends

tech model b.s.
- ✓ usually low debt if any
- ✓ cash rich
- ✓ analyze deferred revenue

In technology investing, balance sheets aren't usually too relevant as most technology companies don't have massive debt positions (you don't need factories to sell software on the Internet). We tend to analyze deferred revenue a lot with tech companies. What is deferred revenue? It is revenue that you can't recognize today. Huh? Well you can only account or record revenue on your income statement when you get the benefit of selling the product in this financial period. Huh huh? Well if you sell 1 years worth of software today and your customer will pick up only 1 box of software this quarter and will come back to pick up the other box next quarter, then the box not picked up becomes deferred revenue so that you can only account for it in next quarter's financial statements (and not in this quarter's financial statements). Until then it is a liability on your balance sheet. Once you recognize it in your income statement then it is no longer a liability.

tech model c.f.
- ✓ usually tracks net income
- ✓ important for subscription companies
- ✓ some companies are seasonal.

Since tech companies don't usually have much debt, then cash flow is usually very close to net income…..so we don't have to bother creating a cash flow statement! Yep that's right.

You always want to model at least 5 years into the future. Ask yourself this basic question before doing any due diligence: "In 5 years is this company going to be more relevant or less relevant that it is today?" If you do this then you will make a killing owning companies like Amazon or LinkedIn and not lose your short shorting these companies in a bull market! Huh? Well in my LinkedIn financial model, I can get to $50 in earnings in 5 years so LinkedIn's stock is

what about valuation?
- ✓ value investors suck at tech.
- ✓ smart money models 5+ years out.
- ✓ use revenue, eps and cf multiples.

only trading at 5x my 5 years earnings per share (EPS) estimate and is a bargain! Well if I looked at LinkedIn and Amazon on this year's earnings (bad idea) then I would think that both companies are ridiculously expensive.

If you are valuing non tech companies, you still want to look 5 years out but you might be more inclined to make a discounted cash flow analysis instead of a p/e or p/sales based target price.

We already know that the best accounting resource on the web is www.sec.gov .Use this resource a lot to get detailed financial information on every publically traded company. We will do this in great detail next chapter.

what about non tech valuation?

✓ dcf

✓ smart money models 5+ years out.

✓ use revenue, eps and cf multiples.

Select search in the top right hand corner of www.sec.gov .

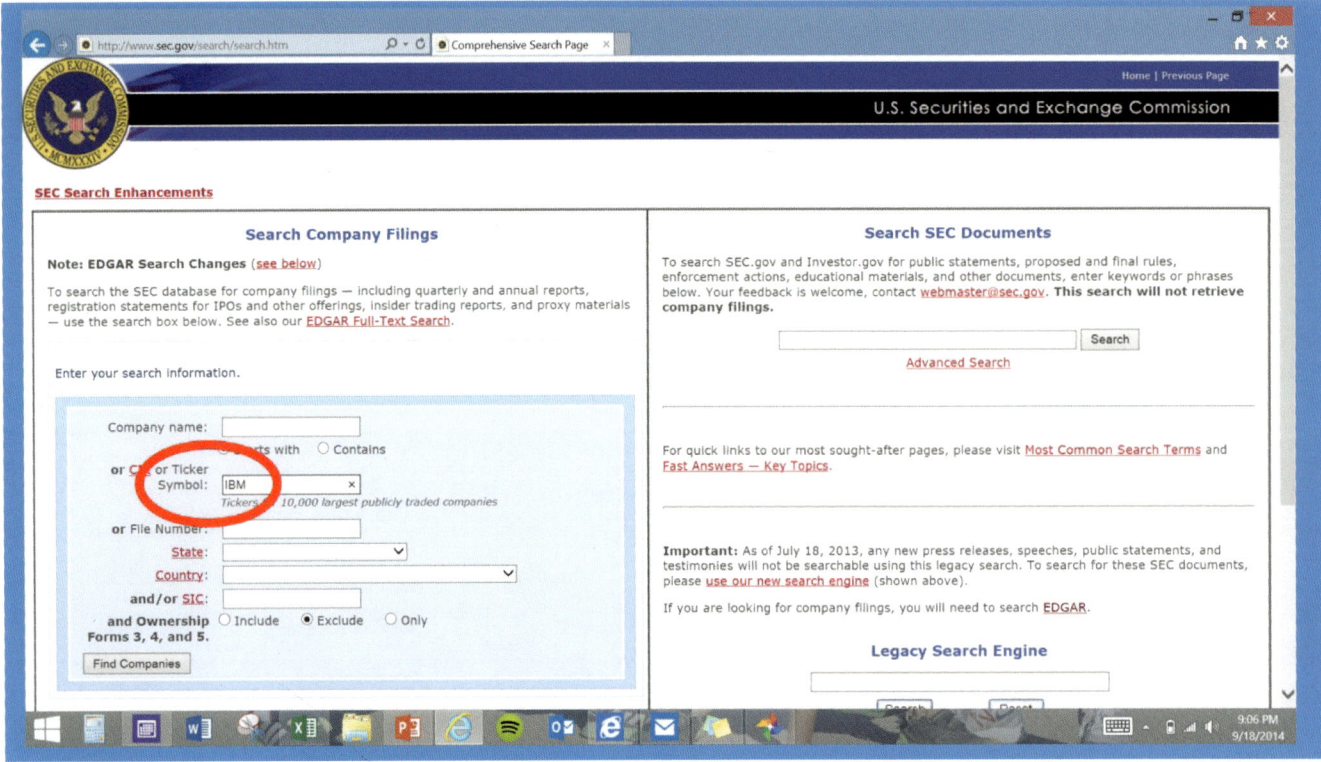

Then enter your ticker, for example, IBM.

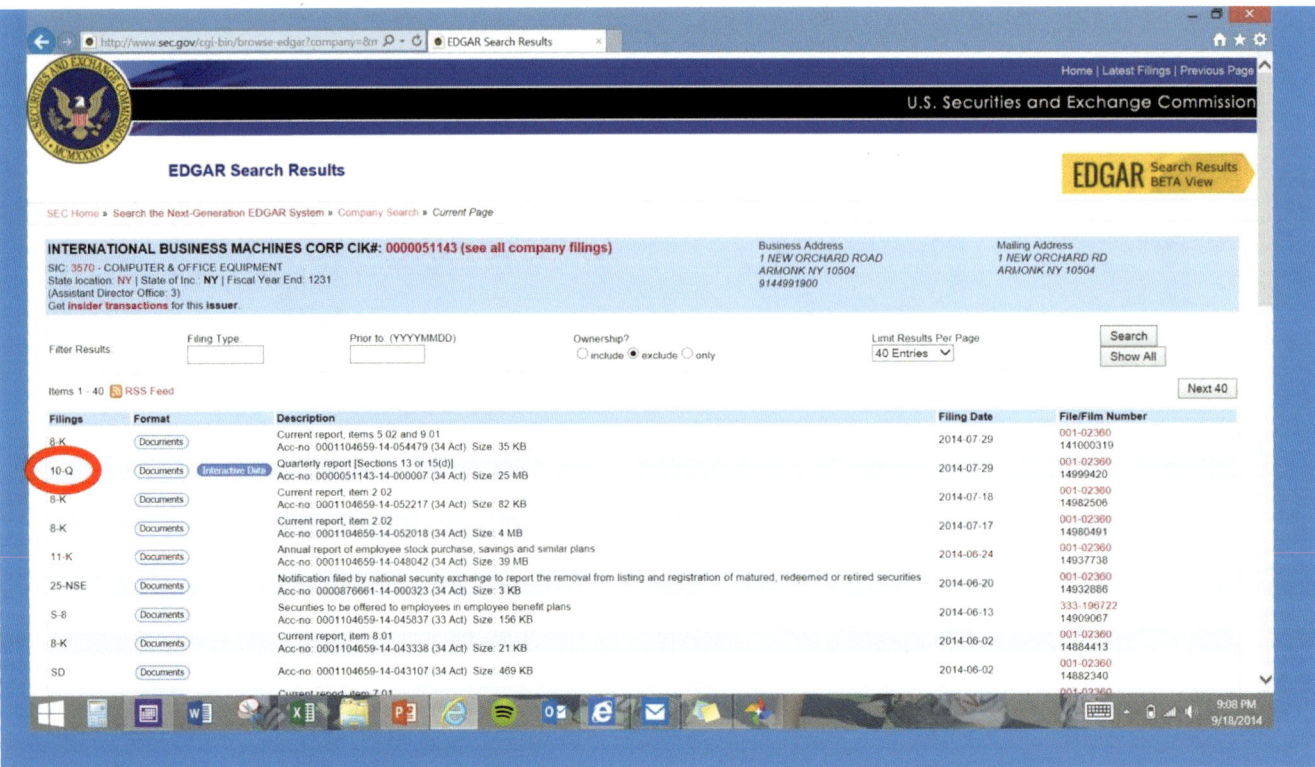

This is a wealth of resources for all relevant quantitative and qualitative stuff. We will talk much more about this next chapter.

Questions Based on Chapter 10:

1: When doing due diligence on a company, it's important to:

   a) Do your own research and form your own opinion.
   b) Listen to the experts because their opinion becomes your opinion.

2: Value investors only buy expensive stocks.

   True   or   False

3: The best investors value companies based on estimates in 5+ years.

   True   or   False

CHAPTER SUMMARY

Chris Haroun @chris_haroun
quantitative tools = target price based on estimates in 5 years. look for trends. form your own opinion on all investments. DON'T LISTEN TO OTHERS! Sec.gov =great resource

> **this topic is worth repeating...**

> **are you looking for a job?**

Don't send in your resume anymore. Huh? It's too competitive and you have similar chances of winning the lottery. You need to set up many informational meetings using LinkedIn.

Every year I tell my students during the first day of class that I could guarantee them a job if they do 20 informational meetings with strangers at firms that they want to work for during the school semester. I ask them all who would do this if I would guarantee that you got the job of your dreams? Of course every single hand goes up! Then during the last class, I ask how many students actually did this? Usually only 1 or 2 hands go up and these students always get a great job! They are never the top students in the class either. Remember the Steve Jobs video. If you want something in life you need to ask for it! Ask and you shall receive.

> **be persistent on in and ask to please meet for a coffee. say you are a student.**

> **to do: set up informationals.**

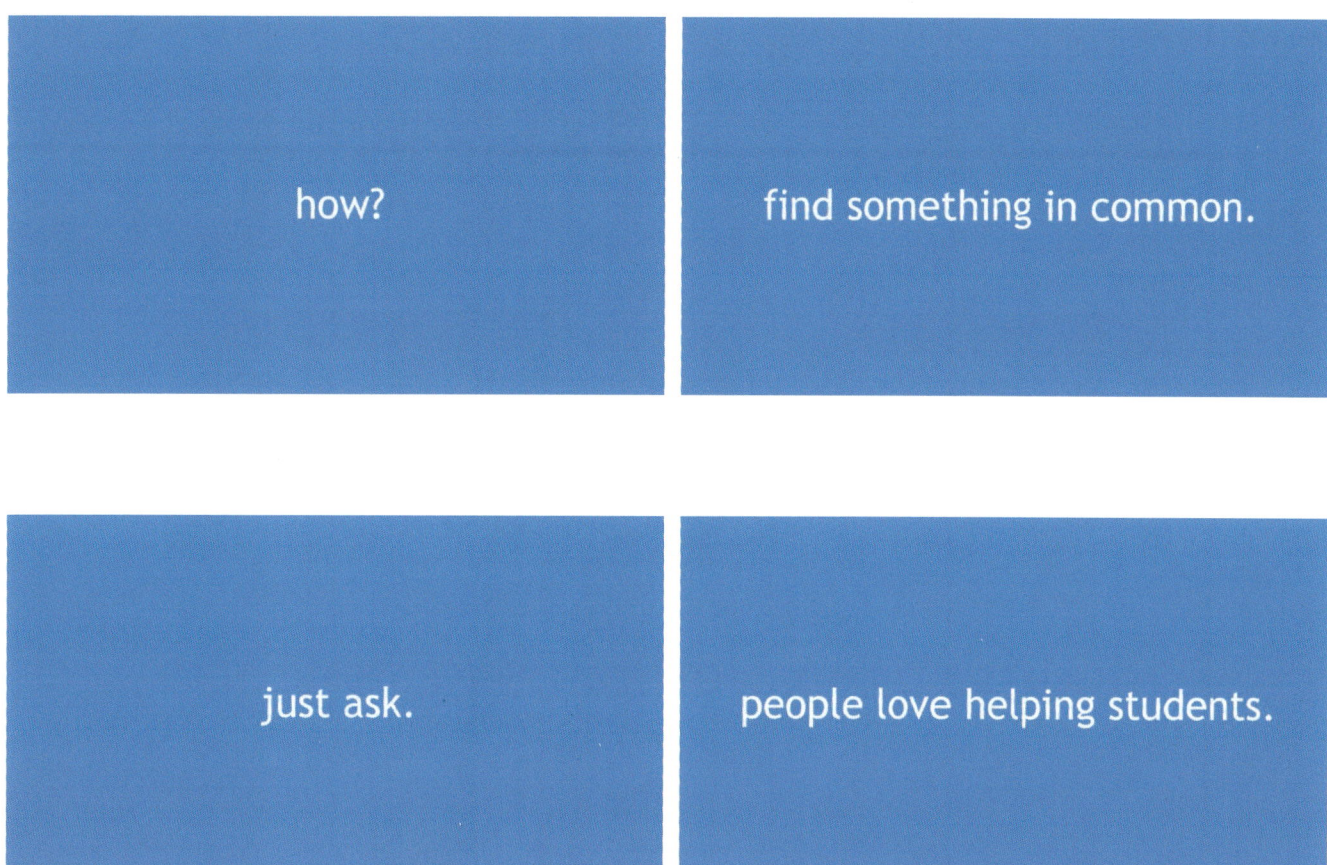

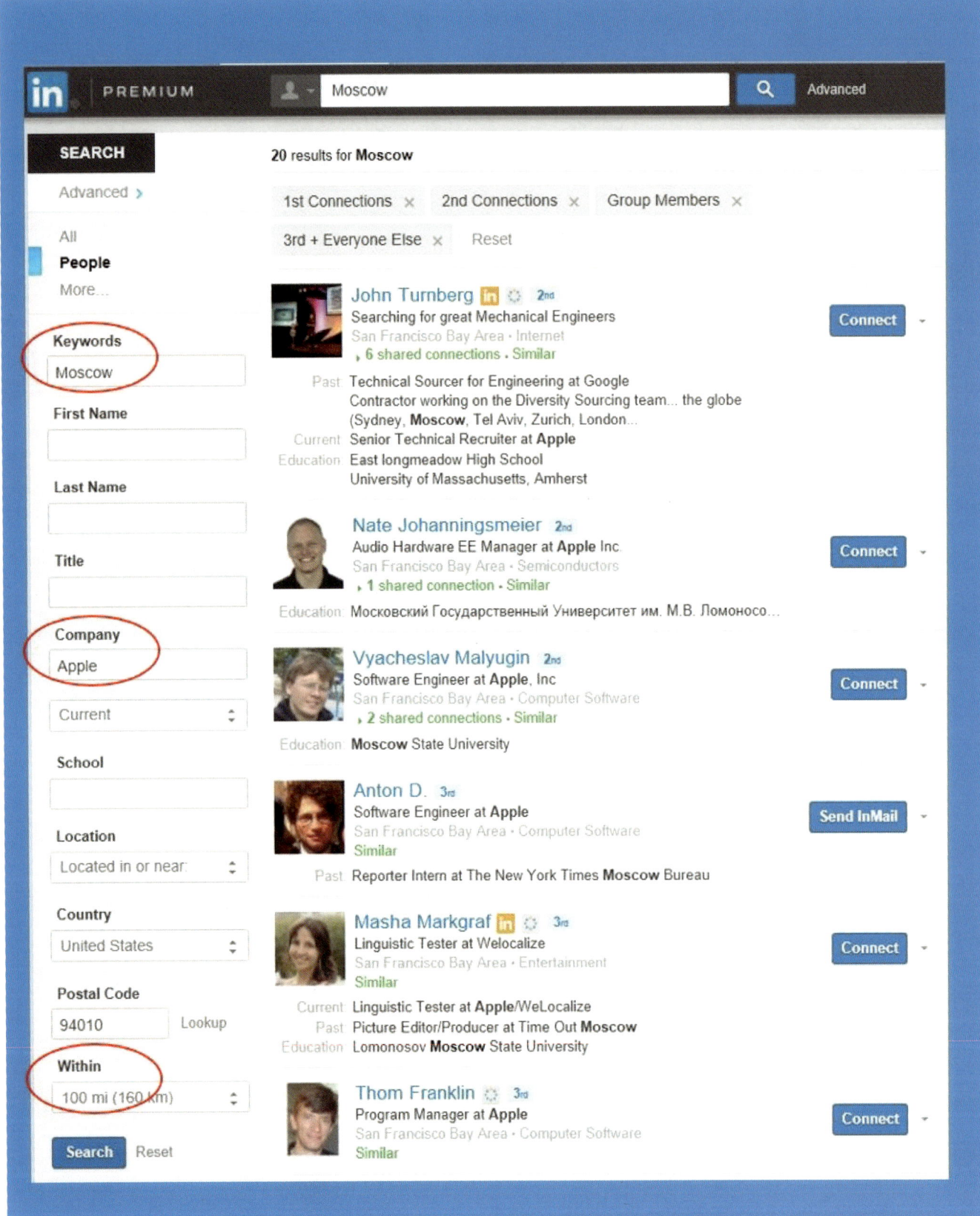

www.tiny.cc/chris79

Confidence is not an American thing....but it is fascinating how American students (whether or not they were born in the US) are the most confident and with confidence comes the ability to sell yourself, raise money, reinvent an industry....etc. Please read the section on confidence in the last chapter of this book for more details on this crucial concept.

Chapter 11: Modeling and Valuation

"Valuation is an art, not a science."

- *Mohandas Pai*

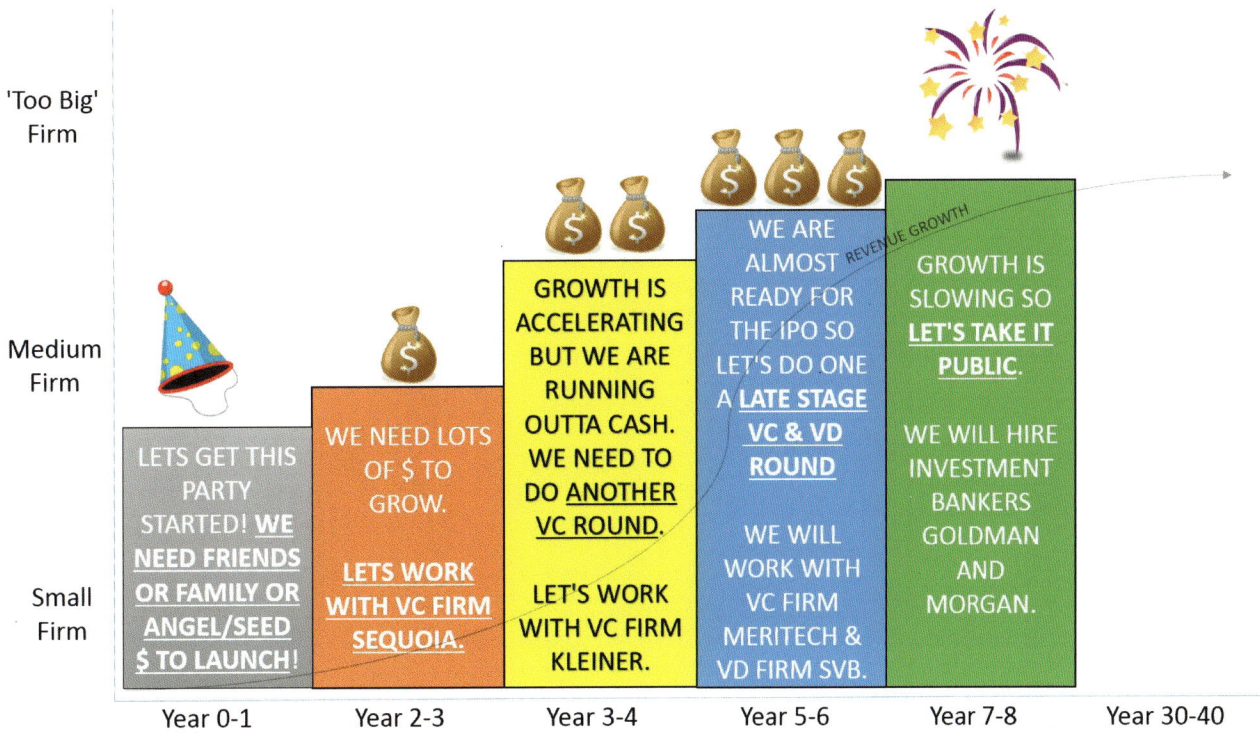

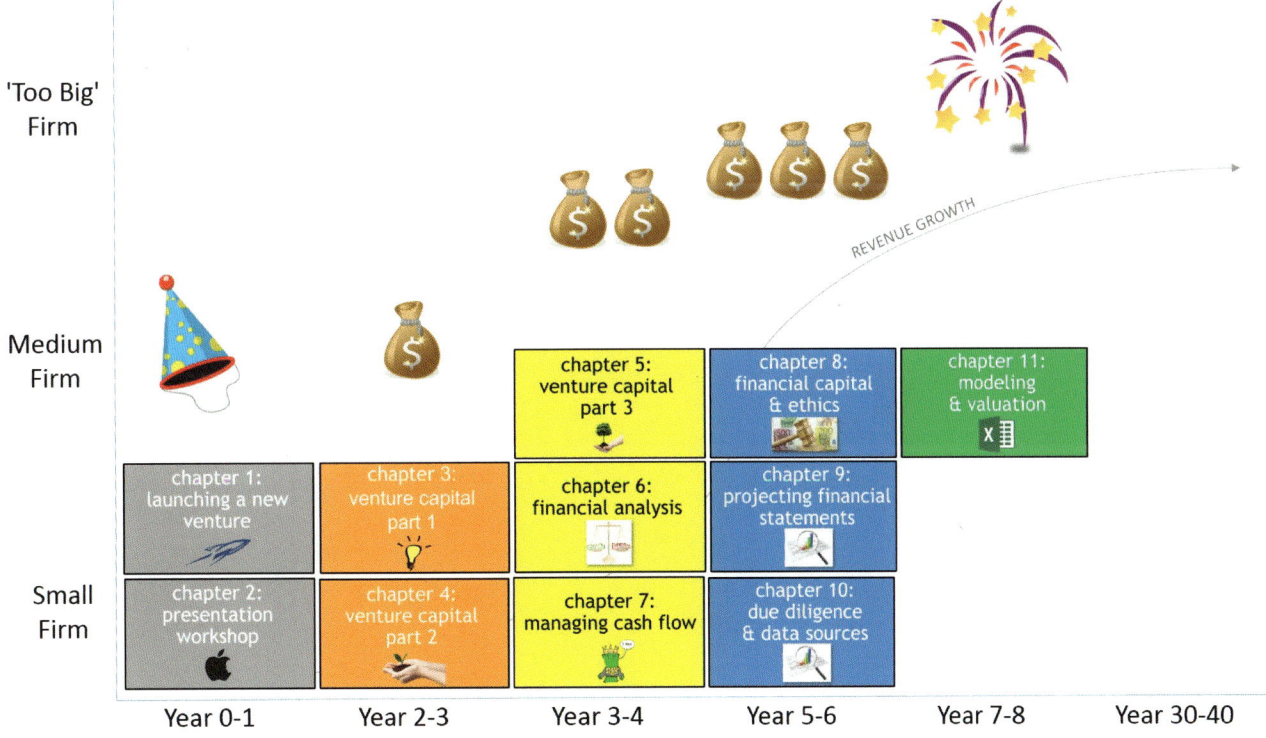

BUILD FINANCIAL MODELS AND VALUE COMPANIES THE EASY WAY

BREAKING NEWS!

Microsoft's investment bankers just approached us and Microsoft might want to buy our company! We need to decide if we should do an IPO or just sell to Microsoft!

I created an online version of this chapter as well at: www.tiny.cc/chris80

In the previous chapter we modeled and came up with the appropriate valuation for our private company. **We will be going public soon and we will discuss the entire IPO process. Before we do so, let's discuss how to value and model Microsoft, a company that is already public.**

We will make the process very easy to understand! In fact, we will make this chapter more Pinterest like versus previous chapters where we covered the basics of valuing a private company. The difference here is we have WAY more information available!

how do wall street analyst make financial models and..	how do they value companies?
you are no longer students.	that's right.
you are financial analysts today in this chapter.	you will learn exactly how wall street analysts work...
what are their secrets?	how do they do due diligence on companies?

a good analyst <u>doesn't need</u> others to form their opinions

a great analyst does a sh*t load of due diligence <u>alone</u>.

when analyzing an investment...

the last thing you should do is speak to management....

...why?

because they are incredible salespeople.

don't trust them.

be skeptical until your research is complete.

- start with the annual report (also called the 10k).
- understand the risks.
- understand the market.
- we will learn how analysts model companies
- we will learn how analysts analyze sectors
- we will learn how analysts assess management
- we will learn how analysts get access to information...
- strap in!

| let's do it! | www.tiny.cc/chris81 |

| theory |  |

No theory in this section! We will create a model and value Microsoft the way I did it in the hedge fund industry.

| what is investor relations? | Investor relations is a function that exists to help YOU the investor decide whether or not to invest in a company. All large companies have investor relations folks. Smaller companies outsource to investor relations firms. |

| building a model | what are the sources? |

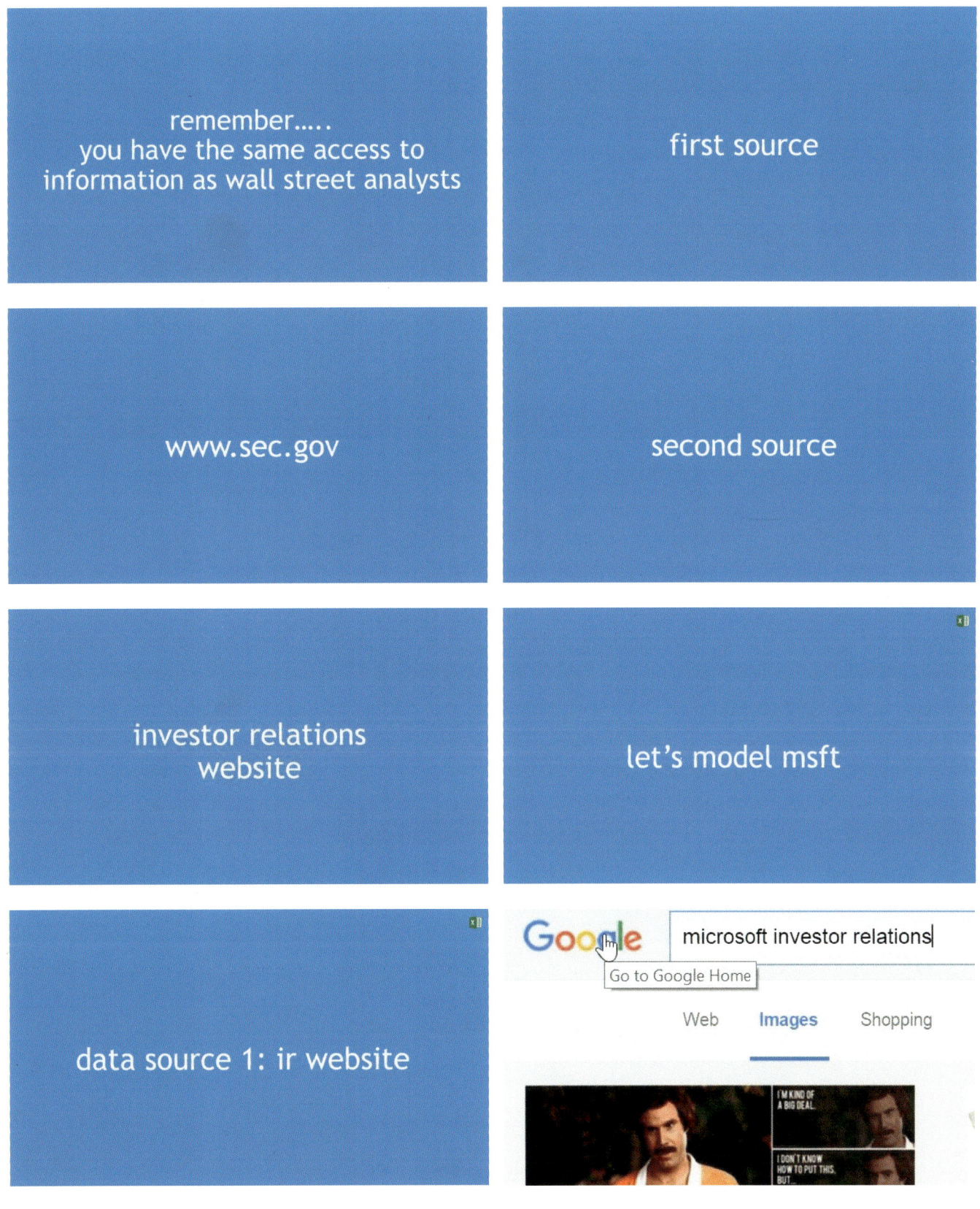

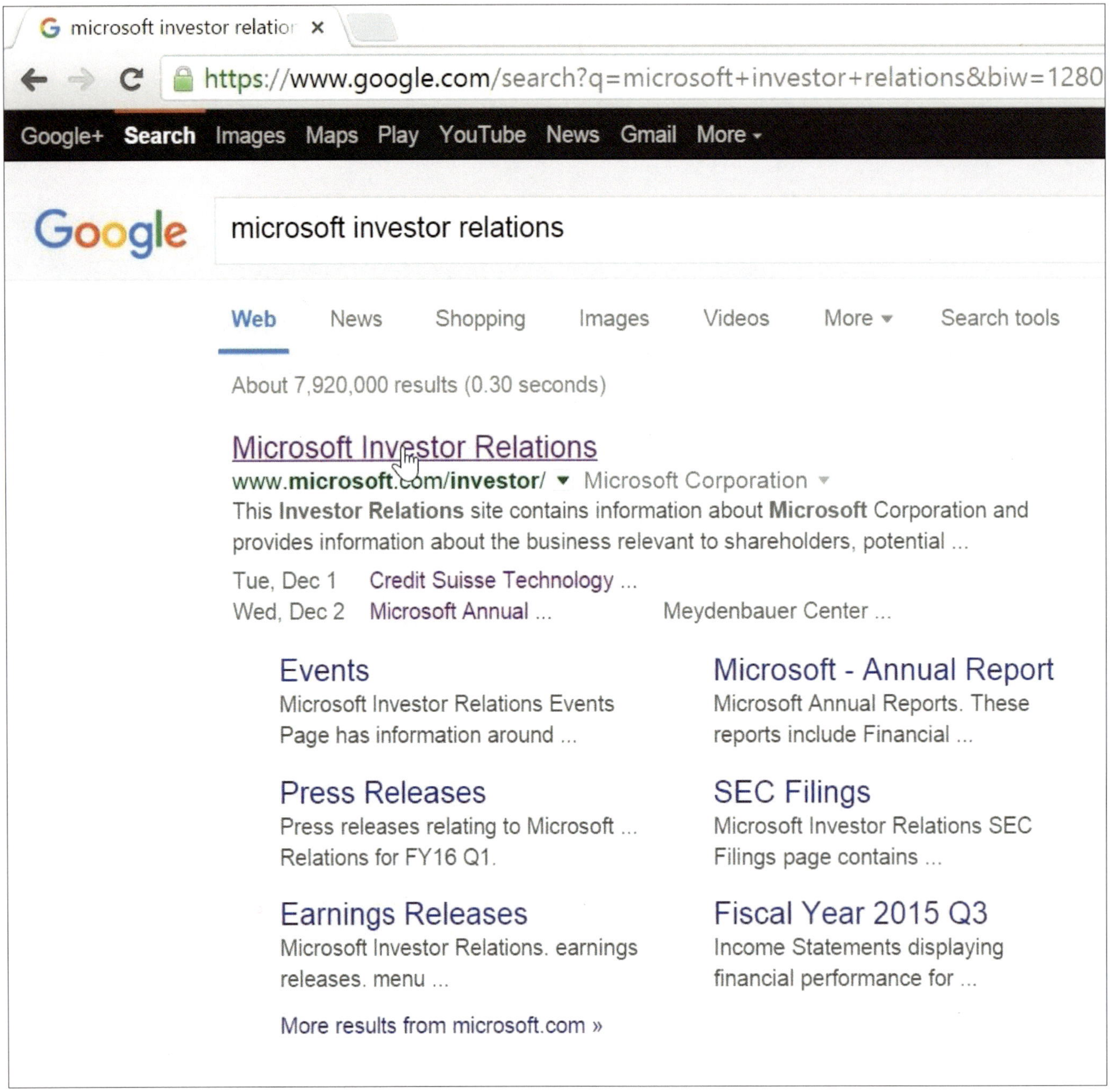

The Ultimate Practical Business Manual

…arningsAndFinancials/Earnings/FinancialStatements/FY16/Q1/IncomeStatements.as…

Earnings Release FY16 Q1

Income Statements | Comprehensive Income | Balance Sheets | Cash Flows |

Segment Revenue & Operating Income

Income Statements (in millions, except per share amounts) (Unaudited)

		Three Months Ended September 30,	
		2015	2014
Revenue	$	20,379 $	23,201
Cost of revenue		7,207	8,273
Gross margin		13,172	14,928
Research and development		2,962	3,065
Sales and marketing		3,333	3,728
General and administrative		1,084	1,151
Impairment, integration, and restructuring		0	1,140
Operating income		5,793	5,844
Other income (expense), net		(280)	52
Income before income taxes		5,513	5,896
Provision for income taxes		893	1,356
Net income	$	4,620 $	4,540
Earnings per share:			
Basic	$	0.58 $	0.55

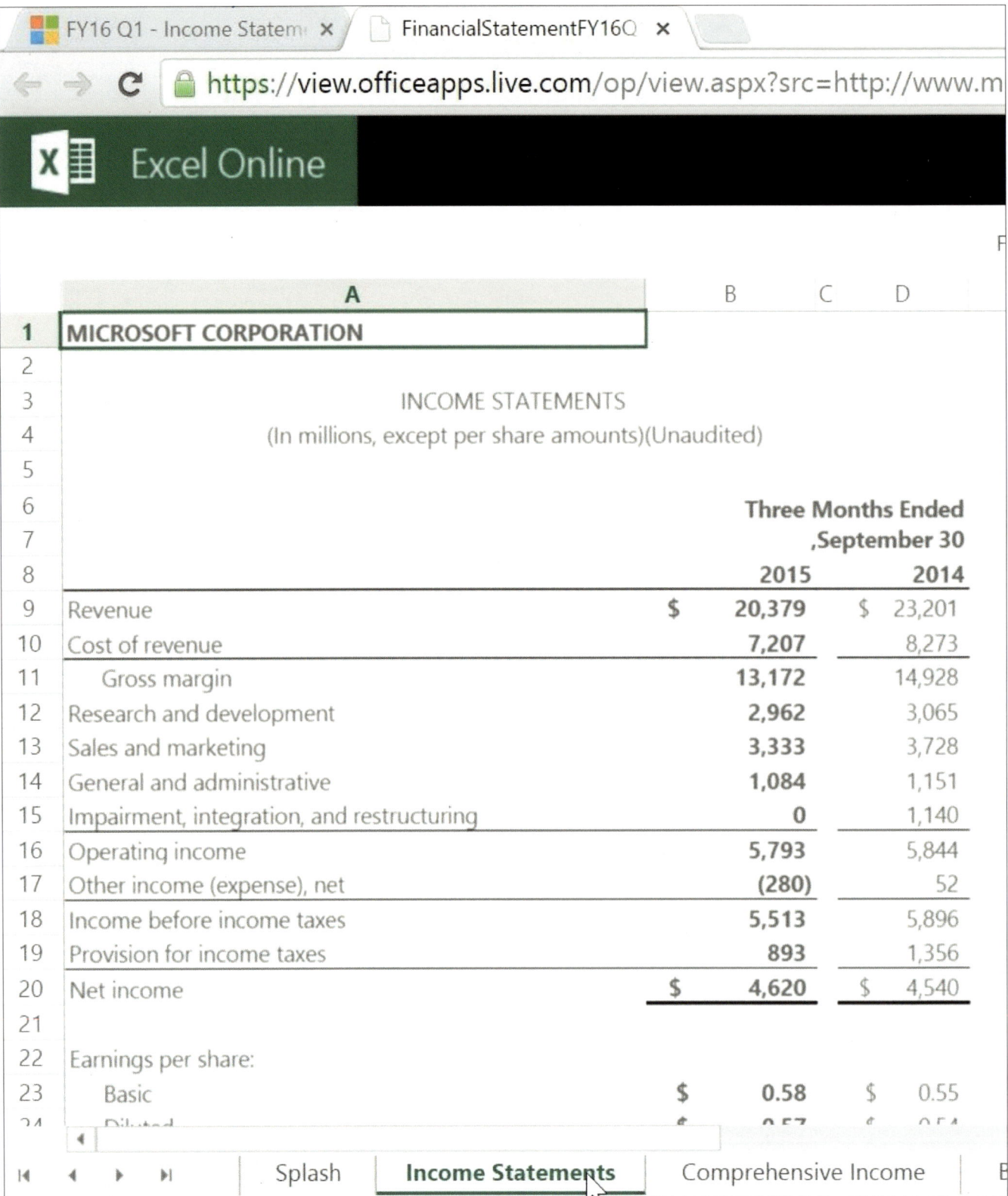

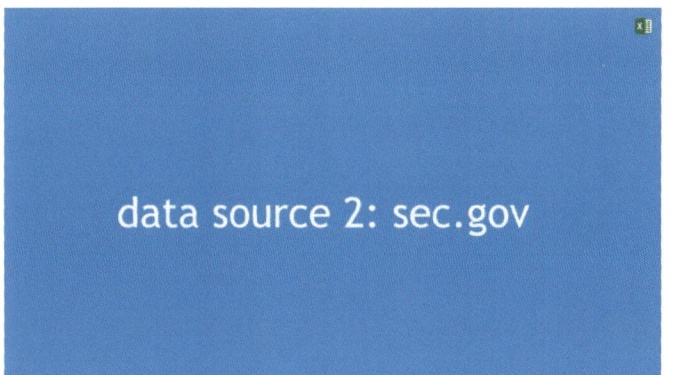

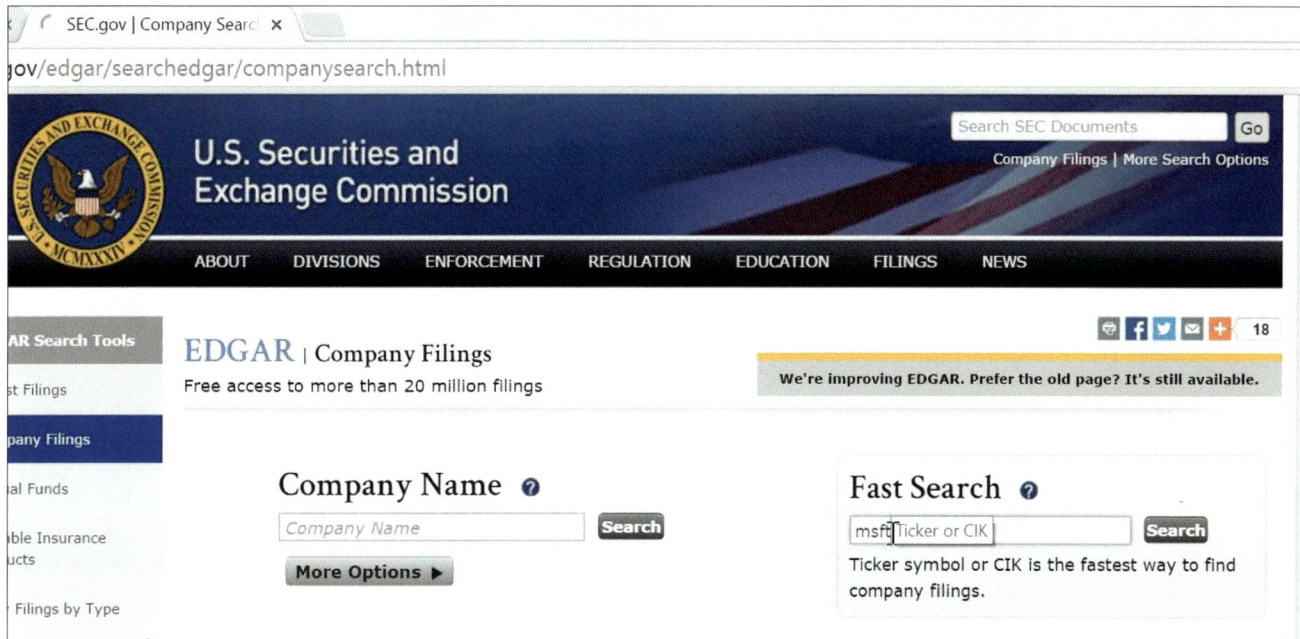
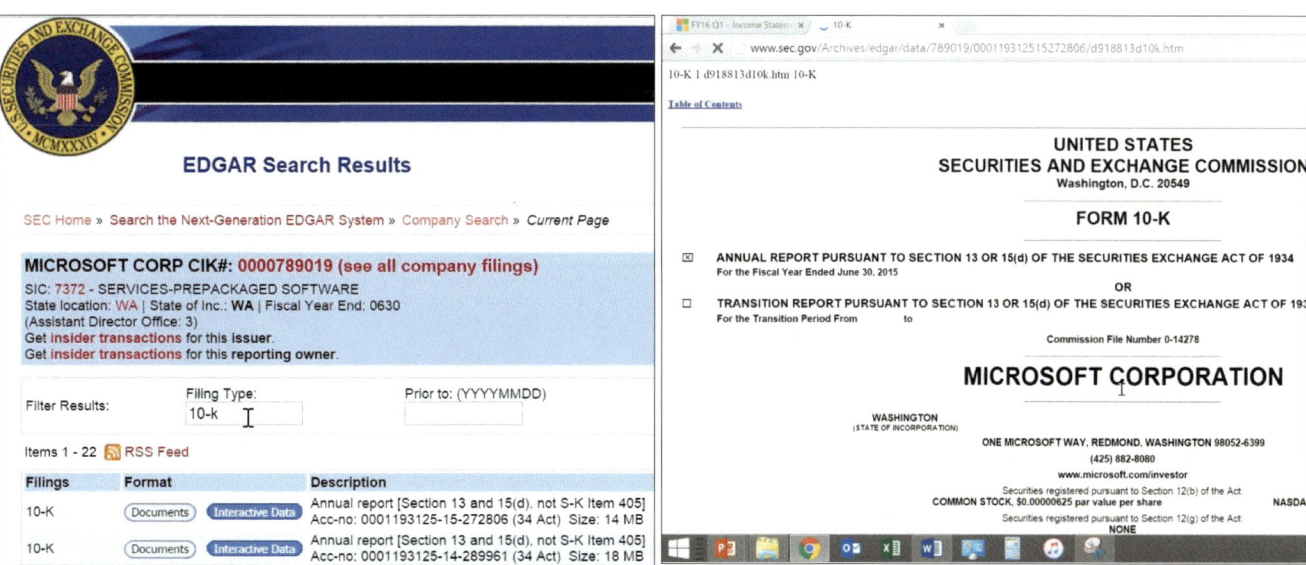

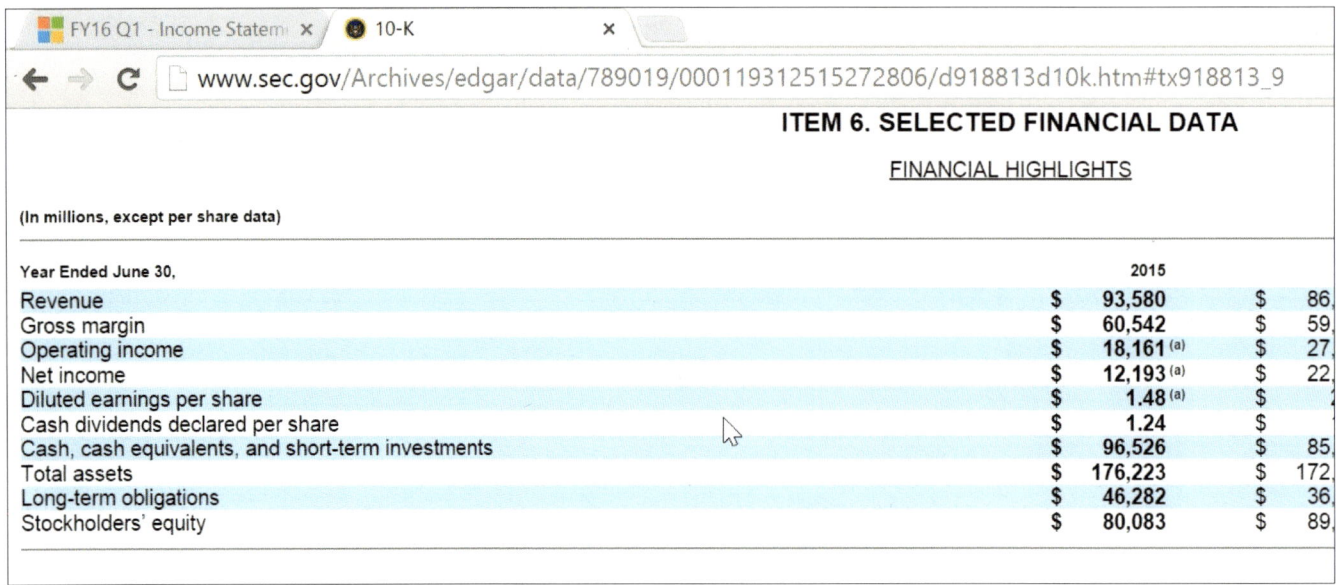

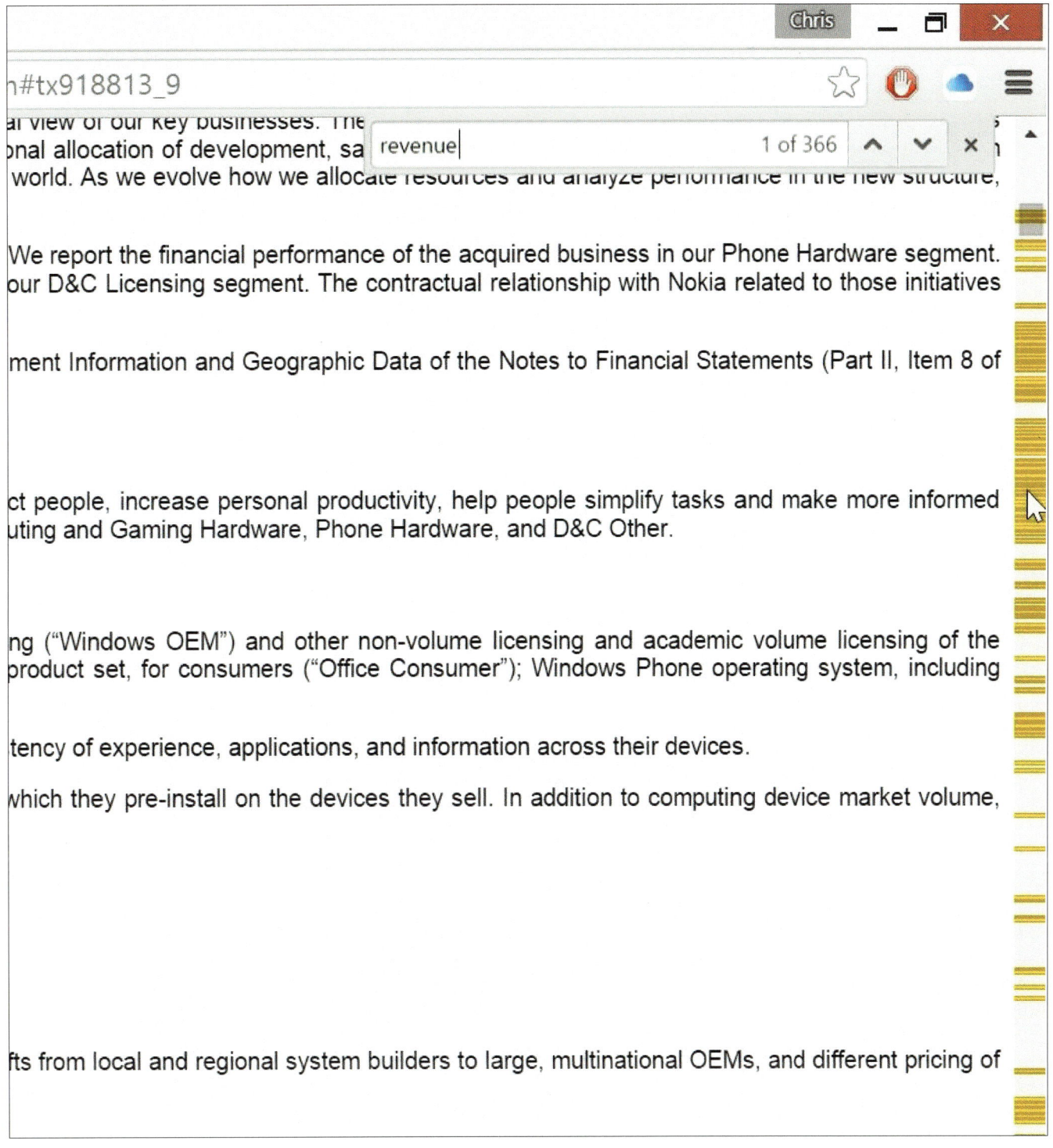

If you hit control+F while in your browser and type any key word (i.e., revenue), you can see in the scroll bar in yellow all of the results in the lengthy SEC filing of the word revenue. Use the Chrome browser for this feature as it makes navigating financial statements online much more fun.

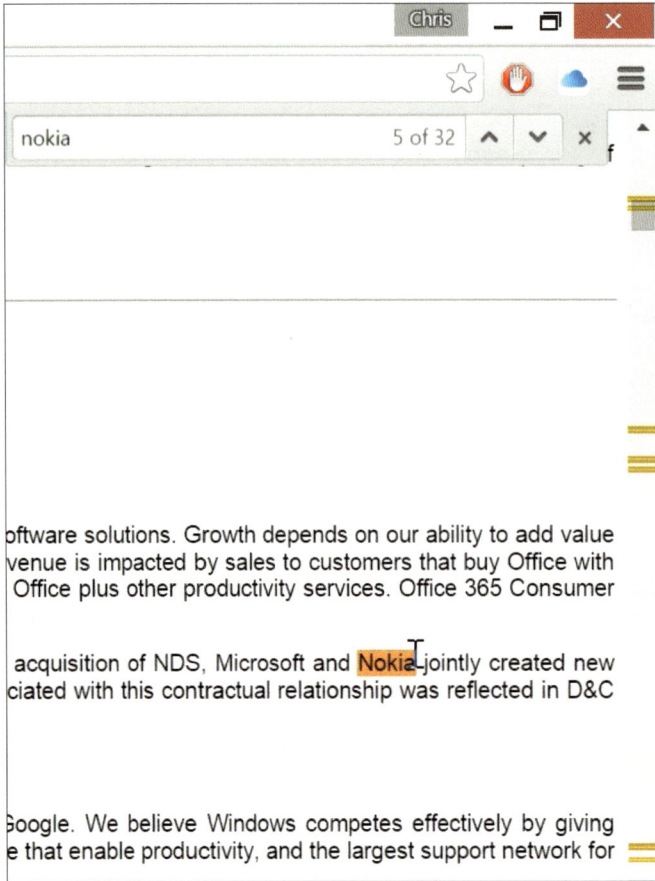

You can search the 10-k for 'Income Statement' etc..

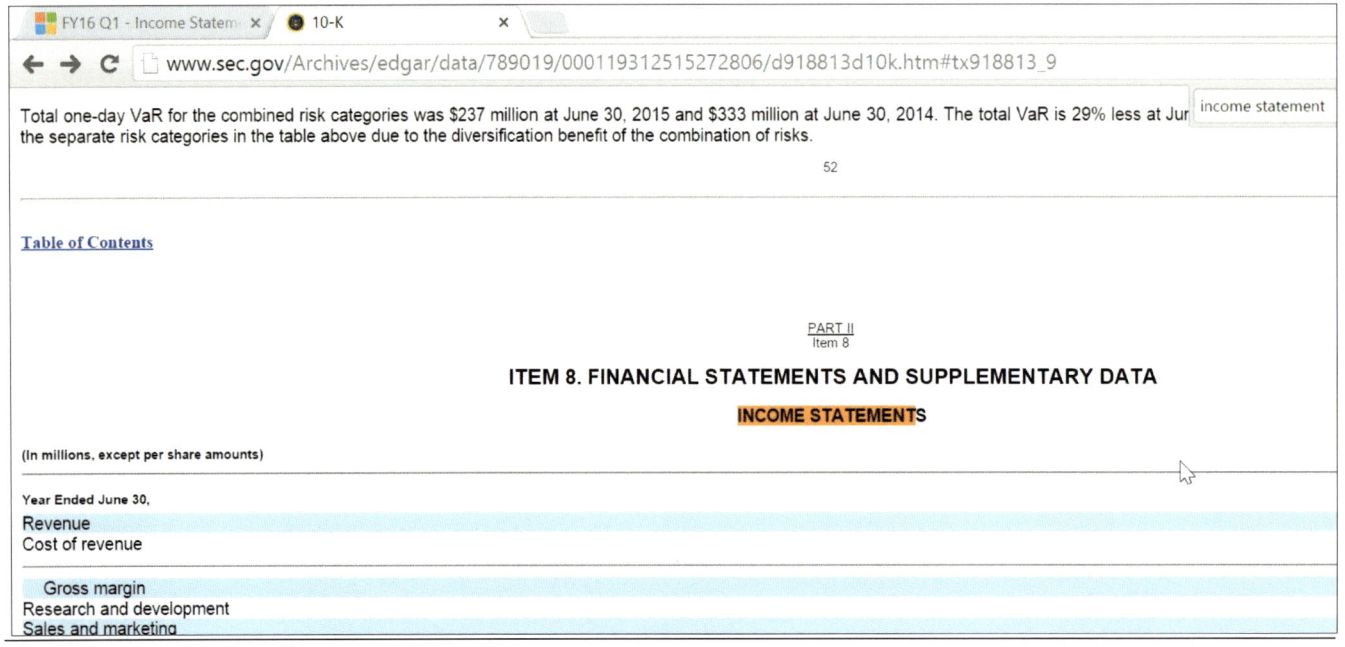

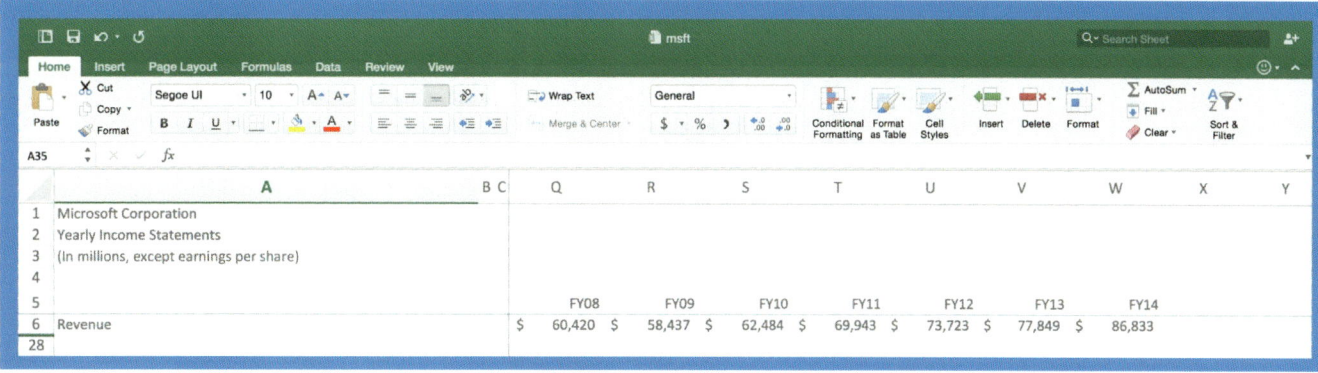

Start with revenue.

and add layers.

Home
Insert
Page Layout
Formulas
Data
Review
View
Paste
Cut
Copy
Format
Segoe UI
10
Wrap Text
Merge & Center
General
A37
fx
A
B C
Q
R
S
T
1 Microsoft Corporation
2 Yearly Income Statements
3 (In millions, except earnings per share)
4
5 FY08 FY09 FY10
6 Revenue $ 60,420 $ 58,437 $ 62,484 $
7 Cost of revenue 11,598 12,155 12,395
25

modeling is very easy...

it all comes down to
1
simple
rule

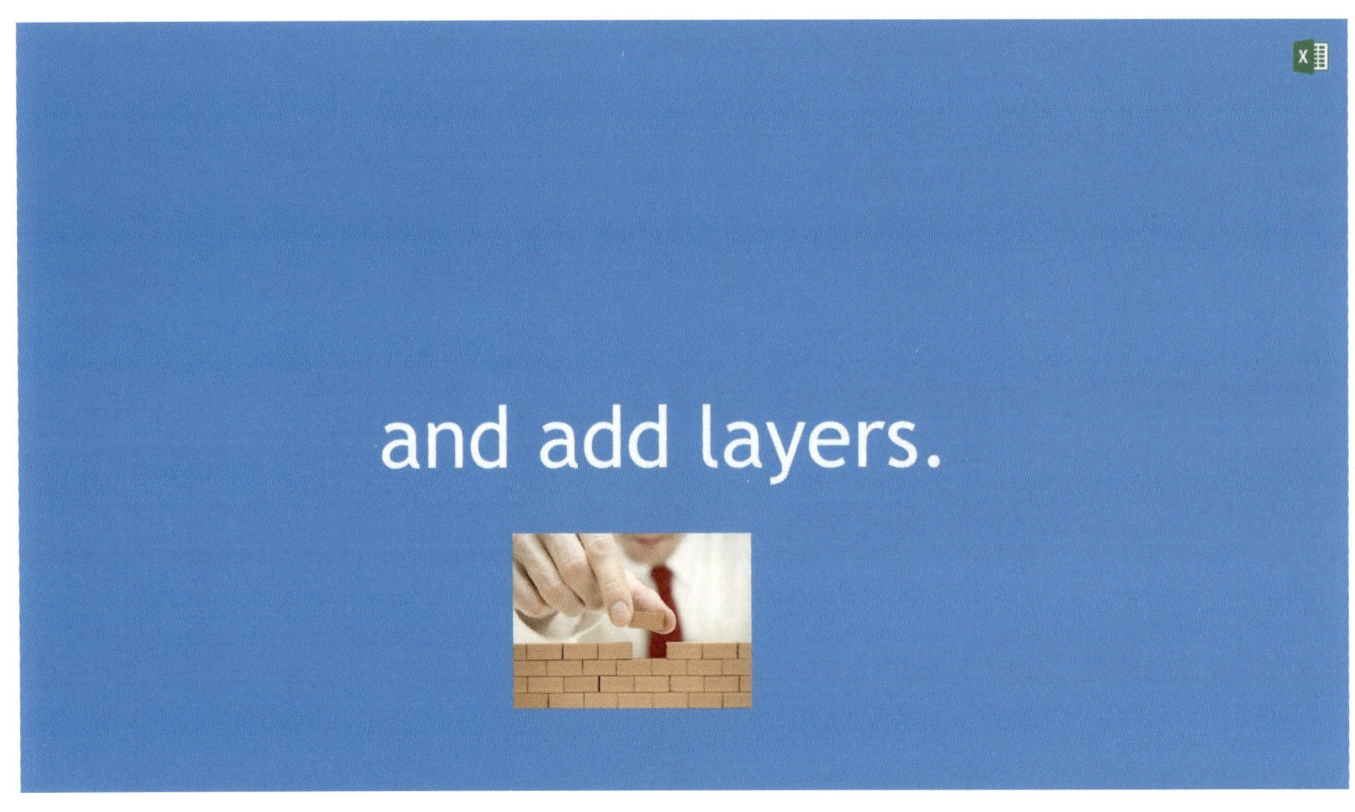

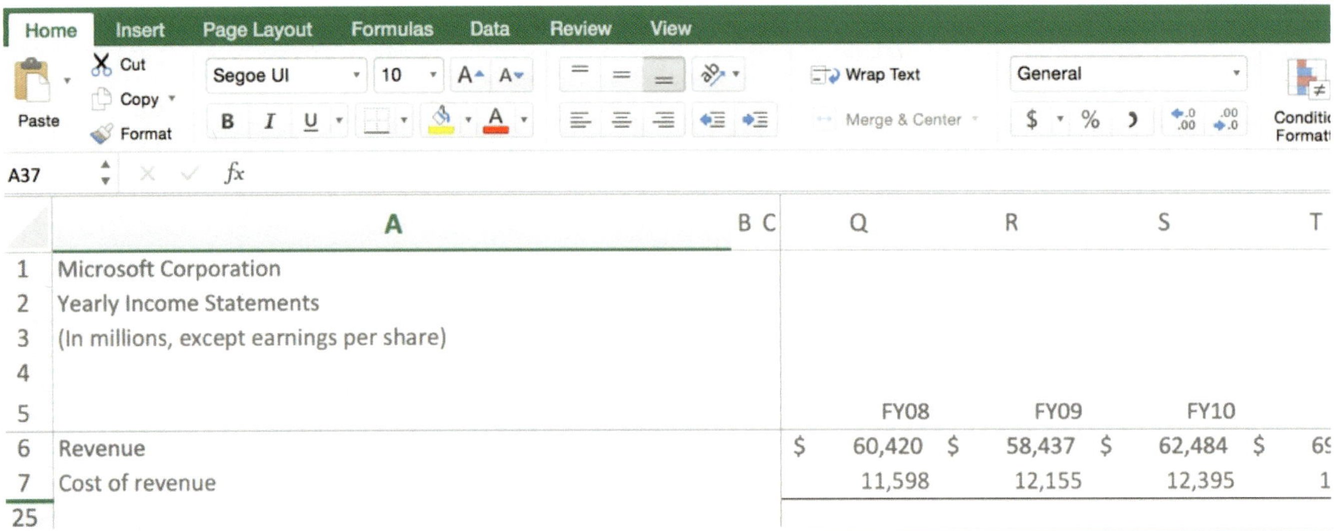

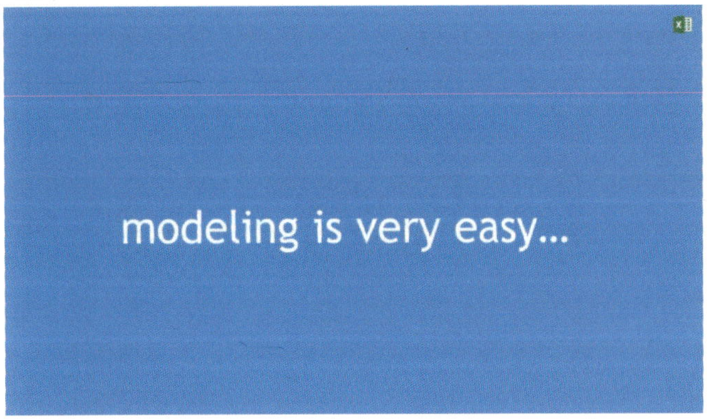

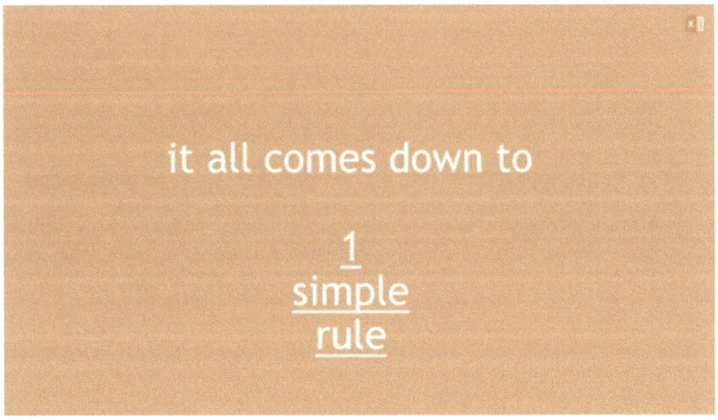

then you make basic assumptions about the future (meaning what percent of sales each line item will be and why)

this is easy!

name your revenue row

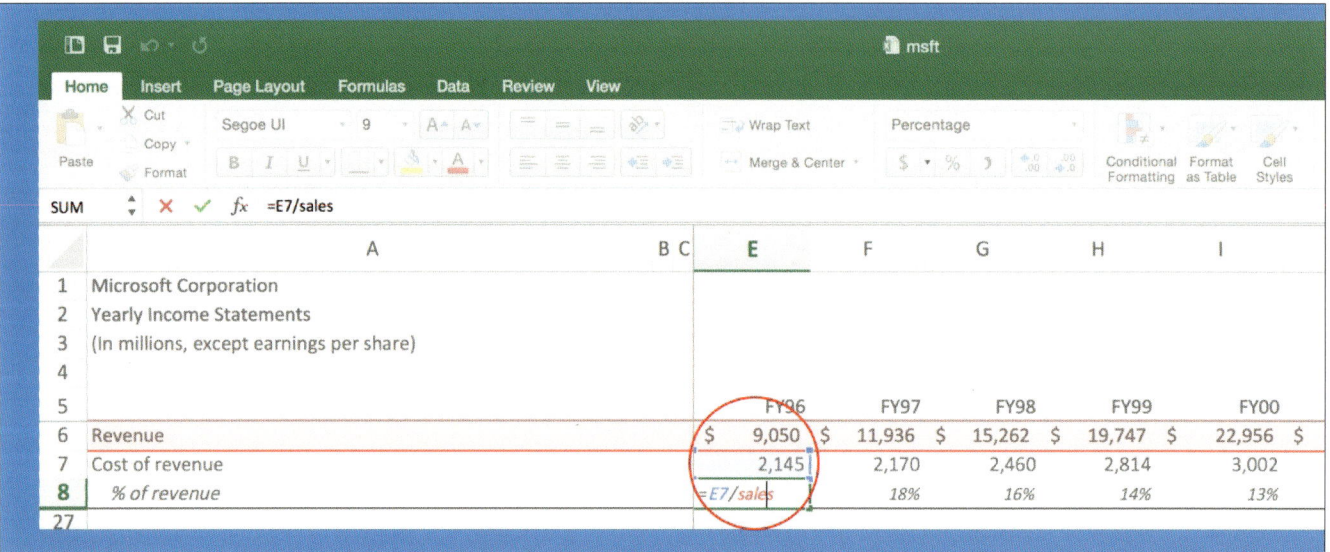

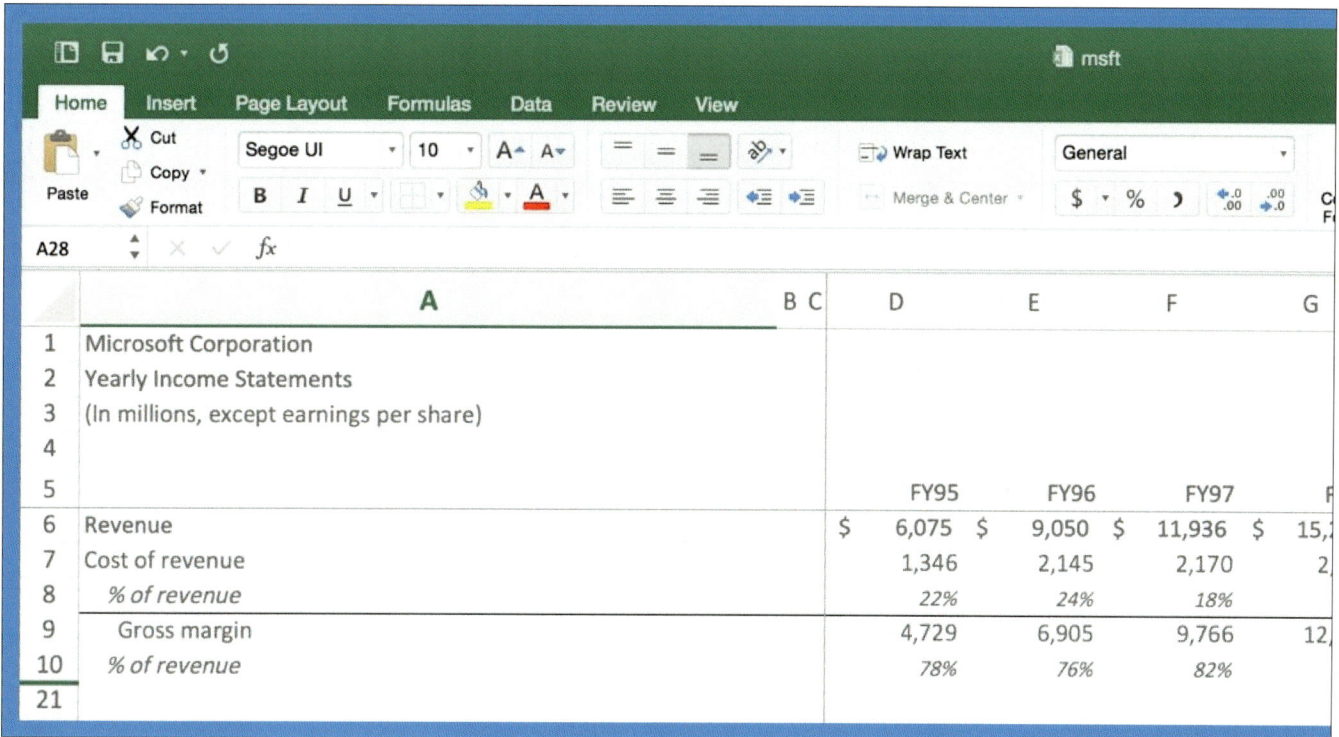

Put in operating expenses now:

Now complete the rest of the historical statement (you can get all this information online at Microsoft's investor relations site.

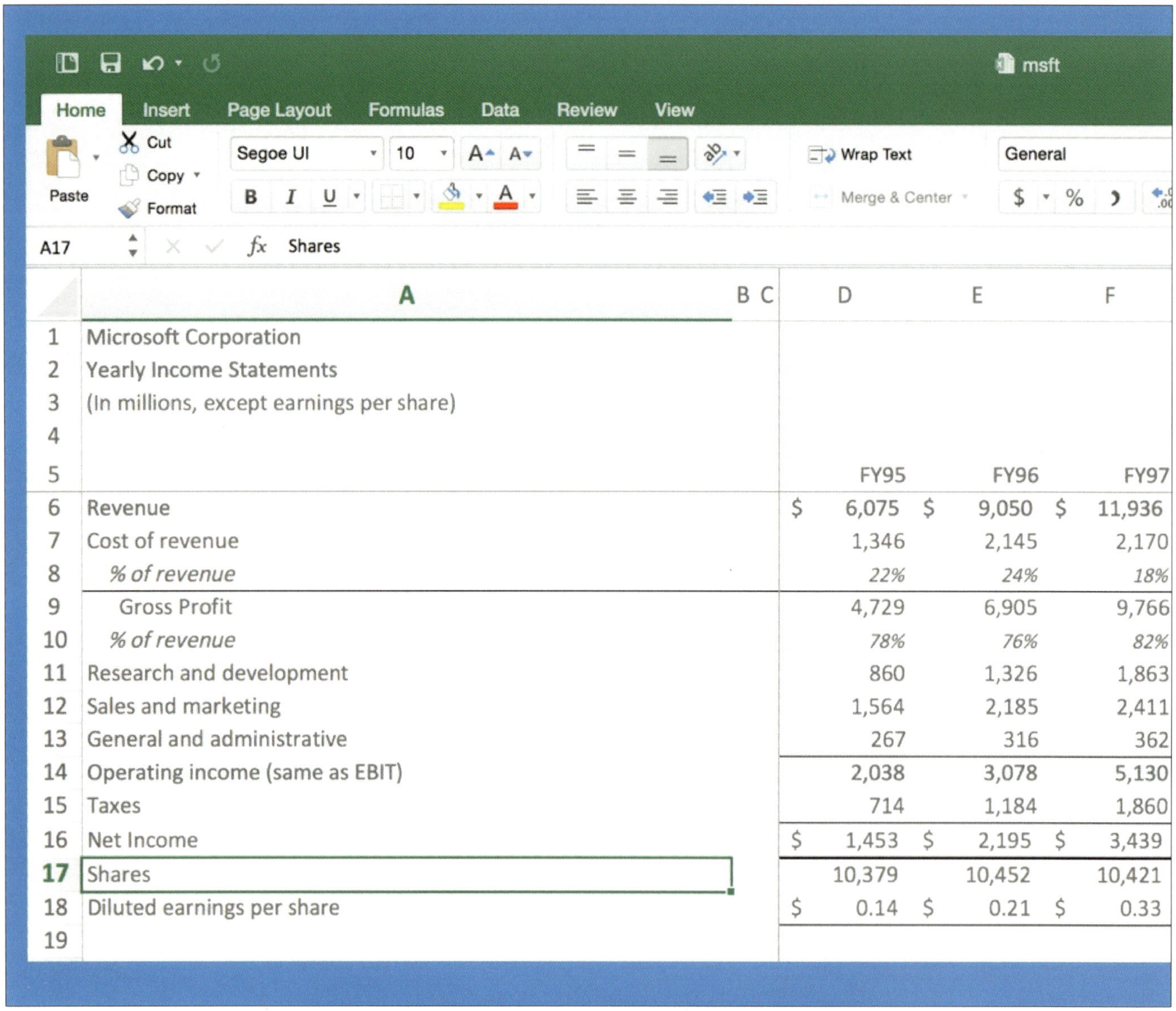

	A	B C	D	E	F
1	Microsoft Corporation				
2	Yearly Income Statements				
3	(In millions, except earnings per share)				
4					
5			FY95	FY96	FY97
6	Revenue		$ 6,075	$ 9,050	$ 11,936
7	Cost of revenue		1,346	2,145	2,170
8	% of revenue		22%	24%	18%
9	Gross Profit		4,729	6,905	9,766
10	% of revenue		78%	76%	82%
11	Research and development		860	1,326	1,863
12	Sales and marketing		1,564	2,185	2,411
13	General and administrative		267	316	362
14	Operating income (same as EBIT)		2,038	3,078	5,130
15	Taxes		714	1,184	1,860
16	Net Income		$ 1,453	$ 2,195	$ 3,439
17	Shares		10,379	10,452	10,421
18	Diluted earnings per share		$ 0.14	$ 0.21	$ 0.33
19					

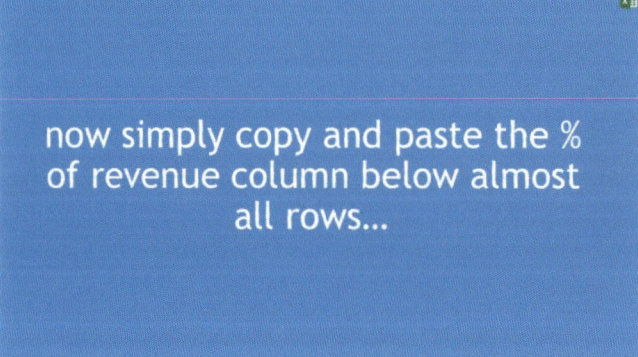

now simply copy and paste the % of revenue column below almost all rows...

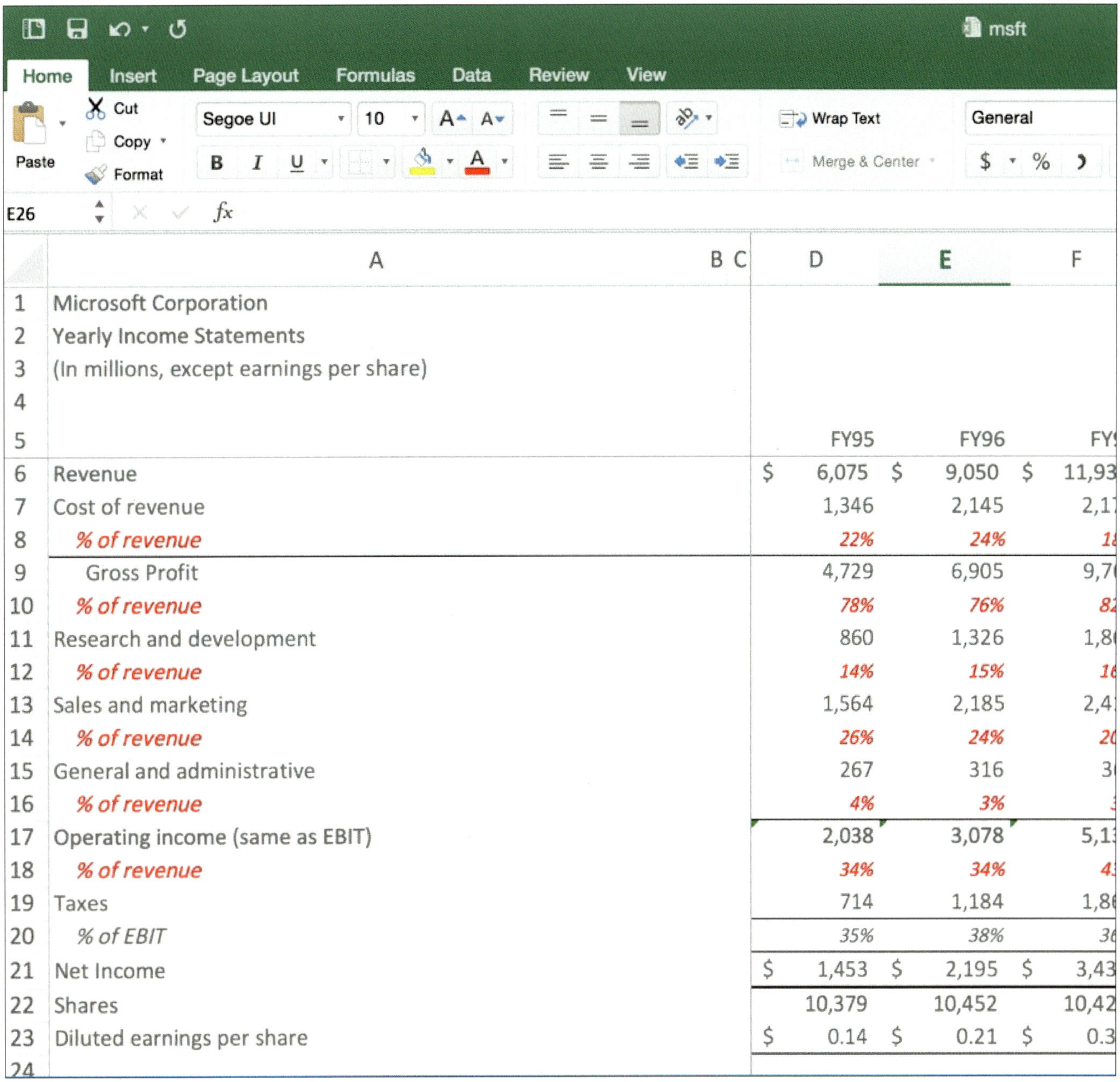

	A	B C	D	E	F
1	Microsoft Corporation				
2	Yearly Income Statements				
3	(In millions, except earnings per share)				
4					
5			FY95	FY96	FY9
6	Revenue		$ 6,075	$ 9,050	$ 11,93
7	Cost of revenue		1,346	2,145	2,1
8	*% of revenue*		*22%*	*24%*	*1*
9	Gross Profit		4,729	6,905	9,7
10	*% of revenue*		*78%*	*76%*	*8*
11	Research and development		860	1,326	1,8
12	*% of revenue*		*14%*	*15%*	*1*
13	Sales and marketing		1,564	2,185	2,4
14	*% of revenue*		*26%*	*24%*	*2*
15	General and administrative		267	316	3
16	*% of revenue*		*4%*	*3%*	
17	Operating income (same as EBIT)		2,038	3,078	5,1
18	*% of revenue*		*34%*	*34%*	*4*
19	Taxes		714	1,184	1,8
20	*% of EBIT*		*35%*	*38%*	*3*
21	Net Income		$ 1,453	$ 2,195	$ 3,43
22	Shares		10,379	10,452	10,42
23	Diluted earnings per share		$ 0.14	$ 0.21	$ 0.3
24					

let's add the YoY % change now

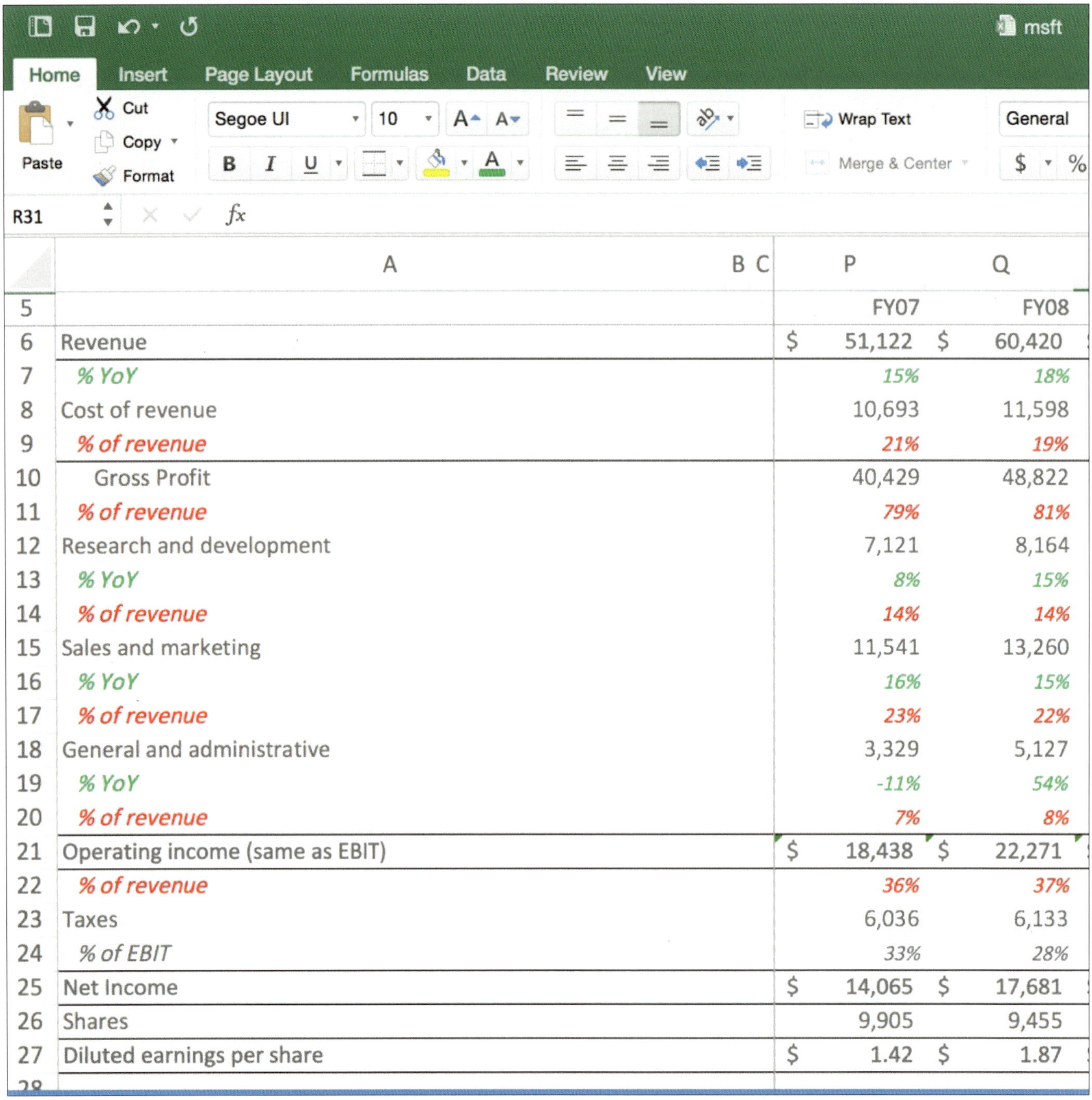

	A	B C	P	Q
5			FY07	FY08
6	Revenue		$ 51,122	$ 60,420
7	% YoY		15%	18%
8	Cost of revenue		10,693	11,598
9	% of revenue		21%	19%
10	Gross Profit		40,429	48,822
11	% of revenue		79%	81%
12	Research and development		7,121	8,164
13	% YoY		8%	15%
14	% of revenue		14%	14%
15	Sales and marketing		11,541	13,260
16	% YoY		16%	15%
17	% of revenue		23%	22%
18	General and administrative		3,329	5,127
19	% YoY		-11%	54%
20	% of revenue		7%	8%
21	Operating income (same as EBIT)		$ 18,438	$ 22,271
22	% of revenue		36%	37%
23	Taxes		6,036	6,133
24	% of EBIT		33%	28%
25	Net Income		$ 14,065	$ 17,681
26	Shares		9,905	9,455
27	Diluted earnings per share		$ 1.42	$ 1.87

isn't cash flow and earnings different?

no! they are the same in the long run!

but what about the BS, CF statement and the other confusing data they give us?

who cares!

why?

because in the very long run earnings and cash flow are the same!

but wait a minute...what about debt and cash balance?

ok...if they are HUGE then we can deduct or add them to our target valuation later....

....but they are usually not that relevant.

wait – if you aren't including a lot of other stuff in your model, then won't your target price be wrong?

no! it might be a few percent off but who cares...it's only a few percent.

close enough is good enough. you have a 1 in a 1,000,000 chance of predicting the exact target price...

Yep; a 1 in a million chance....

www.tiny.cc/chris82

Make sure you see the forest from the trees!!!

back to the model...getting there

ok we have everything we need to make forecasts now!

assume we are at the start of 2015 for this exercise

A	B C	T	U	V	W	X
		FY11	FY12	FY13	FY14	FY15e
Revenue		$ 69,943	$ 73,723	$ 77,849	$ 86,833	
% YoY		*12%*	*5%*	*6%*	*12%*	
Cost of revenue		15,577	17,530	20,249	27,078	
% of revenue		*22%*	*24%*	*26%*	*31%*	
Gross Profit		54,366	56,193	57,600	59,755	
% of revenue		*78%*	*76%*	*74%*	*69%*	
Research and development		9,043	9,811	10,411	11,381	
% YoY		*4%*	*8%*	*6%*	*9%*	
% of revenue		*13%*	*13%*	*13%*	*13%*	
Sales and marketing		13,940	13,857	15,276	15,811	
% YoY		*5%*	*-1%*	*10%*	*4%*	
% of revenue		*20%*	*19%*	*20%*	*18%*	
General and administrative		4,222	4,569	5,149	4,677	
% YoY		*4%*	*8%*	*13%*	*-9%*	
% of revenue		*6%*	*6%*	*7%*	*5%*	
Operating income (same as EBIT)		$ 27,161	$ 27,956	$ 26,764	$ 27,886	
% of revenue		*39%*	*38%*	*34%*	*32%*	
Taxes		4,921	5,289	5,189	5,746	
% of EBIT		*18%*	*19%*	*19%*	*21%*	
Net Income		$ 23,150	$ 16,978	$ 21,863	$ 22,074	
Shares		8,606	8,489	8,474	8,393	
Diluted earnings per share		$ 2.69	$ 2.00	$ 2.58	$ 2.63	

wait! I want to add more detail on revenue to my model...

....because msft provides us with revenue line items for each part of the company (consumer, xbox, companies, crappy nokia etc).

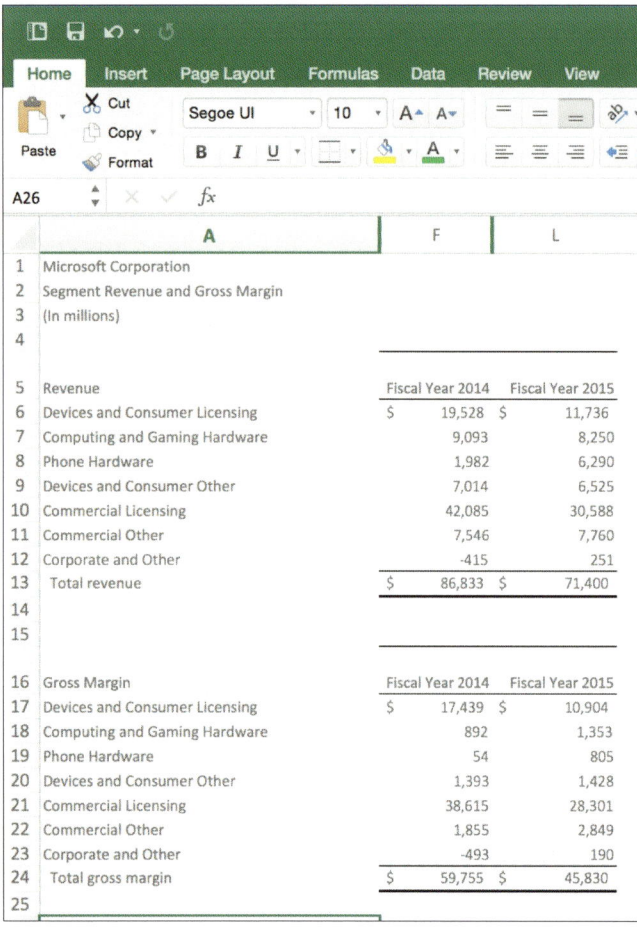

we can add this too..

copy + paste the historicals into your spreadsheet.

but let's not do this as it will take too much time for today's session.

before we make forecasts, let's look for trends in the data

learn to *enjoy* reading financials like a good

understand why revenue grew or contracted.

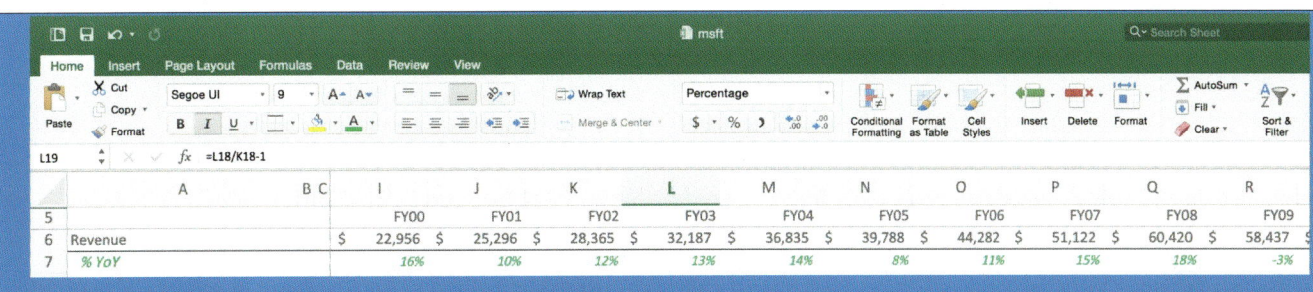

why did revenue growth slow in 2001 and 2009?

The answer because of two horrific recessions. Look for patterns in the data. Look for trends.

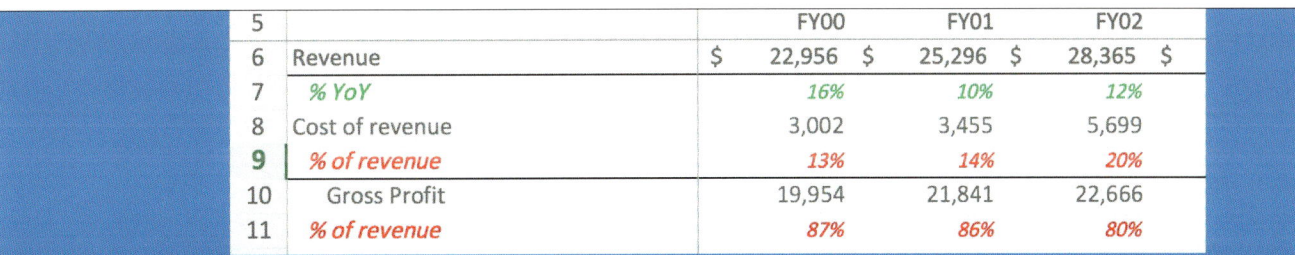

why did gross profit % decline as a percent of revenue?

This occurred because of the release of the first Xbox. Hardware margins suck compared to software margins.

check out the share count:

		FY97	FY98	FY99	FY00	FY01	FY02
5							
6	Revenue	$11,936	$15,262	$19,747	$22,956	$25,296	$28,365
7	% YoY	32%	28%	29%	16%	10%	12%
26	Shares	10,421	10,624	10,925	11,068	11,130	11,156

		FY08	FY09	FY10	FY11	FY12	FY13	FY14
5								
6	Revenue	$60,420	$58,437	$62,484	$69,943	$73,723	$77,849	$86,833
7	% YoY	18%	-3%	7%	12%	5%	6%	12%
26	Shares	9,455	8,993	8,933	8,606	8,489	8,474	8,393

what patterns do you see?

Microsoft started buying back a lot of shares!

ok let's forecast revenue

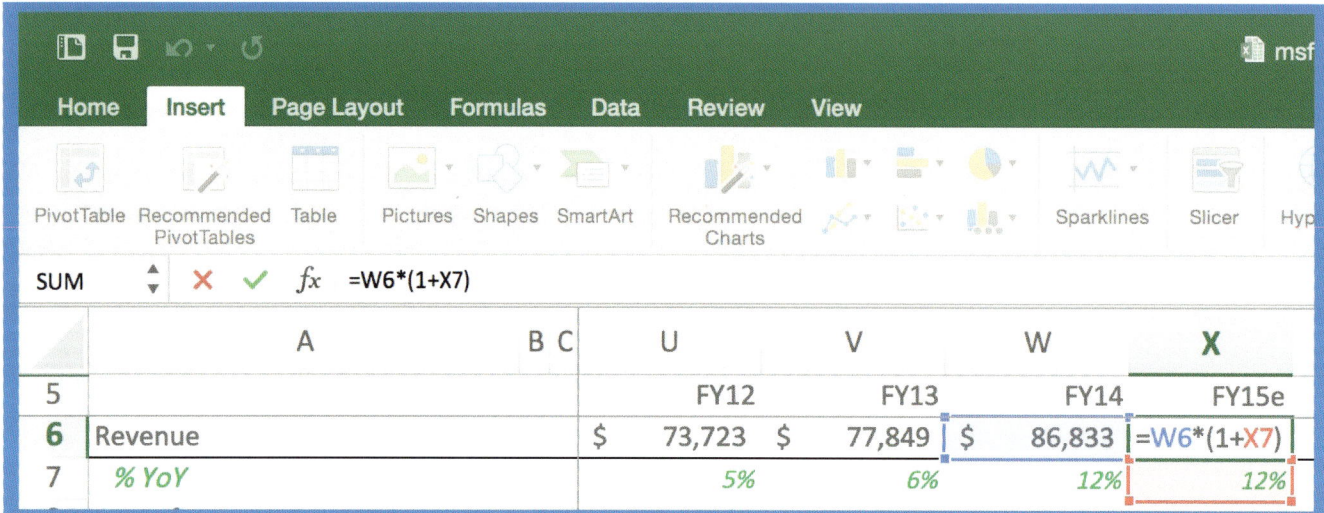

add assumptions (i.e., why the forecasted number)...

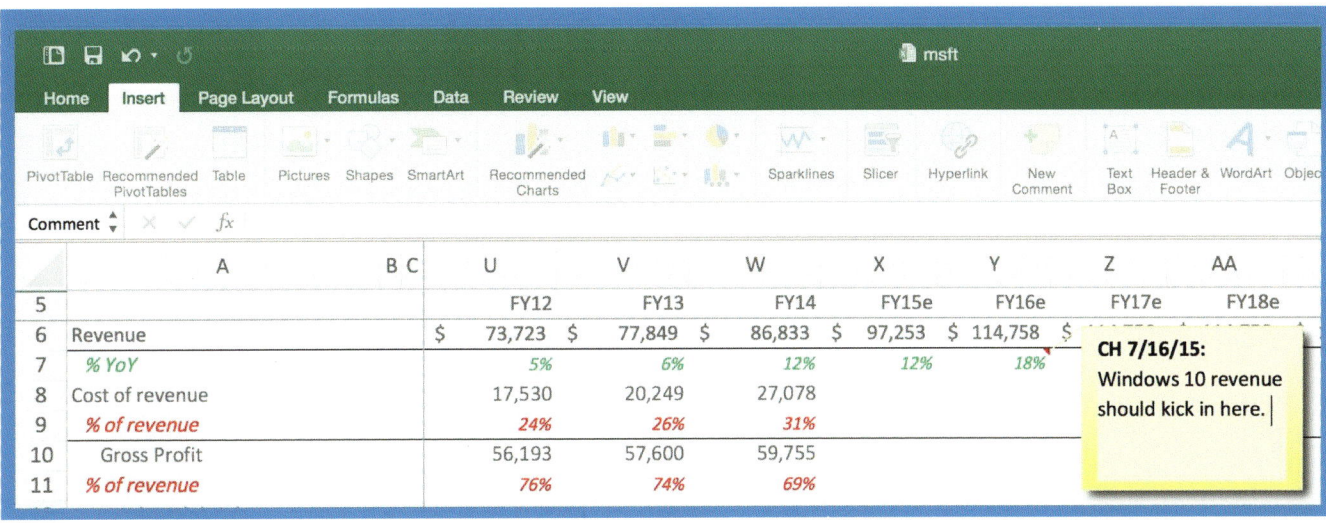

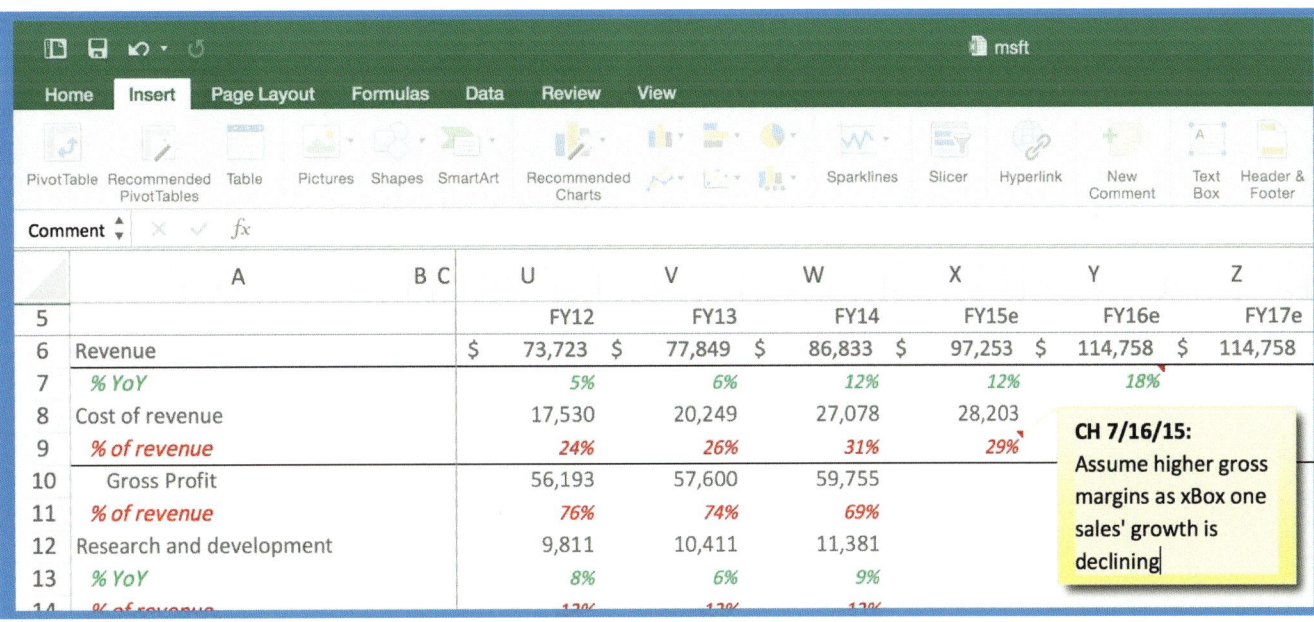

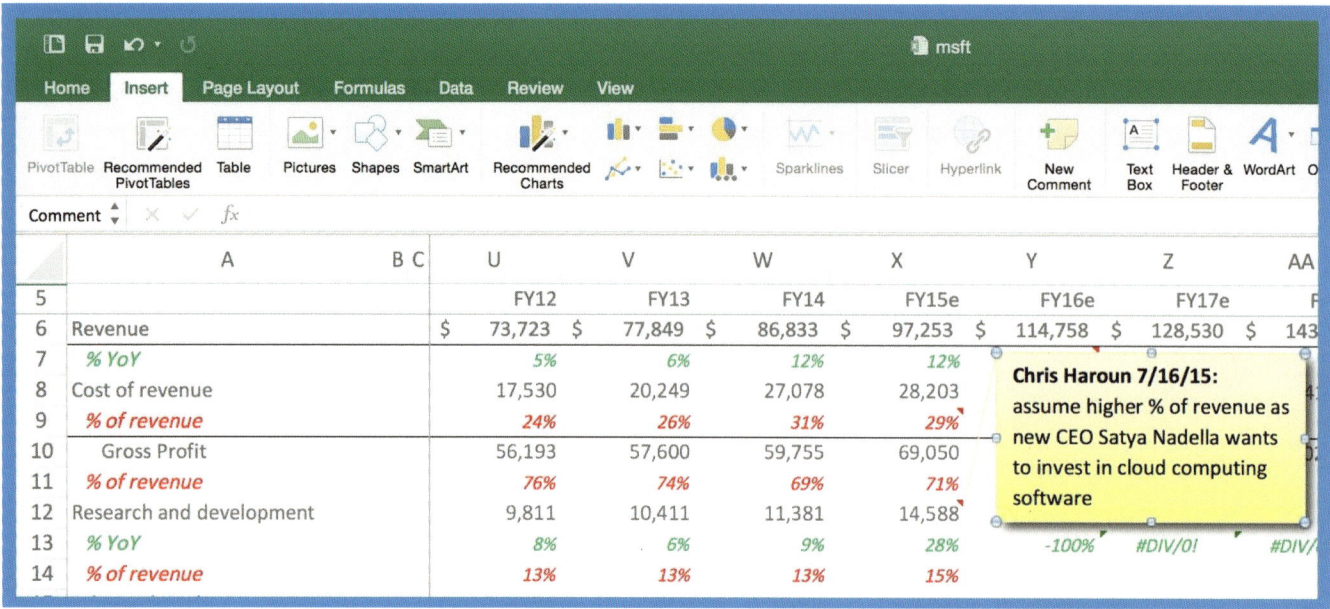

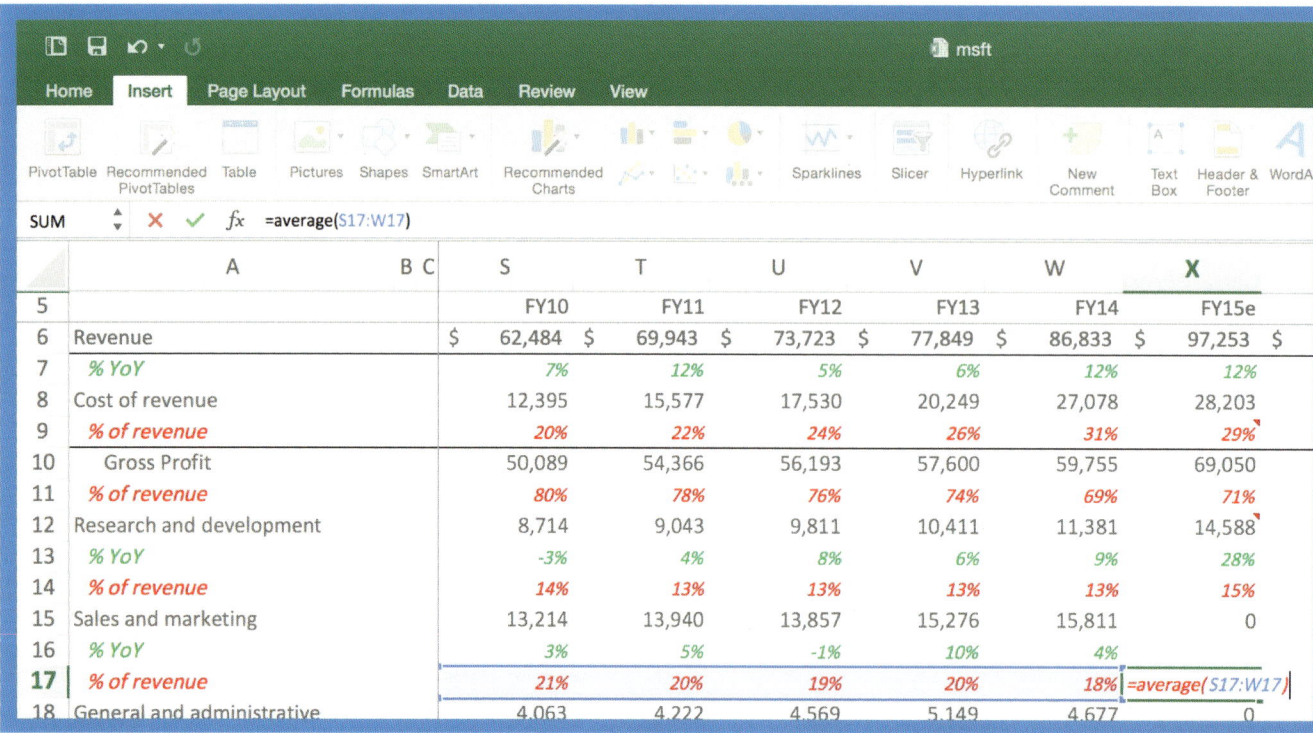

If you have no clue on how to forecast a certain expense line item, then start with taking an average of all prior percents of revenue (per the previous image)!

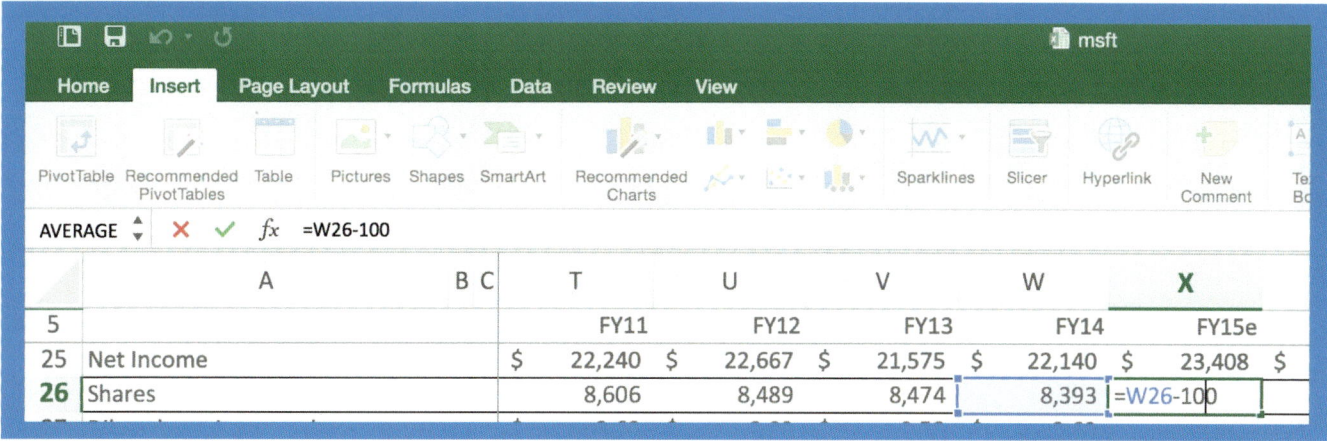

Look for patterns....an object in motion will stay in motion...oki dokki in this case it looks like Microsoft is buying back about 100,000,000 shares per year. Wow!

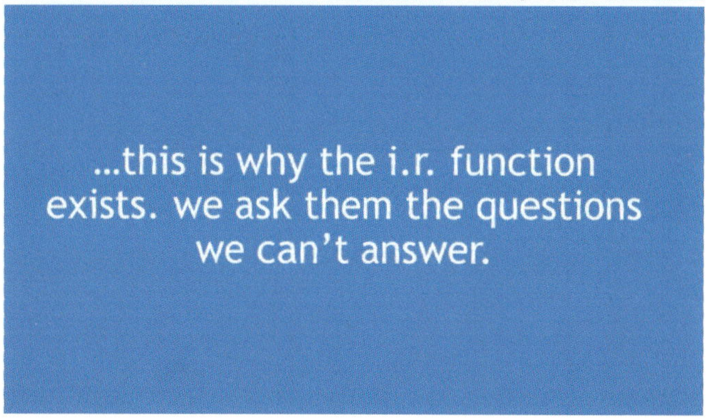

we are done with the model!

that was easy

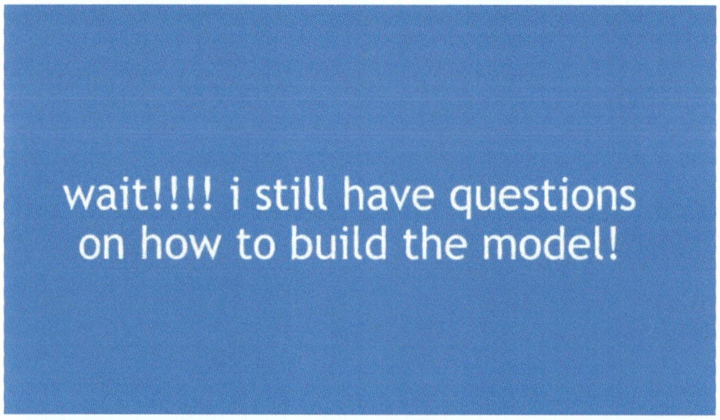

wait!!!! i still have questions on how to build the model!

ok...read the 10k and look at their website and listen to the saved earnings calls on the ir website....

...help – i did all of that stuff but i still have questions!

...this is why the i.r. function exists. we ask them the questions we can't answer.

call i.r. as it's their job to help you

why call management towards the end of your due diligence?

because CEOs and CFOs are the best salespeople in the world...

...do your own research before calling them or listening to anyone (especially the media)!

everyone has their own bias...

http://tiny.cc/chris110

capiche?

don't be intimidated by financial modelling.

you have the same info access as wall street analysts.

reg fd.

modeling and valuation is **very easy** to do.

next topic:

valuation

	FY19e	FY20e	FY21e	FY22e	FY23e	FY24e	Assumptions
Revenue	$ 161,227	$ 180,575	$ 202,244	$ 226,513	$ 253,694	$ 284,138	you can list revenue assumptions here too
% YoY	*12%*	*12%*	*12%*	*12%*	*12%*	*12%*	
Cost of revenue	46,756	52,367	58,651	63,424	68,498	73,876	
% of revenue	*29%*	*29%*	*29%*	*28%*	*27%*	*26%*	
Gross Profit	114,471	128,208	143,593	163,089	185,197	210,262	
% of revenue	*71%*	*71%*	*71%*	*72%*	*73%*	*74%*	
Research and development	20,960	23,475	26,292	29,447	32,980	36,938	you can list r&d assumptions here too
% YoY	*4%*	*12%*	*12%*	*12%*	*12%*	*12%*	
% of revenue	*13%*	*13%*	*13%*	*13%*	*13%*	*13%*	
Sales and marketing	27,409	28,892	32,359	36,242	40,591	45,462	you can list s&m assumptions here too
% YoY	*6%*	*5%*	*12%*	*12%*	*12%*	*12%*	
% of revenue	*17%*	*16%*	*16%*	*16%*	*16%*	*16%*	
General and administrative	8,061	9,029	10,112	11,326	12,685	11,366	you can list g&a assumptions here too
% YoY	*12%*	*12%*	*12%*	*12%*	*12%*	*-10%*	
% of revenue	*5%*	*5%*	*5%*	*5%*	*5%*	*4%*	
Operating income (same as EBIT)	$ 58,042	$ 66,813	$ 74,830	$ 86,075	$ 98,941	$ 116,496	
% of revenue	*36%*	*37%*	*37%*	*38%*	*39%*	*41%*	
Taxes	11,668	13,365	14,880	17,177	19,775	23,284	you can list tax assumptions here too
% of EBIT	*20%*	*20%*	*20%*	*20%*	*20%*	*20%*	
Net Income	$ 46,373	$ 53,448	$ 59,951	$ 68,898	$ 79,166	$ 93,213	
Shares	7,893	7,793	7,693	7,593	7,493	7,393	you can list shares assumptions here too
Diluted earnings per share	$ 5.88	$ 6.86	$ 7.79	$ 9.07	$ 10.57	$ 12.61	

Don't forget to add many comments…which you can also do in an assumptions column.

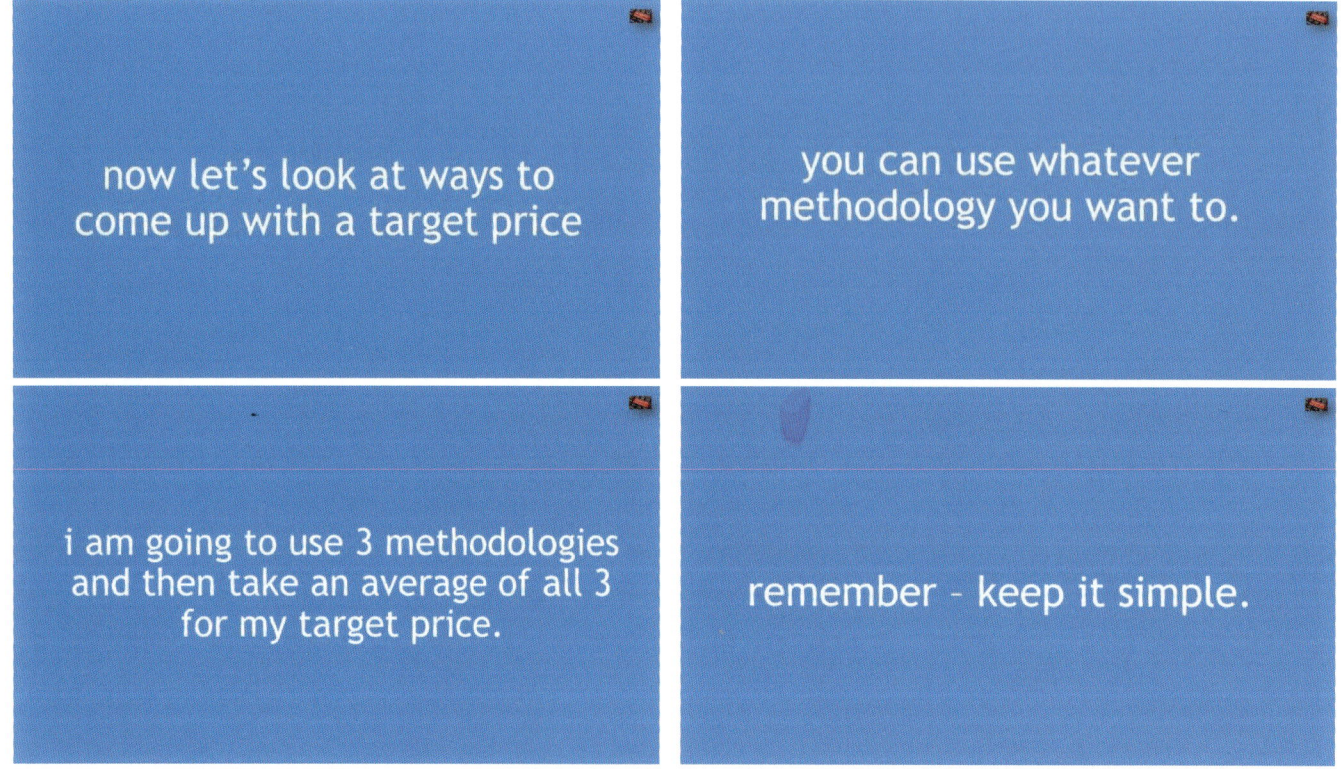

valuation methodology # 1

p/e

your target price should be based on estimates 5 year from now.

in 5 years earnings are growing 12%

so our target price should be 12x's that eps number.

Stocks usually trade near their earnings growth rate. Huh? Well if a company's earnings are growing 20% next year, then the stock should trade at about 20x's that year's earnings at that point in time. If a ocmpany is growing at 8% earnings, then the stock should trade at about 8x's that earnings number that year. Simple enough eh!

A	B C	Z	AA
		FY19e	FY20e
Diluted earnings per share		$ 3.93	$ 4.90
			YoY EPS %: 12%

12 x $4.90 = $59

assume msft is $47 today.

in 5 years we expect 25% appreciation to $59.

seems reasonable as msft is a mature company.

valuation methodology #2: p/r

assuming the average software company trades at 5x revenue in 5 years….

and msft is a big mature company with 70% of the growth of the average software company.

therefore it should trade at a discount at say 3.5x revenue in 5 years (versus sector at 5x).

so the market cap should be $504bn in 5 years.

the market cap is $372 today. so this means about 35% upside.

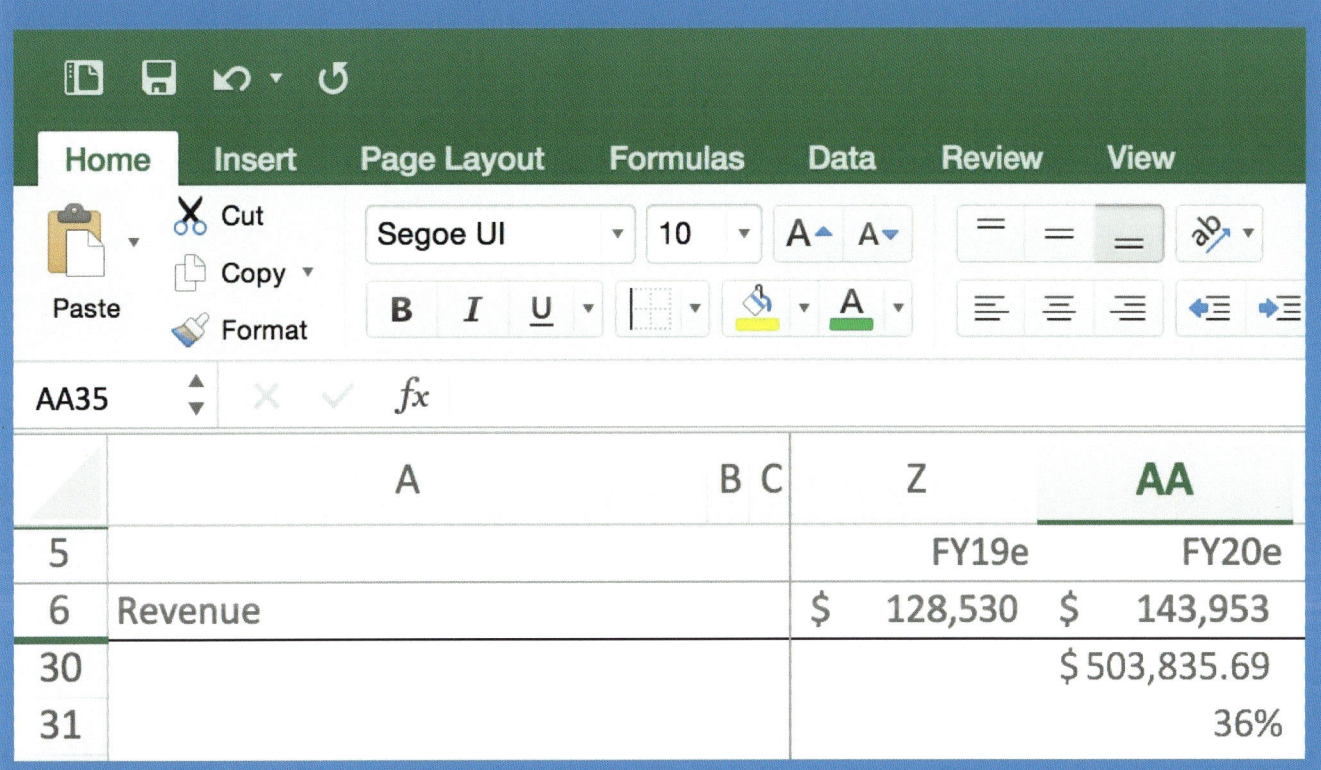

recall valuation methodology #1 predicted 25% upside

now let's do valuation methodology #3 and take an average of all 3 approaches.

dcf

[not an exact science...and i am not a fan...but let's do it anyway]

but let's look at an important pie chart first

i'm going to make dcf easy.

I know I know I know. Not funny!

earnings and cash flow are the same in the long run

great! so we don't need to forecast the bs or the cf statements!

A	B	C	X	Y	Z
			FY15e	FY16e	FY17e
Revenue			$ 97,253	$ 114,758	$ 128,530
% YoY			*12%*	*18%*	*12%*
Cost of revenue			28,203	33,280	37,274
% of revenue			*29%*	*29%*	*29%*
Gross Profit			69,050	81,479	91,256
% of revenue			*71%*	*71%*	*71%*
Research and development			14,588	17,214	19,279
% YoY			*28%*	*18%*	*12%*
% of revenue			*15%*	*15%*	*15%*
Sales and marketing			19,004	22,056	24,520
% YoY			*20%*	*16%*	*11%*
% of revenue			*20%*	*19%*	*19%*
General and administrative			5,978	6,973	7,820
% YoY			*28%*	*17%*	*12%*
% of revenue			*6%*	*6%*	*6%*
Operating income (same as EBIT)			$ 29,479	$ 35,235	$ 39,636
% of revenue			*30%*	*31%*	*31%*
Taxes			6,071	6,880	7,851
% of EBIT			*21%*	*20%*	*20%*
Net Income [SAME AS FREE CASH FLOW]			$ 23,408	$ 28,356	$ 31,786
Shares			8,293	8,193	8,093
Diluted earnings per share			$ 2.82	$ 3.46	$ 3.93

A	B	C	X	Y	Z
			FY15e	FY16e	FY17e
Revenue			$ 97,253	$ 114,758	$ 128,530
% YoY			*12%*	*18%*	*12%*
Cost of revenue			28,203	33,280	37,274
% of revenue			*29%*	*29%*	*29%*
Gross Profit			69,050	81,479	91,256
% of revenue			*71%*	*71%*	*71%*
Research and development			14,588	17,214	19,279
% YoY			*28%*	*18%*	*12%*
% of revenue			*15%*	*15%*	*15%*
Sales and marketing			19,004	22,056	24,520
% YoY			*20%*	*16%*	*11%*
% of revenue			*20%*	*19%*	*19%*
General and administrative			5,978	6,973	7,820
% YoY			*28%*	*17%*	*12%*
% of revenue			*6%*	*6%*	*6%*
Operating income (same as EBIT)			$ 29,479	$ 35,235	$ 39,636
% of revenue			*30%*	*31%*	*31%*
Taxes			6,071	6,880	7,851
Net Income [SAME AS FREE CASH FLOW]			$ 23,408	$ 28,356	$ 31,786
Diluted earnings per share			$ 2.82	$ 3.46	$ 3.93

ok. so let's now come up with the wacc!

The WACC stands for the weighted average cost of capital….basically what is the cost of renting money for Microsoft. Note: it will be a heck of a lot less than for a private company as Microsoft is pretty stable. We then use the WACC to find out what Microsoft's future net income or cash flow is worth today (rember that a dollar in the future is worth a heck of a lot less than it is worth today…..the trick is to find the right WACC to discount future net income or cash flow to today).

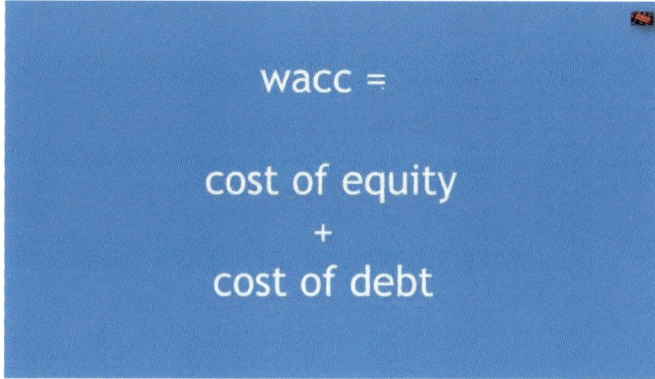
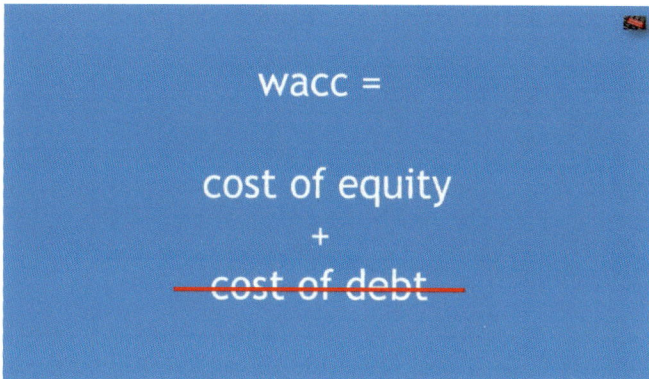

Rmember tech firms don't usually have much debt. If they have some then deduct the debt from your target market capitalization (after accounting for the cash balance)…..I know that this is not an exact science but it is close enough for government work! With Microsoft I am bearish on the company longer term as the founders don't run the company any more so I will just assume that growth will be anemic and they will use their cash balance to keep buying back shares.

cost of equity =

risk free rate

+

(stock market return - risk free rate)

*

beta (how volatile our company is)

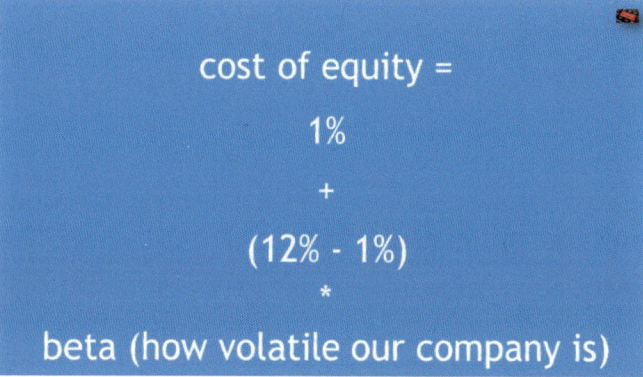

Let's just assume that the stock market goes up about 12% per year. Microsoft is likely to grow slower than the stock market in the long run and it is likely less volatile as it is a stable old company….so I expect the beta to be less than 1. The market's beta or volatility is 1. Your stock is either more volatile (meaning higher beta and riskier) or less volatile than the market (meaning lower beta and less risky than the market).

what is our beta?

You can find a company's beta at Yahoo Finance or any good finance website. In fact, I used to pay $25k per year for Bloomberg's financial data system when I was running my company but I ditched Bloomberg because you can get almost everything that Bloomberg provides online now for free!

finance.yahoo.com
Home
Mail
Search
News
Sports
Finance
Weather
Games
YAHOO!
FINANCE
Microsoft Corporation (MSFT) - NasdaqGS
Watchlist
46.66 0.90(1.97%) 4:00PM EDT
After Hours : 46.86 0.20 (0.43%) 7:59PM EDT
Prev Close: 45.76
Open: 46.01
Bid: 46.80 x 200
Ask: 48.00 x 1200
1y Target Est: 50.13
Beta: 0.78
Next Earnings Date: 21-Jul-15
Day's Range: 45.97 - 46.69
52wk Range: 40.12 - 50.05
Volume: 26,271,673
Avg Vol (3m): 34,249,200
Market Cap: 378.55B
P/E (ttm): 19.37
EPS (ttm): 2.41
Div & Yield: 1.24 (2.70%)
Quotes delayed, except where indicated otherwise. Currency in USD.

cost of equity =
1%
+
(12% - 1%)
*
0.78

cost of equity =
9.58%

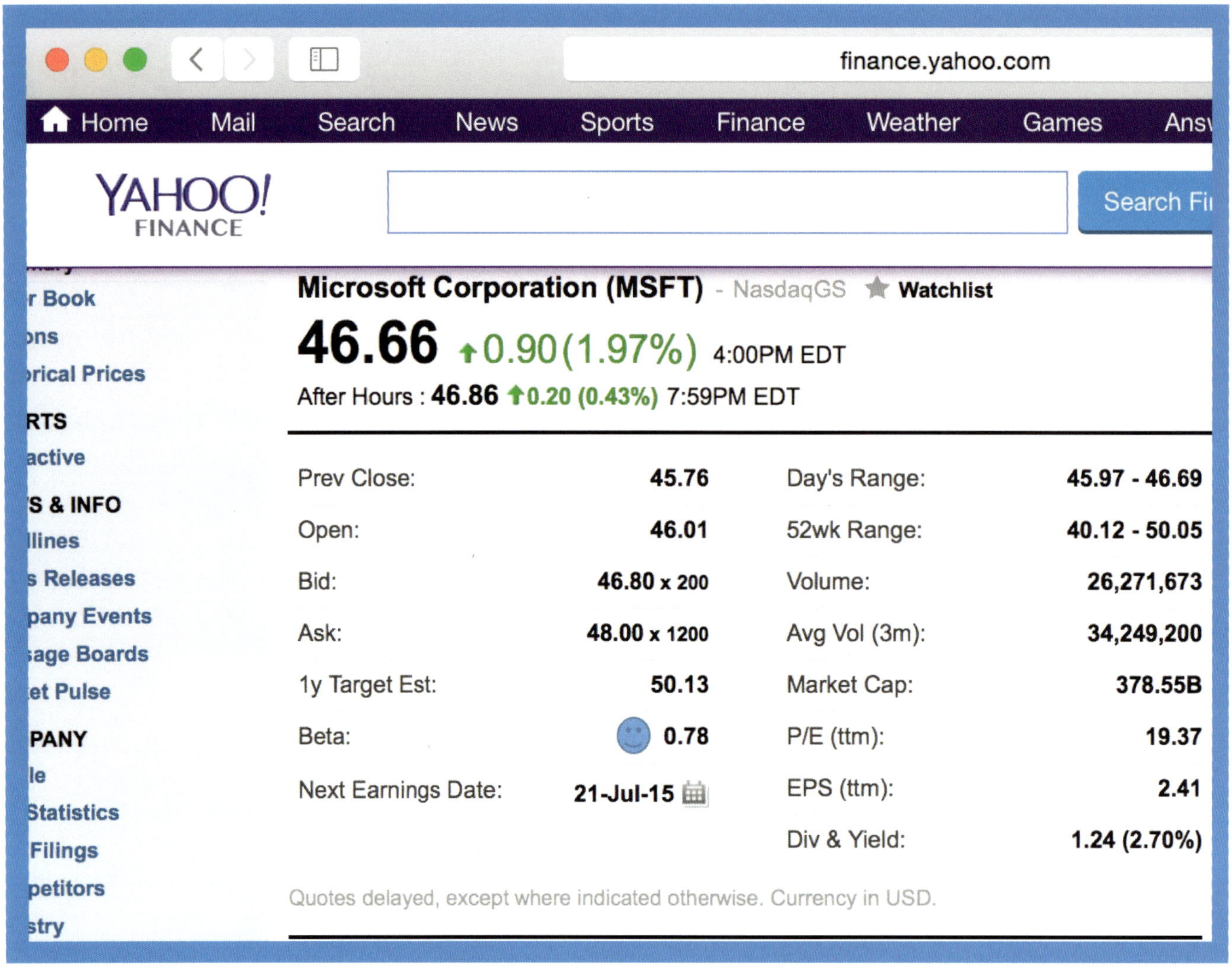

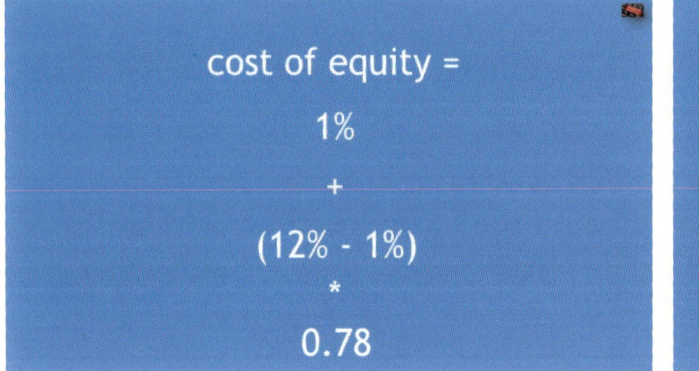

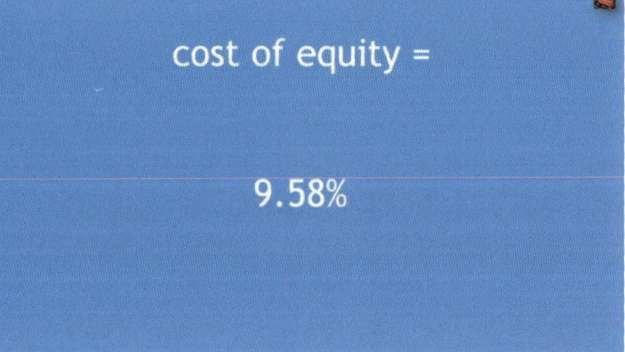

we use 9.58% as our discount rate = "r"

Alright now we need to discount our future net income to today's value. We discount next year's earnings by 1 year. We discount the following year's earnings by 2 years. We discount the year after that's earnings by 3 years......all the way up to 10 years from now per the discounted cash flow formula on the right →.

What about years 2025 to infinity? Don't worry about it...see the first image on the next page for calculating cash flow from years 2025 to infinity!

http://tiny.cc/chris112

$$dcf =$$
$$cf2015e/(1+r)^1 +$$
$$cf2016e/(1+r)^2 +$$
$$cf2017e/(1+r)^3 +$$
$$cf2018e/(1+r)^4 +$$
$$cf2019e/(1+r)^5 +$$
$$cf2020e/(1+r)^6 +$$
$$cf2021e/(1+r)^7 +$$
$$cf2022e/(1+r)^8 +$$
$$cf2023e/(1+r)^9 +$$
$$(cf2024e + tv)/(1+r)^{10}$$

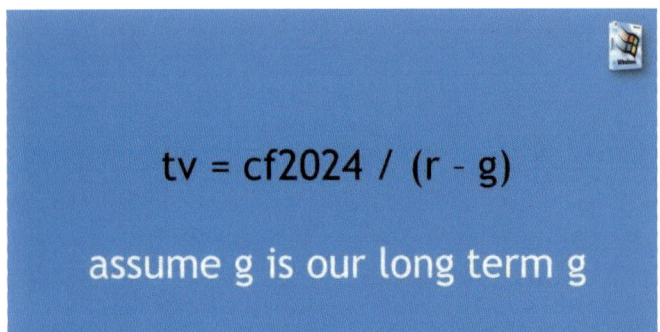
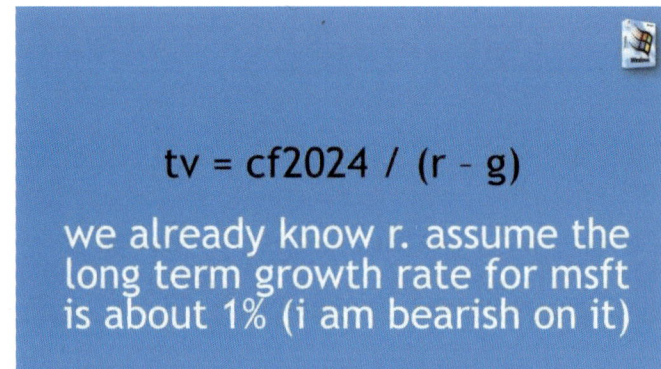
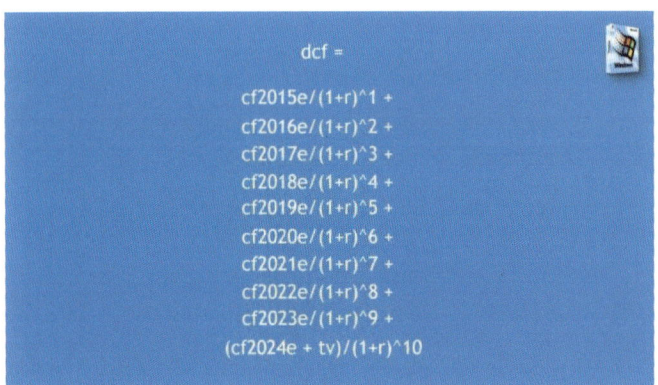
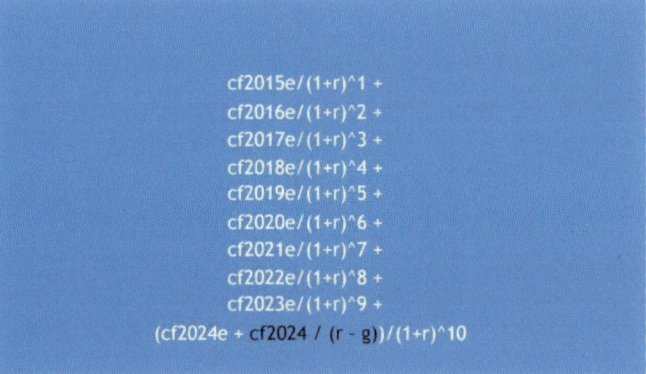
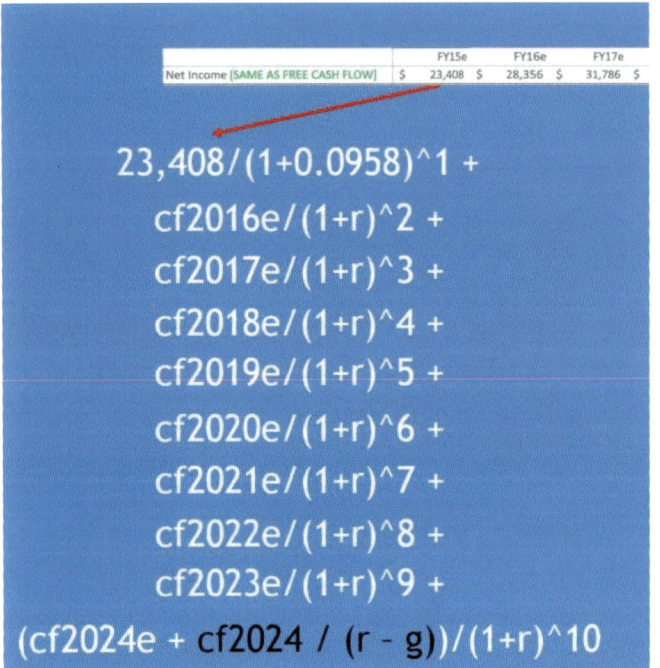
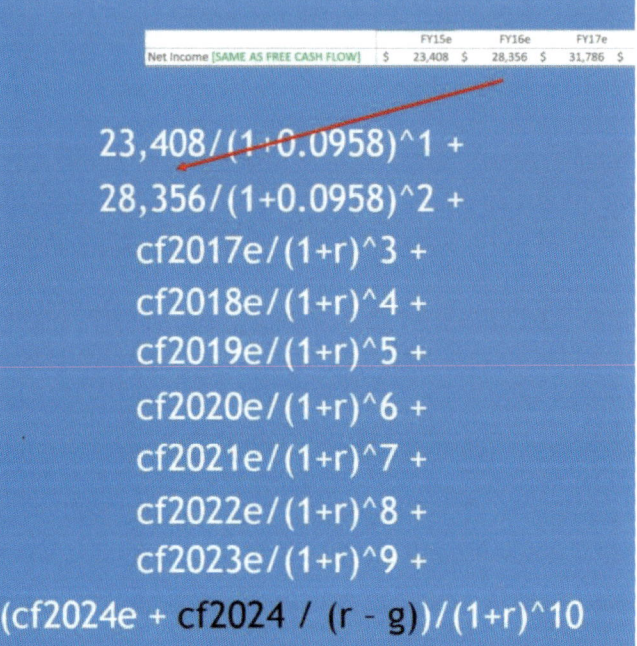

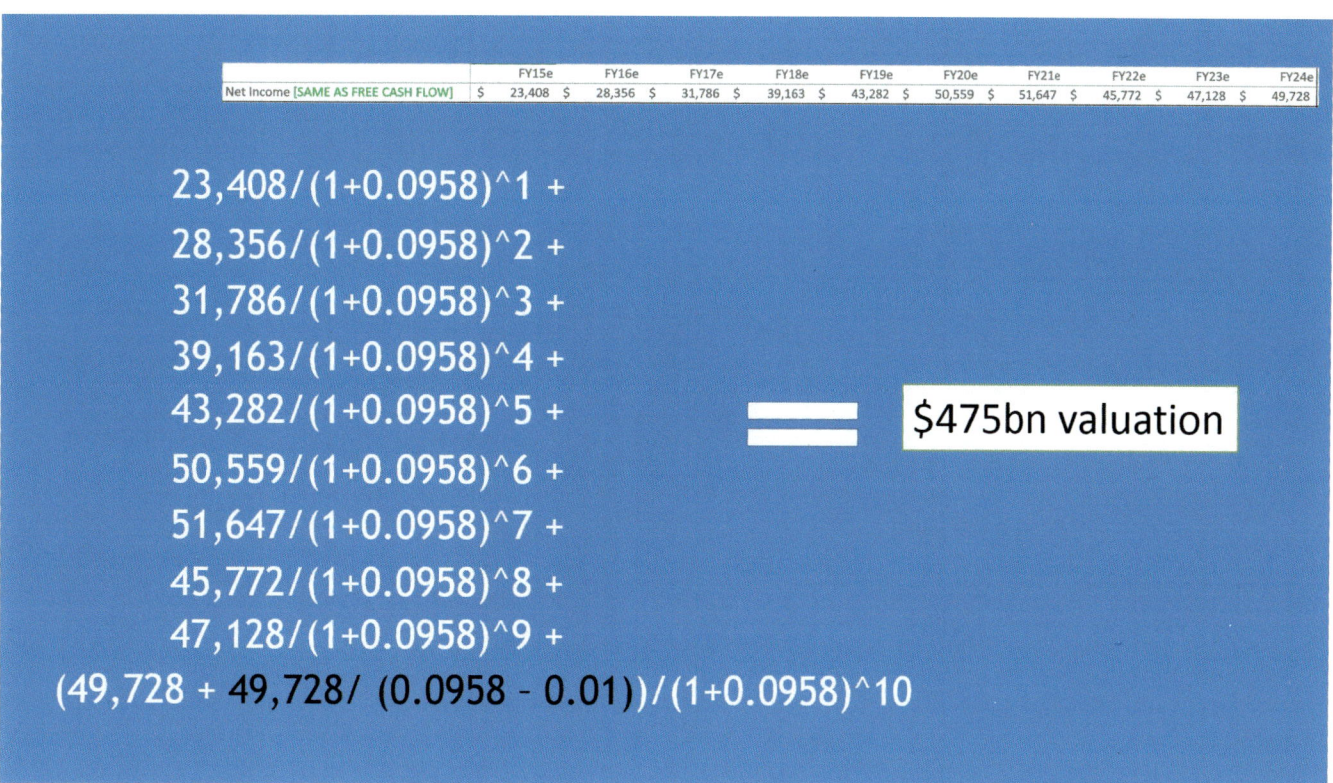

so our 3rd valuation methodology (dcf) implies a value of $475bn
or
25% upside to a target price of
$58.50

What's awesome is that we can do all of the DCF calculations using a very cool quick formula called Excel's NPV formula (Net Present Value). This NPV formula needs 2 inputs: all of the future net income or cash flow values and the interest rate we use to discount them, which was 9.5%:

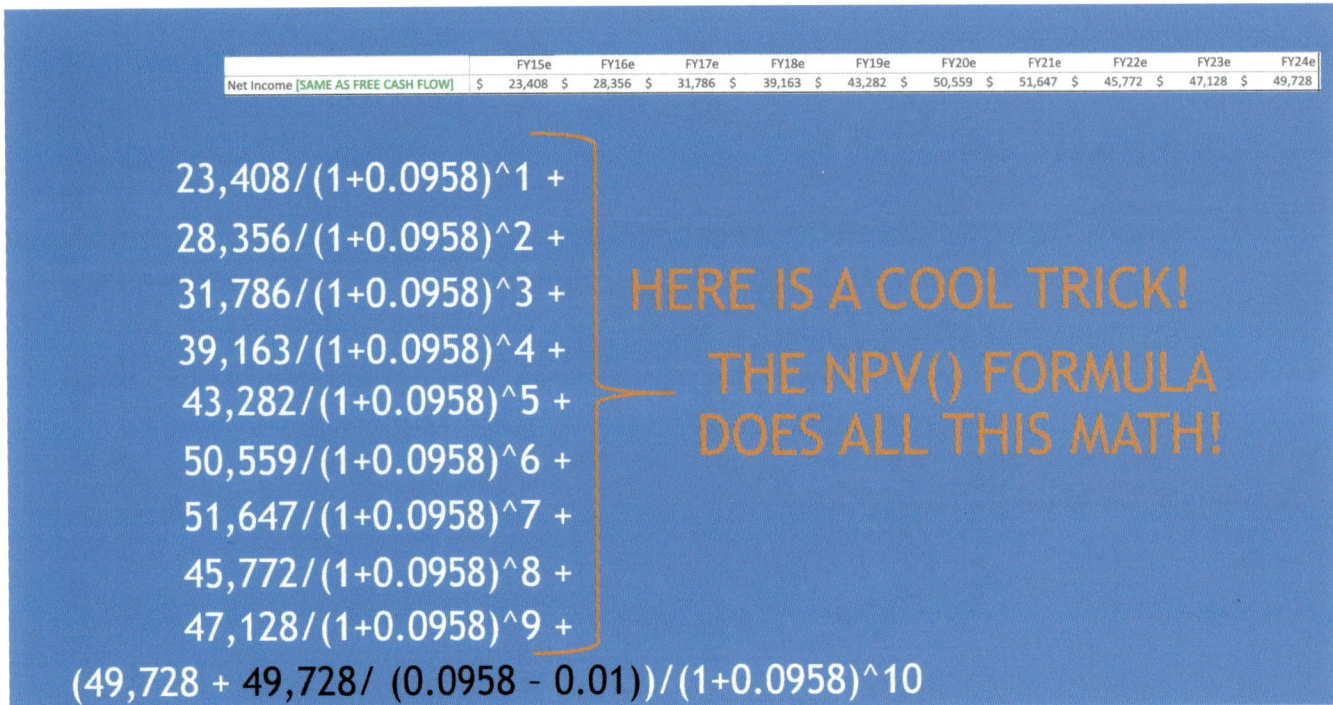

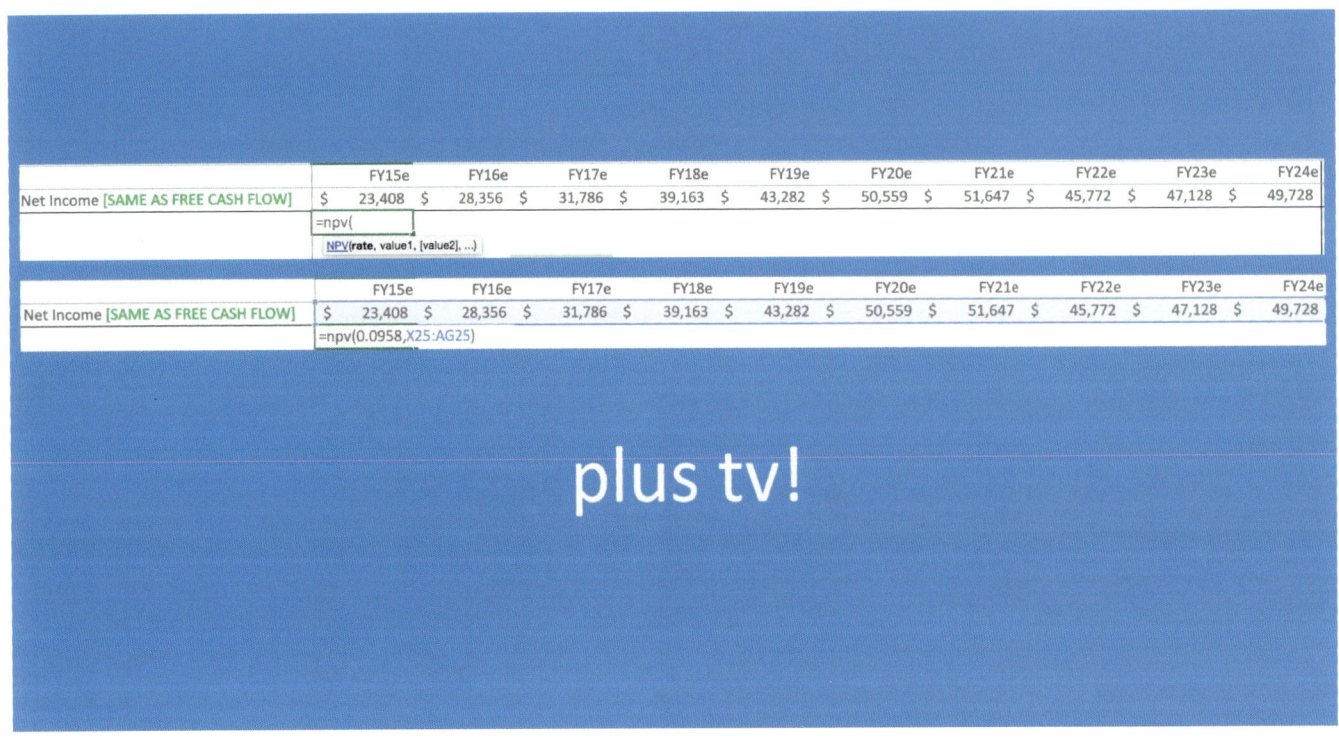

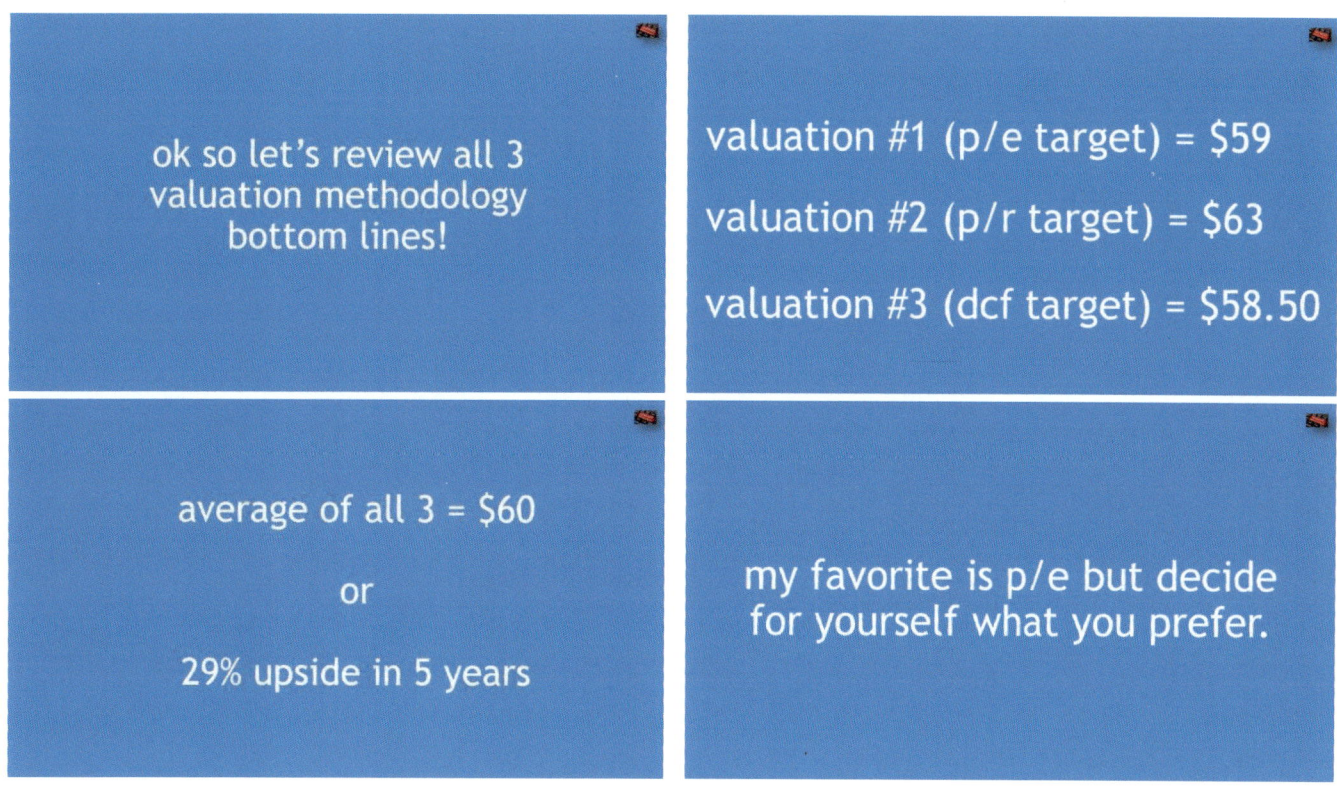

If you are in a class room or large corporate group, divide yourselves into two groups. Team Blue and team Red and see who answers the following questions first using only www.sec.gov

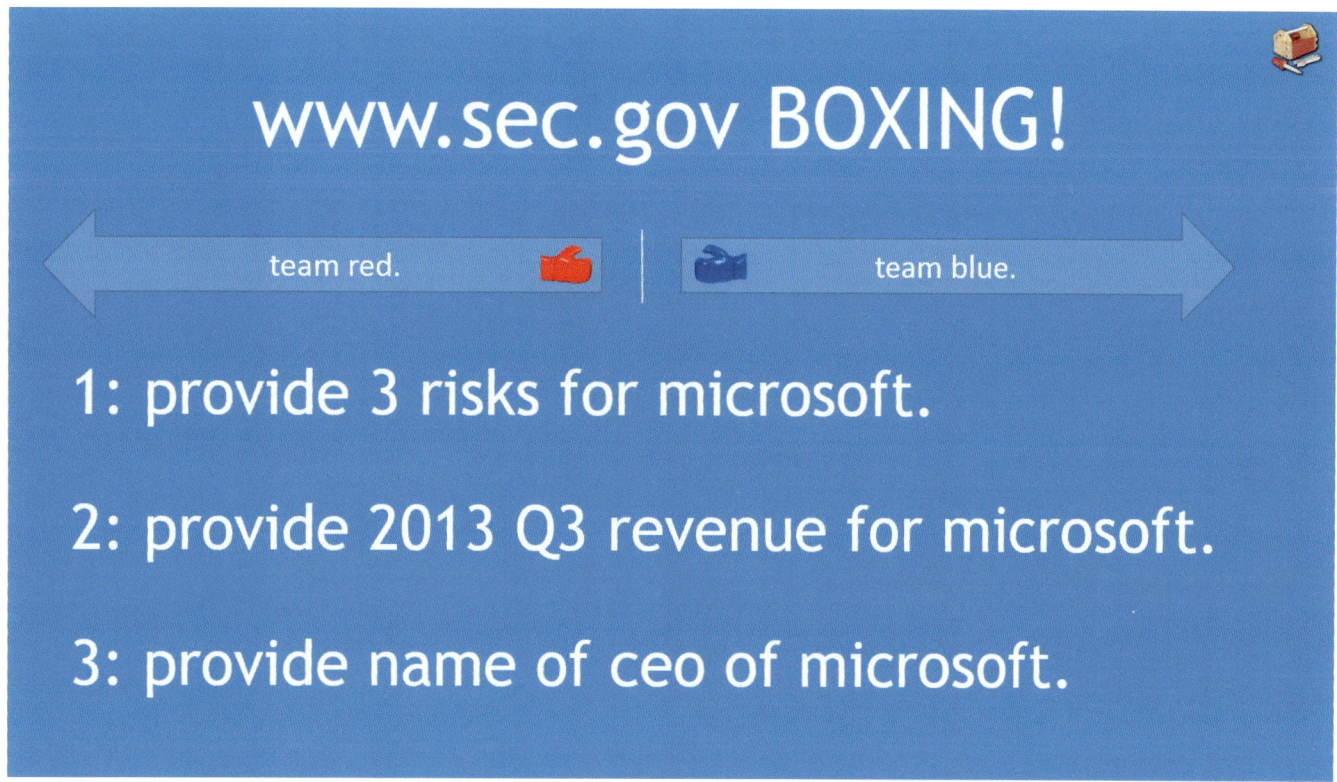

Come on blue! www.tiny.cc/chris84

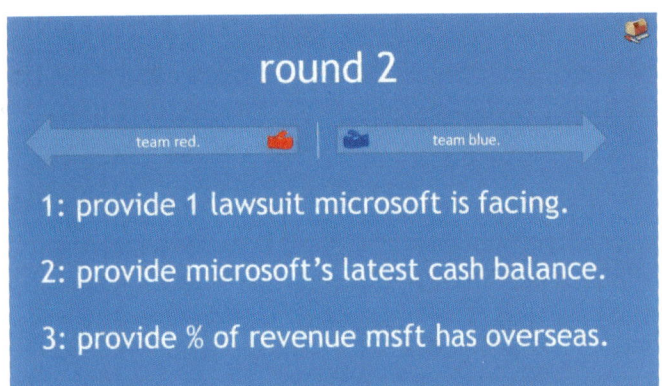

Don't give up blue! www.tiny.cc/chris85

You're my boy blue! www.tiny.cc/chris86

Questions Based on Chapter 11:

1: The best sources for building a model are:

    a) Morningstar.com and sec.com
    <u>b)</u> Sec.gov and I.R.
    c) I.R and CNBC
    d) CNBC and Bloomberg

2: All individual investors have the same access to public market investment information in the US as the big mutual funds and hedge funds have.

    <u>True</u>   or   False

3: You should talk to a company's management team first before doing due diligence on that company.

    True   or   <u>False</u>

CHAPTER SUMMARY

Chris Haroun @chris_haroun
valuation and model projections is not hard. simply forecast revenue and make most expenses a percent of revenue. valuation targets can be from p/e, p/r and dcf. u chose!

Chapter 12: Initial Public Offering and Valuation

"The New York Stock Exchange is the only store in the world where consumers sell stuff when it goes on sale."

- *Warren Buffett*

The Ultimate Practical Business Manual

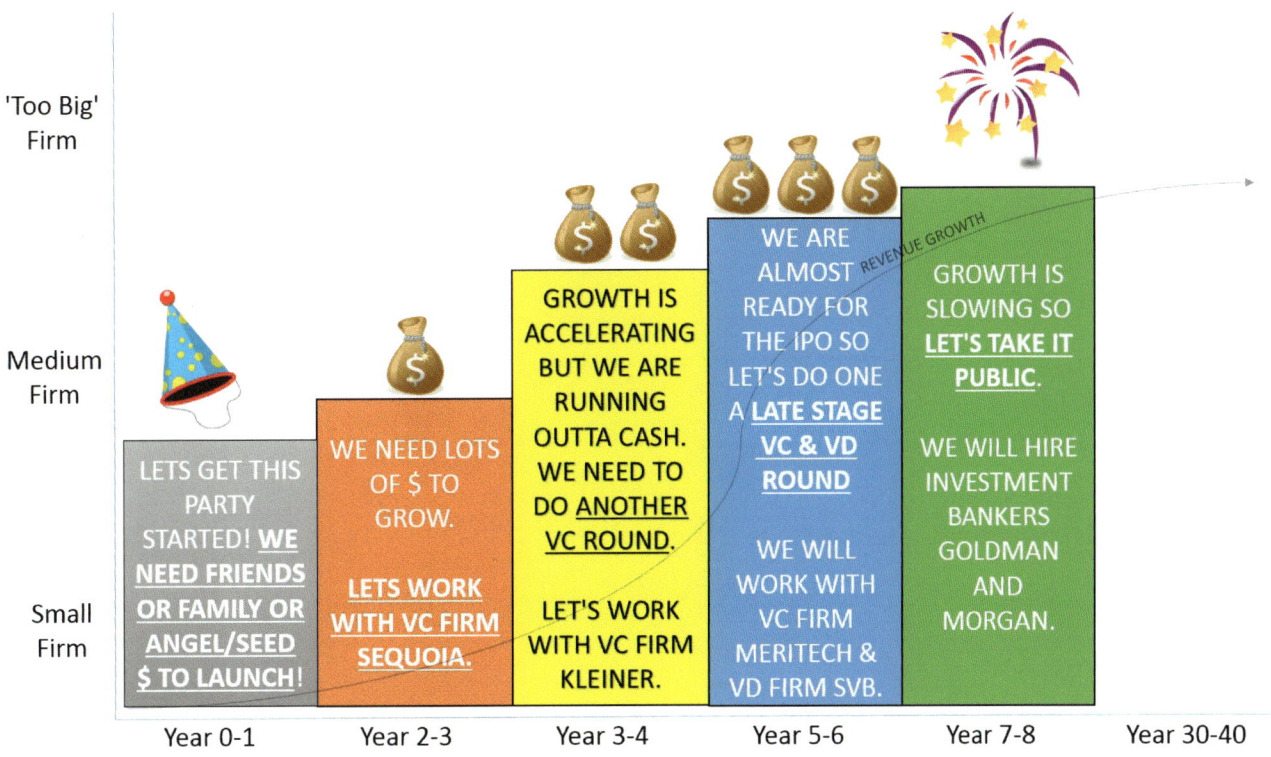

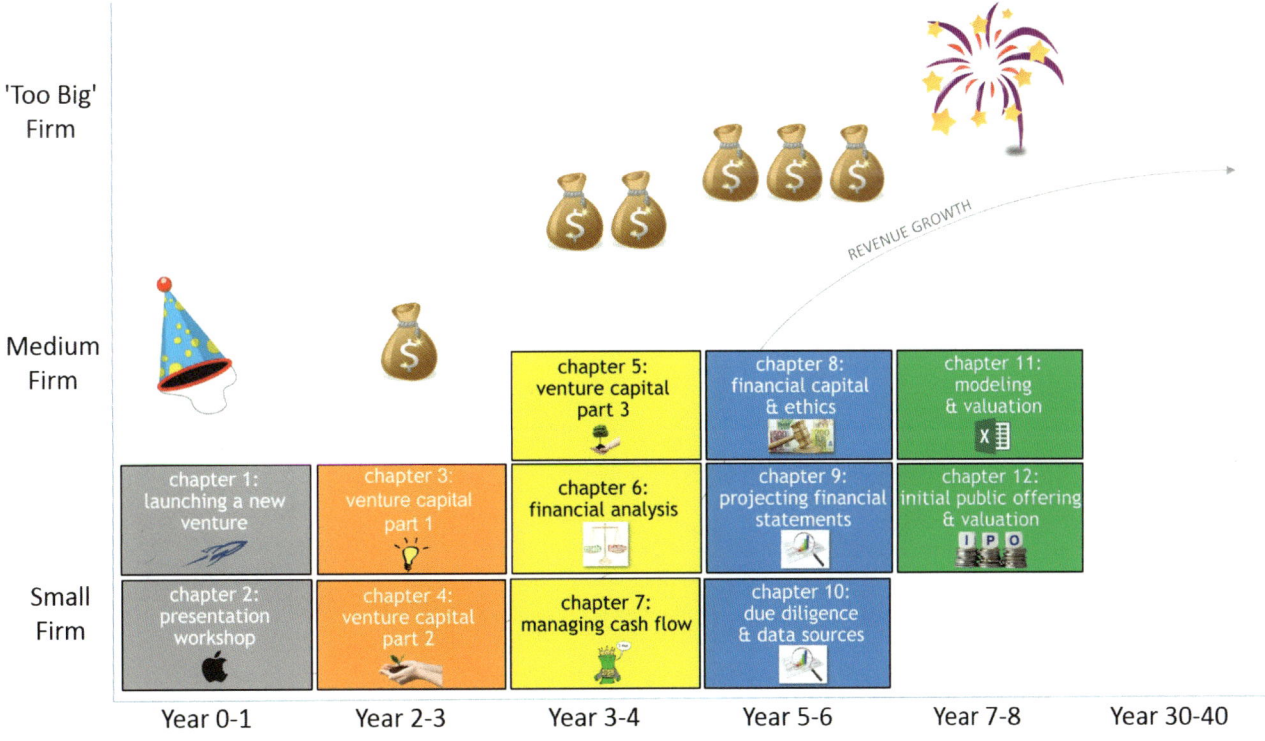

Microsoft offered us $1bn in cash to buy our company! Screw that though cuz we is worth way more than that!

Before we talk about how Goldman Sachs is going to take our firm public, let's try to understand tech valuations through a quick case study on Facebook's purchase of Instagram:

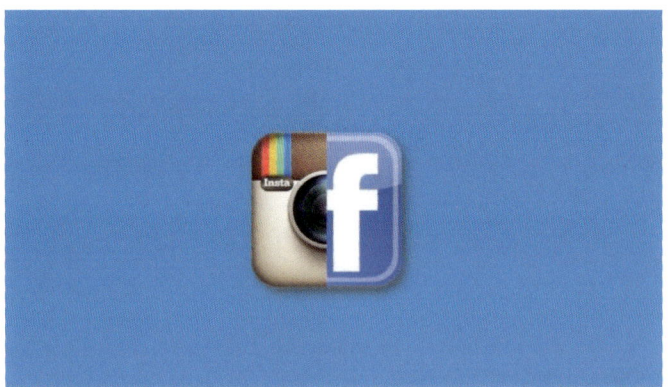

Before we jump in, let's see what Mark Zuckerberg has to say about the acquisition: www.tiny.cc/chris87

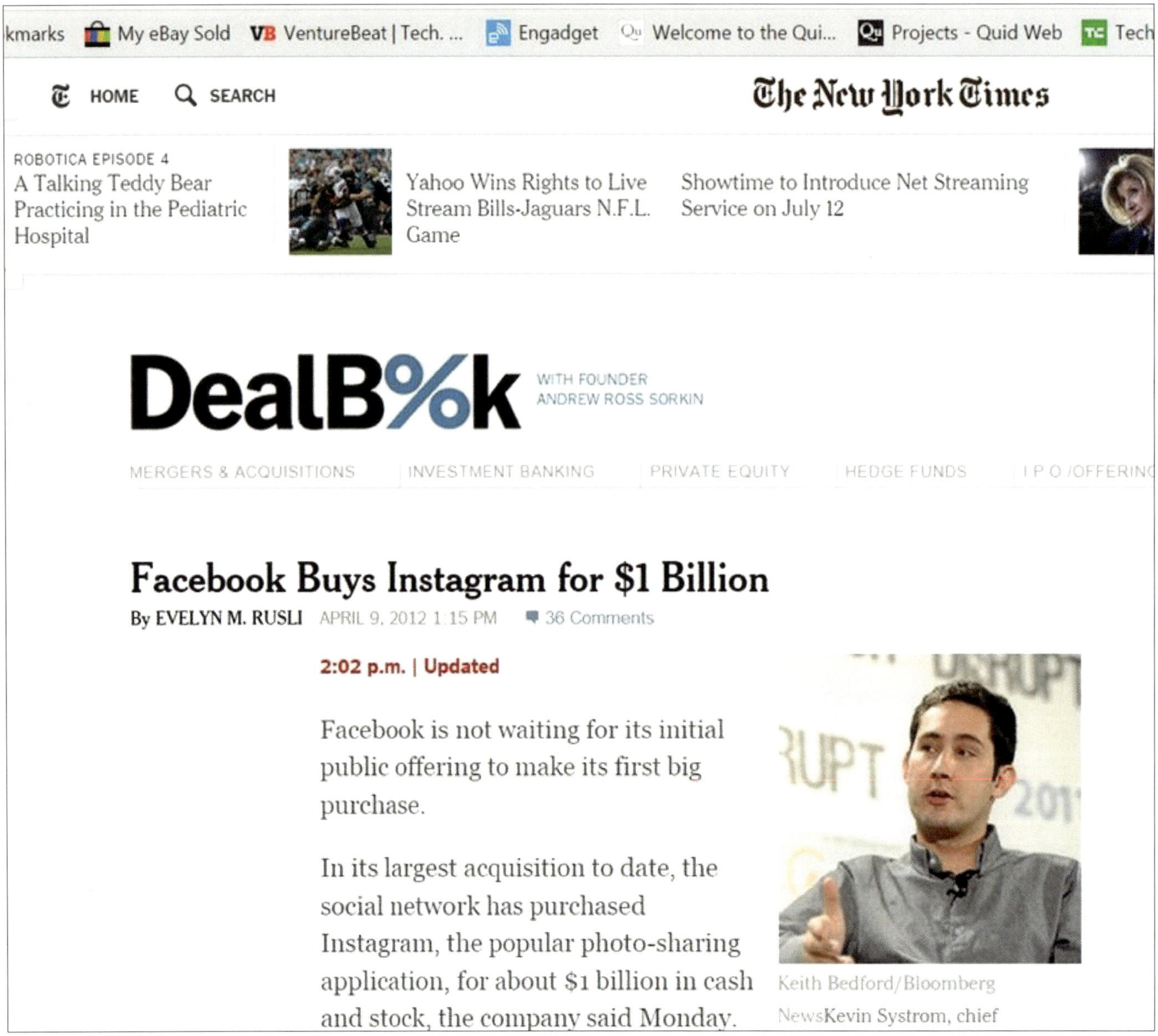

kmarks My eBay Sold VentureBeat | Tech. ... Engadget Welcome to the Qui... Projects - Quid Web Tech

HOME SEARCH The New York Times

ROBOTICA EPISODE 4
A Talking Teddy Bear Practicing in the Pediatric Hospital

Yahoo Wins Rights to Live Stream Bills-Jaguars N.F.L. Game

Showtime to Introduce Net Streaming Service on July 12

DealB%k WITH FOUNDER ANDREW ROSS SORKIN

MERGERS & ACQUISITIONS | INVESTMENT BANKING | PRIVATE EQUITY | HEDGE FUNDS | I.P.O./OFFERING

Facebook Buys Instagram for $1 Billion

By EVELYN M. RUSLI APRIL 9, 2012 1:15 PM 36 Comments

2:02 p.m. | Updated

Facebook is not waiting for its initial public offering to make its first big purchase.

In its largest acquisition to date, the social network has purchased Instagram, the popular photo-sharing application, for about $1 billion in cash and stock, the company said Monday.

Keith Bedford/Bloomberg NewsKevin Systrom, chief

$1bn for Instagram which had no revenue is a HUGE bargain when Facebook bought them in 2012! Why?

2011 instagram users of 1mn

and over 100mn in 2012!

facebook market cap
/
facebook users ("subs")
=
value per sub

$231,000,000 (then)
/
1,400,000,000
=
$165 per subscriber!

instagram acquisition price
/
instagram subs
=
value per sub

$1,000,000,000
/
100,000,000 (in 2012)
=
$10 per subscriber!

Facebook only paid $10 per subscriber versus its own valuation of much much higher per Facebook subscriber!

$1,000,000,000
/
300,000,000+ (today)
=
<$5 per subscriber!

if facebook was valued at $165 per subscriber....

...and assuming instagram is worth at least $80 per sub...

$80 per sub times 200m subs=

$16bn+ valuation for instagram today!

instagram is worth $16bn-$32bn

That $1bn acquisition was very acretive per sub acquired for Facebook. Check out Instagram's user growth:

ok i get it. valuation for high growth consumer tech is based on subs.
what did facebook pay for what's app?

~$20bn

Facebook had to buy Instagram and they had to buy Sequoia backed WhatsApp as Facebook's growth is decelerating. Facebook is much less relevant to younger demographics.

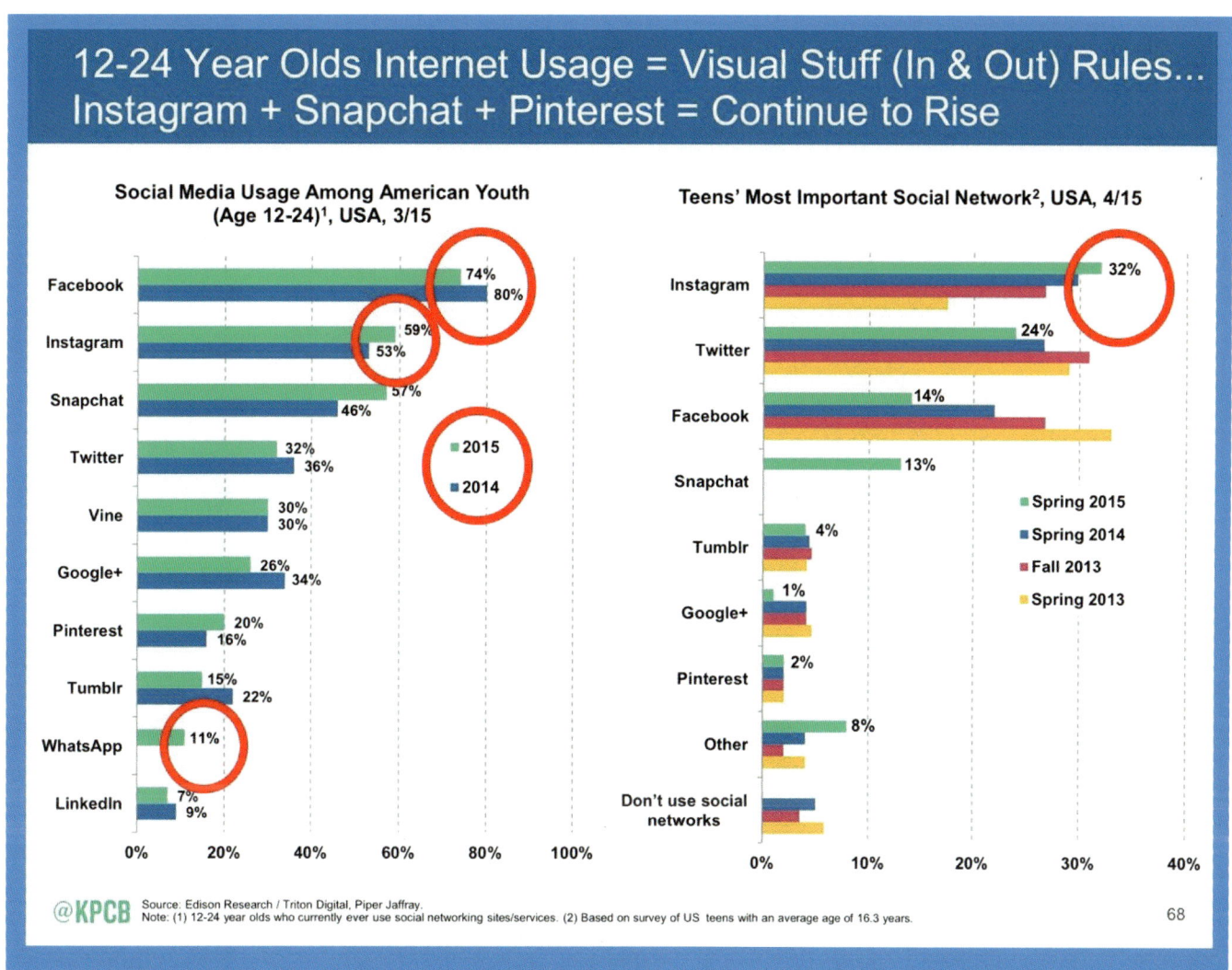

~$20bn/700mn subs

= $28 per sub!

Facebook got another bargain by paying only $28 per subscriber for WhatsApp. This deal was "accretive" to Facebook's value per subscriber.

> **valuation methodologies differ based on the industry**

Valuing companies in the short term always differs based on the sector that the company competes in. In consumer technology, we look at the value per subscriber.

VALUATION DRIVERS

> **short term valuation drivers:**
> - consumer tech = subs
> - enterprise tech = revenue
> - semis tech = earnings
> - hotels = revpar

> **short term valuation drivers:**
> - industrials = earnings & volume
> - telco = arpu
> - retail = earnings & SSS
> - biotech = FDA approval

The hotel industry's valuation driver is "REVPAR" which stands for Revenue Per Available Room. In the telco market we look at "ARPU" which stands for Average Revenue Per User. In biotech we look at the probability a company will get FDA approval, which is why investing in biotech stocks is like a binary event at times. In the retail sector, we look at "SSS" which stands for Same Store Sales as we only care about the growth of each individual store on a YoY or year over year basis. This is why investors loved it when McDonald's started serving food 24 hours a day or when McDonald's started selling high margin coffee beverages.

> **long term valuation drivers:**
> - tech and telco = earnings & cf
> - financials = earnings & cf
> - retail = earnings & cf
> - <u>all</u> sectors = earnings & cf

In the long run all we care about from a valuation perspective in all industries is earnings and cash flow.

The Ultimate Practical Business Manual

additional valuation methods.	we are in late 2019 now.
our private company's valuation	we turned down microsoft's 'insulting' $1bn acquisition offer. go big or go home! let's put a dent in the universe. **we want to go public now.**

Let's take the plunge! Let's go public!!!!!!

We will ask our awesome VC investors Sequoia, Kleiner and Meritech who we should select for our initial public offering (IPO). They all tell us to go with Goldman Sachs as they are the best company when it comes to helping technology firms go public. Goldman puts together a group of investment banks to work with for the IPO, which is called the IPO syndicate. They do this as our IPO is going to be massive and Goldman wants to spread the risk by partnering with and sharing the economics with several firms. We also want to decide whoever does the best job of all the investment banks in the syndicate who to compensate a bit more so than the others. Competition is always good for us, the consumer.

Investment bankers work with lawyers and create all the legal documents required to take us public. They list all of the risks as well in the legal filings so that our investors can't sue us or Goldman if something goes wrong.

Recall when we went to www.sec.gov when we were building our model we used the 10-k (the annual report) to analyze the company we were modeling. At the same website we can search for an "S-1" which is legal filing code for the IPO document that contains everything investors need to know about our firm in order to make an intelligent decision on whether or not to buy our stock in the IPO!

Here is the actual S-1 filing for Facebook's IPO: www.tiny.cc/chris88 . You can see that Morgan Stanley is listed first so they led the IPO for Facebook.

Goldman's investment bankers work with our management team and advise us on how to go public and when to go public and who to sell our shares to. At Goldman there is a team called ECM or Equity Capital Markets that summarize the lengthy S-1 that the bankers created into a few pages called the Sales Memo.

ECM then teaches the salesforce at Goldman how to sell the company going public to their clients. The Goldman salesforce works on the Goldman trading floor beside Goldman's army of traders. ECM tells the Salesforce what the risks are with the investment in our company as well as the positive selling points.

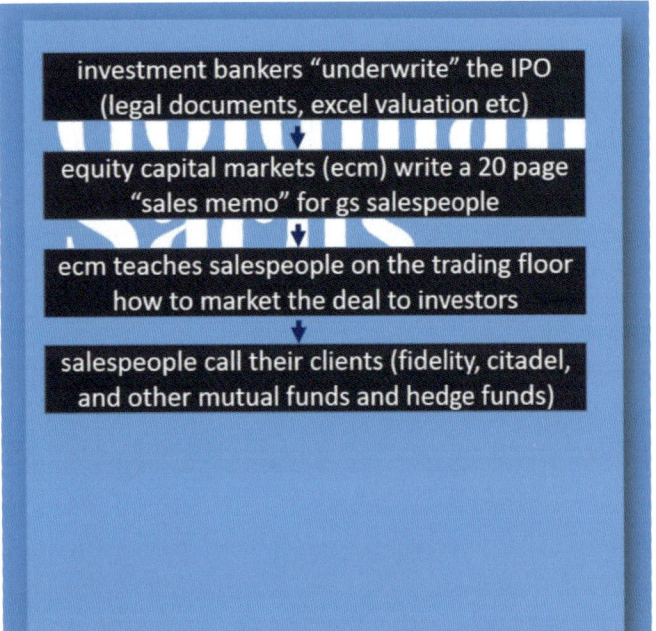

Then the Goldman salesforce calls their customers and market the deal to their mutual fund and hedge fund clients (their clients manage billions of dollars in retirement savings, pension fund money, endowment money and rich people's money etc.).

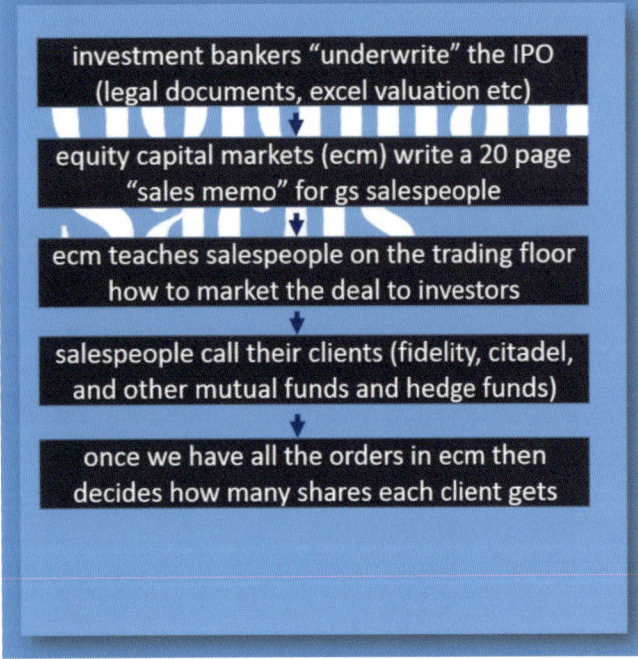

The Goldman salesforce then collects all the orders for the IPO from their customers and articulates the orders to ECM. The larger customers like Fidelity or T.Rowe or Citadel get larger allocations as they pay Goldman more via trading commissions over time. Some companies going public tell the salespeople at Goldman that they only want to participate if the price is low. Others say they don't care about the price and they will buy a large chunk of the IPO with little pricing sensitivity.

Customers know that a deal is hot if they don't get the amount of shares that they ask for. When I used to work at a prominent hedge fund, if a salesperson during an IPO process called me to tell me that I should be happy that I got allocated exactly what I asked for in a deal, then I would be worried as this basically signals that demand for the IPO was anemic (watch out for signals)!

ECM and the company going public ultimately get to decide which clients get which allocations. Management of the company going public usually wants the potential shareholders that they met with that have the best understanding of the business model in the long run to receive large allocations. Why?

Because they are less likely to be tourists in the stock and panic if it goes down and sell it. Goldman will help the company understand which shareholders stick around in IPOs in the long run and which firms 'flip' or quickly sell previous IPOs. Since companies that buy stocks have to file their long position holdings every 3 months or so, it is quite easy to track this information online.

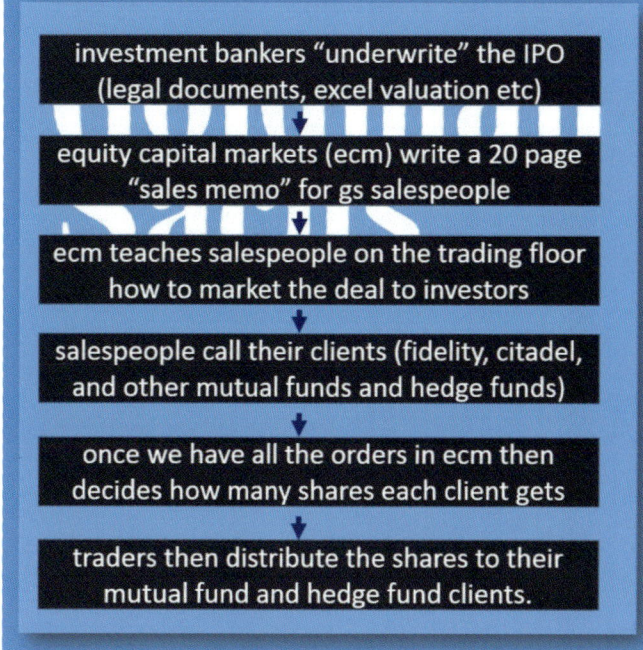

Then the traders on the Goldman trading floor distribute the shares to customers like Fidelity and the Goldman salespeople call their customers to inform them what their allocation was. Then 30 days later the Goldman equity research analyst can initiate coverage on the company with a Buy, Hold or Sell rating which is dependent of course on the valuation of the underlying company at the point of initiation.

after the process is done, goldman wires the ipo proceeds to us (less fees)

oh no…..

goldman tells us that a few mutual funds need to see a dcf which ecm wants to put in their ipo sales memo for the salesforce.

ugh.
fine. but many investors prefer p/e or p/s
we will take an average p/e, p/s and dcf for our valuation

There are so many independent variables when calculating a DCF, which is an issue. If I told you that X+1=3, of course you know that X is 2. If I told you that X+T+Y+Q=3, then you have no idea what X is! The same can be said for DCF as there are so many independent variables like the WACC, the Terminal Value etc.

> so many indep varables in dcf is problem.

> after dcf done we trangulate p/e and p/s and get average.

> dcf is pretty easy...as our company's net income is very close to cash flows anyway.

> lets do a dcf for our firm

> dcf is the value of all future cash flows discounted

> we need to look at the cf from years 2020-2025

> but first we need to calculate the wacc

wacc =

cost of equity
+
cost of debt

We have no debt so there is no need to account for the cost of debt in our DCF.

wacc =

cost of equity
+
~~cost of debt~~

cost of equity =

risk free rate
+
(stock market return - risk free rate)
*
beta (how volatile our company is)

cost of equity =

1%
+
(12% - 1%)
*
beta (how volatile our company is)

what is our beta?

For some reason, the investment bankers think that our beta should be similar to storage company betas as there is a storage element to our product. Fine. We will take the average beta of a few storage companies and that is the beta we will use in our wacc when calculating our DCF valuation.

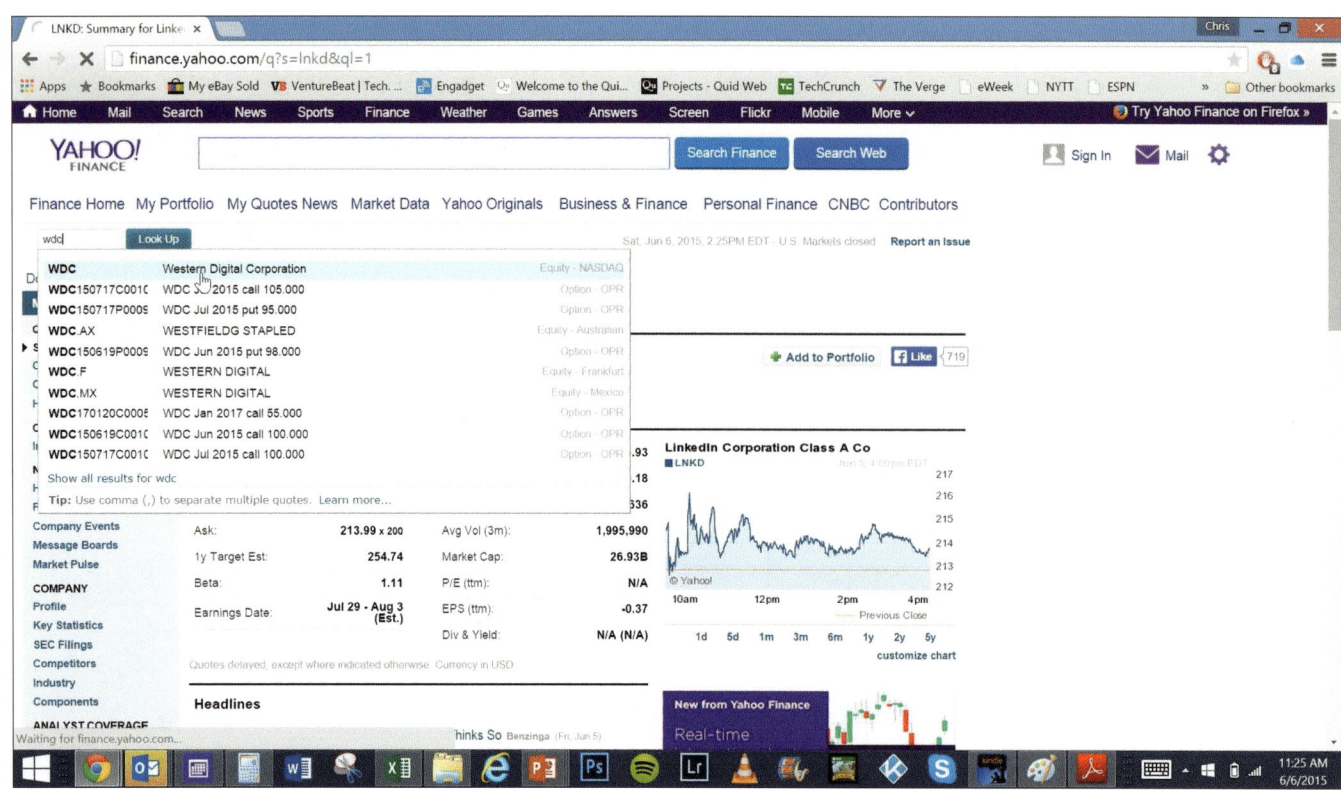

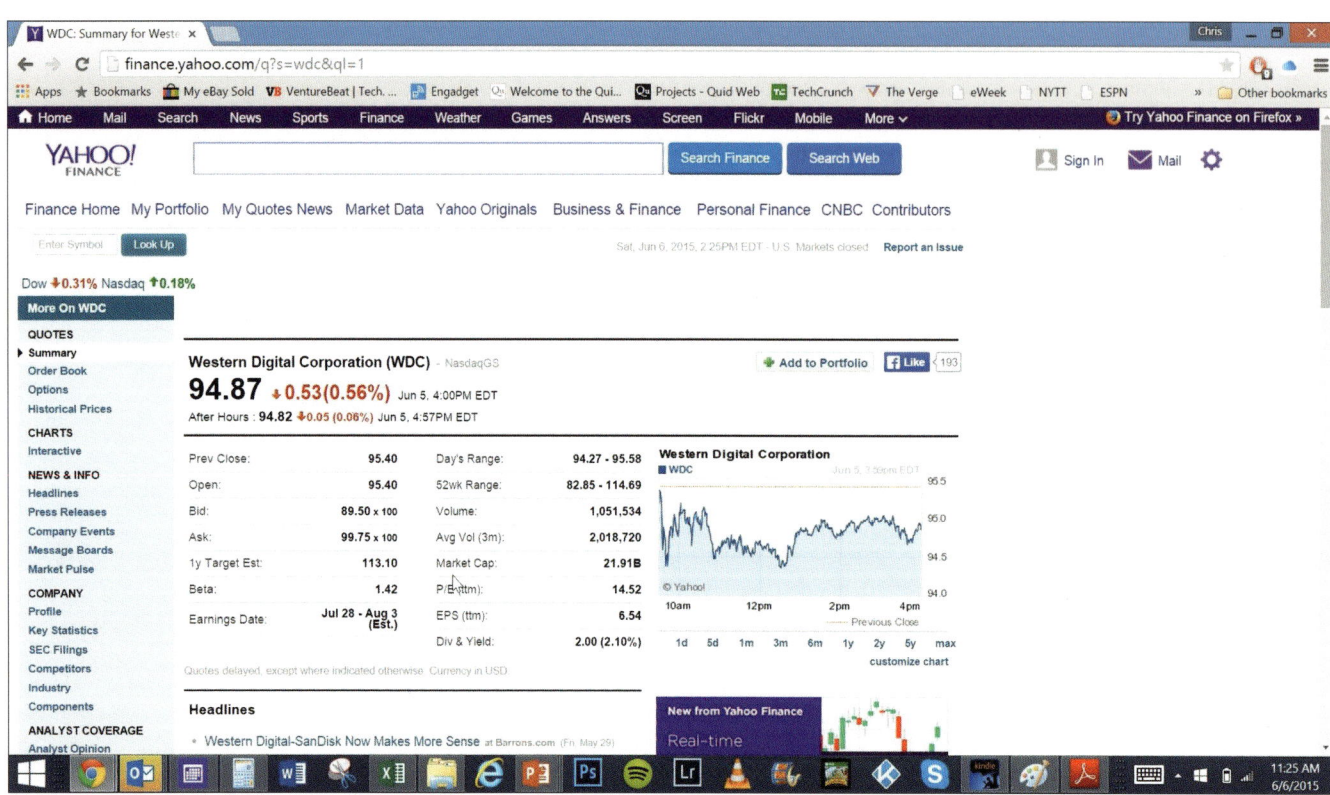

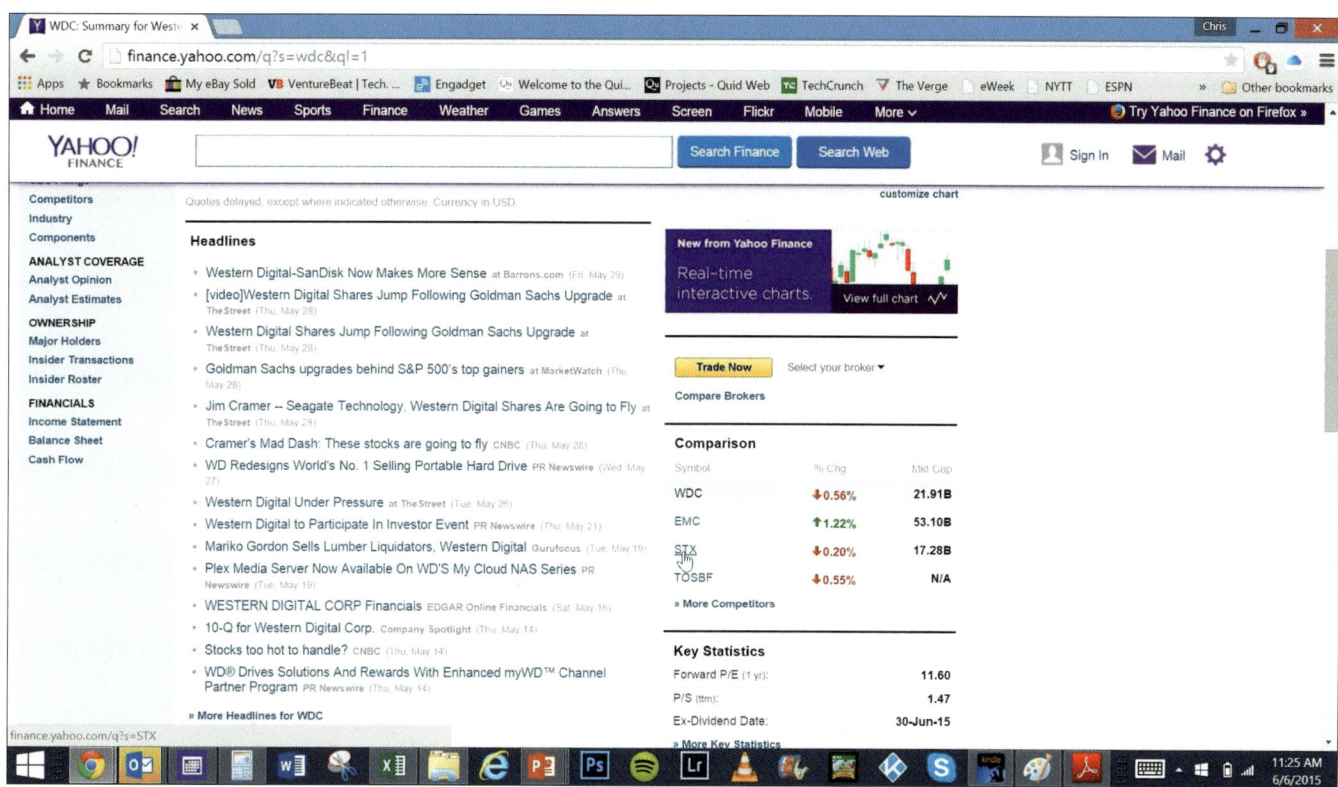

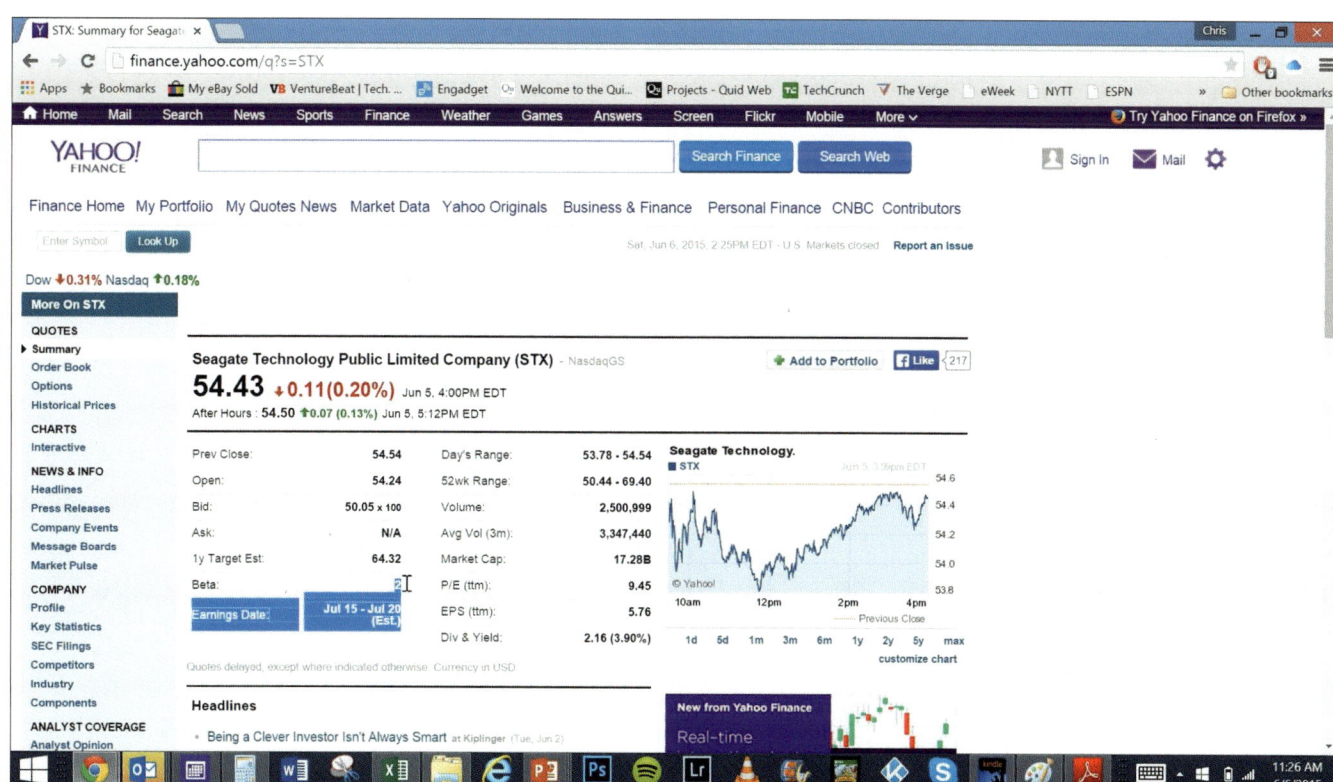

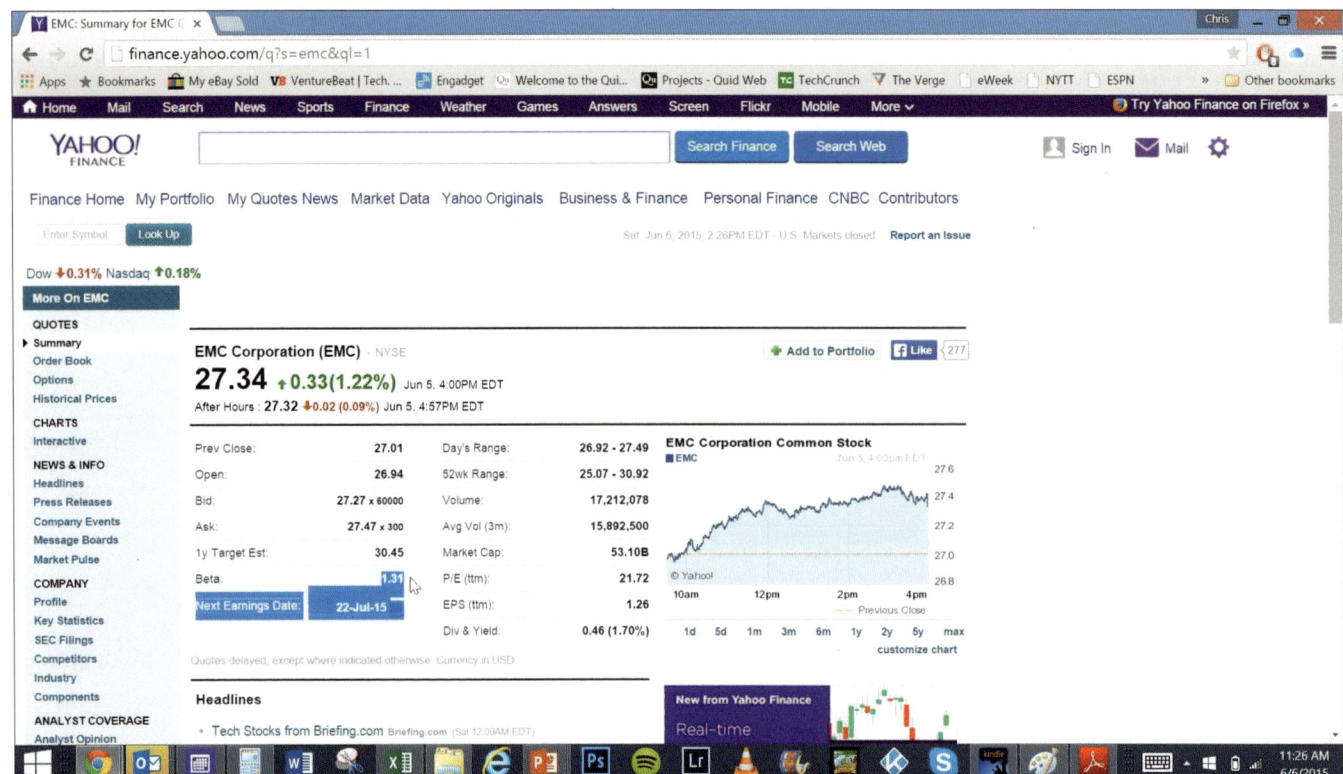

Ok. We calculated the average beta of companies that the bankers think are similar to us…..the average beta is 1.57.

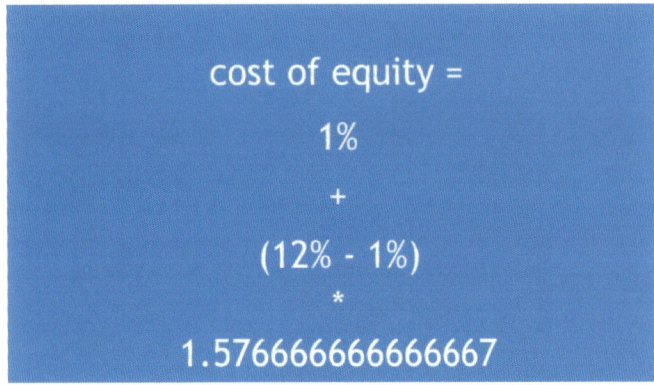

Our beta ends up being way above 1 which makes sense as we are a newer and riskier and likely more volatile stock, unlike Microsoft, which has a beta of under 1.

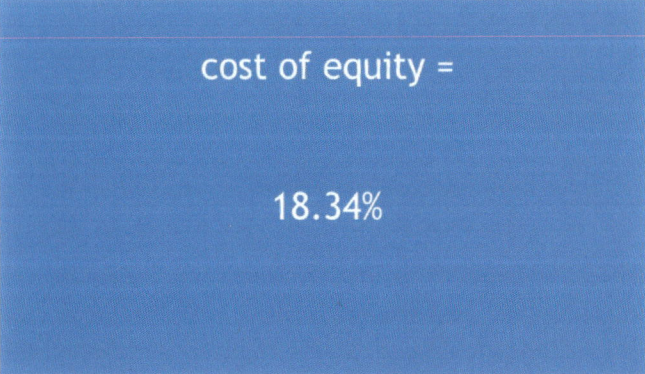

Notice that our cost of capital or wacc is about twice as high as Microsoft's. This is the case as we are a much riskier investment. As a result, we need to discount our future net income or cash flow using a much higher interest rate. This will result in a lower valuation than if we used Microsoft's interest rate. Again, this makes a lot of sense as we are a much riskier investment than stable Microsoft (MSFT) is.

We decided to use the ticker 'BLUE' for our firm as we are huge fans of Will Ferrell.

we use 18.34% as our discount rate = "r"

$$dcf = cf2020/(1+r)^1 + cf2021/(1+r)^2 + cf2022/(1+r)^3 + cf2023/(1+r)^4 + (cf2024 + tv)/(1+r)^5$$

$$tv = cf2024 / (r - g)$$

assume g is our long term g

terminology: r-g is called the cap rate

$$dcf = cf2020/(1+r)^1 + cf2021/(1+r)^2 + cf2022/(1+r)^3 + cf2023/(1+r)^4 + (cf2024 + cf2024 / (r - g))/(1+r)^5$$

	2015	2016	2017	2018	2019	2020	2021	2022
Revenue	$ 2,000,000	$ 20,000,000	$ 350,000,000	$ 661,500,000	$ 999,600,000	$ 1,399,440,000	$ 1,889,244,000	$ 2,066,360,625 $ 1,948,28
% YoY		900%	1650%	89%	51%	40%	35%	9%
COGS	$ 1,800,000	$ 16,000,000	$ 175,000,000	$ 264,600,000	$ 299,880,000	$ 279,888,000	$ 358,956,360	$ 371,944,913 $ 331,20
GM pct	10%	20%	50%	60%	70%	80%	81%	82%
Gross Profit	$ 200,000	$ 4,000,000	$ 175,000,000	$ 396,900,000	$ 699,720,000	$ 1,119,552,000	$ 1,530,287,640	$ 1,694,415,713 $ 1,617,07
Operating Expenses:								
S&M	$ 500,000	$ 4,000,000	$ 66,500,000	$ 112,455,000	$ 159,936,000	$ 209,916,000	$ 264,494,160	$ 268,626,881 $ 233,79
% of sales	25%	20%	19%	17%	16%	15%	14%	13%
% YoY		700%	1563%	69%	42%	31%	26%	2%
G&A	$ 500,000	$ 4,000,000	$ 66,500,000	$ 112,455,000	$ 159,936,000	$ 209,916,000	$ 264,494,160	$ 268,626,881 $ 233,79
% of sales	25%	20%	19%	17%	16%	15%	14%	13%
% YoY		700%	1563%	69%	42%	31%	26%	2%
R&D	$ 4,000,000	$ 20,000,000	$ 25,000,000	$ 25,000,000	$ 40,000,000	$ 35,000,000	$ 35,000,000	$ 35,000,000 $ 35,00
% of sales	200%	100%	7%	4%	4%	3%	2%	2%
% YoY		400%	25%	0%	60%	-13%	0%	0%
Opex Total	$ 5,000,000	$ 28,000,000	$ 158,000,000	$ 249,910,000	$ 359,872,000	$ 454,832,000	$ 563,988,320	$ 572,253,763 $ 502,58
Operating Profit (EBIT)	$ (4,800,000)	$(24,000,000)	$ 17,000,000	$ 146,990,000	$ 339,848,000	$ 664,720,000	$ 966,299,320	$ 1,122,161,950 $ 1,114,48
% of sales	-240%	-120%	5%	22%	34%	47%	51%	54%
Interest	$ -	$ -	$ 85,000	$ 734,950	$ 1,699,240	$ 9,970,800	$ 14,494,490	$ 16,832,429 $ 16,71
Tax	$ -	$ -	$ 4,250,000	$ 36,747,500	$ 84,962,000	$ 166,180,000	$ 241,574,830	$ 280,540,488 $ 278,62
% of EBIT	0%	0%	25%	25%	25%	25%	25%	25%
Net Income	$ (4,800,000)	$(24,000,000)	$ 12,835,000	$ 110,977,450	$ 256,585,240	$ 508,510,800	$ 739,218,980	$ 858,453,892 $ 852,58
% of sales	-240%	-120%	4%	17%	26%	36%	39%	42%
% YoY		400%	-153%	765%	131%	98%	45%	16%

assumptions and revenue drivers | **pro forma income statement** | analysis ratios | ipo valuation

I31 f_x =I27/(1+0.1834)^1

	B	C	D	E	F	G	H	I	J
1			2015	2016	2017	2018	2019	2020	202
27		Net Income	$ (4,800,000)	$(24,000,000)	$ 12,835,000	$110,977,450	$256,585,240	$ 508,510,800	$ 739,218,98
28		% of sales	-240%	-120%	4%	17%	26%	36%	39
29		% YoY		400%	-153%	765%	131%	98%	45
30									
31							dcf each year=	=I27/(1+0.1834)^1	

	H	I	J	K	L	M	N
	2019	2020	2021	2022	2023	2024	
	$256,585,240	$ 508,510,800	$ 739,218,980	$ 858,453,892	$ 852,582,476	$ 943,499,096	
	26%	36%	39%	42%	44%	46%	
	131%	98%	45%	16%	-1%	11%	
	dcf each year=	$ 429,703,228	$ 527,849,336	$ 517,991,077	$ 434,720,521	=M27/(1+0.1834)^5	

f_x =M27/(0.1834-0.05)

C	D	E	F	G	H	I	J	K
	2015	2016	2017	2018	2019	2020	2021	
Net Income	$ (4,800,000)	$(24,000,000)	$ 12,835,000	$110,977,450	$256,585,240	$ 508,510,800	$ 739,218,980	$ 858,45
% of sales	-240%	-120%	4%	17%	26%	36%	39%	
% YoY		400%	-153%	765%	131%	98%	45%	
					dcf each year=	$ 429,703,228	$ 527,849,336	$ 517,99
				tv=		=M27/(0.1834-0.05)		

f_x =I33/(1+0.1834)^5

B	C	D	E	F	G	H	I	J
		2015	2016	2017	2018	2019	2020	
	Net Income	$ (4,800,000)	$(24,000,000)	$ 12,835,000	$110,977,450	$256,585,240	$ 508,510,800	$ 739,2
	% of sales	-240%	-120%	4%	17%	26%	36%	
	% YoY		400%	-153%	765%	131%	98%	
						dcf each year=	$ 429,703,228	527,
					tv=		$ 7,072,706,867	
					discount tv		=I33/(1+0.1834)^5	

	H	I	J	K	L	M
2018	2019	2020	2021	2022	2023	2024
,450	$256,585,240	$ 508,510,800	$ 739,218,980	$ 858,453,892	$ 852,582,476	$ 943,499,096
17%	26%	36%	39%	42%	44%	46%
765%	131%	98%	45%	16%	-1%	11%
	dcf each year=	$ 429,703,228	$ 527,849,336	$ 517,991,077	$ 434,720,521	$ 406,552,635
	tv=	$ 7,072,706,867				
	discount tv	$ 3,047,388,569				
	fcf=	=I34+sum(I31:M31				
		SUM(**number1**, [number2], …)				

	H	I	J	K	L	M
18	2019	2020	2021	2022	2023	2024
0	$256,585,240	$ 508,510,800	$ 739,218,980	$ 858,453,892	$ 852,582,476	$ 943,499,096
%	26%	36%	39%	42%	44%	46%
%	131%	98%	45%	16%	-1%	11%
	dcf each year=	$ 429,703,228	$ 527,849,336	$ 517,991,077	$ 434,720,521	$ 406,551,635
	tv=	$ 7,072,706,867				
	discount tv	$ 3,047,388,569				
	fcf=	$ 5,364,174,366				
		seems logical….but let's compare it to our other valuation methodologies fr				

Our DCF valuation tells us that our company should be worth $5.4bn. Hmm ok let's compare this to what our P/Revenue and P/E valuation targets are.

assume IPO in 2020

growth investors to pay 10x revs
$ 13,994,400,000

value investors (who suck at tech) pay 10x's earnings (which is way too low given the growth rate)   dfcf= $5,364,174,366
$ 5,085,108,000

ok...we are in a bull market now....let's hair cut these by 25% to be conservative and assume we could be in a bear market then

$ 6,997,200,000
$ 2,542,554,000
$ 4,769,877,000

we invested at $350mn valuation
$ 13.63
this means a 14 bagger....and this is very conservative.
what does a mature large cap growth company like salesforce trade at?

wow 9x revenue for salesforce.....and growth is way slower for them....
this $350mn valuation is a bargain!

---

assume IPO in 2020

growth investors to pay 10x revs
$ 13,994,400,000

value investors (who suck at tech) pay 10x's earnings (which is way too low given the growth rate)   dfcf= $5,364,174,366
$ 5,085,108,000

ok...we are in a bull market now....let's hair cut these by 25% to be conservative and assume we could be in a bear market then

$ 6,997,200,000
$ 2,542,554,000
$ 4,769,877,000

we invested at $350mn valuation
$ 13.63
this means a 14 bagger....and this is very conservative.
what does a mature large cap growth company like salesforce trade at?

wow 9x revenue for salesforce.....and growth is way slower for them....
this $350mn valuation is a bargain!

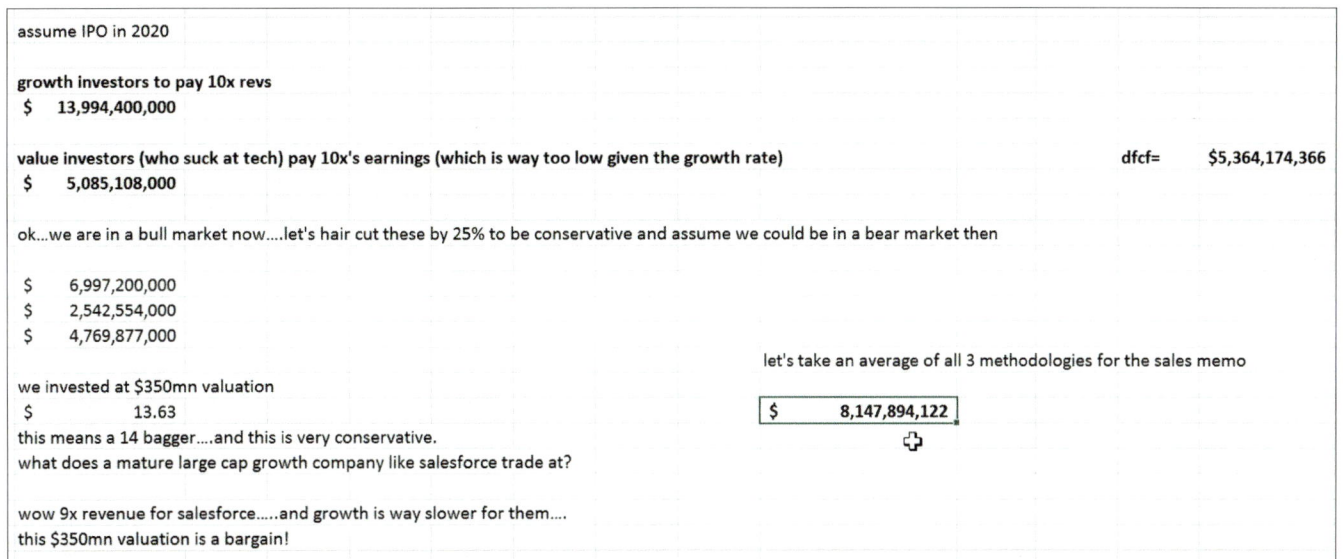

our goldman bankers think the company is worth $8.15bn

but IPOs are priced at a discount....

> gs wants to look good and wants a 30% pop on day 1!

> $8.15bn * 0.70 = $5.7bn

> is there an easier way to do dcf?

> npv formula in excel.

	H	I	J	K	L	M
	2019	2020	2021	2022	2023	2024
	$ 256,585,240	$ 508,510,800	$ 739,218,980	$ 858,453,892	$ 852,582,476	$ 943,499,096
	26%	36%	39%	42%	44%	46%
	131%	98%	45%	16%	-1%	11%
dcf each year=		$ 429,703,228	$ 527,849,336	$ 517,991,077	$ 434,720,521	$ 406,521,635
tv=		$ 7,072,706,867				
discount tv		$ 3,047,388,569				
dfcf=		$ 5,364,174,366				

seems logical....but let's compare it to our other valuation methodologies from last class.

`=npv(0.1834,I27:M27`
NPV(rate, **value1**, [value2], [value3], ...)

We covered this before, but it is worth revisiting.

	H	I	J	K	L	M
	2019	2020	2021	2022	2023	2024
	$ 256,585,240	$ 508,510,800	$ 739,218,980	$ 858,453,892	$ 852,582,476	$ 943,499,096
	26%	36%	39%	42%	44%	46%
	131%	98%	45%	16%	-1%	11%
dcf each year=	$ 429,703,228	$ 527,849,336	$ 517,991,077	$ 434,720,521	$ 406,521,635	
tv=	$ 7,072,706,867					
discount tv	$ 3,047,388,569					
dfcf=	$ 5,364,174,366					
	seems logical....but let's compare it to our other valuation methodologies from last class.					
$ 5,364,174,366.17						

adding complexity to our dcf

deduct non cash items like depreciation.

deduct dividends from cf etc.

how do we look at comps?

a comp for our firm is nmbl

see sec.gov

Comps means comparative or similar companies. We need to look at them so we can make sure that the financial statements we have prepared are not dramatically different. Looks like there is a company Called Nimble Storage, which Sequoia invested in before with an amazing management team and investment syndicate. We can look at Nimble's financials to see if we are thinking about modeling our company the right way. As always, we get this information from www.sec.gov

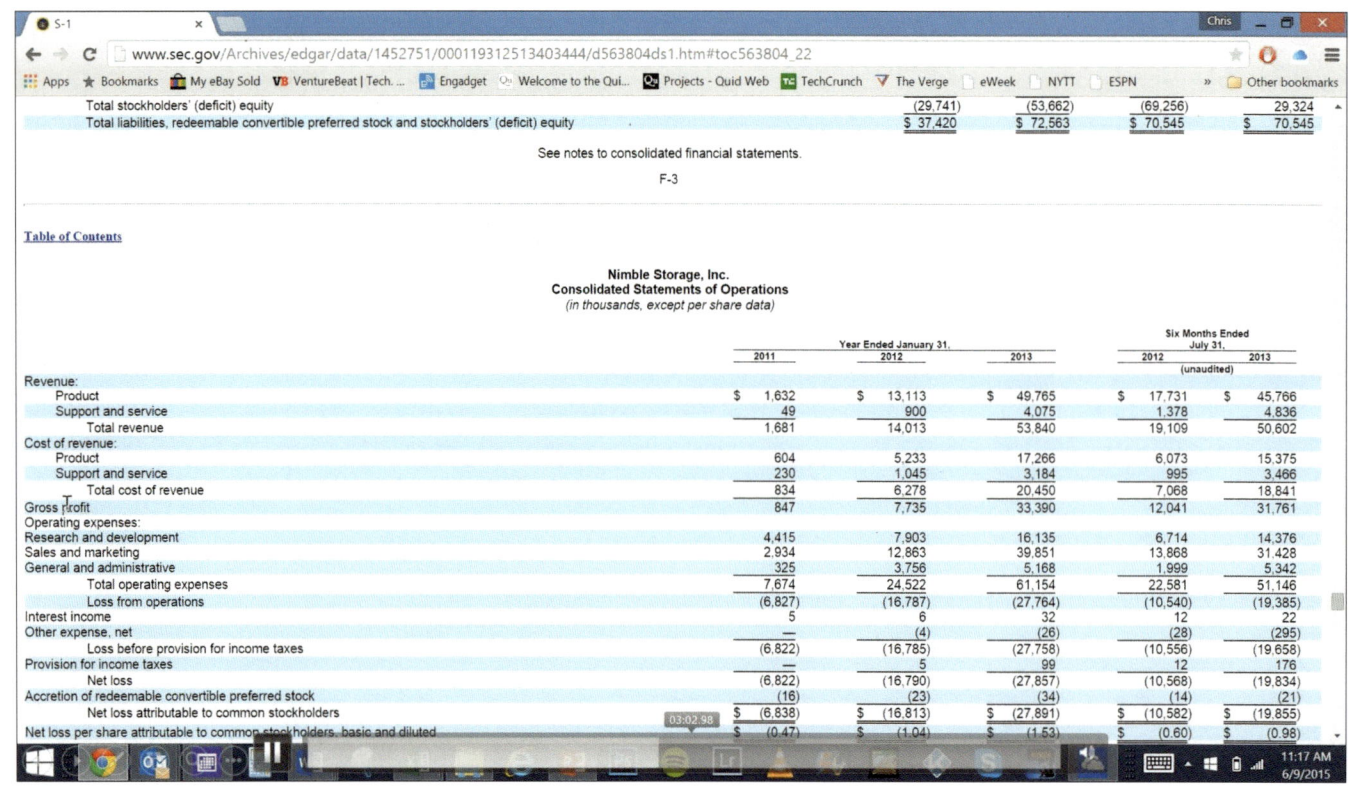

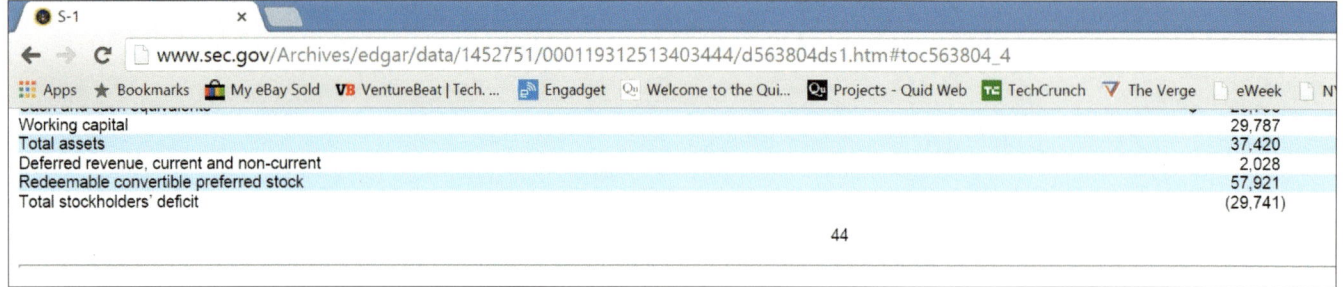

www.sec.gov is an amazing resource. We find S1 IPO filing documents there as well as annual reports (called 10-k's), quarterly reports (called 10-q's) and press releases that companies much disclose (called 8-k's). The beautiful thing about being an individual investor is that we all now have the exact same access to information that the Fidelity's of the world have as well (and at the exact same) time!

Questions Based on Chapter 12:

1: Investment banks usually price IPOs at a discount to what they believe the fair value is of the underlying company.

    <u>True</u>   or   False

2: The NPV formula makes calculating a DCF much easier.

    <u>True</u>   or   False

3: A company with a high beta is less risky and less volatile than a company with a low beta.

    True   or   <u>False</u>

CHAPTER SUMMARY

Chris Haroun @chris_haroun
short term valuation methodologies differ by sector. in the very long run it is all about earnings and cash flow. triangulate different valuation methodologies for IPOs.

Chapter 13: Management Analytical Frameworks

"Option A is not available.

So let's kick the sh** out of option B."

- *Sheryl Sandberg*

The Ultimate Practical Business Manual

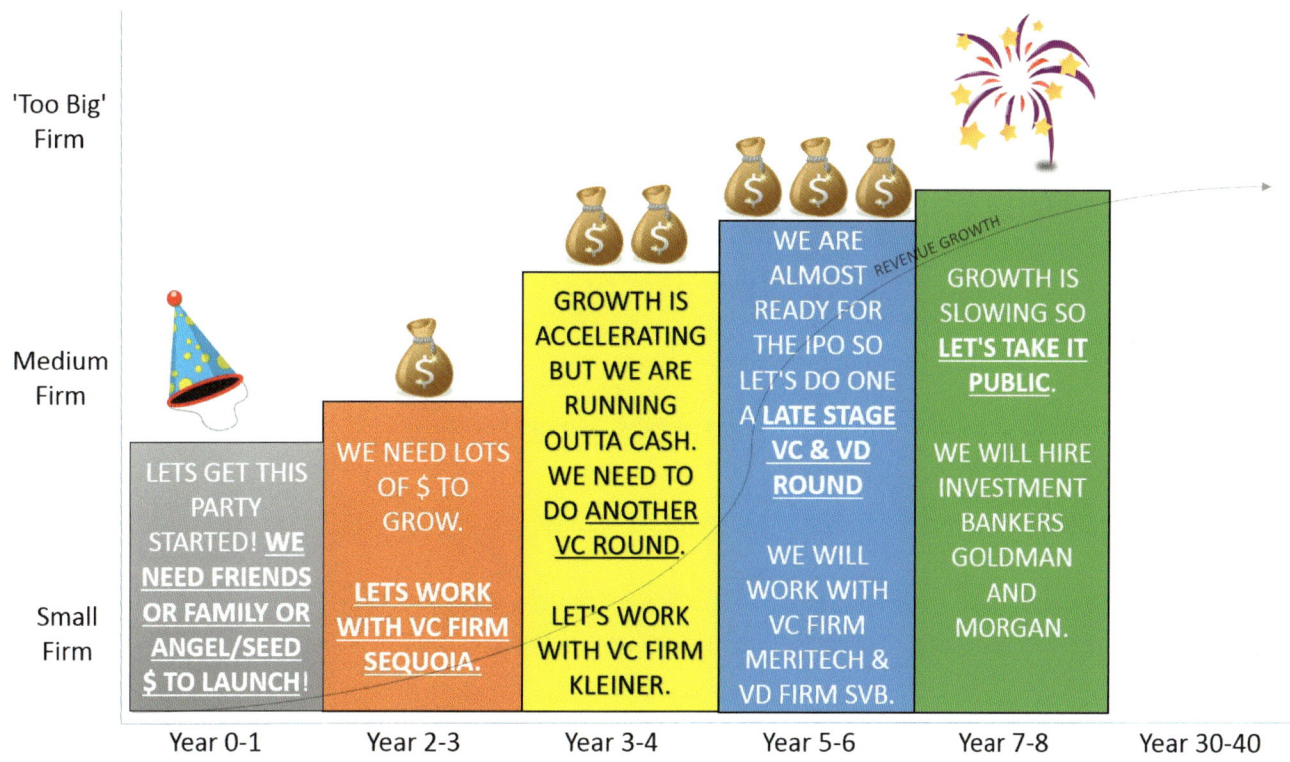

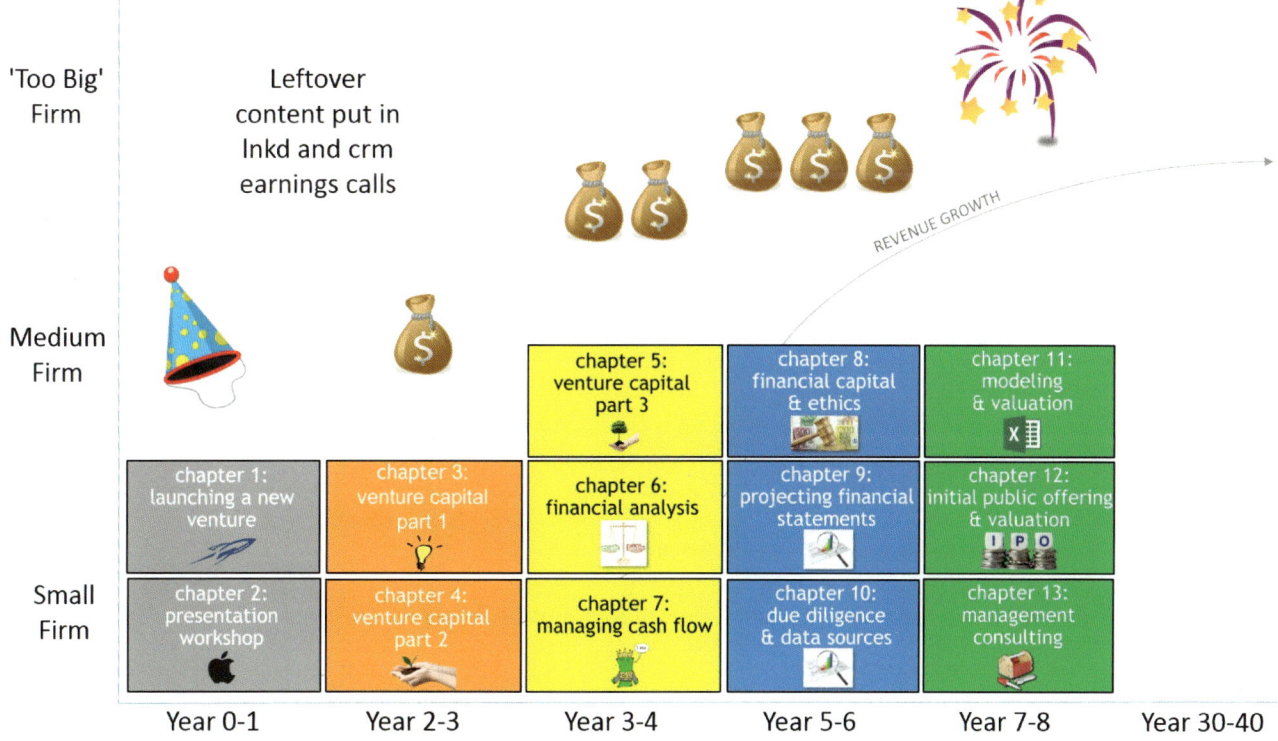

Microsoft tried to buy our company for an insulting $1bn. Oracle just approached us and is considering buying our firm for $10bn! Wow. Why would they do this? Is it because they are not growing anymore and they have to 'acquire growth' in order to appease concerned shareholders? Maybe they are too big to innovate? Tough call. Oracle needs some big time advice….

MANAGEMENT CONSULTING

In this chapter we will cover the role of the management consultant. In fact, you will get the opportunity to be a consultant and help your enterprise technology company client Oracle by offering advice on how they can grow revenue. Let's get started!

you are consultants in this chapter.	you will be armed with consulting frameworks.
which will help you analyze problems.	your mission is to help your client…
ORACLE	a tech relic and…

an old school software firm.	that has awful cloud technology.
how can they compete?	salesforce is eating their lunch!
cloud computing companies are killing them...especially...	salesforce
the largest tech employer in SF.	the most disruptive tech firm.

Salesforce is getting much stronger each year. They are building a massive 'Salesforce Tower' in San Francisco, which will be by far the tallest building in the city!

so strap in

this will be a real life simulation

do you want to be a consultant?	in this chapter you work for McKinsey&Company
consultants use frameworks	they analyze the problems
and suggest solutions	why are they hired?

because their clients cannot solve complex problems.	can you help oracle stay relevant?
let's begin.	about oracle.

Oracle (www.tiny.cc/chris89) is one of the oldest and most successful enterprise software companies in the world. The company has been trying to build on its core database product for years.

The cloud (www.tiny.cc/chris90) presents a threat - especially Salesforce (www.tiny.cc/chris91) and an opportunity for Oracle.

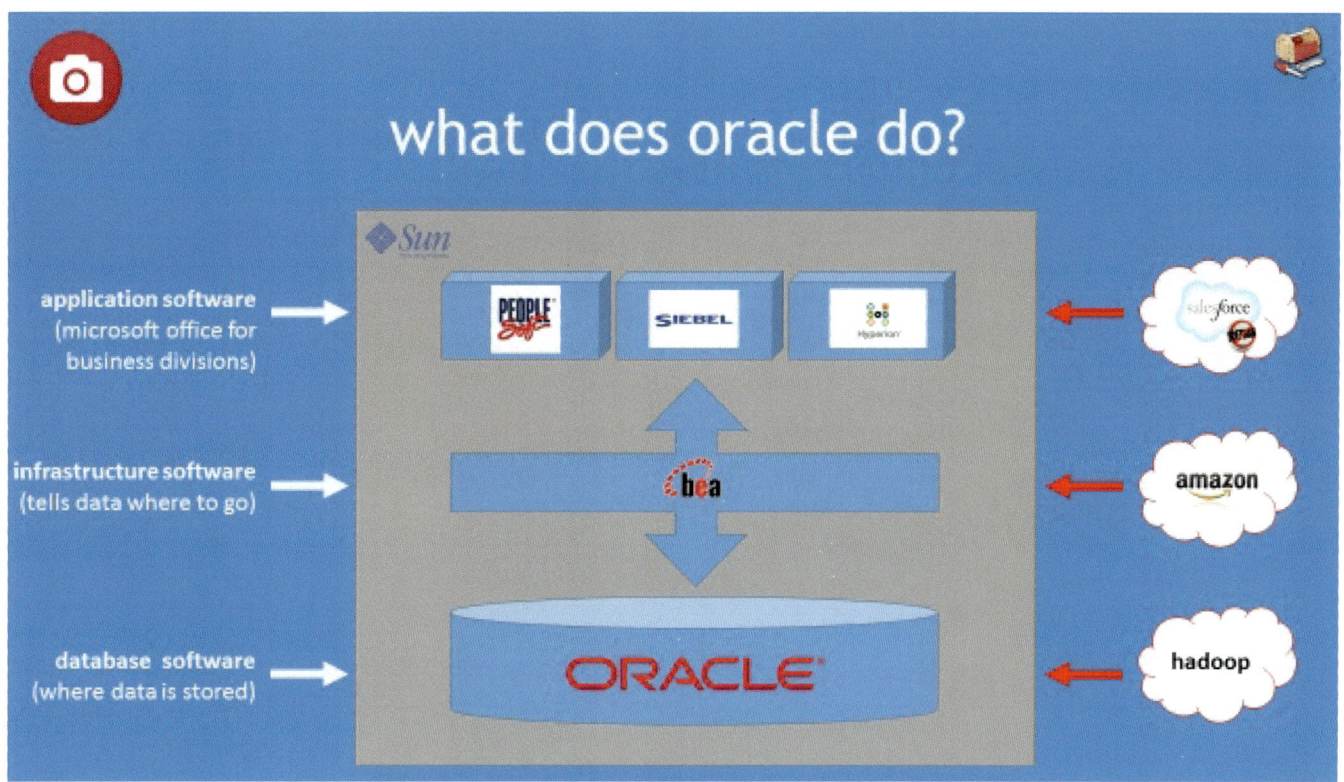

Oracle has been incredibly successful because of their CEO and founder Larry Ellison. You need to watch this video to understand his brilliant cerebral intensity: www.tiny.cc/chris92 .

Unfortunately Larry Ellison is stepping away from managing the day to day activities of the company. Per my article on founders leaving a company in the last chapter of this book, I am always worried about investing in a tech company when the founder is not as active as she or he used to be.

Let's look at an overview of the consulting industry:

consulting tam.

global tam = $420bn.
us tam = $165bn. 130k firms

types of consulting firms.

1: management / strategy
2: financial
3: i.t.
4: h.r. / staffing

management / strategy consulting

- should the government bail out ford?
- should a restaurant change the menu?
- should a hardware company divest?

financial consulting

- financial statement preparation?
- environmental regulation impact?
- should 2 big accounting firms merge?

i.t. consulting

- merger of b of a and nationsbank
- setting up offshore bank for cibc
- online banking access for b of a

I used to work in the i.t. consulting industry at Accenture, which I loved! 3 projects I worked on are listed in the previous graphic. What I loved about the consulting industry is that if you hate your job, it's all good as you can easily move on to another project in 6 months at another client site! Fortunately I loved every second of my employment there!

h.r. / staffing consulting

- should we outsource hiring?
- outsource retirement plan benefits?
- should we let people go?

positives of working in consulting

☺ intellectually stimulating
☺ opportunity to travel
☺ excellent compensation

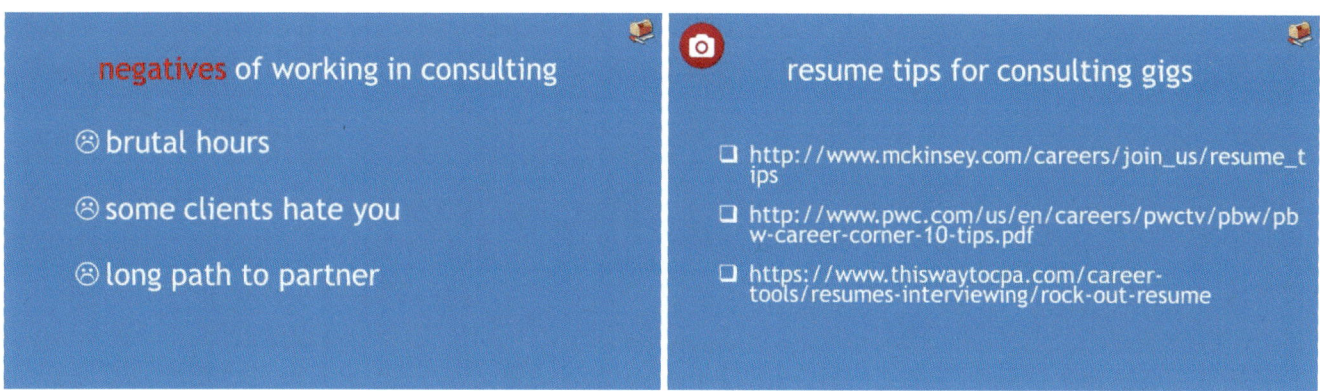

Here are the links from the 3 bullet points on the preview slide (if you are interested in working in the consulting sector that is):

- www.tiny.cc/chris93
- www.tiny.cc/chris94
- www.tiny.cc/chris96

After each course I took during my MBA and undergraduate business education, I would always reflect and try to recall one framework that I could take with me for analyzing business problems. Here are a few:

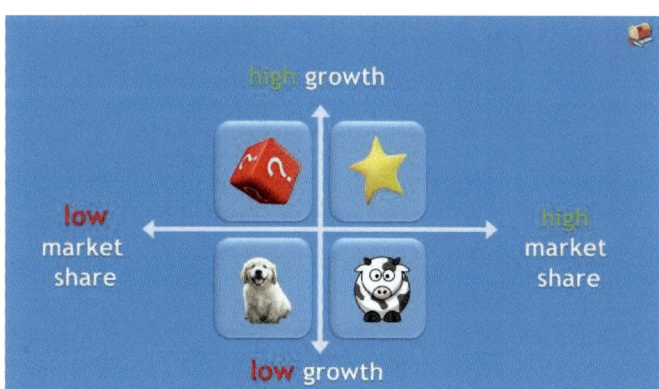

This is the Boston Consulting Group Framework. This framework helps companies categorize if their products or services are high or low growth and if they have high or low market share relative to the competition. Per the following slides, see if you can put each Apple product it the right categories. The categories are called: Question Marks, Stars (my kids tell me the Star logo is from the Mario Galaxy game which is a masterpiece), Dogs or Cash Cows.

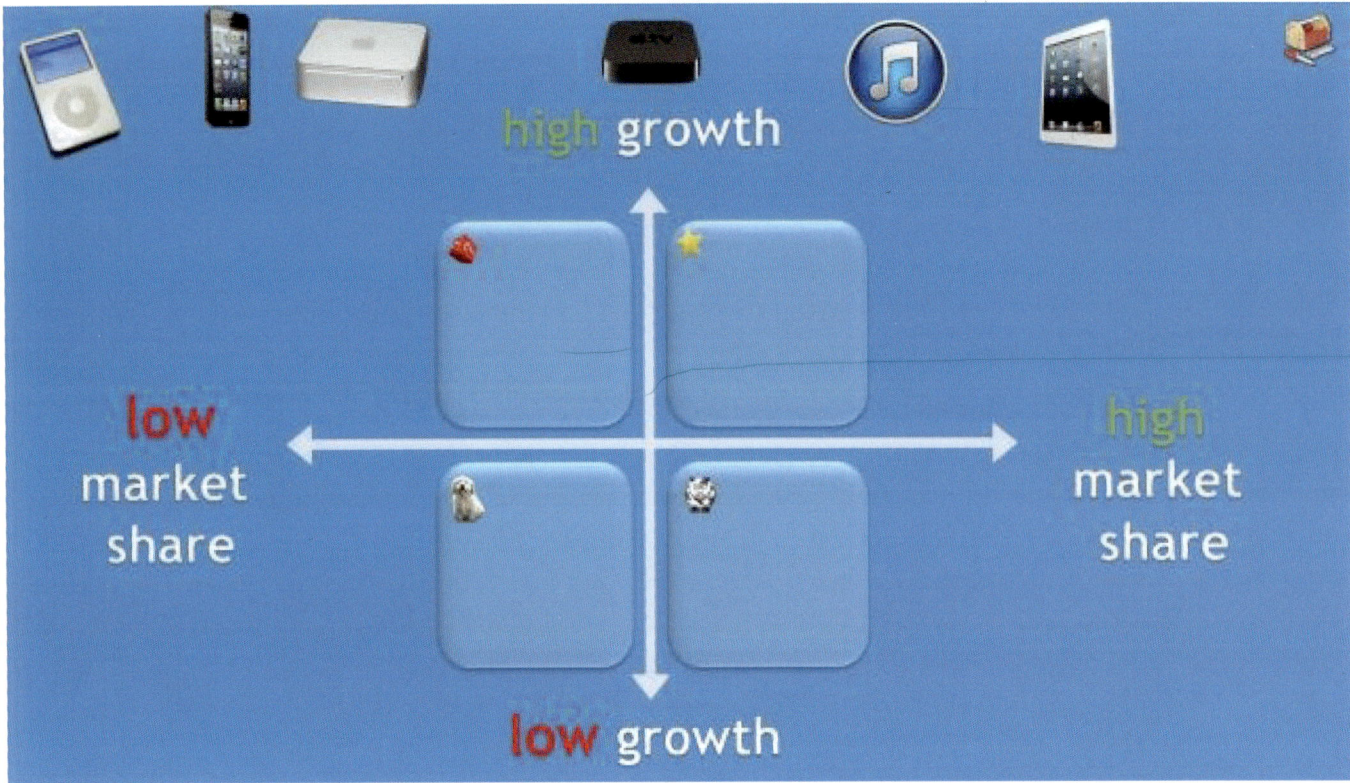

Let's see if you can place each of the Apple products in the image above in the correct Boston consulting Group (BCG) boxes. Again, the categories are: Question Marks, Stars, Dogs and Cash Cows.

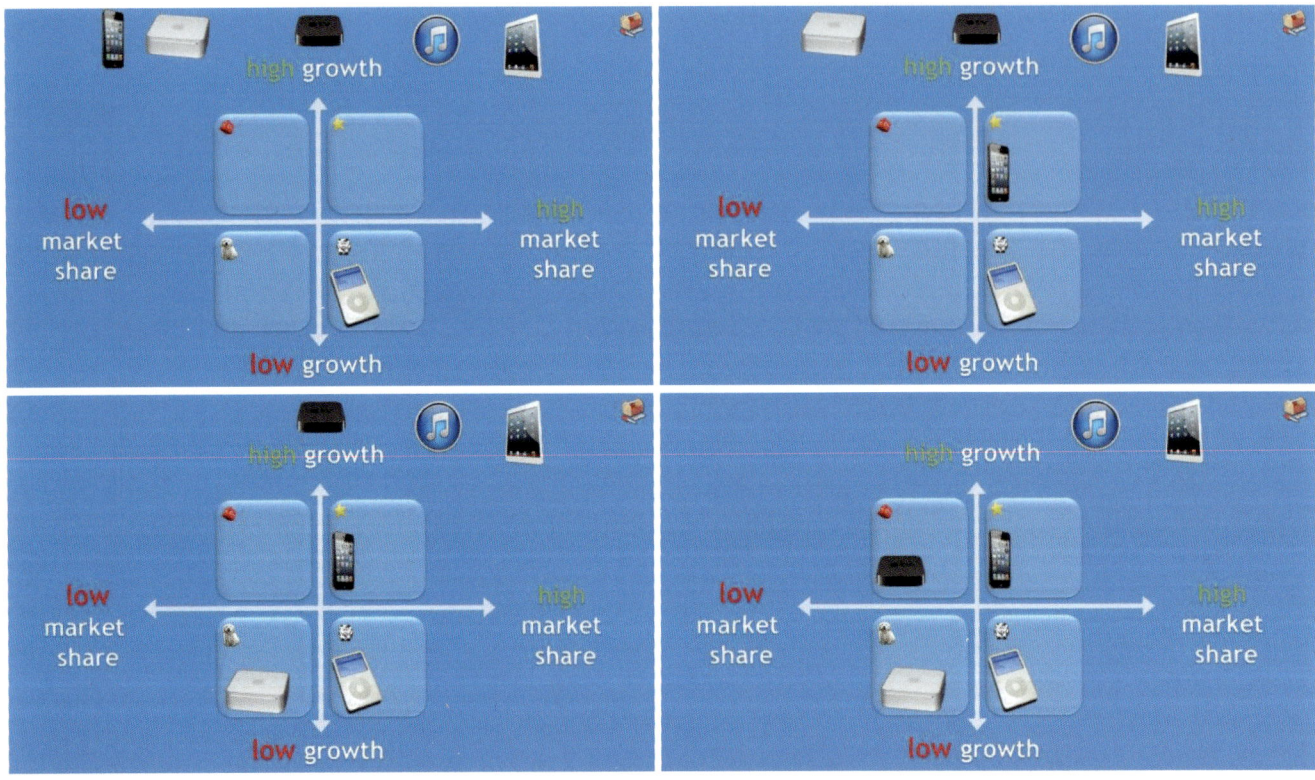

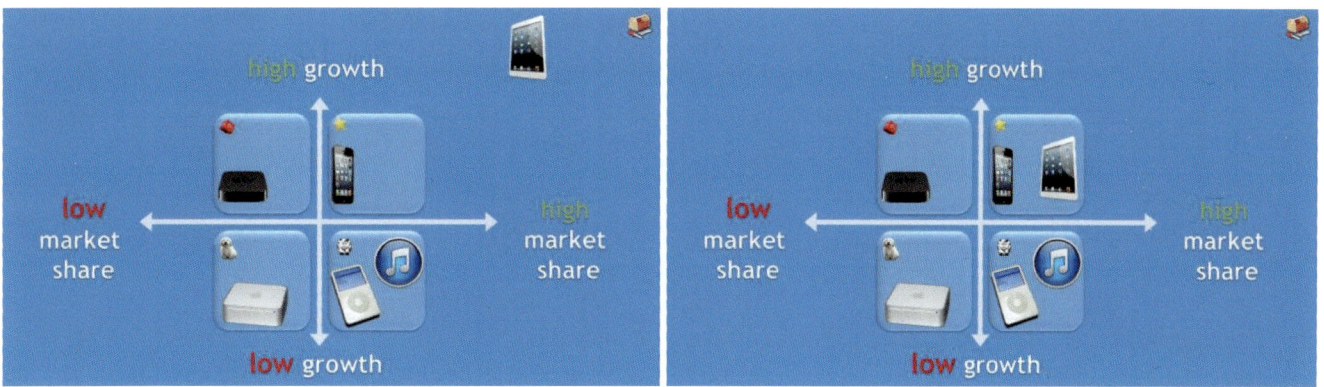

Another cool framework that I like to use is a SWOT analysts, which lets you categorize what a company's Strength, Weaknesses, Opportunities or Threats are.

Here is an example of a SWOT analysis in real (sort of) life here in Silicon Valley: http://tiny.cc/chris113

See if you can do a SWOT analysis for Facebook.

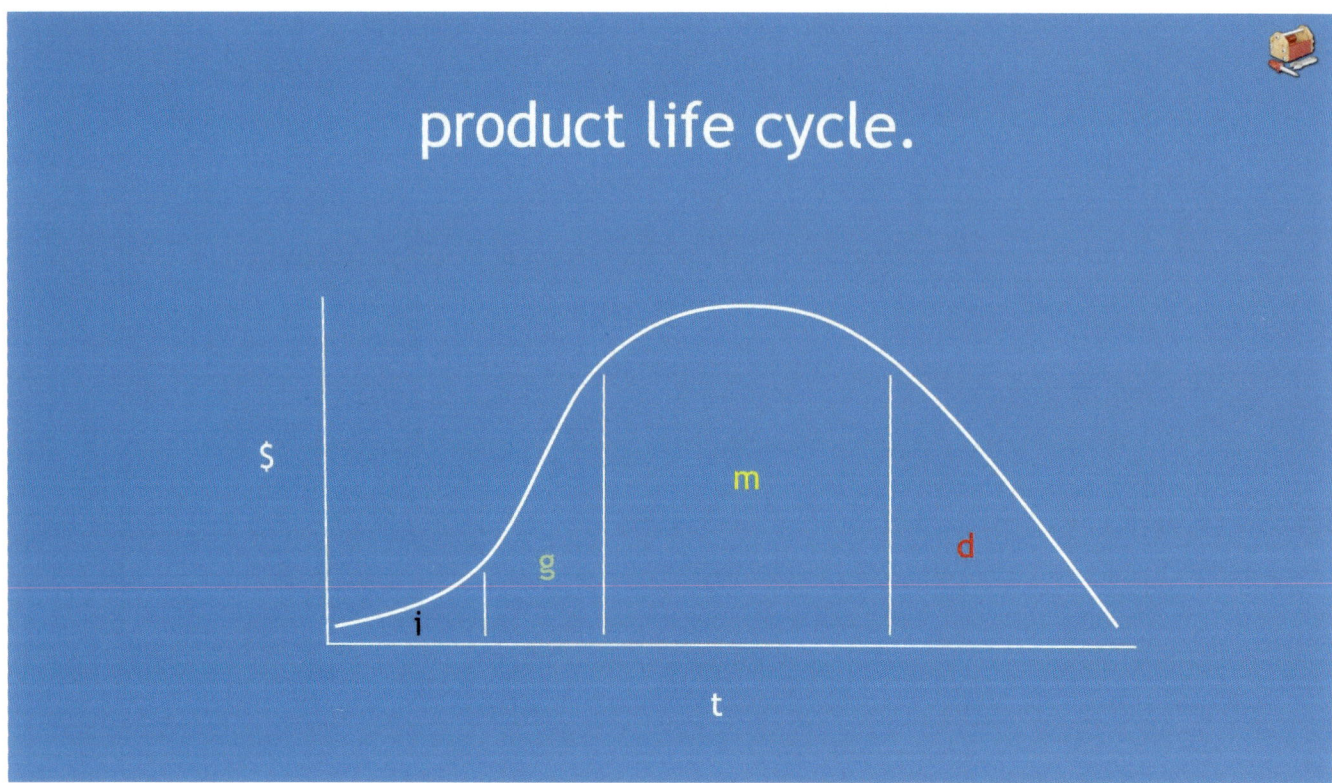

Another framework that consultants use and that I find helpful is the PLC or Product Life Cycle framework. Here you can analyze using time as the x axis and revenue growth as the y axis where companies or products are in their life cycle. The categories are Introduction Phase, Growth Phase, Maturity Phase and Decline Phase. Let's see if you can categorize where the following products are in the PLC: Microsoft Windows, The Apple Watch (our banana watch is way better!), IBM's Mainframe and the Tesla Model S car.

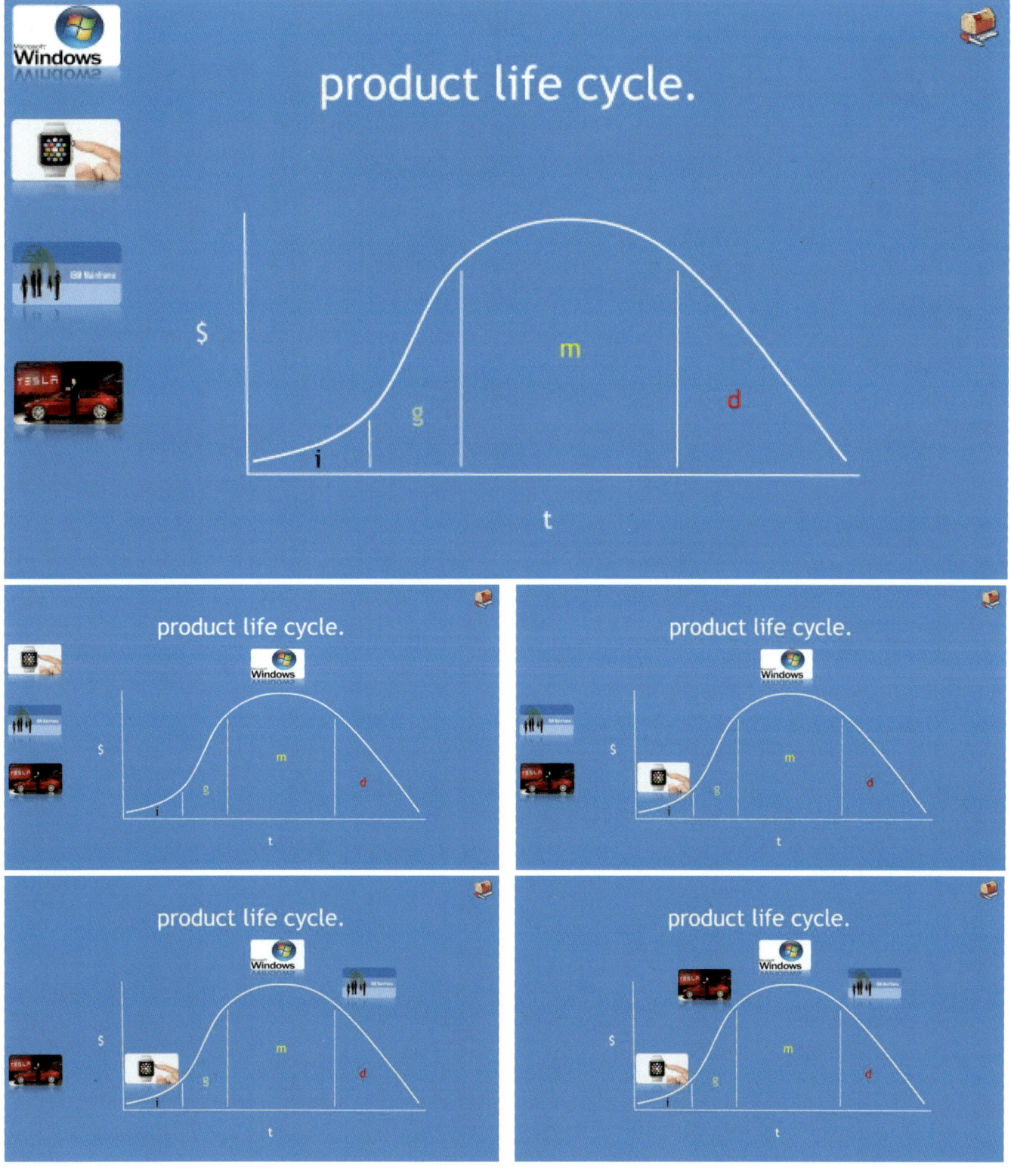

Another popular framework is Michael Porter's 5 Forces Model, where you analyze the following 5 forces have on a company: Supplier Power, Buyer Power, Competition, Substitutes and New Entrants. See if you can analyze Apple using this framework.

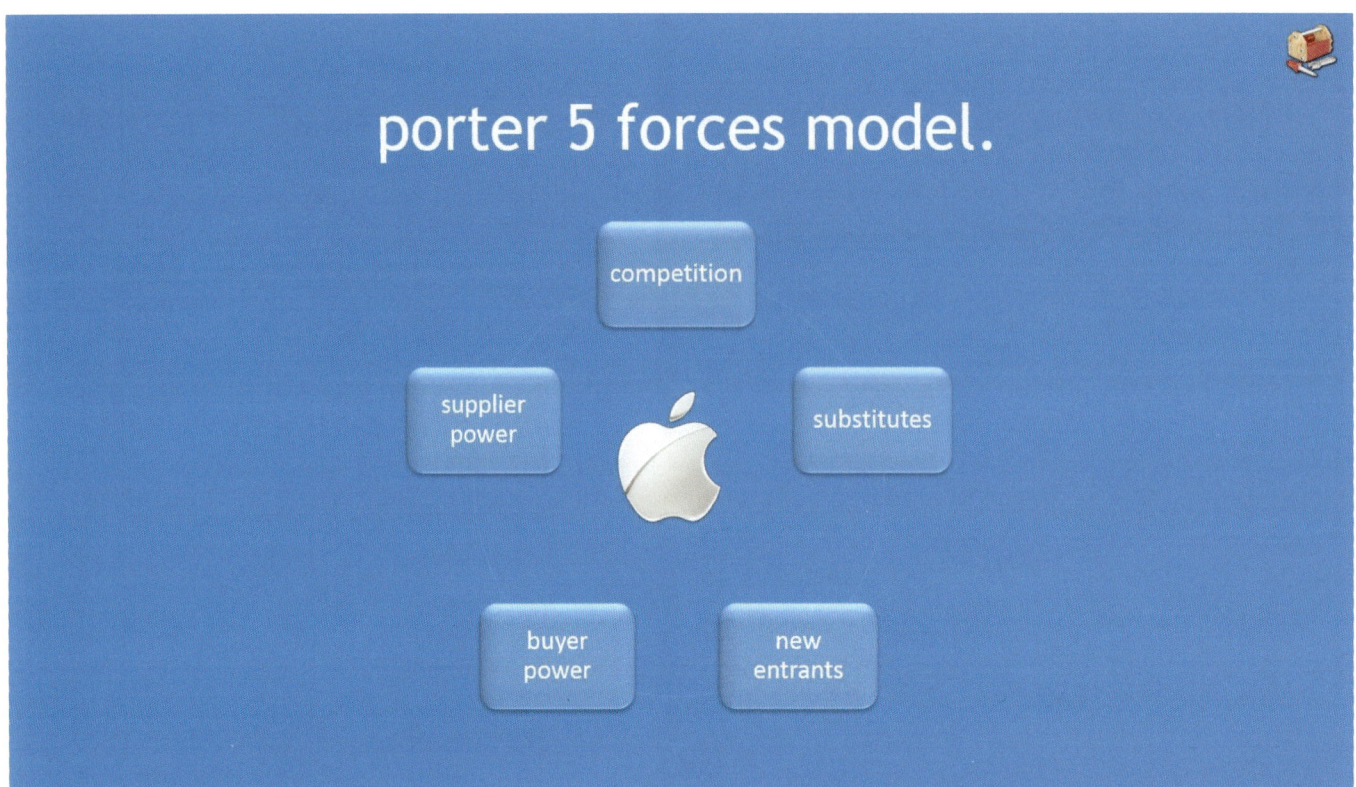

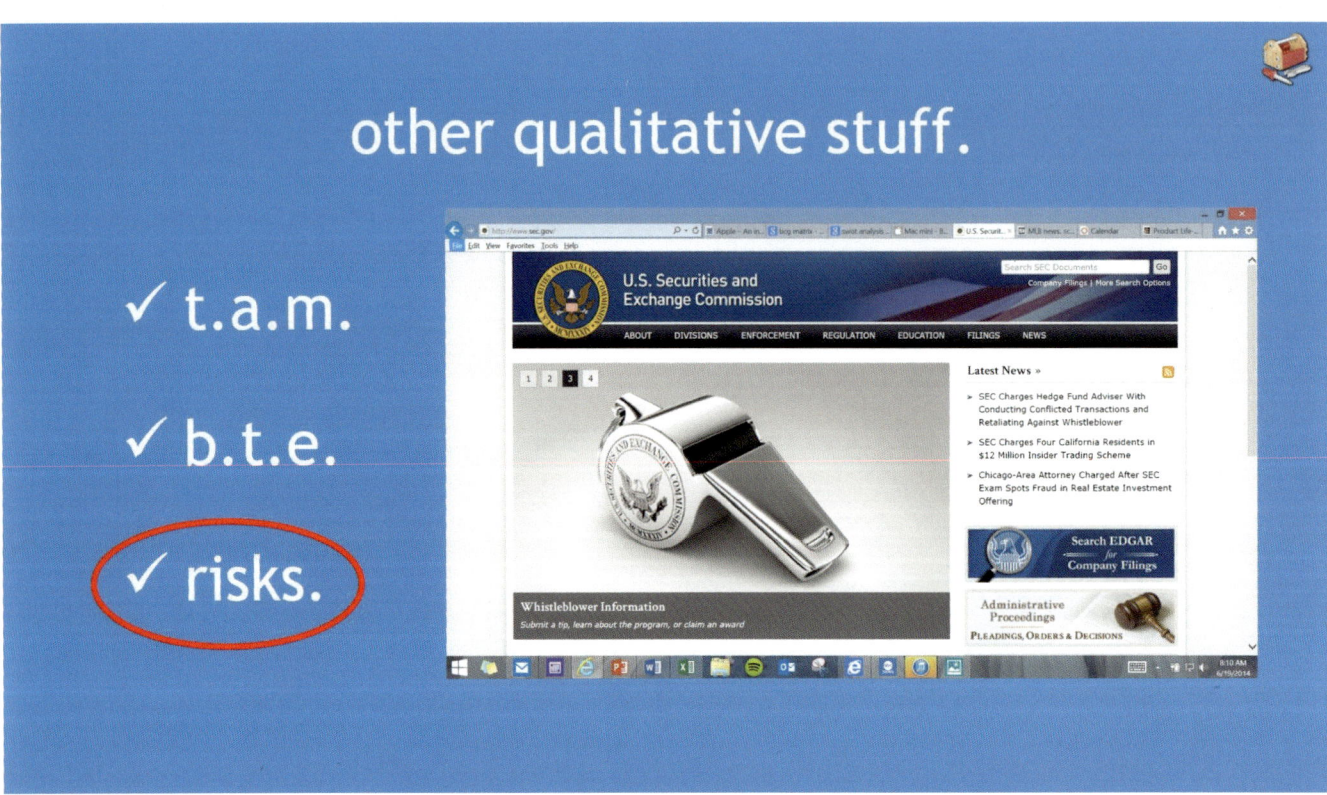

We can analyze a companies' T.A.M. or total addressable market as well, which we have already done earlier in this book. We can also analyze a company's B.T.E. or barrier's to [market] entry. Lastly, we have already used the www.sec.gov website to read about a company's or a company's competitor's risks in 10-k, 10-q, S-1 or 8-k filings. The next image shows some www.sec.gov highlighted risks as filed by Microsoft.

=

PART I
Item 1A

ITEM 1A. RISK FACTORS

Our operations and financial results are subject to various risks and uncertainties, including those described below, that could adversely affect our business, financial condition, results of operations, cash flows, and the trading price of our common stock.

We face intense competition across all markets for our products and services, which may lead to lower revenue or operating margins.

Competition in the technology sector

Our competitors range in size from diversified global companies with significant research and development resources to small, specialized firms whose narrower product lines may let them be more effective in deploying technical, marketing, and financial resources. Barriers to entry in our businesses generally are low and software products can be distributed broadly and quickly at relatively low cost. Many of the areas in which we compete evolve rapidly with changing and disruptive technologies, shifting user needs, and frequent introductions of new products and services. Our ability to remain competitive depends on our success in making innovative products, devices, and services that appeal to businesses and consumers.

Competition among platforms, ecosystems, and devices

An important element of our business model has been to create platform-based ecosystems on which many participants can build diverse solutions. A well-established ecosystem creates beneficial network effects among users, application developers, and the platform provider that can accelerate growth. Establishing significant scale in the marketplace is necessary to achieve and maintain attractive margins. The strategic importance of developing and maintaining a vibrant ecosystem increased with the launch of the Windows 8 operating system, Surface, Windows Phone, and associated cloud-based services. We face significant competition from firms that provide competing platforms, applications, and services.

- A competing vertically-integrated model, in which a single firm controls the software and hardware elements of a product and related services, has been successful with some consumer products such as personal computers, tablets, mobile phones, gaming consoles, and digital music players. Competitors pursuing this model also earn revenue from services that are integrated with the hardware and software platform. We also offer some vertically-integrated hardware and software products and services; however, our competitors in smartphones and tablets have established significantly larger user bases. Efforts to compete with the vertically integrated model will increase our cost of revenue and reduce our operating margins.
- We derive substantial revenue from licenses of Windows operating systems on personal computers. We face substantial competitive challenges from competing platforms developed for new devices and form factors such as smartphones and tablet computers. These devices compete on multiple bases including price and the perceived utility of the device and its platform. Users are increasingly turning to these devices to perform functions that would have been performed by personal computers in the past. Even if many users view these devices as complementary to a personal computer, the prevalence of these devices may make it more difficult to attract applications developers to our platforms. In addition, Surface competes with products made by our OEM partners, which may affect their commitment to our platform.

Alrighty it's that time again. You're my boy blue! :)

www.sec.gov
team red.
team blue.
1: provide 3 risks for oracle.
2: provide 2013 Q3 revenue for oracle.
3: provide name of ceo of oracle.

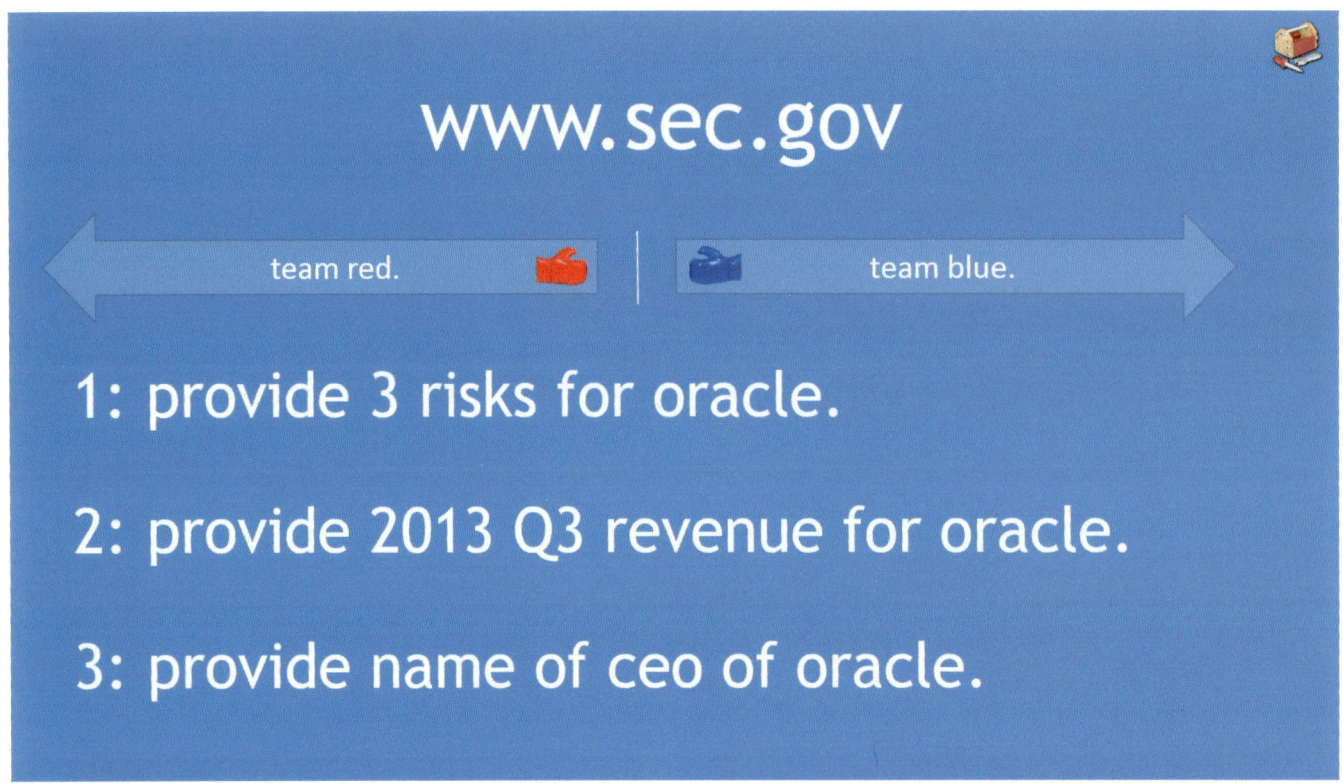

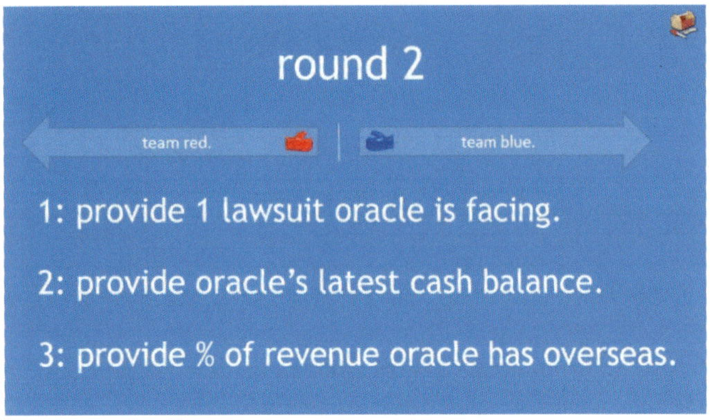
round 2
team red.
team blue.
1: provide 1 lawsuit oracle is facing.
2: provide oracle's latest cash balance.
3: provide % of revenue oracle has overseas.

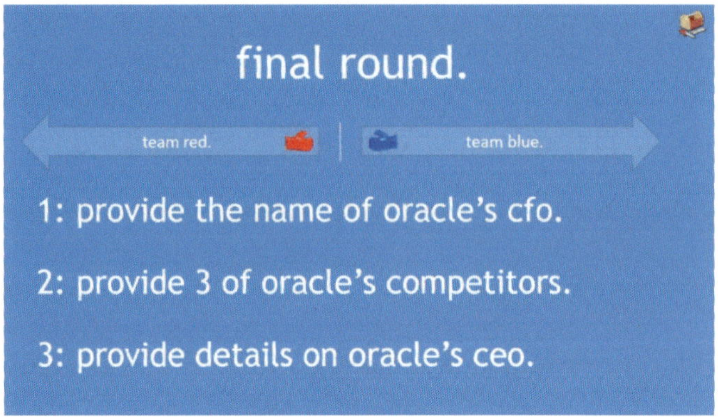
final round.
team red.
team blue.
1: provide the name of oracle's cfo.
2: provide 3 of oracle's competitors.
3: provide details on oracle's ceo.

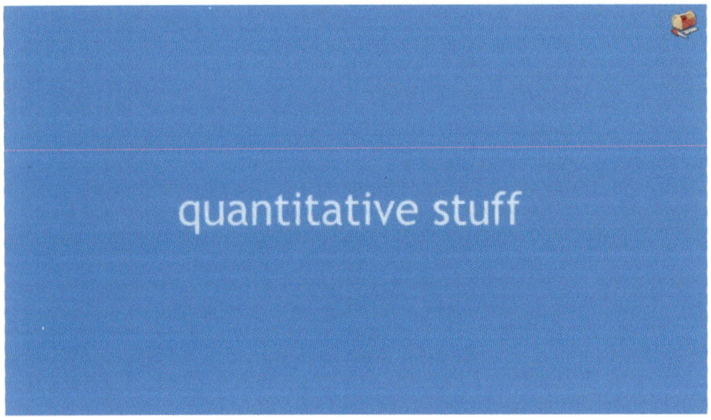
quantitative stuff

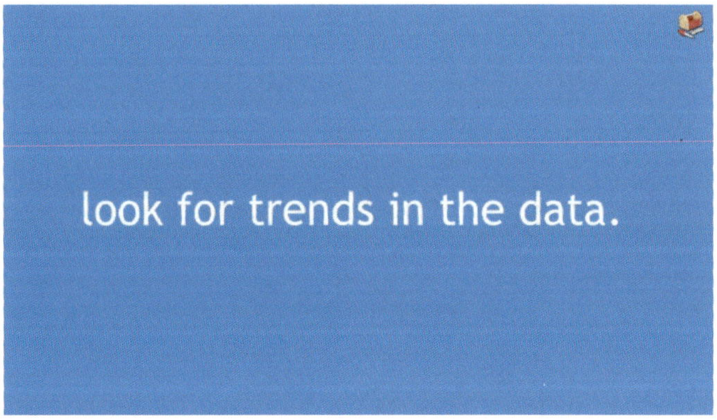
look for trends in the data.

oracle income statement.

[Chart showing Oracle revenue bars from 2009-2014 with acquisition logos: PeopleSoft, Siebel, Hyperion, bea, Sun Microsystems, RightNow (36 in 2011), Taleo (37 in 2012), acme packet (37 in 2013), micros (38 in 2014), with values 23 (2009), 27 (2010)]

Every chart tells a story. We already know that Oracle's organic growth is negative. In fact, if the company didn't make the acquisitions listed above, then actual revenue growth would be negative. The danger with Oracle's acquisition strategy is that they need to make multi-billion dollar acquisitions every single year or else investors will catch on that they have anemic growth. It's not their fault as all great tech companies get too big and it just gets hard to grow given the law of large numbers.

Below is a 10 year P/E chart for Oracle. It looks like Wall St. is catching on as the P/E continues to contract.

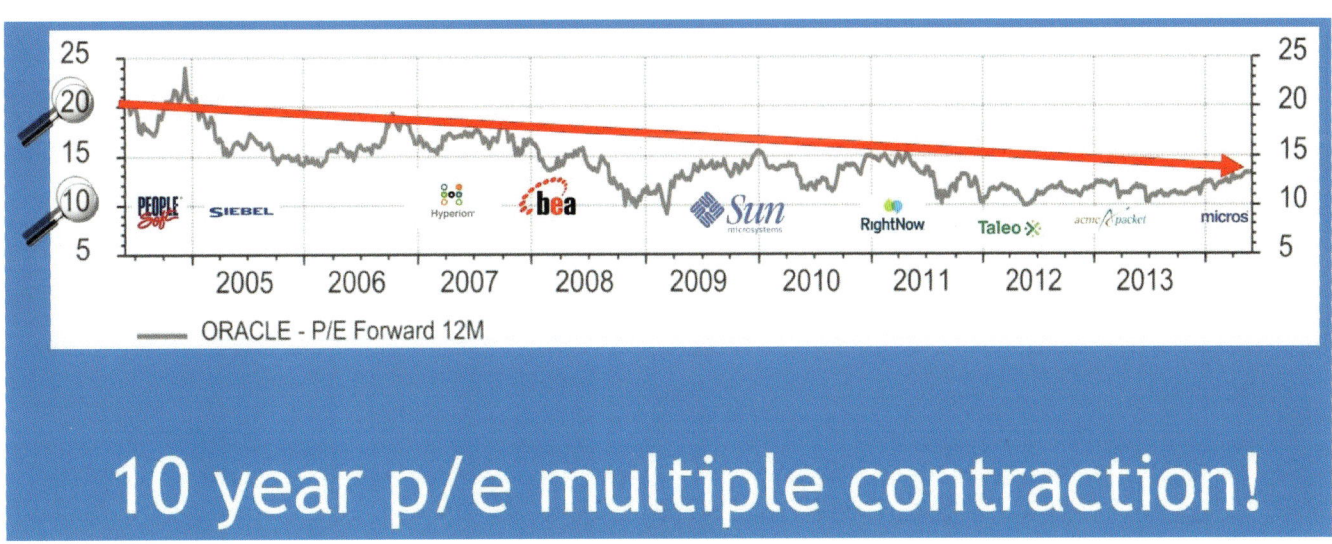

10 year p/e multiple contraction!

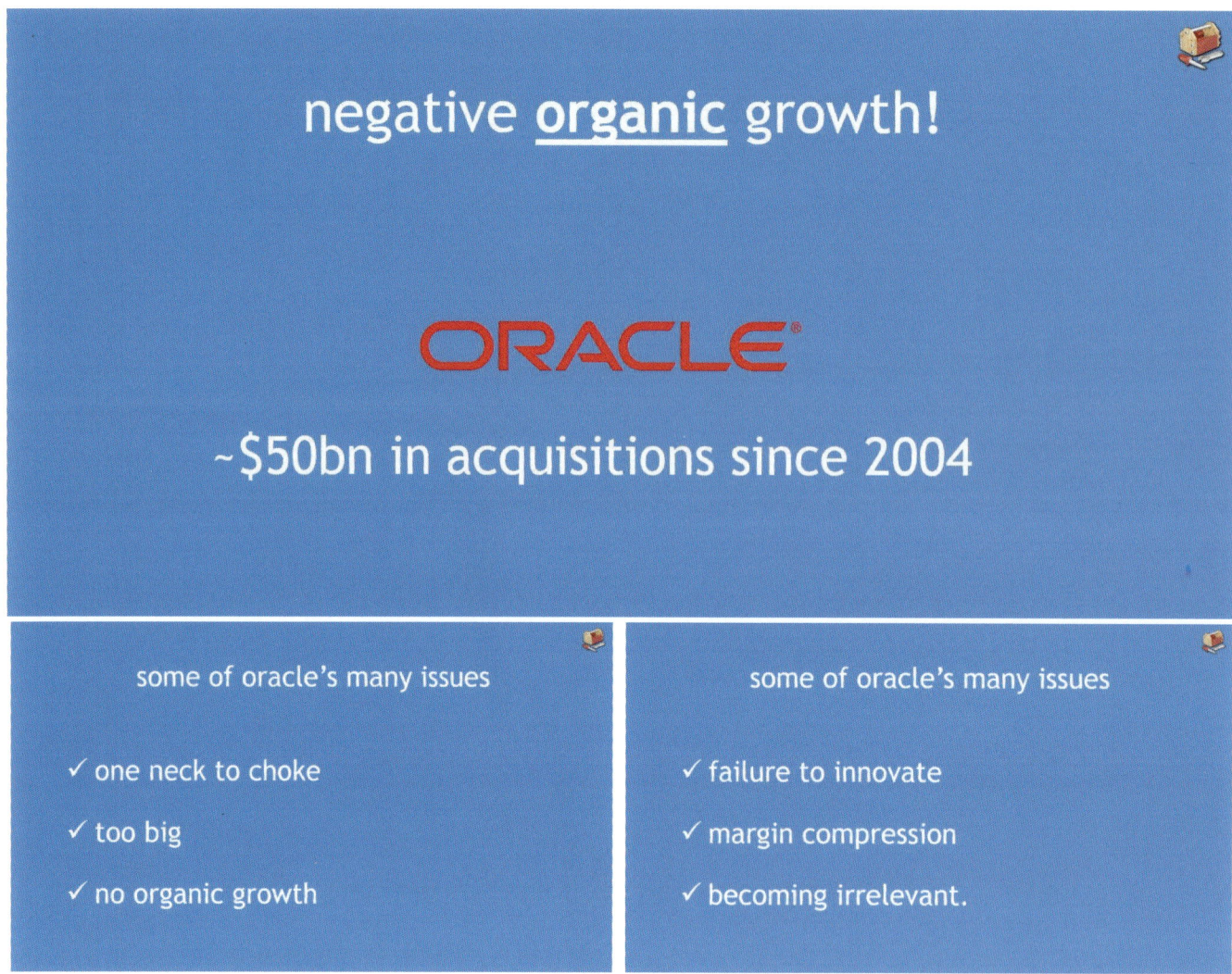

Oracle has many issues, which you as the consultant can analyze. There is a concern that they have way too much market power as many of their customers buy too much from them. We call this a 'one neck to choke' strategy as customers complain to one salesperson at Oracle if they have issues since they buy many products from one firm. However, this can lead to higher prices if a company has too much market power over customers (side note: Is Apple getting this way? Have you ever seen a product on sale in an Apple Store?).

consulting ethics.

A cornerstone of this book is business ethics, which of course are of paramount importance also in the consulting industry as well: www.tiny.cc/chris97 .

orcl today is in secular decline

What would you recommend that Oracle do to stop organic growth from being negative? How would you improve Oracle? What would you recommend they do?

<u>another</u> networking workshop.

getting a job using

www.tiny.cc/chris98

did anyone get an informational meeting?

PLEASE try harder.

HOW TO TELL IF SOMEONE IS LYING

When I worked at a large hedge fund called Citadel, management hired 25 year CIA and FBI veterans to teach us how to tell if a CEO is lying to us. Here are some of the key takeaways:

1: A liar often gives long winded answers to a simple yes or no question.

2: A liar often does not make eye contact when answering a question and the answer contains a lie (unless this is their normal demeanor).

3: A liar often puts their hand on their mouth when answering a question with a lie.

4: A liar often shakes his or her foot when answering a question with a lie (unless they drink too much coffee)!

Questions Based on Chapter 13:

1: Companies often hire consultants because that company can't solve complex themselves.

　　True   or   False

2: Positives of working in the consulting industry might include:

　　a) The ability to travel.
　　b) The ability to receive excellent compensation.
　　c) The work can be very intellectually stimulating.
　　d) All of the above.

3: S.W.O.T analysis stands for: Strengths. Weaknesses. Opportunities. Threats

<u>True</u>   or   False

CHAPTER SUMMARY

Chris Haroun @chris_haroun

qualitative tools = b.c.g, p.l.c., s.w.o.t, management, catalysts, risks and networking. *"relationships are more important than product knowledge!"* www.sec.gov.

Chapter 14: Alternatives and Turnarounds

"We are all in. All the time. 24/7. 365 days a year.

100% heart. 1000% passion."

- *Mike Harden*

The Ultimate Practical Business Manual

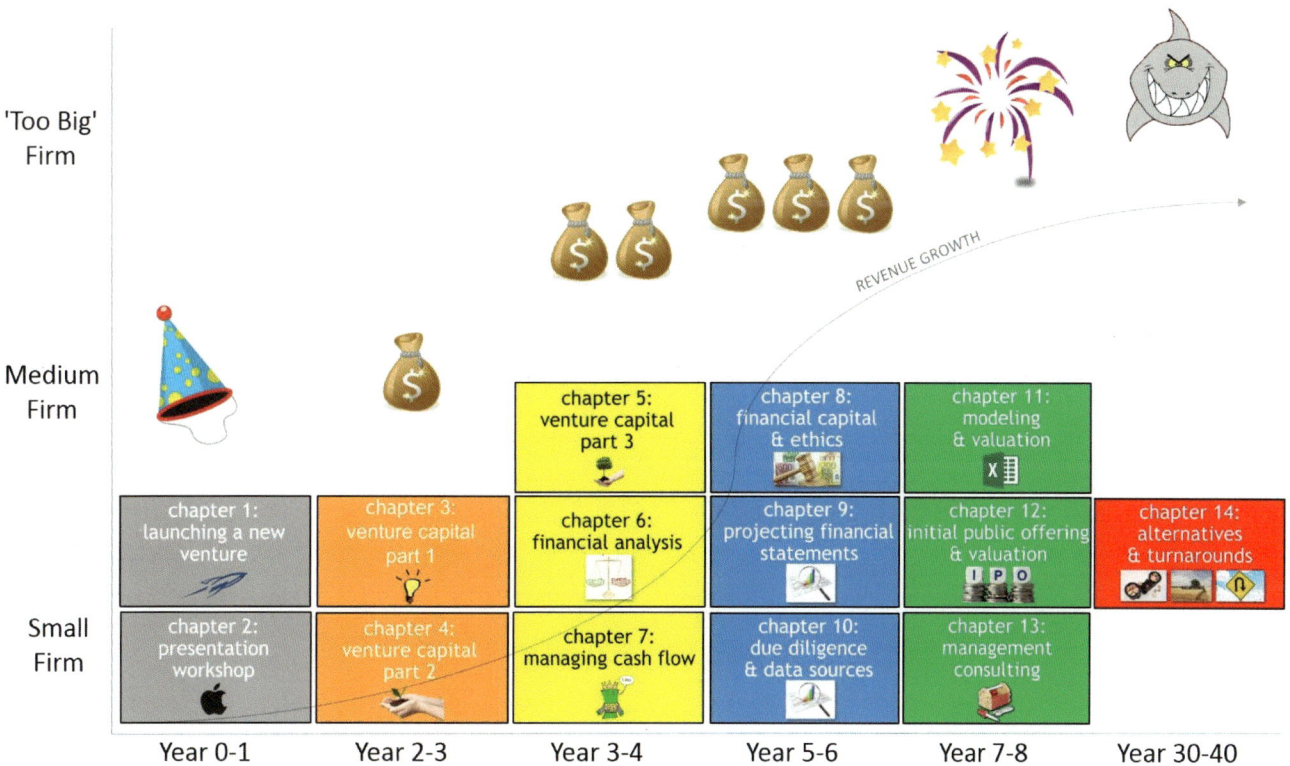

i hope you use the entrepreneurial skills you learn in this book and be your own boss one day.

this video is an inspiration for you to one day be your own boss! :)

www.tiny.cc/chris99

We have started a company in this book. We took the company public. Companies often get too big. When this happens they get too inefficient. Their stock price starts to fall. Investors get upset. Blood is now in the water and here come the sharks.....

this chapter's topic:

financing alternatives / harvesting / turnarounds

topic 1 of 3:

financing alternatives

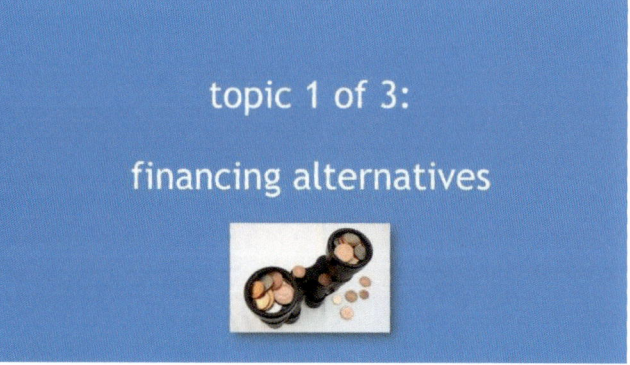

equity investors are better for startups...

...because if you had debt investors and missed just one payment.....

….then your business dies.	ok. let's examine additional sources of financing.
raising money is tough. should you pay upfront fees to a consultant to raise you money?	99% of the time it is fraudulent or doesn't work!
fees after trumps fees before.	in real estate, commissions come after a sale and never before!
you will meet many dishonest people in business. keep your guard up!	commercial & venture bank lending

commercial loans are possible with a few years of operating history.

commercial lenders want to see cash flow projections based on a few years of history.

they care a bit less about the value of your assets unless they are uber liquid.

lenders hate giving money to earlier stage companies as the government harasses them about NPLs.

vc firms love risk.

debt firms hate risk.

wait! there is a bank that has a brand that implies that they lend to venture startups!

svb lends to vc backed startups...

...in return they get interest and more importantly warrants.

for vc firms, equity is the main course.

for vd firms, equity is the sweetener.

entrepreneurs partner with vc

before

entrepreneurs partner with vd

all of the hard work and due diligence was already done by the vc

the vd jumps on the bandwagon.

why u might not get debt financing
- if you don't have 2+ years financials
- if you have few tangible assets.
- if you have low revenue (tech…)
- 1-2 employees are too valuable

credit cards
- 50% of startups use credit cards for debt
- don't get romanced by teaser rates
- if your cr rating sucks, you can't raise d.

foreign investor funding sources
- the us government lets you buy lawful permanent resident status if you invest $1mn in a startup and create or preserve 10+ jobs
- the minimum drops to $500k if it is in a rural or high unemployment region.
- wow…many people buy the american dream
- even easier if foreigner invests in a turnaround!

additional government loans
- for native americans
- for hawaiians
- for women
- for veterans etc

vendor financing

- 'payable in 2, 10 net 30'...
- ...means you get a 2% discount if you pay in 10 days or else it is due in 30 days.
- dumb idea though....
- ...as that 2% discount for 10 days = an annual compound rate of over 40%!

vendor leasing

- kind of like what svb does for loans
- ...except you lease equipment and....
- ...part of payment is in warrants

other financing examples

- mortgage if the company owns the business
- 'direct public offerings'....
- ....means you get a loan of up to $1mn through a syndicate of many investors
- this is basically crowdsourcing [lending club]

bootstrapping

- this means you pay for the start up yourself
- but I advise <u>always</u> advise using O.P.M. ...
- other people's money [unless you are loaded]
- and set up that LLC so your family is protected.

<u>PLEASE</u> don't ever finance an early stage company with a loan... www.tiny.cc/chris100

topic 2 of 3:

harvesting

harvesting an investment

- assets can be transferred to investors
- company can be sold and cash is distributed to investors
- company goes public and shares are distributed 6 months post IPO lockup

planning an exit strategy

- you need to explain liquidity targets to investors when you are raising capital
- otherwise trauma occurs as investors have their own personal liquidity needs
- easy way to value them is using relative multiples [we covered valuation already]

buyouts.

- leveraged buyout (lbo)....
- ...financed using debt
- must have great cash flows to secure loans

buyouts.
- firms like KKR or TPG can help
- many public companies partner with these private equity firms and go private….
- …with the goal of going public again at some point.

buyouts.
- if management drives the buyout then..
- …it's called a management buyout (mbo)
- this took place with nabisco in the 80s with KKR's help (henry kravis)

KKR (Henry Kravis) and LBOs in action

Henry Kravis from KKR created the private equity business, which do LBOs (leveraged buyouts) and can take a public company private, which is the opposite of what IPO investment bankers do! www.tiny.cc/chris101

ESOPs.
- employee stock ownership plans…
- …employees buy the company using leverage
- owned by all employees and not just management

IPO
- we covered this…let's just over a few terms…
- …primary shares in an ipo means new shares (so the firm gets $)
- …secondary shares in an ipo means existing shares are sold (for the vc or for employees that want to cash out).

IPO
- 'underwriting spread' is the fee the investment bank gets (usually up to 7%)
- to list on NASDAQ you need to price at $4+, have over 1mn shares, been in business for a few years, BOD, etc.

topic 3 of 3:
troubled ventures & turnarounds

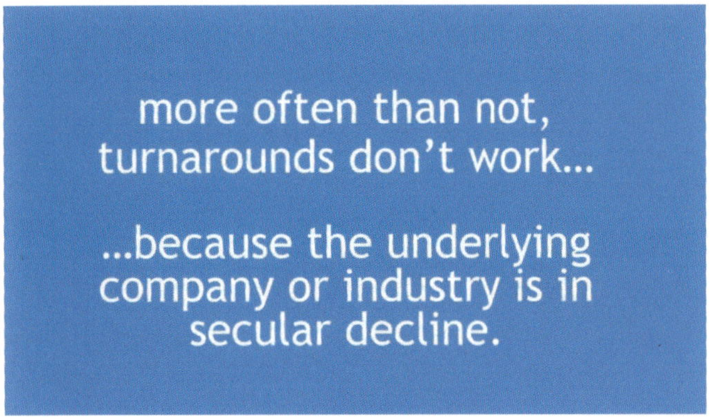

> **more often than not, turnarounds don't work...**
>
> **...because the underlying company or industry is in secular decline.**

Corporate raiders restructure companies in the hope of turning them around (even though I don't believe that turnarounds work in tech, per my article on this topic in the last chapter of this book).

www.tiny.cc/chris102

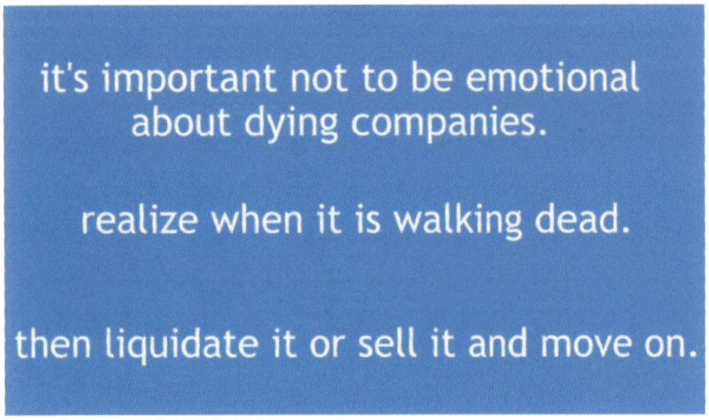

> **it's important not to be emotional about dying companies.**
>
> **realize when it is walking dead.**
>
> **then liquidate it or sell it and move on.**

Learn when to shut down a company. Don't be emotional. Just move on and live to fight another day.

www.tiny.cc/chris103

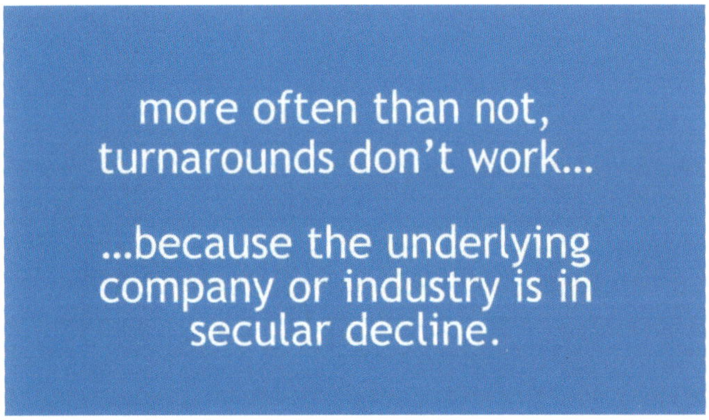

> **more often than not, turnarounds don't work...**
>
> **...because the underlying company or industry is in secular decline.**

> **as a result, corporate raiders break apart the company.**

> **for example, is hp worth more dead than alive?**

> **#1 reason ventures fail?**

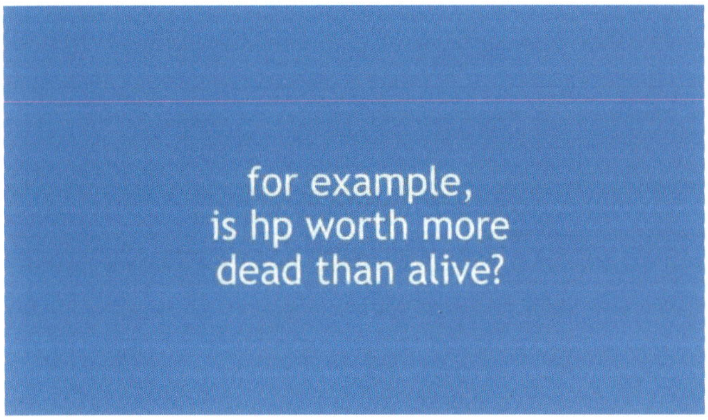

The primary reasons that companies die is that they run out of cash. Cash is king.

why do ventures fail?

"I RULE."

financial distress

when cash on hand is insufficient to pay for current liabilities

loan default

miss one payment and it's over.

acceleration provision

when a firm defaults on just one payment then all future payments are due immediately.

cross default provision

one late payment on one loan causes <u>all</u> loans to go into default

foreclosure

the legal process where lenders collect and take stuff from you

This is the house I grew up in in Mississauga, Canada. On the left is a picture of my friend's house. A wonderful family lived there that owned a few amazing Portuguese delis. Unfortunately my friend's father didn't set up an LLC. The restaurants were in his name. As a result, when he missed just ONE payment, the bank took his house and everything in it. Bastards. They even changed the lock on the door. PLEASE protect your family and hire a lawyer when you start a company. She/he will register your company for you so that your family is protected.

LLC protects your family. equity rules.

insolvent

negative book equity

25% of companies go belly up within 2 years of being founded.

>50% of companies shut down within 4 years of being founded.

WHAT IS 'CHAPTER 11': WHAT IS THIS AND WHY IS IT IMPORTANT TO YOU?

what is all this "chapter this" and "chapter that" stuff in bankruptcy law?

bankruptcy laws is a legal code that has many chapters. i.e.,:
- chapter 7 is how people/firms liquidate stuff
- chapter 9 is how cities deal w/ bankruptcy
- chapter 11 is how firms deal w/ bankruptcy
- chapter 12 is how farms deal w/ bankruptcy

"chris not only is this session incredibly boring but please show me what my life might be like if i don't follow my dreams and be my own boss one day."

www.tiny.cc/chris104

what about the other chapters?

- chapter 1, 3 & 5 are general bankruptcy rules
- chapter 15 = the trustees that help banks
- chapter 13 restructuring personal debt
- most important = 7 (liquidate), 11 (restructure)

chapter 7 liquidation

after a person/company files for bankruptcy then a court supervises the liquidation process

chapter 11 bankruptcy example...

www.tiny.cc/chris105

chapter 11 bankruptcy filing

this temporarily protects a distressed firm so they can restructure or pay off debt

buys you time

operations restructuring

increase revenue
or
cut expenses

asset restructuring

selling assets
or
improving ratios like d/e

asset restructuring

you can also improve ratios like:

days sales outstanding

or

inventory conversion period

financial restructuring

changing terms on debt
(i.e., gimme more time)

---

chris this session is depressing me

can you share a little positive stuff?

YES!

chapter 11 works!

65% reorganize
28% liquidate
and
7% merge with another firm

---

http://tiny.cc/chris114

---

chris this session is so interesting now!

can you walk me through ch 11 steps?

HECK YAH!

1: file for chapter 11 with one of 300 bankruptcy courts

2: a bankruptcy judge accepts or doesn't accept petition

3: if no fraud, the company has 120 days to make a plan

4: 60 days is then given to creditors to accept the plan

5: investors then vote

---

debt sucks early on.

banks don't give a damn.

vc firms care (more)

---

raise as much $ as you can when you can from equity investors.

it's almost impossible raising money in a recession.

A butterfly effect can rip through the global economy causing a damn domino effect....which is what happened to many given the Madoff scandal. Heck his name was 'Made Off' so we should known better eh! :)

with all investors, offer near full transparency for 2 reasons (among others)...

...all you have in business is your reputation/integrity.

...and often the same investors will back you again (even if you were not successful! yes it is true)

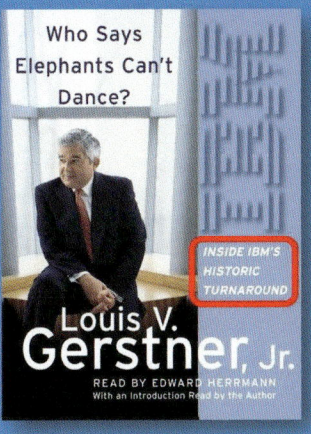

Questions Based on Chapter 14:

1: Most companies that are not fraudulent that declare Chapter 11 status end up benefitting by restructuring.

True or False

2: Most people and entities that claim that they can help you raise money are not legitimate.

True or False

3: Entrepreneurs usually partner with venture debt firms before venture capital firms.

True or False   VC b4 VD

CHAPTER SUMMARY

Chris Haroun @chris_haroun
equity investors trump debt investors early on. additional ways to raise capital. bankruptcy courts can protect your business as you restructure.

CHAPTER 15: LEFTOVER CONTENT

"The harder we work, the luckier we get."

- *Stuart Peterson*

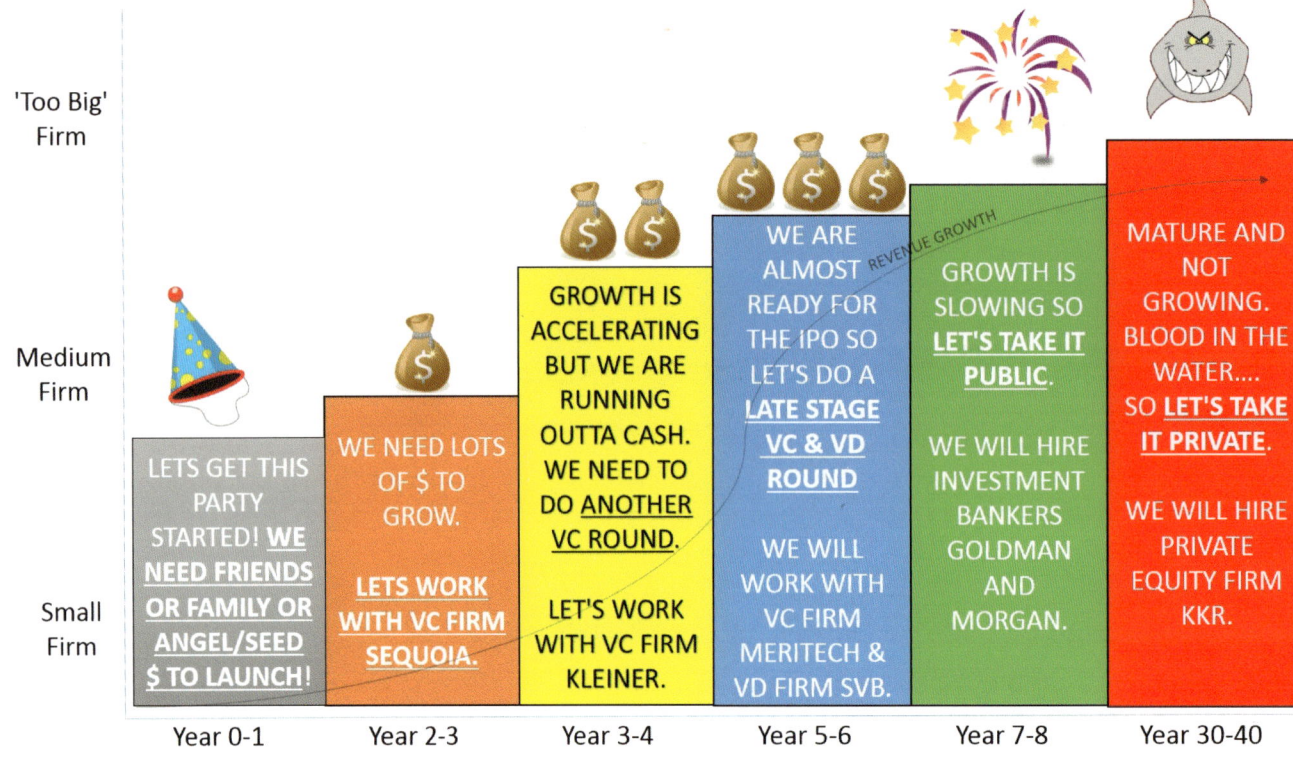
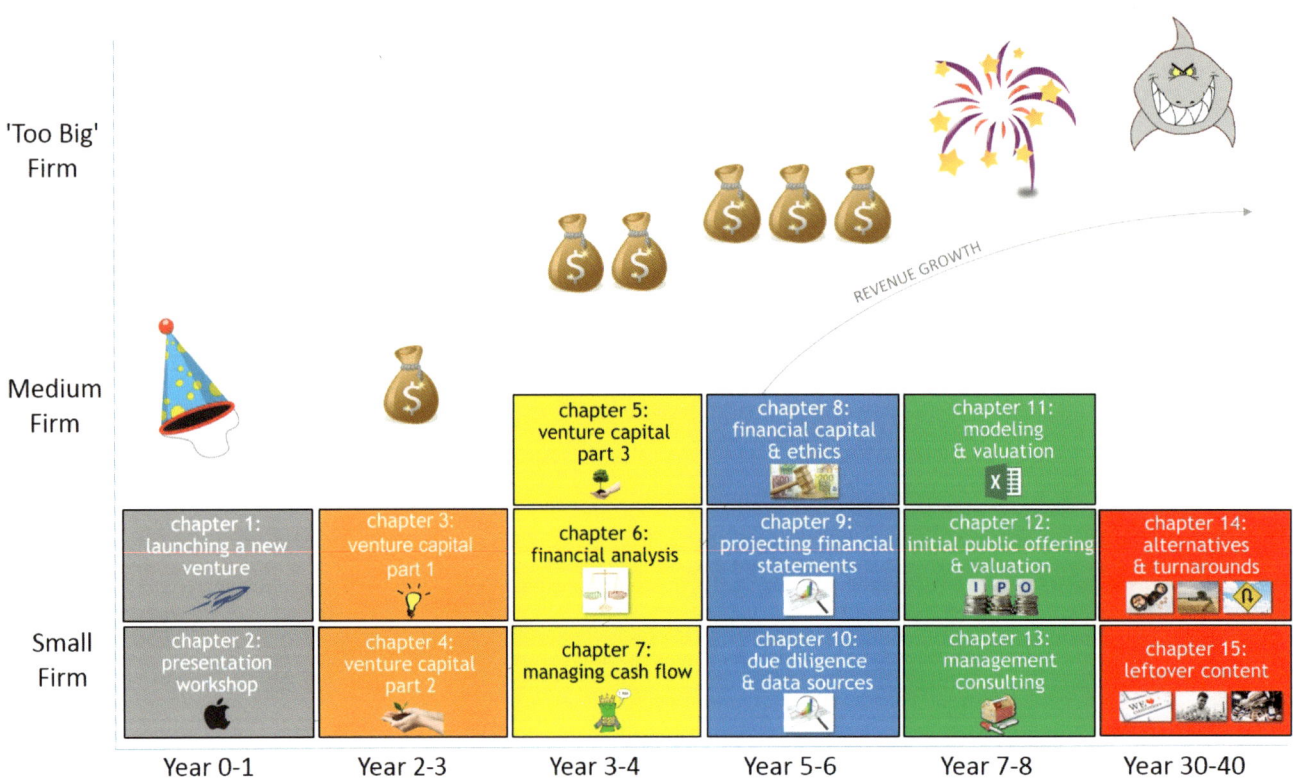

How Do I Make A Term Sheet?

A term sheet is a non-legally binding document that you and your investors sign highlighting the high level terms of an investment by the investor(s) in your company. I highly recommend getting a lawyer to draft all of your documents. However, if you want to know the contents of a term sheet you can make one yourself using an easy to follow step by step process on the web at a great law firm's web site called Wilson Sonsini. This website will automatically generate a term sheet for you for free: www.tiny.cc/chris106

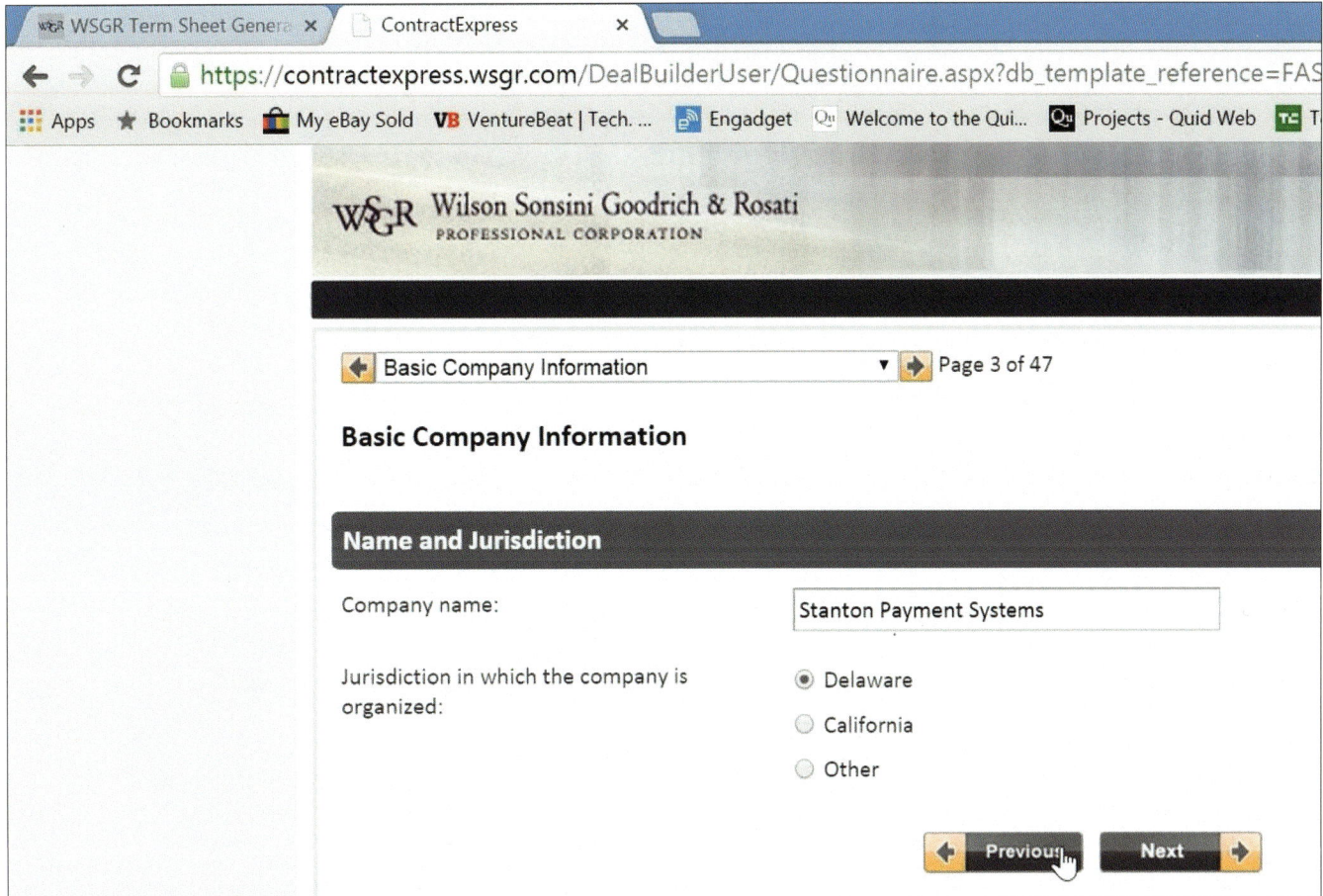

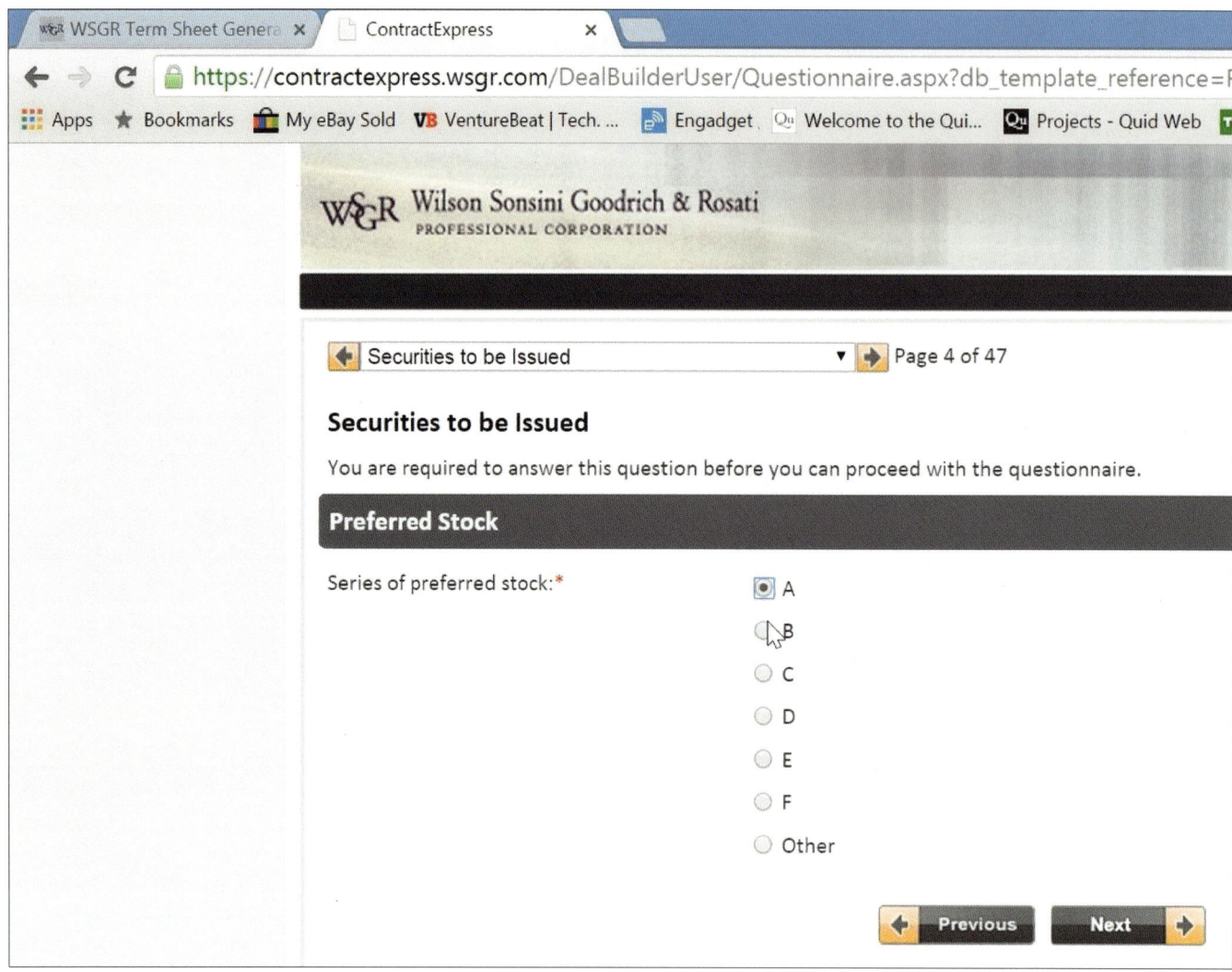

After completing all 47 steps, a PDF of your term sheet is automatically generated (please see the image on the next page):

STANTON PAYMENT SYSTEMS

MEMORANDUM OF TERMS

Except with respect to the provisions entitled "*Confidentiality*" and "*Exclusive negotiations*", which are intended to be, and are, legally binding agreements among the parties hereto, this Memorandum of Terms represents only the current thinking of the parties with respect to certain of the major issues relating to the proposed private offering and does not constitute a legally binding agreement. This Memorandum of Terms does not constitute an offer to sell or a solicitation of an offer to buy securities in any state where the offer or sale is not permitted.

THE OFFERING

Issuer:	Stanton Payment Systems, a Delaware corporation (the "*Company*")
Securities:	Series A Preferred Stock (the "*Series A Preferred*")
Valuation of the Company:	$9,000,000 pre-money
Amount of the offering:	Up to $1,000,000
Consideration:	Cash
Number of securities:	8,000,000 shares
Price per share:	$0.1

THE MOST IMPORTANT INVESTMENT YOU WILL EVER MAKE

You are your biggest investment. Don't be cheap when it comes to education and self-improvement. Continuous improvement is of paramount importance when it comes to your success in business or in life in general.

Spend more than you think you can afford on education, including degrees, online education, books, audio books, podcasts etc. Whatever it takes. You do have time to read. Yes you do; you can listen to audio books during your commute to work or at the gym. You can also watch many online lectures. In fact, most online lectures are free and my favorites are inspiring Ted Talks. If you have Wi-Fi and a stationary bike at home you can watch online courses at www.Udemy.com or even on YouTube.

Be a voracious reader. Read as many books as you can on successful business people and humanitarians. What are their secrets? Learn from them and watch your career take off.

Follow these People…

I have always been a voracious reader of biographies of successful people. I love learning from them. What are their recipes for success? How did they do it? Did they lead a well-balanced life on the road to their success? Although I am incredibly busy, I listen to many biographies of successful people in the car, and in the kitchen.

Use Twitter to follow your business heroes. They often tweet incredibly motivational quotes that resonate well with me. I love their short snippets of optimism, hope and best practices.

I find it incredibly motivating to know as much as I can about these successful people as most of them came from very uncompromising backgrounds. I love the poor, smart and hungry rags to riches stories. I feel empowered when thinking about them; there are no limits to what you can achieve. These people are no smarter than you are. They all have very positive attitudes, which I love!

I Have Never Met a Successful Person With…

You will never meet a successful person with a negative attitude. If they didn't believe in themselves and in their goals, then they would never have been successful. The quintessential example of this is Richard Branson. I just finished his latest audio book and my goodness does he ever have an amazing positive attitude! In fact, what I have learned from most of the audio books that I have completed on successful people is that the secret of their success is that they all believe that there are no limits to what you can achieve!

I have spent a lot of money on many biographies of successful people over the years and this was probably my best investment ever. So what is the biggest takeaway of the many biographies that I have read? How did all of these positive people all maintain a positive attitude with so many negative people around them? **Their secret is that many of them believed that unjustified criticism is a disguised complement**? How prophetic! Successful people often see criticism as a complement!

I used to get a bit sensitive when others would criticize me in business. I don't let this bother me anymore. In fact, the more successful in life you become, the more this will happen to you. How should you react? Well first of all I hope this happens to you more often because it is a reflection of your success. You almost want this to happen more often as it is incredibly flattering. Your coworkers or competitors might develop a very slightly condescending tone with you over the years the more successful you become as well. You almost want to reach out and thank them for the disguised complement! Don't worry because maybe they just feel threatened by you which is a euphemism for a huge complement.

Successful people are criticized all the time. The ones that are the happiest and have the best peace of mind are those that see criticism as nothing more than a disguised complement. So bring it on doubters! :)

The most important investment you will ever make is you! Be a voracious reader of published works written by or written on your business and humanitarian heroes. **Follow their success blueprints and one day others will follow and read about you as part of the most important investment they ever make!**

A Company is Only as Good as Its Customer Service

I have never heard of anyone that had a bad customer experience with Amazon, Apple, Costco or Salesforce. The aforementioned companies are incredibly successful due, in large part, to a material focus on the customer experience. Not surprisingly, the stock market has handsomely rewarded these four companies over the past decade.

Amazon is so customer focused that it will literally send you a replacement for a lost package immediately without ever implying that the customer is at fault. The result is a consumer experience that is so optimal that Amazon is the only place where many consumers decide to shop online.

The same can be said for Apple when it comes to the in store experience. Apple employees are so passionate about their products that I feel like I am talking to a polite tech enthusiast in the Apple stores and not Apple employees! The result is incredibly brand loyal customers. When was the last time we heard of a consumer switching from using primarily Apple products to non-Apple products? Apple's in store Genius Bar customer support concept is brilliant and I can't understand why more companies don't do it. The result is Apple having the highest sales per square foot of any retailer in the U.S. at close to $5,000 per square foot per year!

The customer experience at Costco is also superb. In fact, Costco has the best return policy in the retail industry. We only buy televisions from Costco given the company's multiyear return policy. Costco also doesn't even bother asking for a receipt when you return items (given their digital receipt policy). In addition, Costco has never raised prices on its fast food products; you still pay only $1.50 for the hot dog and drink combo, which was the same price Costco charged consumers 30 years ago! Most consumers don't know that you can even trade in your old consumer electronic devices at Costco and receive a 'Costco Cash Card' in return. A friend of mine jokes that "if you can't find it at Costco, then you don't need it!"

Not surprisingly, Salesforce, whose roots are in the customer relationship market, also has superb customer service. In fact, Salesforce is so customer focused and so transparent that the company will publicly disclose in real time when its cloud services are unavailable or having reliance issues. Consumer trust is of paramount importance as 'transparency builds trust'. For more details, please see the following link for real time Salesforce outages:

https://trust.salesforce.com/.

How good is Salesforce's customer experience? Here is what happens when you start typing 'salesforce customer support' in your browser address box or in Google:

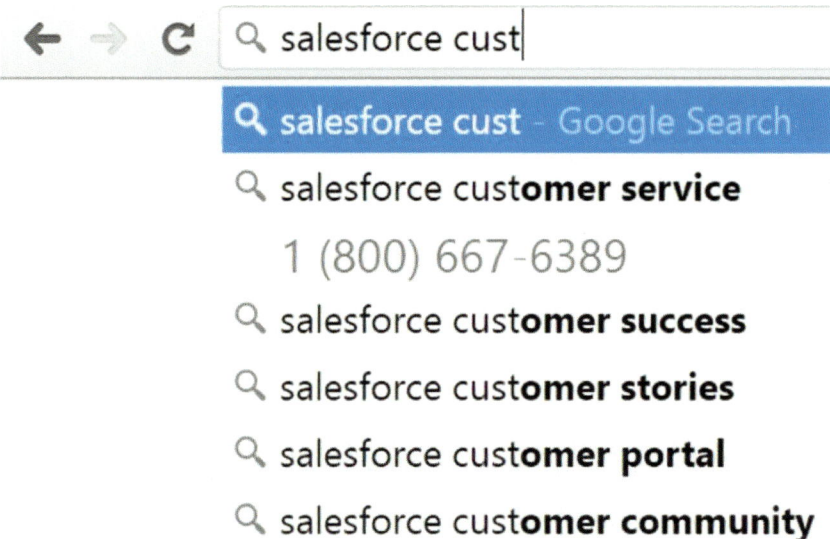

In conclusion, a superb customer experience begets more loyal customers that will no doubt spend more money on a company's products or services in the long run. A superb customer experience also leads to higher stock prices over time. In this digital social media age, if a customer has a poor experience, all of their online contacts might find out about it very quickly. It can take 30+ years to build a brand and just a handful of poor customer experiences to destroy it; a company is only as good as its customer service.

3 Reasons to Be Long-Term Greedy

When I worked at Goldman Sachs my mentors would always tell me to "**be long-term greedy.**" I didn't fully appreciate it at the time but it makes perfect sense to me now, especially when it comes to investing. Here are 3 reasons to be long-term greedy:

1: If you think long-term, then you can think like the founder does.

My favorite investments are the ones run by founders that don't care about quarterly earnings. Rather, they think about long-term strategies only (especially after the IPO). This is why I love Google and Amazon as both companies don't really care about short-term guidance metrics for investors. I love this quote from Amazon's incredible CEO, Jeff Bezos: "*If we have a good quarter it's because of work we did 3, 4 or 5 years ago. It's not because we did a good job this quarter.*" When you invest in a company, you are investing in the management team. Hence, we must think like the founder does before considering investing. In the technology sector, if all of the founders have left the firm, then the company is not a worthwhile investment in my humble opinion.

2: If you think long-term, then you can ignore irrational market volatility which purges 'tourist investors'; this creates buying opportunities so that you are not fooled by randomness.

Warren Buffet is the best long-term investor in the history of the stock market. My favorite quote of his is "*the New York Stock Exchange is the only store in the world where consumers sell stuff when it goes on sale.*" Brilliant! Mister Buffett also said "b*e greedy when others are fearful and fearful when others are greedy*." This is a euphemism for being a contrarian; don't buy stocks everyone else buys as there will be fewer incremental buyers. Being a long-term investor lets you focus on the company's destination and not on the path.

3: If you think long-term, then your outlook on the company's prospects will not be the same as consensus.

Before I do due diligence on any company as a potential investment candidate, I ask myself one very basic question: *"In 5 years will this company be more relevant or less relevant than it is today?"* Sounds pretty simple! It should be because the best investors see the forest from the trees and understand that investment trends last much longer than we think. I always ask myself this basic 5 year question before I do any due diligence on companies.

Nobody is better at being a wise long-term investor than Warren Buffett. I remember when I was an MBA student at Columbia University in 1999 and Warren Buffett was teaching one of our classes on value investing. One of my classmates pitched a technology stock to him. He very politely interrupted 30 seconds after my classmate pitched the stock and said *"Son thank you very much for the idea but I don't have enough visibility where this company is going to be product cycle wise in 3, 5, 10 or 20 years."* He was right as 6 months later the technology company my classmate was pitching went belly up; there is a reason Warren Buffett is called the *Sage of Omaha.*

Mister Buffett ended his presentation to us with this prophetic investing quote: "<u>*The longer the view, the wiser the intention*</u>".

WEALTH = HEALTH + GRATITUDE + HAPPINESS

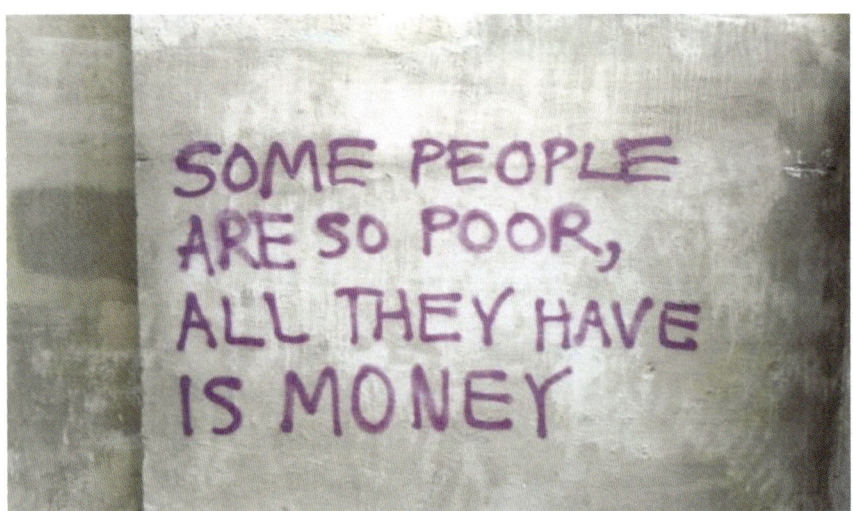

MONEY DOES NOT = HAPPINESS

When I started my second company, I was stressed out and I took a drive alone down the beautiful California coast. I stopped by Carmel and I went for a long walk as I often do to come up with personal and professional goals. I stopped by a beautiful old church and I sat down and collected my thoughts.

A priest was there and sat down next to me. We spoke for a while about what I was trying to accomplish in life. I mentioned that I wanted to make as much money as possible so that I could give my children the standard of living that I wanted them to have. What he told me that day was incredibly prophetic and just what I needed to hear:

"Chris, 50 years from now your children will not look back on you and remember how much money you made. They will look back and reflect how good of a father you were."

I was blown away by his comment and I thanked him profusely for imparting this incredible wisdom on me. I now know in my heart that money does not equal happiness. Please don't make it your primary goal. Find your passion in life and the money will come whether you want it to or not! Then you can focus on giving it away and making the world a better place.

I have seen money destroy friendships and families so many times. Money can destroy your relationship with many people including your children. Give most of your money away to charities and only keep enough to keep your family happy as counterintuitive as that might sound.

PERSONAL GRATITUDE AND HAPPINESS

You will be much more successful in business if you have sincere personal gratitude for what you have. Years ago I read *The Art of Happiness* by the Dalai Lama. He said that in western society people are so unhappy as we tend to compare ourselves to those that have more than us. By contrast, those that live in second, or third world countries are happier than we are as they focus on what is important in life, like family and friends and a beautiful day!

If we are grateful for at least one different thing in our lives every day and help others that are less fortunate, then we will all lead more fulfilled lives. At night when I say prayers with my 3 wonderful children, I always make them thank God for something different every day.

If we spend more time helping others that are less fortunate, we will all be much more fulfilled and we will be much more successful in life.

All Your Wealth Can't Buy You Health

If you are happy in your life personally and professionally, then you will be much more productive. However, in order to be happy you need to find time to exercise daily (no excuses) and focus on nutrition (no excuses) and get 7-8 hours of sleep per night (no excuses).

I promise you that your productivity and level of happiness will increase materially if you exercise daily. Nothing is more important. Exercising daily helps you think more clearly and be generally happier at work. That positive attitude will remain elevated with exercise.

The Dalai Lama, when asked what surprised him most about humanity, answered:

"Man. Because he sacrifices his health in order to make money. Then he sacrifices money to recuperate health. And then he is so anxious about the future that he does not enjoy the present; the result being that he does not live in the present or the future; he lives as if he is never going to die, and then dies having never really lived."

Wealth = Health + Gratitude +Happiness

TURNAROUNDS DON'T WORK IN TECH

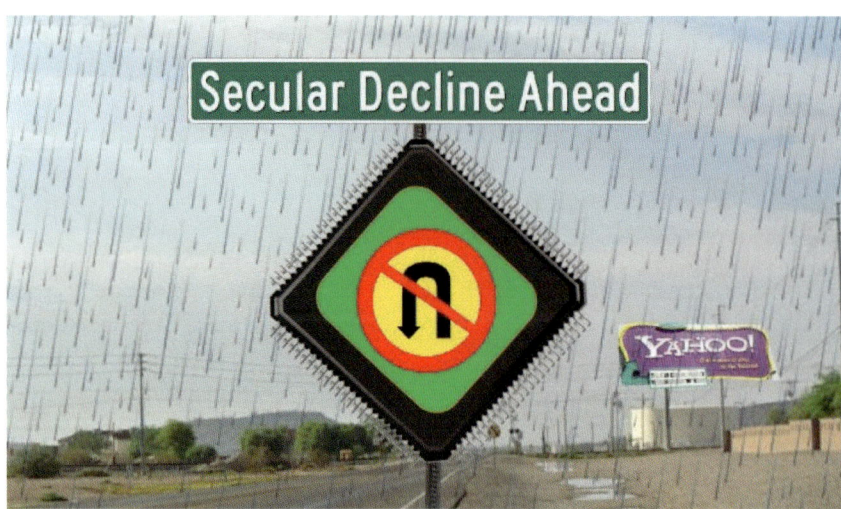

Yahoo, Dell, RIM, HP and Computer Associates are all technology companies that are in secular or terminal decline as they continue to lose market share to companies like Apple, Google and Salesforce. When a technology company is in secular decline, then the road ahead is filled with potholes, false hope and empty promises. Only 1 turnaround in the technology sector tends to work each decade in the public markets. Last decade it was Apple only because Steve Jobs returned to the company and in the 1990s it was IBM under Lou Gerstner, the brilliant former McKinsey consultant.

Once consumers sense that a technology company is in secular decline, they gradually use the product less often regardless of what new products are introduced by the company in secular decline. This is what happened with BlackBerry's parent Research in Motion. Many executives, especially on Wall Street, used the BlackBerry as their very first smart phone. Then the iPhone and Android handsets were released which had awesome app stores, unlike the BlackBerry. Then for a while executives carried a BlackBerry and either an Android or iPhone device. Then executives phased out the use of their BlackBerries entirely. The biggest problem with the BlackBerry was that its app store paled in comparison to Apple or Google's app stores. BlackBerry had trouble trying to be a decent software company as well as a decent hardware company. Most companies can't effectively produce high quality software and hardware products. Apple is probably the only company in the world that can be a great hardware and a great software company at the same time. Google was smart enough to know that it is a software company and therefore partnered with Samsung and other hardware companies to make Android-based smart phones. Google is trying to change this though by acquiring hardware related start-ups including Nest while retaining some of the patents from its Motorola acquisition.

The same argument can be said for enterprises; where there's smoke there's fire. Once an enterprise decides that a technology company might be in secular decline, then they no longer purchase products from the company. In many cases they even rip and replace the technology company's products as they are fearful that they won't be able to get the proper support for the underlying products in the long run. When I used to work in the technology consulting sector at Accenture as a software engineer, I would always be neutral when it came to the decision of which database to use and I would leave it up to my clients to decide. Clients would always ask me which company is most likely to be in business in the long run. As a result, we usually chose to deal with Microsoft's SQL Server database or IBM's DB2 database or Oracle's database Instead of Sybase, which had a less rosy long term outlook (this was a wise choice as the company was later acquired by SAP). The same can be said for today when it comes to antiquated technology companies like CA (Computer Associates). Forward thinking enterprises prefer to use cloud-based solutions from incredibly forward thinking companies like Salesforce.com, Workday or NetSuite. We all know that the cloud is the future and that the mainframe and antiquated client server products from companies like CA are in secular decline.

Consumer and enterprise companies will be well served to ask themselves one very basic question before purchasing a technology product, which is this: *"in five years is this technology company going to be more relevant or less relevant that it is today"*. This is a simple question but it has a lot to do with future technology purchases. As a result, IT purchasers might decide not to use products from companies that have structural or secular issues including Hewlett-Packard or CA, among others.

We can use the same logic when it comes to investing in technology companies. Technology investors should never invest in a company that they believe is not going to be more relevant in 5 years. This is why investors tend to flock to Apple, Amazon, Salesforce and Google instead of HP, Yahoo, CA, RIM or Dell (when it was publically traded). Quite often we see investors lose their shirts by getting seduced into investing in companies in secular decline because their valuations seem attractive. What we often overlook when chasing 'value traps' is the fact that the earnings estimates by Wall Street analysts for these companies for this year and next year and the year after are usually way too high. As a result, the valuations of these companies are incorrect. Investing in a technology company because valuation seems attractive this year or next year is not a winning proposition.

Investors are far better served to create a financial model and value a company on earnings at least five years from today. Why? Once a consumer or an enterprise has decided that a technology company is in secular decline, it is almost impossible to convince them to go back and use the products they thought were once relevant. If you disagree, then why don't we all wear fashions that were in style in the 70s like bell bottom pants? How many of us that used to use Yahoo as our search engine and then switched to Google have ever switched back to using Yahoo? Exactly! How many of us that used to use a Windows laptop and then switch to using a Mac have switched back to using a Windows laptop? How many of us that used to go to Barnes & Noble and then switched to Amazon have decided to go back to shopping only at Barnes & Noble for books? Lastly, how many of us print more documents using HP printers since we purchased our first tablet? Exactly!

Companies that are in secular growth mode are those with superb customer service too. I have always believed that a company is only as good as its customer service is. The companies that are in secular growth mode like Apple and Amazon have the best customer service. Those that are in secular decline (including Comcast) have very poor customer service. Perhaps this is due to low employee morale given the difficult outlook for the company they work for

Smart money investors value companies off of their earnings estimates at least five years in the future. If you disagree talk to hedge fund portfolio managers who have tried to short Amazon over the past decade because the stock seemed expensive. The smart money investors in secular growth companies love Amazon because earnings will be much much higher in at least five years from today. The same can be said for hedge funds that shorted Netflix because valuation seemed lofty. Don't ever bet against secular growth companies (unless we are in a horrific bear market, in which case almost all tech stocks will fall).

Valuing secular growth tech companies based on this year's earnings is illogical. What matters much more is valuation based on your earnings estimates at least five years into the future. Many investors get tempted to invest in companies in secular decline given their relative attractive valuation. Most of the time, this is a huge mistake. Investors might be fooled by randomness and profit once or twice from this strategy but this is usually due to the markets rallying and all ships or all stocks rising as well. More often than not, investors buying turnarounds in tech are merely 'tourists' and give up investing after realizing that there are better secular growth opportunities elsewhere; they learn their lessons from 'renting' and losing money investing in the companies in secular decline.

Given the slippery slope that technology companies face once they enter the secular decline phase of their life, it's no wonder why value investors are usually not very good investors in technology companies. Rather, growth investors that love to invest in secular growth companies that might appear expensive on this year's earnings and next year's earnings do far better when investing in technology companies than value investors do. If you disagree with statement, then look at the historical price earnings chart for Hewlett-Packard over the past decade. Investors that argue the stock might have been cheap at 18 times earnings lost their shirts as price earnings multiple contraction always occurs over time to companies in secular decline. Investing in technology companies because you believe you will see price earnings multiple expansion is not prudent. All that should matter is if your estimates are higher than Wall Street estimates up to five years from today.

So how do we know if a technology company is in secular decline? There are a few ways. If you notice that fewer people are using a technology product today than they did a year or two ago then chances are that the company is in secular decline. Another way to tell if a company is in secular decline is if the company misses several quarters in a row versus Wall Street estimates (unless we are in a recession). When I used to work in the hedge fund industry we would always say that software companies never miss just once. Another way to tell is if many employees start resigning because they are on a sinking ship. Check out www.glassdoor.com and see if the employee reviews of the company they work for deteriorates over time.

So should you invest in technology companies that think they can improve their business prospects once they are in secular decline? Absolutely not. There's usually only one company per decade that can buck this trend; I don't like those odds. If a founder comes back to the company then there is a small chance that the company will no longer be in secular decline, but the odds are against it. When you hear Wall Street analysts or other pundits telling you that a technology company is a turnaround play, be very skeptical as the chances of a turnaround working in technology is extraordinarily low. Where there is smoke there is fire; turnarounds almost never work in technology.

SUCCESS = APPLE'S SIMPLICITY + INTEL'S PARANOIA

Some of the best investments in history have had a combination of Apple's simplicity and Intel's paranoia. In fact, both Apple and Intel had a healthy dose of paranoia and simplicity under CEOs Steve Jobs and Andy Grove respectively, which is a winning combination. Other companies that have showed similar characteristics include Microsoft, Nintendo and Netflix.

In 1997 Andy Grove wrote his masterpiece, 'Only the Paranoid Survive' which stipulated that a company contains the seeds of its own destruction and that success, in fact, breeds complacency. Complacency then tends to breed failure. As a result, companies must be paranoid in order to survive by either disrupting their own markets or being overly paranoid of the competition. Steve Jobs was paranoid of employees leaking products ahead of product launch dates and even had many secret code words for the same product so that he would know who leaked a product name should the press write about it. Grove was incredibly paranoid about the viability of his company's business when it came to competing with the Japanese, who were much more aggressive with pricing. Grove reacted accordingly and reinvented the company in the processor market.

Steve Jobs' genius was the simplicity of his products' designs and marketing efforts. He was the quintessential communicator and he was famous for his simple catch phrases. He believed that 'less is more' and he was adamant about having only one physical method for entering information in hand held devices, unlike the post Jobs products which are a bit more complex (including the Apple Watch which is slightly confusing to use at first and the stylus on the new larger iPad). In fact, Jobs believed in product portfolio simplicity by having relatively few products to sell. The number of Apple products that the company sells increased from 12 four years ago prior to the passing of Mr. Jobs to 24 today. Under Andy Grove, Intel created the brilliant yet simplistic 'Intel Inside' advertising campaign with the Intel jingle, creating consumer brand loyalty for a chip that consumers never see! Simply brilliant.

Microsoft also had a healthy dose of Apple's simplicity and Intel's paranoia under Bill Gates as he believed that Microsoft was always one and a half years away from bankruptcy. Under Gates, Microsoft simplified the process of using computers with the release of Windows. In the post Bill Gates Microsoft era, the number of products has also grown materially leading a slightly more complex product portfolio.

Nintendo, similarly, has prided itself on very simple video game designs while being incredibly paranoid since its founding in 1889. For many years Nintendo has had a multi-billion dollar cash balance that many investors feel is unnecessary. In fact, Nintendo is so paranoid when it comes to its cash balance that the company could actually operate at a $250mn annual deficit for more than 35 years if needed! I met the CFO of Nintendo in Tokyo about 8 years ago and I asked him why they have such an enormous cash balance while the Nintendo Wii was a huge success. He told me that they are always paranoid about companies that they compete with that are much larger than they are, including Microsoft and Sony. The Wii U, which is the follow up to the Wii, has been such a flop that it would cause many competitors to declare bankruptcy, which happens often in the video game sector (i.e., Sega). I now appreciate and understand why the company is now in its third century of existence!

Netflix is yet another example of a company that has embraced simplicity in all of its platform solutions on multiple devices while using paranoia to its benefit. Netflix's streaming business was created in order to cannibalize its cash cow DVD rental business years before competing streaming devices could do so. Founder Reed Hastings was paranoid that his DVD rental business would not be viable in the long run, so he preemptively destroyed his own cash cow. Please leave a comment at the bottom of this article if you can think of a company that has ever reinvented itself as well as Netflix has.

Companies run by CEOs that have a healthy dose of Apple's simplicity in its products and marketing tend to outperform those that do not. Similarly, companies run by CEOs that have a healthy dose of Intel's paranoia withstand the test of time and remain relevant. Companies that have a healthy dose of simplicity and a healthy dose of paranoia are extraordinarily rare and are superb investments. Simply put, only the paranoid survive.

SUPERB MARKETING BEATS GREAT PRODUCTS

Remember the days when we used to talk about the type of processor we had in our computers? Nobody really cares or knows anymore what processor our iPads or iPhones or laptops or Samsung products have. Superb marketing almost always beats great products; this trend exists in the technology sector, the clothing market, academics and even in politics!

Windows 3.1 was released in 1992 and it certainly paled in comparison to Apple's 'Mac 84'. The same can be said for Windows 95. So why did Microsoft Windows have materially higher market share than Apple back then? One of the reasons was that Microsoft then had much better marketing strategies than Apple did. Microsoft's Steve Ballmer was a marketing genius. Most people don't realize that prior to joining Microsoft, Ballmer was a Product Manager on the Duncan Hines cake mix product at Procter and Gamble. He managed to get Duncan Hines to the #1 product in the sector by market share by simply making the box bigger! In fact, per the image below, Steve Ballmer made the size of the Microsoft Windows box exactly the same size as the Duncan Hines box which was larger than competing products! Marketing was a key reason why Microsoft was so incredibly successful then.

Microsoft's marketing savvy has since deteriorated, in part, due to founder Bill Gates resigning. In fact, when all the founders leave a company, both the marketing and product quality deteriorates; remember how much more dominant Nike's marketing efforts were prior to founder Phil Knight retiring? There are many examples of this in the technology sector, clothing sector and many other industry verticals.

IF BO JACKSON TAKES UP ANY MORE HOBBIES, WE'RE READY.

The 'superb marketing trumping great products' trend is also very much apparent in politics where the person that often wins an election does so because he or she has a much better marketing campaign than the competition does. In fact, think of most political leaders since the Nixon Kennedy's televised debate in the 1960s and we might conclude that many elections around the world were won by candidates that had better marketing campaigns and by candidates that were more affable; the quality of their product or policies doesn't seem to be the primary driver for election success. Superb marketing beats great policies in politics too.

The same trend can be said for academics. In many cases, students with the top grades are not the most successful in life. Rather, students that have superb 'Marc Benioff-esque' personal marketing skills tend to prosper the most. Their grades (or their diploma product) is not nearly as relevant compared to their personal marketing skills.

It is extraordinarily rare for a company to have a combination of superb marketing and superb products. When this occurs, we get companies that tend to dominate their sectors at least until the founder is no longer running the company. Companies that have this killer approach of having superb marketing and superb products almost always knock out the competition and offer superior investor returns.

LESS IS MORE IN BUSINESS

President Lincoln delivered the Gettysburg Address on November 19, 1863 on the battlefield near Gettysburg, Pennsylvania. This speech was incredibly powerful yet it was only 272 words! Less is more.

Steve Jobs was the quintessential communicator and entrepreneur. He firmly believed that for a product or idea to be widely adopted, it needed to have a simplistic design. The iPhone and iPad have only one button. His presentations usually have 3 bullet points or 3 images per slide and that's all.

In this day and age we are so inundated with information that 140 character bottom line summaries are more relevant than lengthy write-ups. This is why Twitter has been so incredibly successful. The best business model presentations that I see as a venture capitalist have a maximum of 10 slides with only 3 bullet points per slide; less is more works.

Executives and potential investors have extraordinarily short attention spans in this day and age given the many screens that we are addicted to like smart phones, tablets, laptops, watches etc. You need to get your point across in as few words as possible.

Pretend that each message that you send costs you $100 per word. With this in mind you will definitely embrace the winning methodology of less is more in business.

TIMING IS CRUCIAL IN BUSINESS

Since I am Canadian, I have to quote the greatest hockey player of all time, Wayne Gretzky. Gretzky was incredibly successful not because he skated to where the puck is. Rather, he skated to where the puck is going to be. Companies that have incredible foresight into a market that will have an enormous total addressable market (T.A.M.) are essentially subscribing to Gretzky's forward thinking strategy. This is what Bill Gates and Paul Allen did in the 1970s when they read the cover story of Popular Mechanics and knew in their hearts that there would be a day in the not too distant future that we would all have computers on our desks.

The right idea at the right time is a major driver of success. Yahoo's purchase of Broadcast.com for $5.7bn in 1999 could have had YouTube-like returns for investors. Similarly, Yahoo's purchase of social media pioneer GeoCities for $3.6bn in 1999 could have produced Facebook-like returns for investors. Unfortunately the timing of the two aforementioned acquisitions by Yahoo was way too early.

The same can be said for Apple's Newton product, which was several years too early or Microsoft's early tablet computer strategy or even Oracle's brilliant but failed Network Computer strategy in the 1990s. There are also so many amazing environmentally friendly clean tech companies out there that might be decades too early to succeed; I am certainly hopeful that they do. Timing is everything.

I had the privilege of speaking with Silicon Valley legend Andy Bechtolsheim about the drivers for success. Many people, myself included, believe Andy is the most successful technology entrepreneur in Silicon Valley history. Andy was not only the very first investor in Google, but he was also the first employee at Sun Microsystems and a founder of so many unbelievable companies that are public or have been acquired, including Arista, Granite, DSSD etc. As I always do when I meet incredibly successful entrepreneurs, I ask for reasons for their success. Andy has never had a failed startup and he very humbly told me that **timing is one of the most important drivers of success**.

Timing also matters when it comes to venture capital investment opportunities in cyclical economic downturns. During the recession of 2001 there was 1 notable company that venture investors felt safe investing in, which was Google, which went public in 2004. The same can be said in 2008 when we were within 24 hours of bank machines not working! Venture capital investors then wanted to back a sure thing, which of course was Facebook. Of course we know that Google and Facebook succeeded for many reasons, including brilliant management teams and execution, but timing helped them as well.

So how do we know if our timing is good enough to succeed? It comes down to several factors, including a huge consumer or enterprise appetite for a product or service which can be quantified through an enormous T.A.M. Component or input prices for products needs to be low enough as well, which is a reason why Android and Apple smartphones have been so incredibly successful. Years ago I read an incredible McKinsey study about how all component prices in computers, phones and TVs drop in price close to 1% every single week! The hard part is assessing through focus groups when prices for consumer or enterprise products or services will be low enough to entice them to buy the products or services.

Timing might be a bit less relevant in technology today for a reason aside from the price of purchasing the product or service. What I mean by this is that many technology companies are copying the magazine subscription business model and renting or allowing consumers or enterprises to effectively subscribe to use their products, which is superb from a revenue visibility perspective. A two year subscription to a smart phone might cost close to $1,000. By having consumers subscribe to products on a monthly basis, the sticker shock risk is mitigated. As a result of subscription business models from companies like Apple or Salesforce, timing is a big less of an issue today.

Timing has a lot to do with success; we need to skate to where the puck is going to be in the not too distant future.

FRUSTRATION IS A GOOD THING IN BUSINESS

If you have a high level of professional frustration in your life then this is a gift to you. It's a gift to you because you are not professionally doing what you are most passionate about.

It's perfectly normal to be frustrated in business. The fun part is figuring out what you love doing in life and what your business purpose is in life. What were you put on this earth to accomplish professionally? How many lives could you help improve if you accomplished your business goals? What would it take for you to no longer feel professionally frustrated?

Find humor in stressful and frustrating business situations and you will live a much longer and happier life! Self-deprecation is an admirable trait. Finding humor in frustration instantly changes your state and helps you to focus on turning a crisis into an opportunity. Rather than be depressed given a perceived failure or frustration, smile and cheer up because your future incredible success in business is a result of that failure. You will be grateful later in life that you 'failed'.

There are so many amazing examples of executives that have failed or have been fired which forced them to realize their dreams by starting their own company. Frustration often leads to breakthroughs in your career.

Here are some incredibly inspirational examples of people that were fired. Thank goodness they were or we wouldn't enjoy the benefits of their future business empire creations:

Tomas Edison was fired by Western Union.

Michael Bloomberg was fired which made him get his revenge by starting his financial empire Bloomberg. Without getting fired he wouldn't have ever become the Mayor of New York.

J K Rowling hated her job as an administrative assistant. She quit and found her passion, which was writing the Harry Potter books.

Walt Disney was fired by a publication he worked for.

Madonna was fired from Dunkin Donuts

Robert Redford was fired from an oil company.

Lee Iacocca was fired from Ford. So he turned around and led Chrysler.

All these amazing people lost their jobs because of a lack of passion or because of frustration with their careers. They then became incredibly successful because they focused on their passion.

What is your calling? What is your raison d'être? Find your passion and you will always be happy in business and in life. If you feel suffocated in your current job, then find your passion, write a business plan and quit.

Frustration leads to breakthroughs.

Frustration leads to reinvention.

Embrace it.

Find your professional passion and end your frustration; welcome to the new you.

SUCCEED LIKE DEREK JETER BY WRITING THESE DOWN

A major reason for baseball icon Derek Jeter's success in every aspect of his life was because his parents made him write down his goals every single year. You need to write down your goals and update them often. If you do, the chances of you achieving your dreams rises materially; most of your competitors won't bother doing this!

In 1953 there was a famous study conducted at Yale University. The graduating class was asked if they had written down their goals. Only 3% had done so. Then 20 years later, a poll was taken and the graduating students from the class of 1953 were asked what their net worth was. The net worth of the 3% that had written down their goals was greater than the other 97% combined!

Write down your goals in your smart phone's calendar and have this calendar entry be repeated daily. Tell your friends or family members what your long term goals are so that it forces you to work towards them and think of your goals often. Consider writing your goals down on paper and then placing them in a sealed and stamped envelope with your address on the envelope. Then give the envelope to a good friend or family member and tell them to mail the letter in 6 months or 1 year.

Think of the most ambitious goal you can achieve in your life. Don't ask yourself if it is achievable; of course it is. Rather, ask yourself what you need to accomplish in order to make this goal a reality. Make a rudimentary gap analysis. Once you know what your goal is then focus on filling the gap, meaning what you need to accomplish in order to make this goal a reality.

When you first think of an incredibly ambitious goal, you are so fired up and excited to start the journey. Before you start the journey you can clearly see the top of the mountain, which is a metaphor for your goal.

Once you embark upon your journey you are full of energy and excitement as with each step you get closer and closer to your goal. Then much later in the journey you become frustrated as you can no longer see the top of the mountain. As a result, your pace deviates a bit and is perhaps slower than it once was.

You wonder what happened to my goal? Why can't I see the top of the mountain anymore? Well the reason is simple; the reason is that you are half way up the mountain and can't see the top of the mountain. Rest assured, your goal is within reach. Finish what you started, be long term greedy and reap the rewards.

Set a goal so big that you can't achieve it until you **become the person that actually can achieve it**. Update these goals often and I promise you will wake up one day and realize that you accomplished all of your goals and more.

We often overestimate what we can accomplish in a year but we significantly underestimate what we can accomplish in a decade. Please write down your short and long term goals and watch your career take off!

TECH INNOVATION THRIVES IN THE US DUE TO YOUTH WITH CONFIDENCE

Tech Innovation Thrives in the US Due to Youth with Confidence

"We are witnessing the downfall of the U.S. economic growth engine as U.S. student test scores are way below test scores of other countries." I have seen the aforementioned quote in countless media publications for my entire life, but the quote is flawed. American students, whether or not they were born in the U.S., are number one globally in the most crucial economic category that nobody acknowledges, which is confidence. Confidence leads to innovation. Innovation leads to entrepreneurship. Entrepreneurship leads to business models getting funded. Business models getting funded leads to risk taking. And risk taking leads to GDP growth.

Most generations criticize the next generation for being too entitled or the previous generation for taking on too much debt. Each American generation blames the one before or makes renegade critical comments like "don't trust anyone over 30!" Each generation has the confidence to disrupt the previous generations' business model empires and the confidence to question authority. This isn't just a Haight Ashbury phenomenon; it transcends generations. The one common link all generations of American students have is the ability to confidently take risk and sell the dream of global innovation or global social justice.

The American Dream is based on the notion of confidence and innovation. Anybody can make it in America regardless of their backgrounds or where they were born. Due to this, there is a belief in the U.S. that anything is possible. Some of the best salespeople in the world were students in America regardless of where they were born. A great CEO is a great salesperson and a great salesperson has above average confidence. In all of our portfolio company investments in venture capital we look for a little bit of Marc Benioff or Steve Jobs, two quintessential, confident, brilliant visionaries and salespeople. Individualism and freedom of expression is embraced in America. Some other countries are more conformist, which leads to the antithesis of individualism and entrepreneurship and we hear of quotes like "the nail that sticks out gets hammered down." In the U.S. failure is not shameful. Rather, entrepreneurs in the U.S., whether or not they were born here and regardless of their age, see defeat as merely a challenge to try again.

Confidence among American students is more apparent today than ever before. It's hard to keep track here in the Bay Area of the number of successful student-founded ventures over the years where a student creates an overnight multi-billion dollar company, such as Facebook, Apple, Google, etc. Also, with ubiquitous mobile broadband offerings, expect the number of new multi-billion dollar disruptive business models to accelerate. In addition, given the extraordinary low cost of cloud computing from companies like Amazon, Google and Microsoft, the barriers to entry for start-ups are also extremely low. As a result, it is significantly easier for larger companies to see their business models disrupted by student run start-ups.

Each generation is given a label from Generation X to Generation Y to the Entitlement Generation, and so on. I refer to the current generation as Generation C for Confidence. With confidence comes innovation, prosperity and continuous generational improvements in economic productivity and social justice; I applaud the sub 25 year old Generation Confidence, as no other generation has had the same positive impact on older generations as the current generation. The cynical pundits that are calling for the long term downfall of U.S. economic growth due to poor student test scores have flawed logic; tech innovation has always thrived in the U.S. due to youth with confidence.

AMAZON AWS: THIS GENERATION'S BERLIN WALL TEARDOWN DEFLATIONARY EVENT

Amazon Web Services (AWS), with its 'Walmartesque' everyday low prices strategy, has single handedly altered the enterprise software pricing model and has created the most important deflationary impact of this century.

The 'old tech' business model was to dominate an industry and then release mediocre upgrades at commensurate pricing points and with minimal worthwhile innovation. The 'new tech' model is to undercut the competition with material value added lower cost upgrades, which is exactly what AWS is doing. Amazon's low cost strategy has influenced many technology companies to also cut prices for their platform solutions, including Microsoft with its competing web platform, Azure, as well as Google Compute. In fact, you could argue that Windows 10 will be free for many users initially because of Amazon's influence.

We are being conditioned to expect to pay nothing or next to nothing for operating system platforms. I can't think of a more deflationary secular trend.

There are so many intriguing free Internet software products available now because of Amazon and there are no historical industry vertical precedents. The optimist in me believes that interest rates are low in part due to the deflationary impact of Amazon Web Services (AWS), and that the impact of low cost cloud platform computing will cause many verticals and software companies to cut prices in the years ahead and, hence, cause interest rates to remain close to historically low levels. AWS in 2015 is this generation's 1989 Berlin Wall tear down deflationary economic event.

Today, enterprise applications and operating system prices are plummeting thanks to Amazon acting as a price cut leader. This deflationary trend has started to accelerate as Microsoft and Google have started to also be price cut leaders by materially cutting the pricing points of their cloud service provider platforms, which are the platforms that some of the most disruptive companies in the world operate on top of. New companies are being created like Uber that charge much lower pricing points due to the inherent cost savings of low cost cloud platform solutions like AWS. This deflationary trend should continue for the foreseeable future. Many disruptive new companies don't use any software from old school tech companies like Oracle or Microsoft as there are widely available free (or lower cost) alternatives that run entirely on AWS. As a result, as consumers, we have so many opportunities to use technology products that now cost next to nothing to use or subscribe to (i.e., Netflix).

Why was the global economy booming in the '90s? It wasn't primarily because of the booming tech sector. Rather, it was mainly because the Berlin Wall fell in 1989 and a plethora of lower-cost, high-quality labor was unleashed from Eastern Europe; this was the reason we had low interest rates then, relative to the booming global economy.

AWS is today's equivalent. And the technology cost savings we're seeing today are commensurate with the deflationary labor cost savings in that era. Instead of the late, great Ronald Reagan prophetically telling Mr. Gorbachev to "Tear down this wall," Amazon has forced the entire enterprise software market to dramatically reduce prices around the walled garden of ridiculously high-margin software prices. Only it was Jeff Bezos telling Mr. Ballmer in 2005, when AWS was released, to "Tear down this wall." The deflationary impacts are remarkably similar.

How is AWS deflationary? Your monthly cable bill is now more than 50 percent cheaper. Your hotel fees are more than 50 percent cheaper. Your server computing bill is more than 50 percent cheaper. The IT cost to start a business is now more than 50 percent cheaper. The list goes on.

Netflix is profitable and is dirt cheap at only $7.99 per month, with superb proprietary content, because Netflix runs on AWS. Airbnb allows us to pay next to nothing for hotels because Airbnb runs on AWS. Dropbox has cut our company's server costs by more than 50 percent because it runs on AWS. As AWS continues to materially cut the pricing point of its platform and applications, we can expect more companies to cut prices and/or new companies to emerge that compete with, and materially disrupt, old school companies that have dominated their respective industries for decades. It's astonishing how much better Netflix's content is today versus a decade ago when its pricing point was much higher; thanks in large part to Netflix running on AWS.

Under Ballmer, Microsoft only cut the price point of Windows three times since it was launched more than 20 years ago. By contrast, Bezos has cut the price point of AWS close to an astonishing 50 times in less than 10 years.

But now, under new CEO Satya Nadella, Microsoft's competing product to AWS, Microsoft Azure, is not just a price cut follower, but also a price cut leader. Google's superb cloud platform, Google Compute, is also now a price cut leader. We have three unbelievable cloud service providers all aggressively cutting prices.

These platforms are the most important cloud operating systems and, thanks to AWS, the deflationary impact of the aforementioned platform price cuts is staggering and unprecedented. This is not an irrational exuberance event.

There is no historical deflationary precedent in any other industry. The impact is commensurate with Ford, GM, and Toyota cutting prices on cars 50 times in 10 years. Or Marriott, Holiday Inn, and Ramada cutting hotel prices 50 times in 10 years. Or General Electric, Sub-Zero, and Maytag cutting prices on their appliances 50 times in 10 years.

In the past, companies were slaves to the enterprise software giants with their "one neck to choke" strategy. Conglomerates like Oracle, with their patched together acquired vertical offerings from the hardware layer (Sun Microsystems), to the middleware layer (BEA) to the enterprise resource planning layer (PeopleSoft and others), would charge hefty annual maintenance fees. Never again. AWS and lower priced deflationary cloud computing options have finally disrupted this model. In the years ahead, we will continue to see cloud service provider platform giants like Amazon, Microsoft, and Google continue to cut prices, furthering the most deflationary event we have seen since that historic event in 1989.

A Brief History of Silicon Valley, the Region That Revolutionizes How We Do Everything

If you live in Silicon Valley, chances are that you are reading this article from your iPhone, while riding in an Uber car to the company you work at that holds the next world-changing technology.

But it goes beyond the technology we see and hold in our hands and includes all the industries the Valley has helped flourish, providing growth for technology that shapes our lives in ways many of us not only don't understand, but don't even know. The minds and innovation that live and thrive here hold the keys to future technology innovation. The San Francisco the Bay Area receives more than 50 percent of the country's VC funding.

Silicon Valley offers unparalleled access to high-quality engineers, a risk-taking culture, venture capitalists and superb universities. But the reason this particular spot ended up at the heart of the technology industry might surprise you. It all starts with Sputnik.

Americans were brokenhearted when Russia beat the United States in the space race with the launch of Sputnik 1. NASA was created, and NASA needed high-powered components to be developed in order to put the first person on the moon. Fulfilling that need was Fairchild Semiconductor, which was founded in the Bay Area in the midst of Cold War competition.

The seminal event was the spark that ignited Silicon Valley's innovative, risk-taking culture five decades ago and it has truly shaped the way our lives have been, and will continue to be, enhanced by technology. If not for Sputnik we would not have witnessed the massive technology innovations that spawned from Fairchild Semiconductor and "Fairchildren" companies like Intel, AMD and NVIDIA. This was just the beginning. A flourishing hardware industry emerged. As a result, the software and Internet industries also flourished.

Bay Area innovation is changing the way we do everything – from Uber disrupting the taxi industry, to Twitter disrupting the media industry and Facebook disrupting the communications industry. One can even argue that Barack Obama is president partially as a result of embracing social media technologies and Salesforce's cloud-based software for campaign management – talk about a political disruption! In truth, you can look at any industry that has yet to be optimized by tech and bet that in the not so distant future it will experience a revolution in part due to innovations from Silicon Valley.

Think about the transportation sector, an industry that hasn't changed much in the last half century, but is on the precipice of complete technological disruption. Automated, self-driving cars are something we already see sharing our Bay Area roads, but in as little as five years these cars will likely be broadly available, instituting a massive disruption in the way we commute. Longer-term, this disruption will also offer a sizable boost to economic growth, with the number of accidents falling because of this sensor-based self-driving technology.

The opportunity for mobile commerce and communication are also limitless. While these are areas that receive a lot of air time, it's breathtaking to think that each of us with a smartphone holds more power in the palm of our hand than every computer we used to put a person on the moon (take that, Sputnik!), or that a child in Africa has more and faster access to information than Bill Clinton did in the 1990s. These revolutionary communications tools have worked to keep rogue governments in check, spurred political revolutions and enabled countries without sophisticated, tech-enabled banking systems to able to flourish, thanks to smartphone computing and the advent of Bitcoin. In short, the disruptive power of technology can, and will, rock every industry as we know it on a global scale.

Still more industry-disrupting companies will be born in the Bay Area over the next decade, leveraging technologies via the Internet of Things (IoT) movement or, in true Valley style, creating an entirely new movement altogether.

As an investor, the best investments are platform solutions because they own the ecosystem and are technologies that have the ability to scale and grow. Facebook, LinkedIn, eBay and even YouTube (as a media platform) are great examples of platform-based approaches that have scaled, with skyrocketing numbers of users, but also content or applications that run on top of them. It starts as one platform and morphs into something much bigger. The healthcare industry is beginning to see the platform tectonic shift that will change the way we all give and receive medical services. Once we address cloud-based security issues, enterprise public cloud computing will also flourish.

Other regions have tried to emulate what the Bay Area has done with little success. The region's technological prowess isn't just due to great minds and high-quality schools like Stanford and UC Berkeley. If this were the case, then Oxford and Cambridge would make London a dominant tech center. Silicon Valley is a fertile technology crescent 50 years in the making. It is the product of Sputnik-induced competition, a 1960s induced cultural renaissance and an open-minded, risk-taking approach where failure is accepted. Silicon Valley cannot be replicated anywhere else, but the effects of its innovation will continue to be shared around the world.

SPUTNIK, HIPPIES AND THE DISRUPTIVE TECHNOLOGY OF SILICON VALLEY

SIT DOWN AND talk with anyone about technology and you'll have little trouble arguing that the San Francisco Bay Area is the quintessential location for tech startups. The area offers unparalleled access to high quality engineers, venture capitalists and superb universities. But the reason this particular spot ended up at the heart of the technology industry might surprise you, and it all starts with Sputnik.

The seminal event was the spark that ignited Silicon Valley's innovative, risk-taking culture more than 50 years ago, and it has truly shaped the way our lives have been and will continue to be enhanced by technology. If not for Sputnik, we would not have witnessed the massive technology innovations that spawned from Fairchild Semiconductors and "Fairchildren" companies like Intel, AMD and NVIDIA. Apple, Google, Oracle, Uber, Twitter, Facebook and many other disruptive technology companies would not exist.

Still more industry-disrupting companies will be born in the Bay Area over the next decade. What Uber has done to the taxi industry is the just the tip of the iceberg. Bay Area innovation will disrupt countless industry verticals with Google and Tesla disrupting the transportation industry with self-driving cars. Then you have Twitter disrupting the media industry; Facebook disrupting the communications industry; LinkedIn disrupting the human resources industry; Salesforce disrupting the political and customer relationship management industries; and many emerging startups disrupting consumer markets via the Internet of Things (IOT) movement.

Silicon Valley has shaped our lives in so many ways that we don't realize. One can easily argue that Barrack Obama is president partially as a result of embracing social media technologies and Salesforce's cloud based software for campaign management. The advent of real-time data and communication allowed him to target specific regions for campaigning and reach out to tech-savvy voters across the country.

We also can't forget the incredibly open nature of the Bay Area, which has led to unprecedented sharing of information and empowering technologies. During the hippie movement of the 60s, Bay Area technology companies became more open minded and embraced the open-source movement and the sharing of ideas. This unparalleled culture has been critical to innovation and the exceptional speed at which new companies have been and will continue to be founded.

Additionally, this open nature mentality has led to a culture that embraces risk-taking where failure is seen as a learning experience and — unlike in other global economic hubs — is not shameful. As a result, risk-taking is embedded in the DNA of Silicon Valley.

Other regions have tried to emulate what the Bay Area has done with little success. The region's technological prowess isn't just due to great minds and high quality schools like Stanford and Berkeley, among others. If this were the case then Oxford and Cambridge would make London a dominant tech center.

Silicon Valley cannot be replicated without the 50-plus years of history it has taken to develop the ideal fertile technology crescent. So if you want to work in technology and change the world, move to the San Francisco Bay Area

WHEN A COMPANY FOUNDER RESIGNS, INVESTORS SHOULD HEAD FOR THE EXIT TOO

Most large tech companies are no longer run by their founders. This is problematic for investors, because a painful corporate bureaucracy develops when a founder leaves and, as a result, risk-taking and innovation deteriorates.

Any large tech company no longer run by its founder that tells you otherwise is being disingenuous to its investors.

Why is this the case? Many tech companies with enormous research and development budgets can't innovate as effectively as a few engineers in a garage if they're not run by their founder. Executives who work at large tech firms are focused mainly on climbing the corporate ladder. If they step out of line to take a risk by innovating and are unsuccessful, then their careers are significantly damaged. If they are successful, they won't get compensated, as HR departments refuse to materially disrupt compensation structures. For non-C-level executives, the best way to get compensated is to quit and join a startup or smaller founder-led private company.

Founders have earned the respect of their investors. They are less exposed to the pressures of having a short-term investment horizon, and they can take long-term innovation risks. They aren't subject to the same politics as executives at big companies, nor do they care. They don't have a job, they have a passion. To quote Steve Jobs, they are crazy enough to think they can change the world.

When a CEO founder leaves a company, passion, innovation, and risk-taking materially deteriorates, which obliterates shareholder value.

But what about Google, Amazon, and Salesforce? Aren't these enormous tech companies that are incredibly innovative? Yes they are, and all are still run by their founders. How are they different? They don't care about short-term quarterly results; they are correctly greedy in the long term, not the short term.

Google is run by a founder, Larry Page, who has given engineers an incredible amount of flexibility by allowing them to spend 20 percent of their time on R&D initiatives that they are incredibly passionate about.

At Amazon, founder Jeff Bezos doesn't allow any meeting to take place that requires more than two pizzas in order to eliminate the "too many cooks in the kitchen syndrome" (otherwise known as bureaucracy).

At Salesforce, founder Mark Benioff emerged as the quintessential cloud evangelist; I look for Mark's passion in all CEO/founders that I meet with when I do due diligence on potential venture capital investments. (As an example, we invested in cloud company Bracket Computing partially due to the visionary passion of cofounder Tom Gillis.)

Many investors believe that we are in a tech bubble. While I can't disagree that valuations on some private companies are lofty, I can argue that part of the lofty valuation is due to the fact that many large-cap tech companies have extremely low organic growth. As a result, and due to their inability to innovate, they have no choice but to make many acquisitions.

Given the large number of mature, large-cap tech companies no longer run by their founders, the number of expensive private market acquisitions has materially increased. The private tech market has caught on to this and, as a result, many tech companies are staying private longer.

The goal of many VCs, and private companies, is no longer to have a sub-billion dollar IPO. Rather, it has been fruitful for VCs to encourage portfolio companies to wait even longer to go public; large-cap tech companies are partially to blame for current lofty valuations, which is indirectly due to the fact that they are incredibly ineffective at innovation.

Does this mean that large-cap tech companies no longer run by their founders are significantly overpaying for acquisitions? Not necessarily, as many large-cap tech companies have more than 50 percent of their revenue overseas, versus many private companies that have almost all of their revenues from domestic sources. Small private companies are better innovators but have problems scaling; large companies are better at scaling but have problems innovating.

How do we address the large company innovation conundrum? Perhaps they should emulate the Google/Amazon/Salesforce practices of giving engineers much more creative freedom, keeping innovation teams small, and ensuring that there is more evangelical passion present.

It's also important for large tech companies to encourage innovation risk-taking by implementing unlimited upside bonus structures for engineering teams, tying them to the upside success of the products and services that they pioneer. Otherwise, your best talent will be incentivized to quit and join a startup run by a passionate founder, and investors will also run for the exits.

You Need Yodas in Order to Succeed in Business and Life

You need many Yodas in your life and in your career. You need mentors and you need to mentor others in order to reinforce what your core beliefs or critical career and life success factors are.

Make sure that your Yodas (or mentors) are in a position that you want to be in one day. Are they successful professionally? More importantly, are they successful personally? Did they achieve a great work/life balance? Are some of their past accomplishments your future goals? Can you trust them? Do you enjoy their company? Can they offer you constructive criticism so that they can help you to seek continuous improvement?

It is extraordinarily rare for an executive to rise to the top of any organization or for any entrepreneur to be wildly successful without many mentors. Hewlett mentored Steve Jobs and Steve Jobs paid it forward too by mentoring Marc Benioff from Salesforce, which is now the largest employer in San Francisco.

Behind almost every single successful business person is a great spouse. You are a team and you have likely only gotten to where you are in life because of their mentoring. Listen to them and thank them often especially this Thanksgiving weekend as they are also one of your Yodas. I often read my emails that I am composing to my wife Christine before sending them. Her feedback always rocks.

Your spouse knows what makes you happy in business. Remind them often what your business passions are. In return, they will remind you what you love in life and reinforce and hence help guide and remind you **what you are on this earth to accomplish in business. What is your purpose?**

Your spouse is your ultimate confidant and life coach. Only your spouse can tell you if what you are wearing went out of style 80 years ago! Only your spouse can tell you that you sound too arrogant when practicing a corporate presentation. Only your spouse can remind you why you wanted to work in the industry you currently work in. Only your spouse can help you achieve your long term goals. So thank your spouse often as you will never get a better life coach / Yoda.

Give and you shall receive. This statement has been true since the beginning of time; those that are generous with their time and mentor others are much more successful than those that are not. Why? First of all it is the right thing to do as others helped you to get to where you are today, but by mentoring others you also reinforce your core beliefs and remind yourself what the drivers of success are.

I am so honored and so humbled to be on the board of a wonderful charity called the LEMO Foundation, whose mission is to eradicate poverty through scholarships to those that are less fortunate. LEMO's core mission statement is brilliant: *"Don't expect to accomplish your dreams unless you help others accomplish their dreams."* I love that; so prophetic and so true! Some call it karma and others call it paying it forward. Everyone should seek mentors and mentor others; you will be much more successful in the long run if you practice what you preach.

People are flattered when you ask them to mentor you. They almost always say yes when you ask them. Ask and you shall receive mentors. They will help you achieve your goals in life. More importantly, there is nothing more satisfying in life than watching people that you mentor become incredibly successful. This is worth repeating: **"Don't expect to accomplish your dreams unless you help others accomplish their dreams."**

WHEN TO CHANGE CAREERS

If you get up in the morning and tell yourself that you are going to work, then you are doing it wrong; you need to change careers. Find out what your passion is. Find out what you were put on this earth to accomplish. It certainly isn't to make a lot of money. Don't worry, odds are that if what you are doing in life is your passion, then compensation will never be an issue. What is your calling?

Success does not lead to happiness; rather, happiness, leads to success. In venture capital when deciding what companies to invest in, we don't look for founders that want to be rich. Rather, we look for passionate entrepreneurs that want to put a dent in the universe. This is their calling. This is their reason d'être.

Don't worry about money early in your career; if you follow your passion, then everything else will fall into place. Many of my business students want to become investment bankers but then they hate it and they are miserable once they start. Focus on what you love doing most in life. The best entrepreneurs don't have a job; they have a passion. Superb examples of passionate entrepreneurs include Sir Richard Branson of Virgin, Mark Benioff of Salesforce, Christian Chabot of Tableau and of course Steve Jobs. The best CEOs and businesspeople in the world are passionate salespeople.

What is your passion? Ask yourself this question "who is a rock star to me but is not a musician?" Sounds out there I know, but for me when I was younger it was Bill Gates….so my passion then as it is now is software!

Don't ever focus on money as your primary career goal or you will never have a happy existence; you will never feel fulfilled. Here is a wonderful quote by the Dalai Lama on this topic:

"Man…sacrifices his health in order to make money. Then he sacrifices money to recuperate his health. And then he is so anxious about the future that he does not enjoy the present; the result being that he does not

live in the present or the future; he lives as if he is never going to die, and then dies having never really lived."

Don't have regrets later in life. Change careers if it will make you a happier person. It's never too late to start over.

Take that Walk & Ponder a Career Change!

Some of the best decisions in life are made on long walks. Steve Jobs used to go on long walks with his friend, Oracle founder Larry Ellison. All US Presidents needed R&R at Camp David to go on long walks to come up with impactful decisions.

Go on at least one long walk per week in order to clear your thoughts and assess where you are in life. When you have a critical decision that needs to be made in life, take a long walk and decide what to do, especially when it comes to your career.

When I worked in the consulting industry, I wasn't passionate about what I was doing and I thought maybe an MBA might help? I played a round of golf alone and in between holes, I wrote down the pros and cons on going to business school on two separate pieces of paper. I then put a score out of ten next to each criteria; 10 was the highest score and 1 was the lowest score. I then added up the scores. The total score on the pros card outweighed the total score on the cons page.

That long walk on the golf course that day in 1997 changed my life.

Should I Go Back to School?

Should you bother getting a graduate business or law or engineering or other degrees? Only if you need another degree in order to change careers. Only if getting a graduate degree will likely get you closer to your goals. If you want to go to business / MBA school and want help on how to get into a top school, please see this course: http://tiny.cc/chris116

When Changing Careers Remember that 'Nobody is Smarter than You!"

Please accept that fact that everything around you in business was created by people that are no smarter than you. I am not asking you to be arrogant. Rather, I am asking you to materially increase your confidence by accepting the fact that you are the smartest person in the world.

Why am I making such an outrageous request? Because if you believe it then you can accomplish any goal that you create in life regardless of how unrealistic others think it is. Actually, who cares what others think anyway!

Quite often the reason people are not successful in business or don't change careers is because they are not confident enough to accomplish their goals.

Please watch this short YouTube video by Steve Jobs as it will change your life:

http://tiny.cc/chris115

Can I do it? People Say I Can't. Avoid 'those" People

Don't let them get you down. That's right. If you can, going forward disassociate yourself with negative people. Friends with negative attitudes are often not worth having. Surround yourself with positive people that believe there are no limits to what they and you can achieve. Surround yourself with people that are incredibly successful as their success, confidence and positive outlook on business and life will rub off on you and vice versa.

Surround yourself with positive people and the chances of you being extraordinarily successful in changing careers rises 1,000,000%. I have never met a successful entrepreneur, investor or CEO that doesn't have a positive attitude. Richard Branson is the quintessential example of a positive role model. I believe that his cheerful and positive outlook in life and business is the primary reason for his incredible success. His positive attitude is the cornerstone of the happy and positive corporate culture at all of his Virgin companies. Try flying Virgin America or Virgin Atlantic or one day Virgin Galactic and observe how amazing the attitude is of all of his employees. A company with an incredibly positive corporate culture will no doubt be much more successful than a company filled with negative people. A negative person would never consider launching a galactic service or taking on the airline industry. Richard Branson clearly avoids hiring "those" people.

I am a firm believer in letting our children do and be anything they want to be in life. Gone are the days of telling children to be doctors or lawyers. It's their lives so they should just do what they are most passionate about. Steve Jobs was passionate about calligraphy and my kids enjoy legos and Minecraft. They can be anything they want to be. My goal is to make sure they do what they are most passionate about in life.

Why are Technology Employees More Passionate than Other Sectors When it Comes to their Careers?

It certainly is fascinating how much innovation has come out of the technology sector versus other sectors. Why is this the case? It is partially due to passionate software engineers that never saw the profession as a job. Lawyers see their daily activities as jobs and the same can be said for most people in other professions, which is why most non-tech industries pale in innovation advancement, by comparison.

In technology it is astonishing how a great engineer can be 10 times as productive as an average engineer. Why is this the case? Because the best engineers love what they do! This is more apparent in the technology industry than any other industry, which is why there are so many passionate CEOs like Marc Benioff in the sector. I bet that none of the parents of technology innovators urged them to be a programmer when they were younger!

Can Someone be too Old to Change Careers?

No darn way! When I was a kid I remember seeing commercials in Canada on TV for 'Freedom 55', which was a retirement savings company. Then as I got older, this age became 65 for those eligible to receive social security benefits. This age is slowly increasing. It's ludicrous that people retire in their 60s or 70s. Heck, I know of many people in their 80s that are much sharper than I am.

We are on the cusp of a biotech and healthcare renaissance were we will see the eradication of many diseases in the next few decades. I think most people alive today will live to be more than 100 if they take care of themselves. I know in my heart that at some point in my life people will live to 150+ years old.

With this in mind, why would you want to retire in your 60s when you have another 100 potential years? You are never too old to start a new career or start a new company. Anybody that thinks otherwise is guilty in my humble opinion of age discrimination. It doesn't matter how old or young you are, leverage your network and reinvent yourself over and over again until you find your passion!

Ok are You Ready to Do this?

Condition yourself to embrace change and enjoy the process. This will help you deal with the perceived stress and profit from adversity while you change careers. If you feel stressed when you start embarking upon the next [augmented] chapter of your life, ask yourself in business "what is positive about this event and how can I enjoy and benefit from it?"

The belief that anything is possible leads to amazing accomplishments.

The glass is not empty.

The glass is not half empty.

The glass is not half full.

The glass is ALWAYS full!

You are never too old to start over. Successfully changing careers is based on having an unbelievably positive attitude. You be you. Welcome to the new you!

Questions Based on Chapter 15:

1: A term sheet is a legally binding document.

    True or False

2: The most important investment you will ever make is:

    a) A value investment
    b) A growth investment
    c) A debt investment
    d) An investment in you! :)

3: Writing down your goals dramatically increases your ability to achieve these goals!

    True or False

4: A company is usually more successful once the founder(s) resign.

    True or False

5: You should mentor many people because this process can help to reinforce your own best practices.

    True or False

The Ultimate Practical Business Manual

PLEASE READ THIS LAST: GOAL SETTING WORKSHOP.

Please write down your <u>10 year</u> business goals….meaning where do you want to be professionally in 10 years. Please PLEASE PLEASE PLEASE PLEASE don't be conservative. There are no wrong answers. Think big and then think **BIGGER**. #DREAMBIG!

10 Year Goal #1: _____

_____

_____

10 Year Goal #2: _____

_____

_____

10 Year Goal #3: _____

_____

_____

10 Year Goal #4: _____

_____

_____

10 Year Goal #5: _____

_____

_____

CLOSING REMARKS

Thank you. I hope you have enjoyed *The Ultimate Practical Business Manual: Everything You Need to Know about Business (from Launching a Company to Taking it Public)* by Chris Haroun.

If you are interested in taking online courses taught by Chris Haroun please visit: www.Udemy.com/user/chris-haroun/.

Other publications written by Chris Haroun are available at:

http://tiny.cc/chris117

If you would like to receive articles and blogs written by Chris Haroun or if you are interested in having Chris as a guest speaker at your school, charity or company, please contact or submit your email address at: www.BusinessCareerCoaching.com.

Thank you :)

CPSIA information can be obtained at www.ICGtesting.com
Printed in the USA
LVIW01n1232060216
474014LV00005B/7